T0399125

From Byzantium to Constantinople

FROM BYZANTIUM TO CONSTANTINOPLE

An Urban History

JOHN MATTHEWS

OXFORD
UNIVERSITY PRESS

OXFORD

UNIVERSITY PRESS

Oxford University Press is a department of the University of Oxford.
It furthers the University's objective of excellence in research, scholarship,
and education by publishing worldwide. Oxford is a registered trade mark of
Oxford University Press in the UK and in certain other countries.

Published in the United States of America by Oxford University Press
198 Madison Avenue, New York, NY 10016, United States of America.

© Oxford University Press 2024

Library of Congress Cataloging-in-Publication Data
Names: Matthews, John (John Frederick) author.
Title: From Byzantium to Constantinople : an urban history / John Matthews.
Other titles: Urban history
Description: First edition. | New York, NY : Oxford University Press,
[2024] | Includes bibliographical references and index.
Identifiers: LCCN 2024034659 (print) | LCCN 2024034660 (ebook) |
ISBN 9780197585498 | ISBN 9780197585511 (epub)
Subjects: LCSH: Istanbul (Turkey)—History—To 1453. | Byzantine Empire. |
Urbanization—Turkey—Istanbul—History—To 1500.
Classification: LCC DR729 .M38 2024 (print) | LCC DR729 (ebook) |
DDC 949.61/801—dc23/eng/20240904
LC record available at https://lccn.loc.gov/2024034659
LC ebook record available at https://lccn.loc.gov/2024034660

DOI: 10.1093/oso/9780197585498.001.0001

Sheridan Books, Inc., United States of America

Contents

Preface

A BOOK SHOULD not enter the world in fear of being misunderstood, and I will begin by making clear the limitations of this one, both in what it hopes to achieve and in what it does not. It is not a history of Byzantium, nor of Byzantine culture, art, or religion, or any version of what is meant by 'Byzantine Civilization' in the broader sense. Though I have an interest in them, I am not qualified in these areas of research, nor am I an archaeologist, though, as will become clear, I greatly respect that profession and much enjoy reading works in archaeology. Still less is it an antiquarian guide to the city of Istanbul, even though it has an antecedent in such a work, based on the same ancient source as this one (Pierre Gilles' *Antiquities of Constantinople*, published in Latin in 1561 and in an English translation in 1729), and will frequently pause to discuss the nature of monuments, where they were in the city, and what they contribute to the urban fabric. I would not mind if my book were treated as a sort of realization of the work of Gilles. I am well aware that scholarly work always leans upon the work of its predecessors, and I would be greatly honoured if Gilles were thought of as such.

The topic came to me as a possible subject of research while I too was looking at the short inventory of the monuments and resources of the city known as *Notitia urbis Constantinopolitanae* and realized that, as lists often are, it is not a static but a cumulative text, recording the state of the city not only as it existed at the time of compilation but also during the period of development that led up to this moment. Not that this was a surprising reflection, for a city will declare its history in its streets, and a description of its monuments and resources will document this; we are well used to the idea of a city as revealing the story of its development in what can be seen of earlier times. Every city is however its own case, and Constantinople is a very special example. Once one has seen that the late Roman inventories of the *Notitia* may contain traces of the period preceding the compilation of the text, one is led to consider not only the city developed by Constantine and his successors during the fourth and early fifth centuries but also the physical resources of the preceding urban settlement that were available to them in their re-founding of Byzantium as the New Rome, and the influence of the Graeco-Roman city on the development of its successor. New Rome was, indeed, grafted upon Old Byzantium, but in terms of urban development, how was this done? What was the existing urban structure onto which a new city could be grafted, and how does this affect the result? The *Notitia urbis Constantinopolitanae*, written under and dedicated to Theodosius II, allows us to trace this history of urban development for as long as it was contained by the walls of Constantine. It offers a control of the physical development of the city, tracing the emergence of Constantinople from its predecessor in Graeco-Roman Byzantium and measuring the urban development of the city down to the early fifth century. Within its restricted though clear-sighted angle of vision, the text is retrospective over a particular, well-defined period before our evidence is overtaken by attitudes and assumptions of an entirely different sort. The period after the construction of the walls of Theodosius in the early fifth century is part of a different story, and the subject of a different book from this one.

I have addressed my subject as a Roman historian trained in the history of the Classical world, used to the methods developed for the study of that world. My picture of Greek and Roman Byzantium is that of the Classical historian working with the sources of that period, and my assumption is that the Byzantium known to Constantine and to his successors was in origin and essence a Graeco-Roman city, and that its early development will reflect these origins. This is the perspective of the *Notitia*, and is the focus of my study. I believe it to be a valid one, both in its respect for the nature of the text, and as a paradigm of urban development over the period that concerns it.

I am of course aware that the Roman empire of Constantine and his successors was in many respects a departure from its predecessor. It was not a complete break, however, and so I begin with a brief historical account of the origins and rise of the founder of what would become the new capital city of the Roman empire. In Chapter 2 I describe the context of the Graeco-Roman history of Byzantium, for centuries an important metropolis of the region that achieved an important role in a Roman civil war, recovered from its choice of the wrong side, and achieved the status of a Roman *colonia* under the emperors of the Severan period. Having described the circumstances of Constantine's re-founding of the city and having given an idea of its initial development as an imperial capital, I move on in Chapter 3 to a survey of the literary and other evidence from later periods of Byzantine history that may help us to understand the earlier city. This chapter is intended only to guide the reader into this complicated subject and not to advance knowledge of it. There then follows an introduction to the *Notitia* that is at the heart of the book (Chapter 4), with a translation of the text and (in Chapter 5) a survey of the Fourteen Regions into which, after the Roman fashion, the city was divided. These regions are then (Chapter 6) taken in groups and used to define the topographical and social character of the city as it expanded from the civic centre established by Constantine in the area of Graeco-Roman Byzantium to the new urban territories established by him and his successors as far as his city walls. This material is then (Chapters 7–9) reworked to trace the urban development in time over the period from Constantine to Theodosius. Chapter 10 breaks down the numbers of the facilities and institutions of the city provided by the *Notitia* to analyse the social composition of the urban area in its various sectors, from palaces and colonnades to harbours and warehouses, and to offer speculative conclusions about the size of the population, its living conditions, and its distribution. The more technical nature and detailed argument of this chapter suggested at one point that it might better be set aside and published separately, but the topic belongs within the scope of the book, and so it has been retained. The best advice I can give to the reader is to be patient and take it slowly. The final chapter (11) is an attempt to redress the formal nature of much of what has preceded by evoking the actual texture of life in the streets of the city and by adding certain topics, such as the origins of the senatorial class of the city and the character of the legal evidence, that have escaped discussion in earlier chapters. The future of this city as post-Classical Byzantium is not one that I am qualified to write.

In venturing to write as much as I have on the earlier city that is the subject of this book, I wish to recognize, and to express gratitude, to the work of others, giants on whose shoulders I have been emboldened to ride. In first place is the great Cyril Mango, for his astonishing command of the sources for a city that he knows like the back of his hand and his ability to make them spring from the page in arresting and often surprising interpretations, argued with the irresistible logic of a master of the subject; it has been a real privilege to know him and to hear as well as read the way he does history. His work appears constantly in the notes of this book, in particular but not only his *Le développement urbain de Constantinople (IVe–VIIe siècles)*, first published in 1985, and in a third edition in 2004. If I can add anything, it is more a matter of perspective than of substance, in my emphasis on the history of Classical Graeco-Roman Byzantium, and an explicit deployment of the *Notitia* as a primary source deserving of study in its own right. Albrecht Berger's 'Regionen und Straßen im frühen Konstantinopel', *Istanbuler Mitteilungen* 47 (1997), pp. 349–414, gives full emphasis to the evidence of the *Notitia*, and his *Accounts of Medieval Constantinople: The* Patria (*Dumbarton Oaks Medieval Library* 24, 2013) is wonderfully helpful in making accessible this extraordinarily complex, difficult, and highly enjoyable material. Wolfgang Müller-Wiener's *Bildlexikon zur Topographie Istanbuls* (1977) has been a constant resource not only for its comprehensive site references but for its illuminating inclusion of photographic records from earlier periods, when more could be seen on the ground than can be seen now. James Crow, Jonathan Bardill, and Richard Bayliss' *The Water Supply of Byzantine Constantinople* (2008) is a memorable and brilliantly conducted study of a complex and essential topic. Ken Dark and Ferudun Özgümüş, *Constantinople: Archaeology of a Byzantine Megalopolis* (2013), gives a comprehensive and generously illustrated listing of individual sites in the western parts of the city adjoining the walls of Constantine and in the intramural region between these walls and those of Theodosius, and it also includes a meticulous (and revealing) study of the site of the church of the Apostles under the tomb of Mehmet the Conqueror that succeeded it in the fifteenth century, introductory chapters on the progress of archaeological research at Istanbul, and a concluding chapter on the general progress of the urban development of the late Roman and early Byzantine city. The results concur with what is suggested below, a progressive development to the Theodosian period of the area within the Constantinian walls, increasing markedly in the fifth and sixth centuries, that is to say after the period of time covered by the *Notitia*, in the areas most adjacent to these walls and beyond them.

I also acknowledge the translation and documentation provided by Michael and Mary Whitby's *Chronicon Paschale, 284–628* AD (1989) and the general series, Translated Texts for Historians (Liverpool), in which it appears; so too the translation of and studies on John Malalas by Elizabeth Jeffreys, Roger Scott, Brian Croke, and others, published by the Australian Association for Byzantine Studies (1986 and 1990), and the presentation of the *Parastaseis* by Averil Cameron and Judith Herrin, *Constantinople in the Early Eighth Century: The 'Parasteis Syntomoi Chronikai'* (1984). I thank the many University Faculties, including the Departments of History and Classics at Yale and the Faculty of Literae Humaniores at Oxford, whose members, students as well as faculty, have responded to my ideas on the origins of Constantinople in seminars, lectures, and conference presentations. And I owe special thanks to Stefan Vranka and Oxford University Press, New York, for their willingness to take on the publication of this book and for the advice of the anonymous readers whose opinions were sought, and their permission to incorporate, with few changes, the substance and content of Lucy Grig and Gavin Kelly's edited *Two Romes: Rome and Constantinople in Late Antiquity* (Oxford and New York, 2012), chapter 4. It also gives me pleasure to add my thanks to my editors at Oxford University Press, Thomas Deva and Tim Beck, for their help in preparing this book for publication. Authors do know, and I am no exception, that the critical and stylistic contributions of editors make a great difference to the outcome of what may be years of work, and I am very grateful.

For reasons that are only too well known, the years in which this book reached its final form have been marked by unusual problems of access to libraries and academic discussion in general. I am grateful for the co-operation I have received during this awkward period, and in particular wish to acknowledge the contribution of the online site academia.edu, which has been systematic, not to say relentless, in making available to me literature of which I was not aware, indeed might never have found without its help.

Like the author of every book on history that was ever written, I am conscious that there will be readers who know more about some, maybe large parts of it, than I do. Late Roman and early Byzantine history is a good example of the proliferation of academic sub-fields, in itself a good indication of the strength of the subject. My response, and I have often wanted to say this, is that my book is written for those who wish to know more about the subject than those who already do know more, and that, while like any book it will have its strengths and weaknesses, it should be judged as for the coherence of its subject-matter and the range of topics that it covers, as much as for any particular aspect of it.

John Matthews

New Haven, Connecticut
June 2024

List of Figures

List of Tables

FIG. 1.1 Colossal portrait bust of Constantine. *Metropolitan Museum of Art, New York.*

I

Introduction

FROM YORK TO BYZANTIUM

IN A SENSE, and it is a startling thought, the history of Constantinople begins at York, for it was there, on 26 July 306, in a city that was both the capital of a Roman province and a legionary headquarters, that the emperor Constantius died and the army proclaimed his son Constantine as his successor (see Fig. 1.1). In the context of the preceding century this was not such an unusual event, but the last twenty years had made an exception of it. It arose from the simultaneous resignations, on 1 May 305, of the long-serving Augusti Diocletian and Maximian, and the failure of the plans they had made for the succession. The resignations— and we should recognize what a remarkable event that was—brought to an end the system of collegiate rule known as the Tetrarchy, which had come into being in stages since Diocletian's accession to the purple in 284: a Roman empire divided into eastern and western parts, each with a senior emperor bearing the title Augustus and a junior emperor, or Caesar, functioning under his authority— 'running around in all directions', as the historian Ammianus Marcellinus later put it, 'in order to execute their superiors' will' (14.11.10). A stable succession would be secured by the promotion of the Caesars to the rank of Augustus and the appointment of new Caesars to replace them. According to the plan, Diocletian and Maximian were succeeded as Augusti by their Caesars, Galerius and Constantius, who were replaced as Caesars by two newcomers: Maximinus in the east and Severus in the west. It is at this point that the fault in the structure was revealed. Whether it was an act of extreme high-mindedness or he was just too trusting, it is not a criticism to say that Diocletian failed to allow for envy and human ambition in passing over the claims of the retiring Augustus Maximian's and the new Augustus Constantius' sons, Maxentius and Constantine. Diocletian's extraordinary capacity to inspire loyalty dissolved with his retirement to a newly built palace at Split near Salona in Dalmatia, where we can still see it, after its conversion into the medieval town of Split and the transformation of the mausoleum of the old persecutor of Christians into its cathedral. Diocletian's miscalculation was corrected by reversion to a traditional process that was meant to

From Byzantium to Constantinople: An Urban History. John Matthews, Oxford University Press.
© Oxford University Press 2024. DOI: 10.1093/oso/9780197585498.003.0001

have been superseded by the system he had established—civil wars in which the neglected candidates claimed their inheritance.[1]

Excluded from Diocletian's arrangements and supposedly threatened by his successor, Constantine escaped from Galerius' dominions to join his father, to be acclaimed upon his father's death not to the subordinate rank of Caesar but directly to the highest imperial office. This is not what should have happened. The nearest we can come to correct procedure would have been for Severus Caesar to move into the rank of Augustus and appoint his own Caesar, in consultation with Galerius if that were possible. This is no doubt expecting too much. What had happened in tumultuary fashion (to use a Roman expression) in distant York could hardly be corrected by an Augustus currently residing at Milan. Its consequence however was that, until he could put forward some broader claim of entitlement, Constantine was a usurper who had seized power, the first part of his reign dominated by conflict with other claimants for it.

Constantine was the son of Constantius and his wife Helena—Constantius a military officer, Helena an innkeeper's daughter (or so they said). He was born at Naissus (Niš, in the Roman province of Moesia), a city on the military high road between west and east; that is, he was a familiar type of late Roman emperor, including Diocletian and Maximian, the founders of the Tetrarchic system of government he was about to demolish. There is a common portrayal of Constantine as just another 'simple soldier' from the Danubian lands, the origin of so many emperors of the preceding period. This is a prejudiced judgement, and leaves out of account two things: first, the intelligence and capacity of individuals, no matter what their origins, in a social system that will provide them with opportunities, as the military career certainly did. In this matter, modern educational snobbery too often agrees with ancient (was not Shakespeare written not by the son of a provincial tradesman but by an educated aristocrat?). Every source speaks of the ambition and forceful urgency of Constantine's mind; there is no doubting the intelligence of this man. Second, there is his upbringing, far from the land of a 'simple Danubian'. When he was made Caesar in 293, Constantius had to divorce his wife to marry a daughter of Maximian. Helena took Constantine off to the east for his education and training in life, especially in the city of Nicomedia, Diocletian's capital. It is there that he spent his formative years. The church historian and later panegyrist, Eusebius of Caesarea, saw him as a 'youth' in Diocletian's entourage during an expedition to Egypt in around 297/8; so he

---

1. For the rapidly moving events of these years see above all the remarkable companion studies by T. D. Barnes, *Constantine and Eusebius* (1981) and *The New Empire of Diocletian and Constantine* (1982); among many biographies of Constantine, see David Potter, *Constantine the Emperor* (2013). I do not document in detail the events of these years, only points of particular interest in their context.

was born around 280 (which is as close as we can get on his date of birth). It is interesting that, having seen him, Diocletian still did not make him Caesar in 305, perhaps thinking him still on the young side for what was after all a weighty role. Perhaps it was also a matter of personal judgement. A master of caution and consolidation, Diocletian might have hesitated to advance a young man whose character seemed in so many ways a contradiction of his own sturdy caution. Perhaps he was inclined to disregard the claims of blood and did not want the empire to fall into rival Tetrarchic factions; or, feeling that he could not appoint one heir apparent without appointing them both, thought it best to appoint neither. From the point of view of the future emperor, however, Constantine was familiar with the east and was as comfortable as anyone could expect in its cultural language, Greek, as well as in the Latin of the imperial court and administration.

One particular aspect of this familiarity is worthy of note. The young Constantine was in the east at the time of the great persecution of Christianity initiated by Diocletian and Galerius in the latest years of their rule, for what reason or reasons we need not go into here. There has been much discussion of the numbers and social eminence of Christianity in Constantine's time. It is in part a regional matter. There were far more Christians in the east (and in north Africa) than in the west (none worth talking about in Britain), and Constantine had seen it where it was strongest. In the areas best known to Constantine, Christianity was a prominent institution, operating in full view of the public, its clergy prominent members of society, its churches fully visible institutions. If it came down to a choice of religion, Christianity was a serious option, and if it could so motivate people as to seek martyrdom, it might (thinking here for Constantine) be an attractive idea to get these people on your side.

With this background, it is time to look more closely at the phases of his rise to power, and at the way in which Constantine presented it (Table 1.1).

In the early years, immediately after the proclamation at York, on the evidence of his inscriptions, Constantine claimed a dynastic connection with the Tetrarchy through his father Constantius, which is just what we would expect. Despite his acclamation as Augustus, he also seemed content with the title Caesar that he would have possessed had he been chosen in the regular way as Constantius' junior colleague.[2]

In the summer of 307, however, old Maximian, whom they said never really wanted to step down from imperial power, emerged from retirement in Italy to

---

2. Inscriptions of this early period (*ILS* 682, 703, etc.) name him 'son of Constantius'. Constantine claims the title only of Caesar in his public relations with Galerius (cf. *ILS* 682). *ILS* 681 (on a gold fibula) names him Caesar and Herculius, the Tetrarchic title shared with Maximian by Constantius.

Table 1.1 Political Chronology of Constantine, 305–24

305/6	Constantine leaves Galerius' domains in the east to join his father Constantius in Britain.
306, 25 July	Upon the death of Constantius, Constantine is proclaimed Augustus by army at York. Inscriptions (*ILS* 682, 703, etc.) name him 'son of Constantius'. Constantine claims the title only of Caesar in his public relations with Galerius (cf. *ILS* 682). *ILS* 681 (a gold fibula) names him Caesar and Herculius, alluding to a title shared by Constantius with Maximian (Herculius).
306, 28 October	Maximian's son Maxentius is proclaimed Augustus at Rome.
307	Maximian makes an alliance with Constantine, who marries Maximian's daughter Fausta and accepts the title of Augustus, around September; cf. *Pan. Lat.* 7(5). *ILS* 684 has him as Constantius' son and Maximian's 'nepos' (son-in-law).
*c.*308/10	Constantine is with Maximian in Gaul.
310, spring/ summer	Maximian commits suicide at Marseille after 'plotting against' Constantine; Maximian's name is erased on *ILS* 684.
310 (probable date)	*Pan. Lat.* 6(7) makes two claims: (1) Constantine's descent is from Claudius Gothicus, revealed as a secret known only to his closest associates (cf. *ILS* 699, 702); (2) Constantine experienced a vision of Apollo with Victory at a sacred (hot-spring) site in Gaul, probably at Grand (Vosges).
?312, summer	Eusebius' *Life of Constantine* (written much later) recounts a vision of a cross in the sky, with the legend 'Conquer in this'. The date and location are vague, but the army is 'on the march' and the context implies the campaign against Maxentius.
312, 28 October	At the battle of the Milvian Bridge, Constantine defeats Maxentius and visits Rome. According to Lactantius, Constantine's dream instructed him to put a Christian symbol on the shields of his army. The campaign is summarized by *Pan. Lat.* 12(9), which also mentions Constantine's 'divine instructions' and concludes with an evocation of an undefined divine power.
313, February	Constantine meets with Licinius at Milan, issuing the 'Edict of Milan', extant in Latin and in Greek translation, both from copies published in the east. Licinius marries Constantine's sister Constantia; their son Licinius the Younger is later named Caesar.
313, April/May	Licinius defeats Maximinus in the east.

313–14	Constantine campaigns in Gaul and Germany and is resident at Cologne and Trier.
314, August	Constantine calls the council of Arles. Letters of Constantine are preserved in Optatus' *Appendix*.
315	Constantine makes second (tenth-anniversary) visit to Rome. The arch of Constantine is erected by the senate and people; the basilica of Maxentius is re-dedicated with a colossal statue of Constantine.
316	First war with Licinius: 8 October, battle of Cibalae, followed by peace agreement.
318	Licinius Augustus and Crispus Caesar made consuls.
319	Constantine Augustus and Licinius (the Younger) Caesar made consuls.
321–24	Constantine's consuls are not recognized by Licinius.
324	Second war with Licinius: 3 July, battle of Hadrianople; July–September, siege of Byzantium; 18 September, battle of Chrysopolis. Licinius surrenders and is later executed at Thessalonica.
324, 8 November	Constantine dedicates Constantinople, planning new walls and naming Constantius as Caesar.

support his son Maxentius and joined with Constantine to promote his interests; it was at this point that Constantine married Maximian's daughter, Fausta, and accepted the title of Augustus from his new father-in-law.[3] This produced a collegiate reign of Maxentius in Rome and Italy (with Africa) and Constantine in Gaul and the west, the whole arrangement underwritten by Maximian. There were advantages in this. Maximian offered a powerful link with the Tetrarchy, but in 310 Constantine destroyed it in obscure circumstances that required him to march south, far outside his field of operation on the Rhine frontier. Maximian was forced to suicide at Massilia (Marseille), a sad end to a conscientious emperor, who was perhaps more afraid of Constantine's ambition than he was indulging his own. The story was put out that he was conspiring against Constantine,

---

3. The alliance with Maximian, around September 307: *Panegyrici Latini* 7(5); C. E. V. Nixon, in his and Barbara Saylor Rodgers' *In Praise of Later Roman Emperors: The Panegyrici Latini* (1994), pp. 178ff. (p. 197 on the rank of Caesar). *ILS* 684 has him as Constantius' son and Maximian's son-in-law. Constantine already had a son, Crispus, by his first wife Minervina.

but it is equally likely that Constantine contrived the whole thing.[4] It may just be a matter of getting your own blow in first. Whatever the truth of the matter, Constantine now had an enemy in Maxentius, and must have expected, sooner or later, to have go to war with him.

At this point precisely, an orator addressing Constantine (that is, speaking for him) in the city of Trier comes up with two arguments, designed in their different ways to promote Constantine's claims. The orator has two announcements to make. In the first, he makes public a newly discovered, obviously fictional, claim of descent from the emperor Claudius II ('Gothicus'), who had a considerable reputation in Gaul since his brief reign in the late 260s. The second announcement concerns the first of Constantine's encounters with the divine, a vision of Apollo at a hot-spring centre somewhere in Gaul—probably at Grand (Vosges), a famous shrine that Constantine could have visited while returning to Trier after the suppression of Maximian.[5] A modest detour from the direct route, it would require advance planning, suggesting that Constantine already had in mind what he expected to happen—especially if he knew of the prophetic qualities of the shrine. According to the orator, Apollo made an appearance to Constantine and offered himself as his personal protector ('Apollinem *tuum*' says the orator), in the company of Victory. The orator claims dynastic and divine support for Constantine at just the moment when, with Maximian's death and war with Maxentius before him, he needs both. We may well ask: if the dynastic claim of a connection with Claudius Gothicus is a clear invention, what about the religious claim? And who but Constantine can be the source of the personal vision reported by the orator?

Apollo, the god who led Augustus to victory at Actium and inspired Nero to sing, is a formidable choice of deity. He shoots the arrows of plague and he heals; with oracular shrines everywhere, he is a prophet; and as Phoebus Apollo, he personifies the sun. The sun is the source of all life, which he bestows without diminution of himself; he returns with each new day and with the seasons of the year. Romans were familiar with the iconographical image of the four-horse chariot (*quadriga*) of Helios passing across the sky from dawn to evening. He is jealous too—a god who can have Marsyas flayed alive for challenging him at singing, and who can destroy Icarus for flying too high; he can kill as well as sustain. And

---

4. Maximian's name is erased on *ILS* 684.

5. The speech, *Pan. Lat.* 6(7), at §§2, 21, makes the two claims; descent from Claudius Gothicus (cf. *ILS* 699, 702), and the encounter with Apollo at the hot-spring site in Gaul; on which, see briefly David Potter, *Constantine the Emperor*, pp. 126–28 (pp. 150–54 on dreams and visions as part of the currency of religious discourse); more fully Nixon, *In Praise of Later Roman Emperors*, pp. 248ff.

he is the Unconquered Sun (*Sol Invictus*), giving victory to those who acknowledge his power.

This meeting with Apollo is the first instalment in Constantine's religious trajectory, which changes over time, as new aspects are grafted onto it. In a letter written much later, Constantine attributed his success to the support of 'the one true god', by which he then meant the god recognized by the Christian church. With this god's help, 'beginning at the remotest shores of the British ocean and the regions where, according to the law of nature, the sun sinks beneath the horizon' (a somewhat loose description of York, suggesting the hand of a draftsman rather than Constantine himself), Constantine had led his army to victory over his rivals in the east.[6] These sentiments are expressed in a letter cited by the church historian and panegyrist Eusebius, long suspected—but its crucial passage is authenticated by a contemporary papyrus. He also, in an account given 'on oath' to Eusebius and heard by others, told of his vision of a cross appearing over the sun, with the words 'Conquer in this' appearing over it. Eusebius gives the words in Greek (τούτῳ νίκα), but the episode was in the west, so (if one can apply this stricture to a miracle) it must originally have been in Latin; it is often given in its inferred Latin form: 'hoc signo vincas'.[7]

Despite or even because of the emperor's oath (a case of protesting too much), Eusebius' account of Constantine's vision is suspect: it was told in his own favour to interested parties up to twenty-five years after the event and contains details that were not true at the time; but it has one convincing element. Seen 'by the entire army marching with him', it locates the apparition in the context of a quest for victory, which can only be the campaign against Maxentius undertaken in 312; historians often think of it as inspired by a meteorological phenomenon witnessed by the army as it crossed the Alps, the sun's rays being refracted into the appearance of a cross by ice particles in the upper atmosphere (the writing could be added later).[8] With this encouragement, Constantine advanced rapidly down

---

6. On Constantine and the one true God, see Eusebius, *On the Life of Constantine* 2.24ff.; on his origins in Britain, see 2.28. The authenticity of the letter was vindicated from a contemporary papyrus by A. H. M. Jones, 'Notes on the Genuineness of the Constantinian Documents in Eusebius' *Life of Constantine*', *Journal of Ecclesiastical History* 5 (1954), pp. 196–200, reprinted in *The Roman Economy*, ed. P. A. Brunt (1974), pp. 257–62. Translations of the relevant passages of Eusebius and Lactantius can readily be found in anthologies, e.g. J. Stevenson, *A New Eusebius* (1957 and reprinted), pp. 298ff.

7. Eusebius, *On the Life of Constantine* 2.28.

8. On the 'solar halo', already in Jones, *Constantine and the Conversion of Europe* (1948), pp. 96–97, see P. Weiss, 'Die Vision Constantins', in *Colloquium aus Anlass des 80. Geburtstages von Alfred Heuss* (1993), pp. 143–69, and 'The Vision of Constantine', *Journal of Roman Archaeology* 16 (2003), pp. 237–59. The phenomenon, seen quite commonly as a halo, can sometimes form a cross over the sun.

Italy to Rome, with passing sieges of Milan and Verona. Then, before the battle of the Milvian Bridge near Rome in late October 312, in a third instance of divine revelation Constantine was instructed in a dream to paint the Christian monogram on his troops' shields and go to battle armed with this symbol. He did so and won the battle.[9]

There are recurrent themes in Constantine's story that help us to understand it. First, he is seeking a divine power that will give him victory, expressed especially in the solar dimension and Apollo. 'Conquer in this' says the writing over the sun; Apollo appears to Constantine with Victoria. The Unconquered Sun (*Sol Invictus*), as worshipped by Aurelian and the Tetrarchs, is a universal symbol of power and victory. Just as important, however, Constantine is seeking a specific expression of that power, not to be confused with anyone else's: 'Apollinem *tuum*', said the orator. The Christian monogram is not an ambiguous sign, to be explained by parallel instances; it is individual and specific, identifying Constantine's support against others'. Heraldic devices, uniforms, flags, and coats of arms are intended to identify their holders, to generate pride in the unit, and to focus loyalties; they both identify and distinguish. And the idea that piety to the gods

FIG. I.2 Constantine and Sol Invictus. Gold medallion of 9 *solidi*. The emperor appears in matching profile with his companion the Sun-God. He carries a shield with solar imagery and on the reverse is the ceremonial act of arrival in a city (Felix Adventus Augusti), preceded by Victory and followed by a legionary standard. The mint is Ticinum/Pavia (Sacra Moneta Ticinensis). The reverse legend recognizes two Augusti (AUGG.NN.), the other being Licinius, whom Constantine had not yet suppressed when the medallion was struck. E. Gnecchi, *I Medaglioni Romani descritti ed illustrate* (3 vols., Milan, 1912), I.2; Berlin, Staatliche Museen).

<hr />

9. This famous passage is in Lactantius, *On the Deaths of the Persecutors* (*De mortibus persecutorum*) 44.3–6. Maxentius is stigmatized as a usurper (*tyrannus*) in *CTh* 15.14.3, if Seeck's amendment of the date is correct (cf. following note).

FIG. 1.3 Inscription of Arch of Constantine. Dedication to the emperor by s(enatus) p(opulus)q(ue) R(omanus), flanked by Dacian prisoners reused from an earlier (second-century) monument.

brings success is common in the Roman mentality; we see it in the taking of the auspices, and in the legend found on coins (see Fig. 1.2), and on the arch of Constantine (see Fig. 1.3): 'pius felix.' There is nothing unusual in Constantine's attributing victory to the support of his god, even if the god is a new one.

IMP · CAES · FL · CONSTANTINO MAXIMO
P · F · AUGUSTO · S · P · Q · R
QUOD INSTINCTU DIVINITATIS, MENTIS
MAGNITUDINE, CUM EXERCITU SUO
TAM DE TYRANNO QUAM DE OMNI EIUS
FACTIONE UNO TEMPORE IUSTIS
REMPUBLICAM ULTUS EST ARMIS
ARCUM TRIUMPHIS INSIGNEM DICAVIT

To Imperator Caesar Flavius Constantinus Maximus, pious and fortunate Augustus, the senate and Roman people dedicated this arch and adorned it with his triumphs, since by divine inspiration and his greatness of mind, together with his army, he at one and the same time defeated the tyrant and all his faction and in just war avenged the republic.

Viewing these events with justified concern was someone not yet known to Constantine: his colleague Licinius Augustus, who since his elevation in 308 had ruled in the Danubian lands while facing a rival, Maximinus, in the east; the latter was the only true survivor of the rapidly fading Tetrarchy, having been appointed Caesar to Galerius in 305 and succeeding as Augustus upon Galerius' death in 311. It was very much in Licinius' interests to be at peace with his forceful western neighbour, and early in 313 he and Constantine came together at Milan to discuss, as their record of the meeting put it, 'many things of advantage to the state'.[10] This record is available to us in the so-called 'Edict of Milan' issued after the meeting, which we possess in two copies of a letter written in the names of the two Augusti; one was published at Nicomedia in Latin, the other at Tyre in Phoenicia, in a Greek translation—both of them eastern cities in the domains of Licinius.[11] Its best-known provisions were the ending of the persecution of Christians, the restoration of the peace of the church and the return of confiscated property. These are the provisions that enter into the history books; less widely reported but critical to an understanding of the edict, was a marriage of Licinius to Constantine's sister Constantia (a son, Licinius Caesar, was born in 315). This shows how important the agreement was to Licinius, who needed Constantine as an ally more than he cared about the persecution of Christians, and who gained the freedom of action to deal with Maximinus. This was quickly accomplished with the latter's defeat and flight as early as May 313, followed by his suicide at Tarsus, probably in July. In a significant lost chapter of eastern history, Licinius then committed himself to campaigns on the Persian frontier, and later against the Goths in the regions of the lower Danube. The campaigns are known from victory titles on inscriptions of Constantine that can only have been won by Licinius and assumed by Constantine as his colleague, and by an inscription in the names of the two Augusti recording defensive works at Adamklissi in the Dobrudja.[12] These are important events, otherwise unknown to us.

---

10. Given the time needed for communication and travel, the window for the meeting is a narrow one, between Constantine's presence at Rome over the winter after the battle (cf. *CTh* 10.10.2, 1 December 312; and 15.14.3, 6 January 313) and Licinius' confrontation with Maximinus in Thrace at the end of April; Barnes, *Constantine and Eusebius*, pp. 62–63 and 318 n. 4; *New Empire*, p. 81.

11. The versions are respectively at Lactantius, *De mortibus* 48.2.1 (Nicomedia, where Lactantius was a teacher of rhetoric) and Eusebius, *Ecclesiastical History* 10.5.2–14 (Tyre). In the west, Constantine followed up the edict with letters such as that to the proconsul of Africa, Anullinus, on the restoration of church property, at Eusebius, *Ecclesiastical History* 10.5.15–17.

12. *ILS* 696, 8942, both from north Africa, in which Constantine is styled 'Persicus Maximus, Adiabenicus Maximus, Medicus Maximus, Armeniacus Maximus, Gothicus Maximus'; *ILS* 8938 (Adamklissi), with Licinius' name erased; Barnes, *New Empire*, p. 81n.

Constantine, meanwhile, turned to Gaul and Italy. In 314 he put his new allegiance to the test by arranging for a council to settle various matters of church discipline, held at Arles in August, and in his second visit to Rome to celebrate the tenth anniversary of his rise to power. These are his *decennalia*, celebrated at the beginning of the year in which they were fulfilled—so in 315 for a proclamation in 306. He no doubt lent his presence, if the work was completed, to the inauguration of a remodelled basilica of Maxentius with his own colossal statue inside, brandishing the sign of the cross that had given him victory; and to the dedication of the arch of Constantine, on which we can still read the inscription declaring (on behalf of the senate) that Constantine had defeated the faction of the tyrant 'by the inspiration of the divinity and his own greatness of mind'; 'instinctu divinitatis, mentis magnitudine' (Fig. 1.3). These phrases, memorable in themselves and in their context, a triumphal arch in the monumental area of Rome, should be taken together; it was to the inspiration of the divinity that Constantine owed his greatness of mind. The text also appealed to an altogether more familiar idea, the support of the army.

By now, Constantine's greatness of mind had lost interest in the pact with his brother-in-law, whom he attacked in the fall of the following year, with hard-fought battles at Cibalae in Pannonia and Hadrianople in Thrace. From there, in a precursor of what was to come, he advanced towards Byzantium, but Licinius outmanoeuvred him and after a further pact with Licinius, concluded in 317, he fell back upon Serdica (Sofia), which became a favoured capital city in these years before his ultimate conquest of the east. The consuls for 317 had already been appointed by Constantine, but the pact is documented by balancing consulships between the reconciled Augusti and their families in 318 and 319. It did not last, however, for in 320, Constantine claimed both consulships for himself and his son, and from 321 to 324 his choices (western aristocrats, whom he must have come to know during his visit to Rome) were not recognized in the east. For his part, Licinius provided another *casus belli*, if it were needed, by reopening his interest in action against Christians, which he had only set aside, if he ever had enthusiasm for it, as part of the agreement he had made at Milan. By increments of territory, Constantine was advancing his frontiers towards the east, and it can have surprised no one when a second war broke out between them. Constantine, the victor already in three civil wars, made his preparations for a fourth in Galerius' old capital at Thessalonica, a great imperial capital and an important harbour. He was not going to be caught out again. Constantine understood that with Byzantium its target, a combined assault by land and sea was needed, and in the summer of 324, almost twenty years after he had left it to join his father, he descended on the east like a whirlwind.

2

From Byzantium to Constantinople

2.1 The City of Byzantium

AFTER A SWEEPING campaign by land and sea, a siege of Byzantium, and naval battles in the Hellespont and Bosporus, Constantine overcame Licinius on 18 September 324.[1] On the following day he received the surrender of his colleague (and brother-in-law), under a promise of safety that he never intended to keep. Political expediency combined with hard feelings, and Licinius, first allowed to live at Thessalonica, was put to death there in the spring of 325. There was talk of insurrection and a renewal of civil war, allegations easily fabricated for the moment, and, since they were false, just as easily resolved.

His victory had made Constantine sole master of the Roman empire, reunited under a single ruler for the first time in a generation. There was not long to wait for the first signs of the new emperor's forceful energy—that 'ingens animus', already known to the west, by which a later source characterized him.[2] On 8 November, less than two months after his victory, in what we are accustomed to call its dedication, Constantine initiated the city that he would build at Byzantium. The historic moment was enacted with a nice sense of theatre. Philostorgius, a fifth-century church historian whose heretical views ensured that his work would survive only in fragments, told how Constantine, spear in hand, led a procession of supporters out from the old city to where he would build the wall of his new one. On and on he went, declaring to his anxious entourage that he would stop only when the guide who was leading him, visible only to himself, came to a halt.[3] When the guide finally did so, Constantine planted his spear fifteen stades, more than 2,500 metres, beyond the existing limits of Byzantium. It was a massive

---

1. For the battles and their sequence, see T. D. Barnes, *The New Empire of Diocletian and Constantine* (1982), pp. 75–76—omitting a sea-battle in the Hellespont, fought while Constantine laid siege to Byzantium (see esp. Zosimus 2.23–24).

2. Aurelius Victor, *De Caesaribus* 41.12.

3. Philostorgius 2.9 (and in later sources); ed. J. Bidez / F. Winkelmann, *GCS*[2] (1972), pp. 20–22.

From Byzantium to Constantinople: An Urban History. John Matthews, Oxford University Press.
© Oxford University Press 2024. DOI: 10.1093/oso/9780197585498.003.0002

extension of the site, a city conceived on a different scale from the already substantial city that stood there now (Fig. 2.1).[4]

The story has a touch of legend about it, but it was a legend made for the occasion. Philostorgius used good sources, and there is nothing impossible about Constantine's piece of theatre; it is easy to surmise that the emperor's invisible guide helped him to make history at the point earlier marked by his surveyors. We might even detect in Constantine's ceremony a relic of a very ancient Roman tradition, the emperor marking the *pomerium*, the ritual boundary, of his new city. The emperor surely had advisers who could tell him about this.

In addition to its physical expansion, the transformation of Byzantium into the city of Constantine was clothed in symbolic gesture. On the same day as his parade of supporters to the site of the new walls, Constantine's 7-year-old son Constantius was promoted to the rank of Caesar, the third of his four sons to bear that title. These were the euphoniously (and confusingly) named Constantine (II), the child Constantius now promoted, Constans, to be promoted in 333, and Crispus, the son of Constantine's first wife Minervina, Caesar since 317. In the later words of the orator Themistius, referring to the promotion of Constantius, the emperor at one and the same time 'clothed his city with a wall and his son with the purple'.[5] In a society well attuned to such signs, it would be impossible to miss the meaning of this one; Constantinople was to be the seat of a dynasty and the home of empire.

In choosing Byzantium as its site, Constantine was in one sense putting into effect the lessons of his war against Licinius. His siege of the city, and what he may have learned of its history, showed its value. This had been understood by Constantine's predecessor Septimius Severus in his war against the pretender Pescennius Niger, and the three-year siege that provides evidence for the character of the earlier city (below, pp. 18–21). More was in play, however, than the lessons of a civil war. In the broader context of his choice—whether one thinks of Diocletian's capital of Nicomedia, where Constantine had spent much time in his early years, or Galerius' Thessalonica, from where he had organized his campaign against Licinius, or indeed Constantine's own flirtation with Serdica (Sofia)— the emperor seems to be obeying a gravitational pull towards the Bosporan region as the locus of imperial power.

As has often been noted, the site presents certain disadvantages. A steady current flows down the Bosporus from the Black Sea into the Propontis, and when a north wind blew in addition, vessels could find it difficult to make

---

4. Zosimus 2.30.4 gives fifteen stades; on the general accuracy of the measurement see the comments of F. Paschoud, *Zosime* (ed. Budé, Vol. 1, 1971), pp. 226–27, n. 41.

5. Themistius, *Or.* 4, 63a.

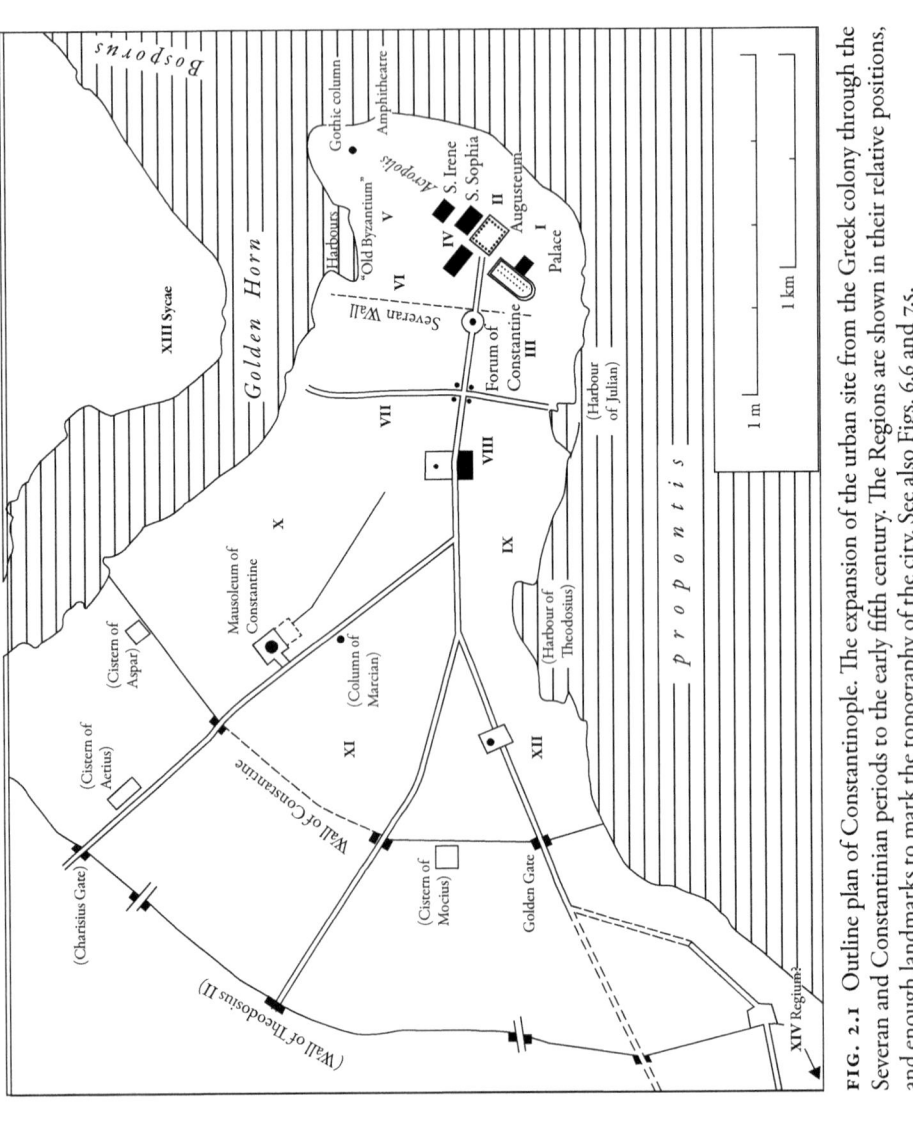

FIG. 2.1 Outline plan of Constantinople. The expansion of the urban site from the Greek colony through the Severan and Constantinian periods to the early fifth century. The Regions are shown in their relative positions, and enough landmarks to mark the topography of the city. See also Figs. 6.6 and 7.5.

harbour—one pagan activist, a famous philosopher and an adviser of Constantine, was executed for 'chaining the winds' by magic and holding the grain-ships out at sea (below, pp. 33, 217). Eunapius, the writer, hostile to Constantine, who recorded this episode, adds the useful observation that the city was difficult of access by sea except when the wind blew from the south.[6] This aspect of sailing conditions on the Bosporus is very well described by Thomas Russell in his recent book on *Byzantium and the Bosporus*, with citation of a sailing manual of 1920:

> Without a favourable southerly wind, the *Black Sea Pilot* notes, a sailing ship cannot sail north through the Bosporus, 'as it is impossible, even with a smart vessel well handled, to proceed out once through the Bosporus against a foul wind, owing to the strength of the current'.[7]

One does not sail the length of the Bosporus from the south to reach Byzantium, but the combination of northerly current and wind, both of them at their strongest in the summer when the grain ships were at sea, presented serious problems of accessibility. We will see attempts to alleviate the problem by establishing harbours on the southern coast of the peninsula, where the current was less direct and the city itself provided shelter from the north wind.

Despite the earlier judgment of Tacitus (*Ann.* 12.63) among others, Byzantium does not possess a very fertile territory, and with a hinterland extending in only one direction, its water supply is insufficient for a very large settlement. Like other, more southerly Mediterranean cities (Syracuse, Carthage, and many other African cities are examples), Constantinople came to depend on storage cisterns rather than (like Rome) on aqueducts of endlessly flowing water, and as it grew its sources became ever more distant, and its cisterns larger and more numerous. This extension of the water supply is one way in which we can trace the growth of the city (below, Chapter 7, pp. 130–4).

These were handicaps to be overcome, but it was worth the effort, for, taking the strategic view, it is a prime location, as others too had noticed. According to a famous story first told by Herodotus (4.144), the people of the Hellespont remembered the Persian commander Megabazus for a remark he made, when he learned that Chalcedon, on the Asiatic side of the Bosporus, was founded seventeen years before Byzantium. Its settlers must indeed have been blind, he said, to

---

6. Eunapius, *Lives of the Sophists* 462–63 (ed. Loeb), pp. 382–85. On the limitations of the site, see esp. Cyril Mango's Introduction to the volume of papers, *Constantinople and its Hinterland* (ed. Mango and G. Dagron, 1995), pp. 1–6. For the Bosporus current, see for example Cassius Dio 75.10 (ed. Loeb, Vol. IX), pp. 192–97.

7. Thomas Russell, *Byzantium and the Bosporus* (2017), p. 30; the citation is from *Black Sea Pilot*, p. 105.

neglect the site of Byzantium and settle where they did, ignoring the worse site for the better! Tacitus ascribed the same sentiment to a recommendation from the Delphic oracle to the Megarian colonists who consulted it, in saying that they should 'seek a place opposite the land of the blind', and thereby came to settle Byzantium. Whether or not Megabazus actually made this remark, and whether or not the Delphic oracle ever made this utterance, it expresses the perspective of an imperial power, considering the site in a strategic context not relevant at the time of the foundations of Chalcedon and Byzantium. Greek settlers of the seventh century BCE were concerned not with empire but with survival and prosperity, which both the 'blind Chalcedonians' and the Byzantines achieved very well. Indeed, at the time of the foundation of the cities, Chalcedon might well have seemed the safer bet, given the exposure of Byzantium to hostile threats from the Thracian inhabitants of the interior. However, it was not as a Greek colony but in a larger arena of imperial power, whether under Persia, Athens, or Rome, that Byzantium came into its own.

It is important to recognize the success achieved by Byzantium, both strategic and economic, in that earlier period. It was a rich prize for those who could control it. Captured by the Greek allies as a first priority after their victory in the Persian Wars, it was for some years the centre of an independent principality of the Spartan king-in-exile Pausanias. Under the fifth-century Athenian empire it held a garrison, played an important role in Athenian trade with the Black Sea, and paid a substantial *phoros* (payment or contribution) of 21 silver talents, to be explained not so much as the result of its territorial wealth or fishing industry as of the city's ability to exact customs dues and fees from commercial traffic in the difficult waters of the Bosporus—we might call it protection money, in the same way that the assessment of the tribute to the Athenian empire was protection money paid to that increasingly predatory institution.[8] The scale of tribute paid by Byzantium demands attention; the only comparable figures recorded in the tribute lists are those of the large island of Thasos, with its mining resources, at 30 talents and 'big spenders' like Aegina, Abdera, and Paros, at 30, 15, and 18 talents respectively. In the later period, shrewdly measuring its support for Hellenistic kings and for Rome (it enjoyed good relations with Ptolemy Philadelphus and, from the time of the Macedonian Wars, an alliance with Rome), Byzantium emerged into the phase of its history that concerns us here, the Graeco-Roman city of the first two centuries of the Roman empire.[9]

---

8. R. Meiggs, *The Athenian Empire* (1972), pp. 71–73 with 465–68, 206, etc. For a summary account of the earlier history of Byzantium, see John Freely, *Istanbul* (1996), ch. 2; more especially, in rich detail and with a powerful appreciation of the economic context, see Russell, *Byzantium and the Bosporus*.

9. On this Russell's *Byzantium and the Bosporus* is not supported by its subtitle, for it has little to say on Roman Byzantium before the foundation of Constantinople.

The advantages of its position will not have escaped an intelligent observer, whether Megabazus the Persian, Pausanias the Spartan, Athenian imperialist, or Hellenistic king. Through its control of the Bosporus, the city connected east and west, as is obvious. Less obvious at first sight, it also connected north and south, for it offered access to the lower Danube and its armies, and to what is now Ukraine, by Constantine's time occupied by Gothic settlers. Ancient history again offers precedent; when Xerxes' predecessor Darius the Great threw a bridge of boats over the Bosporus, it was against the Scythians, living where the Goths now lived, that he was leading his armies.[10] The Byzantines understood their advantages perfectly well. As they observed in a deputation to the senate in the time of Claudius, adducing their long history of service to Rome, they lived in a region through which all armies must march, fleets sail and supplies be carried: 'ea loca insiderent quae transmeantibus terra marique ducibus exercitibusque, simul vehendo commeatu opportuna forent' (Tacitus, *Ann.* 12.62).

In the light of such an appraisal, descriptions of the city as 'a small Greek town [on] the eastward tip of the promontory' or 'an obscure provincial village in the middle of nowhere' are serious understatements of its importance and historical role in the Greek and Graeco-Roman periods.[11] The envoys would have been amazed by such descriptions of their city. So too would the geographer Strabo, who, referring to Byzantium as a 'famous city' and repeating the story of the 'land of the blind', also tells of the famous tunny-fish (*pelamys*) which descend in vast numbers from the Black Sea and, avoiding the Chalcedonian and carried by the current to the opposite shore of the Bosporus, 'provide revenue to Byzantium and the Roman people'.[12] The fish were caught by shore-based systems of nets laid out like a marine maze, driving them into traps where they could be killed and gutted, to be sold in the market or sent for preservation and export. The 'revenue to the Roman people' must be the result of taxation.[13]

---

10. Herodotus (4.87) records that the Byzantines took the inscriptions set up by the king at his place of crossing and used them to build the altar of Artemis Orthosia, except for one block, in 'Assyrian' letters, that was left by the temple of Dionysus. The temple of Artemis was on the acropolis, see below, pp. 183f. It is unfortunate that Russell's map of the Bosporus at *Byzantium and the Bosporus*, p. 20, misplaces Byzantium on the southern coast of its peninsula. The map source, *Barrington Atlas of the Greek and Roman World*, Map 53 (Clive Foss), is correct.

11. Respectively R. Krautheimer, *Three Christian Capitals* (1983), p. 42; and Jaś Elsner, 'The Itinerarium Burdigalense', *JRS* 90 (2000), p. 104. Even Thomas Russell, whose research has done much to prove the opposite case, refers to Byzantium as a 'minor Greek *polis*' surrounded by hostile Thracian tribes—not so under the Romans; see his *Byzantium and the Bosporus*, pp. 165–7 and elsewhere.

12. Strabo 7.6.2 (ed. Loeb, Vol. III), pp. 282–83.

13. For the techniques and manner of exploitation, see Russell, *Byzantium and the Bosporus*, pp. 152ff.

The provincial status of Byzantium under Rome is unusual, reflecting the peculiar nature of its position. A letter written to Trajan by Pliny as governor of Bithynia shows that despite its location on the European side of the Bosporus, the city and its territory belonged to the Asiatic province of Bithynia, where it also owned lands and competed with Cyzicus on the southern side of the Propontis (Figs 2.2–3). It was a matter of practical common sense that the communities on each side of the Bosporus, an economic zone requiring co-operation among them, should be under the same administration, but Pliny's letter opens up a new horizon, in the direction of the Roman armies of the lower Danube. It was the custom of the city, Pliny reminds the emperor, to send an annual embassy of good wishes to the legate of Moesia, a courtesy that Pliny, in accordance with his mandate as governor, proposed to put an end to on grounds of expense. Trajan agreed: 'the governor of Moesia will excuse them', he wrote to Pliny, 'if they are less lavish in their expressions of respect'. Since Moesia, like Bithynia at this time, was an imperial province receiving its mandate directly from the emperor, there is no reason to doubt that its governor accepted the advice.[14] In another letter, Trajan suggested to Pliny that he might secure the services of a surveyor, needed for a construction project at Nicomedia, from the legate of Moesia.[15] Even after Thrace was reorganized as a praetorian province separate from Moesia (between 106 and 114), Byzantium remained part of Bithynia; but the gravitational field of the lower Danubian region, transmitted by the military roads connecting them with the east, was powerful, and a defining feature of the role of the city in the Roman period.

In the last decade of the second century Byzantium entered the mainstream of Roman history when it led its region in support of the imperial claimant Pescennius Niger against Septimius Severus. It is a moment for historians to step up and describe the city, and they do not disappoint. Byzantium is described by Herodian as at that time the largest and most prosperous city in Thrace, with a formidable defensive wall, its stone blocks 'fitted together so closely that one might think it carved from a single block of stone' (3.1.6–7). We are already far from the 'small Greek town' or 'obscure provincial village' described by the modern writers cited above. An older and more conscientious authority than Herodian, Cassius Dio, came from nearby Nicaea and had seen the walls of Byzantium both before and after their ultimate demolition by Severus (75.10–14). Dio gives a detailed account of the long and harrowing siege, surviving intact in its Byzantine epitomators, in which the strength and resources of the city, focused on its great walls defended by artillery, five hundred men-o'-war, and two harbours on the Golden

---

14. Pliny, *Ep.* 10.43 and Trajan's reply at *Ep.* 10.44, with Sherwin-White's commentary, *The Letters of Pliny* (1966), p. 625.

15. *Ep.* 10.42.

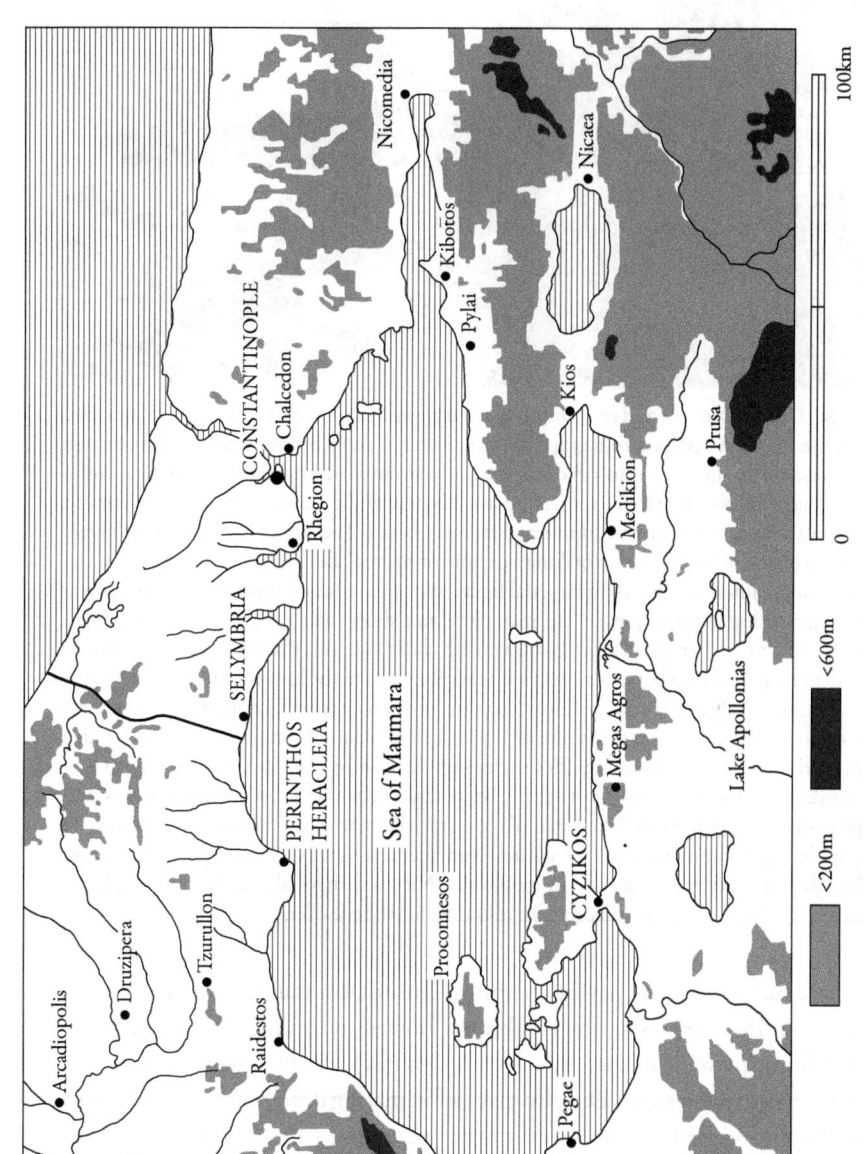

FIG. 2.2 Constantinople and its hinterland.

FIG. 2.3 Constantinople and environs in the Peutinger Map. Despite its extremely distorted format, the Peutinger Map, a topographical panorama of the Roman empire and its eastern neighbours, drawn up in the mid-13th century from a late antique original incorporating earlier material, is a priceless guide to the settlement, road system and distances of the Roman empire. The detail above shows Constantinople and its neighbours. The city is shown in the conventional pose of an enthroned figure making a gesture of address. Beside it is the column of Constantine, surmounted by a standing imperial figure with spear and what must be understood as an orb symbolising imperial power. The map could not show the solar crown with which the statue was equipped, but the column is shown with the iron bands that were placed on it after an incident in 416, when a large stone block was displaced from the lower courses and fell to the ground. Immediately to the west is shown Regium, its distance from Constantinople correctly shown as 12 miles, and above the figure of Constantinople an inlet representing the Golden Horn. To the east is the Bosporus, with the cities of Chalcedon and Chrysopolis, where Constantine defeated Licinius in a sea-battle. The Bosporus curves north-east and finds its way past the 'promontory' to the Black Sea, the north coast of which, with the Sea of Azov, is shown as a strip at the top of the map. Below Chalcedon is an inlet reaching Nicomedia past Libyssa and, south of this, divided by the inlet and by mountains, Nicaea with its lake, and Prusias. Each city carries a symbol indicating the nature of its resources for the traveller.

Horn, are plain to see. It may be rhetorical enthusiasm that led Dio to write of 'stones from the theatres and whole bronze horses and statues of bronze' being thrown from the walls in the city's defence (75.11.4), but he knew the place and what was to be found there. Dio also gives a fascinating description of the famous echo effect produced by the seven towers extending from the Thracian Gate to the sea. Only from the first of the seven towers could the effect be produced, but there, if one shouted or threw a stone at the wall, the echo was passed on from tower to tower all the way to the sea, as if the towers were speaking to each other. Dio's understanding of acoustics may be imperfect, but he had personally heard the 'talking towers' before they were demolished. The 'Thracian Gate' must be the gate through which Constantine led his supporters in the procession of 8 November 324, with which this chapter began.

Byzantium was punished by Severus for supporting his enemy, by the loss of civic rights and juridical subjection to nearby Heraclea/Perinthus (a compatriot of Dio's named Priscus, who had designed the artillery machines used in its defence, was condemned to death but then spared, to make his engineering gifts available to Severus for his campaigns in the east). Later, however, in a significant change of mind Byzantium received back its civic status. Its walls were rebuilt and the city was developed on a monumental scale.

The restoration of Byzantium by Severus has been doubted by historians of the city, but there is good reason to accept it. It is attributed by the late fourth-century Historia Augusta to the influence, in his father's lifetime, of the young Caracalla (joint emperor with Severus from 198 and his successor from 211 to 217). The Historia Augusta is a collection of imperial biographies from Hadrian in the early second century to Carus in the late third, composed by a single author, probably writing in the late fourth century, under the purported names of six authors of the age of Diocletian and Constantine. It is hard to imagine a stranger literary situation, and more questions arise as to the character of the work and motives of its author (why such a pretence?) than can possibly be discussed here. Especially in the later series of *Lives* beginning with Severus Alexander (222–35) the production has a well-deserved reputation for romance and invention, but this is less true of the earlier *Lives* down to Caracalla and Elagabalus. It is here important to assess the value of individual items and of their likely source, who on this occasion is the early third-century biographer Marius Maximus. Named in full L(ucius) Marius, L(uci) f(ilius), Maximus Perpetuus Aurelianus, he is one and the same man as the general who had led Severus' forces against Byzantium; 'dux exerciti Mysiaci [*sic*] aput Byzantium', says his most informative inscription from Rome, where after a distinguished career he was urban prefect under Caracalla's successor and the father of a consul of 237.[16] This evidence transforms our understanding of Marius Maximus' vantage point. He was at the heart of events, had an interest in the city, and his historical work is known to have covered this period. One can hardly imagine a better-placed source for an action taken by Severus and Caracalla with respect to Byzantium.

A second source is the sixth-century historian Hesychius, fragments of whose work survive in the collection of Byzantine sources known as *Scriptores originum Constantinopolitarum* or 'Patria', to be discussed in Chapter 3 below.

---

16. *Life of Caracalla* 1.7; *ILS* 2935. Marius Maximus' vantage point is not acknowledged by Cyril Mango, 'Septime Sévère et Byzance', *Comptes Rendus de l'Académie des Inscriptions et Belles-Lettres* (2003), pp. 593–608; similarly, T. D. Barnes, *The Sources of the* Historia Augusta (1978), pp. 88, 101–2. In its view of Marius Maximus, my position on the 'Historia Augusta question' differs from that of Ronald Syme, *Ammianus and the Historia Augusta* (1968) and elsewhere; see Anthony Birley's translation of the earlier *Lives* in the series; *Lives of the Later Caesars* (1976 and reprinted), pp. 14–15.

What remains of Hesychius' paragraphs on the foundation and early history of Byzantium is of value only as a source for later mythologizing, but when the summary arrives at the Severan period, its character changes. It produces brief but serviceable accounts of Severus' war against Pescennius Niger and of the emperor's change of mind when, having first punished Byzantium by dismantling its walls and making it subject to Heraclea, he built public baths and a Hippodrome for the newly favoured city.[17] As long as Severus and his son lived, according to Hesychius, the city was known as Antonina, but reverted to its old name after the deaths of these emperors. This detail of nomenclature is a priceless item, suggesting the promotion of Byzantium as a Roman *colonia* with an appropriate addition to its nomenclature; the name Antoninus, borne by Caracalla and not by his father, would match the statement in the Historia Augusta that it was Caracalla (rather than Severus) who was responsible for the restoration of the city. There is a further reason for pausing on Hesychius' account. His reference to the emperor Severus and his son as being 'enrolled among the gods' upon their death is a correctly expressed description of Roman practice, long obsolete by the time of Hesychius. Writing in the sixth century, he preserves the authentic terminology of an earlier period.[18] In a further detail, Hesychius wrote that after its reduction by Severus forces, the 'crown of the walls' was removed. If this refers to a complete demolition, it cannot have lasted for long. A Roman *colonia*, as Byzantium was to become, required the dignity of city walls, and it is obvious from the sequel down to the time of Constantine that the city was well defended. Perhaps Hesychius meant that only the 'crowning glory' of the walls, that is to say their more decorative upper registers, was removed.

Some of these details are confirmed, and others added, by our third source, the historian Zosimus, a slightly older contemporary of Hesychius. Zosimus' time of writing has been held against him as evidence for the earlier city, but this is not a valid objection, given his well-established reliance on the much earlier Eunapius. The architectural features described by Zosimus, including a new agora in the area south of the acropolis and double colonnades leading to a city gate in a refurbished wall, will call for discussion later, when the evidence is more completely assembled Chapter 6. There is more here than can be dismissed as a later invention. In the meantime, we should appreciate the significance of the Severan period in the urban development of Byzantium. We need not join those historians who think of Septimius Severus (or his son) as a sort of 'proto-Constantine' (whether real or legendary), to appreciate the importance of

17. Hesychius 35–38 (in *Patria* 1.34–36; ed. Th. Preger I, pp. 15–16; Berger, pp. 20–23). The Byzantine lexicon known as the Souda twice refers to the city under the name 'Antonia', s.v. A(ntonia) 2721 and S(everus) 181 (ed. Adler I, p. 247 and III, pp. 334–35).

18. Hesychius 36 (in *Patria*, Preger I, p. 16; Berger, p. 23). The full colonial titulature of Severan Byzantium is not known. Berytus, a *colonia* since the time of Augustus (see below), added the name 'Antoniniana' under Caracalla. Hesychius 43 is also correct on the 'Troadensian porticoes', located in relation to the Constantinian city wall.

Byzantium long before the days of that emperor.[19] Byzantium was an important city both locally and in its broader context, and its monuments of preceding periods were a significant element in the Constantinian urban landscape.

In one sense, a new city named after the emperor who established it is not so remarkable an occurrence—the Roman world was filled with such commemorations of emperors and princes, accumulating over centuries. A glance at a map reveals them, from all periods of the empire—Juliopolis, Claudiopolis, Hadrianopolis (not to mention fully Greek names like Sebastopolis) among many from earlier times, Diocletianopolis and Maximianopolis from the generation preceding Constantine; the list is endless, and continues into the future.[20] It was regular practice also for emperors' names to be added to cities that were re-founded or promoted in status, as with Aelia Capitolina (Jerusalem, named after Hadrian upon its re-settlement as a colony), or the many cities that added to their own nomenclature names like Iulia, Ulpia, Aurelia, and so on, almost as if they had been 'adopted' into the families of the emperors who favoured them. In the early fourth century preceding the foundation of Constantinople, two cities, Arelate in southern Gaul and Cirta in Numidia, added 'Constantina' to their existing names (the latter, a major city in Algeria, is still 'Constantine'), while after the death of Constantine, the Italian town of Hispellum became 'Flavia Constans' after Constantine's son and successor, in recognition of the benefits it had received—an annual festival with gladiatorial games, a temple in honour of the imperial family.[21] It is the regular pattern of imperial munificence, and could produce elaborate results, as a city's nomenclature expanded with the honours it had received. The full title of Roman Beirut, founded as a colony in the time of Augustus, was 'Colonia Iulia Augusta Felix Berytus', that of Tyre, promoted under Septimius Severus, was 'Tyrus Colonia Septimia Severa Metropolis'—'Metropolis' to designate it as the chief city of the region, another prized honour. As we have just seen, Byzantium itself was for a time known as 'Antonina', after Severus' son and successor Caracalla, reflecting its promotion to the status of a colony.[22]

An especial connection was reserved for cities to which emperors were attached for some personal reason, for example as the origin of their family.

---

19. For Severus as a 'proto-Constantine', see G. Dagron, *Naissance d'une Capitale* (1974), pp. 15–19; and Cyril Mango, *Le développement urbain de Constantinople* (1959), p. 19; in *Patria*, Berger, p. 289, n. 50: 'This well-known Byzantine legend is historically incorrect, for the rebuilding of Byzantion took place only long after Severus' death', etc.

20. For instance Grenoble, ancient Gratianopolis, Theodosiopolis, Arcadiopolis, and places called Justinianopolis.

21. *ILS* 705, lines 41ff. The titulature at the head of the inscription gives to Constantine and his three sons the family name 'Flavius', which Constantine had taken over from his father to produce what is known as the second Flavian *gens* (cf. *ILS* 642ff., 682ff.).

22. Berytus: *RE* III, col. 322: Tyre; *RE* VIIA, col. 1900. Berytus added 'Antoniniana' under Caracalla.

A prime example, relevant to Byzantium for the scale and character of its development (see Chapter 6, pp. 106–8, below), is Tripolitanian Lepcis Magna in the time of Septimius Severus, who was descended from an equestrian family already prominent in the city in the first century; others are Philippopolis in Arabia under the Emperor Philip, and Constantine's own birthplace, Naissus in Moesia—'which town he later adorned magnificently', as one source says. The birthplace of Galerius in Dacia Ripensis was renamed Romuliana after his mother Romula, and Constantine himself named a city after his mother, Helenopolis, formerly Drepanon, in Bithynia.[23]

Some cities became centres of administration and thereby acquired some of the status of capital cities. The term 'capital city' is neither formally nor exactly used, but it does direct our attention to the new political landscape that is emerging in the course of the third and fourth centuries. Examples are Nicomedia, promoted as his capital by Diocletian, as were Thessalonica by Galerius, and Trier in the Mosel valley by Constantine in the early years of his rule. It was in this last city that an orator, invoking the name of Rome to raise the profile of an imperial capital in the provinces, declared to Constantine:

> I see a Circus Maximus to rival, I believe, the one at Rome. I see basilicas and a forum, palace buildings, a seat of justice, raised to such heights that they promise to be worthy of the stars and sky, whose neighbours they are. All these things are without question the gifts of your presence. Whatever places your divinity illuminates most frequently by its presence, in these places all things—men, city walls, grants of privilege—are increased.

Circus Maximus, basilica, forum, palace, seat of justice, city walls, an influx of population, grants of favour—the orator could almost have been describing Constantine's city to be founded in the east.[24] The same remarks could have been made of Galerius' Thessalonica or Diocletian's Nicomedia—which indeed is compared by Ammianus Marcellinus to a region of the 'eternal city' itself, such was the splendour of its public and private buildings after the expenditures of the emperors who had resided there.[25]

---

23. Naissus: *Anonymus Valesianus* 1.3; 'quod oppidum postea magnifice ornavit'; Romuliana: *Epitome de Caesaribus* 40.16. The re-foundation of Drepanon as Helenopolis is dated to 327 by Jerome's *Chronicle* and *Chronicon Paschale* (translation and notes by Michael and Mary Whitby, in TTH 7 (1989), p. 15), adding immunity from taxation for 'as far as could be seen from the city'.

24. *Panegyric Latini* 6(7).22.5, of 310, commented by C. E. V. Nixon in Nixon and Barbara Saylor Rodgers, *In Praise of Later Roman Emperors* (1994), p. 252.

25. Ammianus Marcellinus 22.9.3, contrasting its ruinous state after a catastrophic earthquake (17.7.1–7).

We are witnessing the emergence of a new political geography of the Roman empire. In a process looking back to the second and third centuries, the city of Rome had shown itself progressively less able to combine the strategic and ideological needs of its empire. It was in no sense a failure of affection or loyalty to the old capital, but practical questions of time and distance; the city was too far from the frontiers to claim the emperors' presence in times of extended warfare. As the emperors spent less time there and visited less often, Rome had given way to better-located provincial cities, some of which we have seen—Trier in the Rhineland, Arles in southern Gaul ('Gallula Roma Arelas', the poet Ausonius called it); Milan in north Italy; Sirmium, Thessalonica, and Serdica in the Danubian and Balkan regions; Nicomedia and Antioch in Asia Minor and the east. Wherever the emperor resided might be thought of as a sort of Rome, as he took there the institutions of state and government; army, treasuries, supplies, and administrative services followed the emperor to whichever provincial centre required his presence, and the idea of Rome was re-created; Rome, it might be said, was wherever the emperor was.[26]

The case of Constantinople is of a different order. We have seen the scale of expansion of the site initiated by Constantine as well as the involvement of his dynasty. and the phrase 'altera Roma', 'second Rome', used of the city by a poet writing close in time to its dedication, a man connected with the emperor, well informed and eager to please, puts the familiar image into a new and sharper focus.[27] We are looking not at a literary device adaptable to any city that might be said to resemble Rome but at a more exacting comparison, and at the direct expression of the intentions of an emperor.

2.2 A New Rome

After five and a half years of intense activity since its dedication, what we now think of as the consecration of the new city took place on 11 May 330, a day henceforth observed as the birthday of Constantinople, like the Roman Parilia of 21 April. The ceremonies, focusing on a procession to the newly completed (or re-commissioned) Hippodrome followed by chariot-races, are described in two

---

26. E. Mayer, *Rom is dort, wo der Kaiser ist. Untersuchungen ze den Staatsdenkmälern der dezentralisierten Reiches von Diocletian bis zu Theodosius II* (2002); Sylvain Destephen, *Le Voyage Impérial dans l'Antiquité Tardive* (De l'Archéologie à l'Histoire 67, 2016), and 'From Mobile Center to Constantinople', *DOP* 73 (2019), pp. 9–23, pointing out that the role of Constantinople as an imperial residential centre was achieved in stages.

27. T. D. Barnes, 'Publilius Optatianus Porfyrius', *AJP* 96 (1975), pp. 173–86; Barnes, *The New Empire of Diocletian and Constantine*, p. 76. Barnes' argument that Porphyrius was writing before the promotion of Constantius as Caesar in 324 is not compelling; his poem refers to the existing Caesars (Crispus and Constantinus) as military figures ('coruscos ... duces'), and Constantius (born 7 August 317) was too young to be described like this so early a date. For Porphyrius' biography and connections with Constantine, see A. Chastagnol, *Les Fastes de la Préfecture de Rome au Bas-Empire* (1962), pp. 80–82.

sources; the sixth-century *Chronicle* of the Antiochene John Malalas, an account repeated with minor variations in the *Chronicon Paschale* or 'Easter Chronicle', compiled in the early seventh century.[28]

The connections between these texts spring to the eye from a side-by-side comparison, as is presented below (bearing in mind that the text of Malalas that we possess is itself a condensation of the original). Some discrepancies are noted, as in the dating of Constantine's building programme in *Chronicon Paschale* to 328, as opposed to the year 330 given by Malalas. It may be that this is simply a matter of continuity in the narrative, *Chronicon Paschale* having inserted a crossing of the Danube for a campaign against Goths and Sarmatians over a newly built bridge;[29] or else the author, perhaps also Malalas in his original version, may have thought it appropriate to mention Constantine's building programme at Constantinople before the actual consecration of the city, by which time a significant part of it must have been complete. It is also a reminder that an emperor has many things to think about, for example the military campaigns just referred to and, not least, the visit to Rome to celebrate Constantine's twentieth anniversary of rule (*vicennalia*), a visit that did not turn out quite as expected, seeming to result in a rejection of Rome that cannot have been intended. Malalas' statement that Constantine left Rome in a long *processus* as if in an extended ceremonial progress formally transferring power from the old Rome to the new may be misleading, but is an intelligible description of his movements; having initiated the building of Constantinople, he visited Rome and on returning to the east continued to use Nicomedia as his capital city until his new one was ready.[30] It was a time of intense activity on many fronts, as a building programme in the making since Constantine's choice of his new capital city accompanied the performance of the traditional duties of a Roman emperor. War across the Danube was one of these, but there were also new concepts of imperial duty, as Constantine's attendance

---

28. Malalas, p. 322 Bonn; Elizabeth Jeffreys, Michael Jeffreys, and Roger Scott (eds), *The Chronicle of John Malalas*, p. 175; *Chronicon Paschale*, p. 528 Bonn; Michael Whitby and Mary Whitby, *Chronicon Paschale*, pp. 17–18.

29. The same notice appears in Theophanes' *Chronicle* under the year 329. The bridge, at Oescus-Sucidava, was obviously made for repeated use; M. Kulikowski, in Noel Lenski (ed.), *Cambridge Companion to the Age of Constantine* (2006), pp. 360–63; *Barrington Atlas of the Greek and Roman World*, sheet 22 5B. Despite the doubts of the author, I think that the bridge shown on the 'small bronze medalette' minted at Constantinople, fig. 6B of Lars Ramskold, 'Coins and Medallions Struck for the Inauguration of Constantinople, 11 May, 330', *Niš and Byzantium* 9 (2011), pp. 136–38 must be intended to suggest the bridge at Oescus.

30. Barnes, *The New Empire of Diocletian and Constantine*, pp. 78–80, thoroughly documents the activities of Constantine in these years. He was at Nicomedia in Feb.–Sept. 325 and July 327–March 328, in the meantime at various places including Rome in July–Aug. 326.

at the council of Nicaea and his own letters of this period show, but proper distinctions are respected. The founding of a city has its own procedures and ceremonies, in no way to be confused or amalgamated with those of a church council. Constantine's presence at Nicaea preceded both the visit to Rome of 326 and the consecration of Constantinople, but it did not influence the ideological character of either event.

Malalas 13.7–8; pp. 319–21 Bonn 330 (Jeffery and others, pp. 173–75).

Chronicon Paschale pp. 527–29; Bonn, s.a. 328 (Whitby and Whitby, pp. 15–18).

During his reign, during the consulship of Gallicanus and Symmachus [330], the former Byzantion was dedicated. The emperor Constantine made a lengthy *processus*, going from Rome to Byzantion. He reconstructed the earlier city wall, that of Byzas, and added another great extension to the city wall and, joining this to the old city wall, he ordered the city to be called Constantinople. He also completed the hippodrome and adorned it with bronze statues and with ornamentation of every kind, and built in it a *kathisma*, just like the one in Rome, for the emperor to watch the races. He also built a large and beautiful palace, equally on the pattern of the one in Rome, near the hippodrome, with the way up from the palace to the *kathisma* in the hippodrome by the staircase known as the Kochlias.

In the time of the aforementioned consuls, Constantine the celebrated emperor departed from Rome and, while staying at Nicomedia the metropolis of Bithynia, made visitations for a long time to Byzantium. He renewed the first wall of the city of Byzas and, after making considerable extensions also to the same wall, he added them to the ancient wall of the city and named it Constantinople. He also completed the Hippodrome, adorning it with works in bronze and with every excellence, and made in it a box for imperial viewing, in the likeness of the one which is in Rome. He made a great Palace near the same Hippodrome, and the ascent from the Palace to the box in the Hippodrome by way of the Kochlias, as it is called.

(Malalas)

(*Chronicon Paschale*)

He also built a large and very beautiful forum, and set up in the middle a marvellous column, all of porphyry. On this column he set up a statue of himself with seven rays upon its head. He had this bronze statue brought from where it had stood in Ilion, a city in Phrygia. Constantine took secretly from Rome the wooden statue

He also built a forum which was large and exceedingly fine; and he set in the middle a great porphyry column of Theban stone, worthy of admiration, and on top of the same column a great statue of himself with rays of light on his head, a work in bronze which he had brought from a city in Phrygia.

known as the Palladion and placed it in the forum he built, beneath the column which supported his statue. Some of the people of Byzantion say that it is still there. He made a bloodless sacrifice to God, and the Tychē of the city which had been restored and built and named after himself, he called Anthousa.[31] This city had originally been built by Phidalia; and she at that time had called its *tychē* Keroe [digression on Phidalia and her marriage to Byzas the king of Thrace].

The same emperor Constantine secretly took away from Rome the Palladium, as it is called, and placed it in the forum built by him, beneath the column of his monument, as certain of the Byzantines say who have heard it by tradition. After making bloodless sacrifice, he named the Tychē of the city renewed by him Anthousa.

Constantine built from the entrance to the palace up to his forum two splendid colonnades decorated with statues and different kinds of marble, and he called the place with the colonnades the Regia.[32] Nearby he also built a basilica with great columns and statues outside; this he called the Senaton. Opposite this he set up a statue of his mother Helena as Augusta, on a low porphyry column. This place he called the Augusteion.

The same emperor also built two fine colonnades from the entrance of the Palace as far as the Forum, adorned with statues and marbles, and he named the place of the colonnades the Regia. Nearby he also built a basilica with an apse, and set outside great columns and statues; this he named the Senate, and he named the place Augustaeum because he had also set up opposite to it a monument of his mother, Helena Augusta, on a porphyry column.

Likewise he completed the public bath known as the Zeuxippon, and decorated it with columns and marble of many colours and bronze statues. He had found the public bath unfinished; it had been begun formerly by the emperor Severus.

Likewise he completed the bath called Zeuxippon, adorning it with columns and varied marbles and works of bronze.

(Malalas)

He also built the hippodrome and many other buildings. When he had finished everything he celebrated a race-meeting.

---

31. Tychē is the Latin Fortuna. 'Anthousa' translates Flora, the 'secret name' of the Fortuna of Rome. The story about the Palladium is later legend.

32. At Antioch also, Malalas' home city, the colonnades leading from the public parts of the city to the palace were called 'Regia'.

He was the first to watch the spectacle there and he wore for the first time on his head a diadem set with pearls and precious stones, since he wished to fulfil the prophetic words which said, 'You placed on his head a crown of precious stone' [Ps. 20.4]; none of the previous emperors had ever worn such a thing.[33]

The descriptions of the building of the city given by Malalas and *Chronicon Paschale* are complemented by their narratives of what we understand as its consecration. The two accounts are again shown in parallel columns. Especially notable in *Chronicon Paschale* are the multiple forms of dating, and the careful differentiation of the ranks of Constantine's sons; in this respect at least, they have the air of official accounts. The reign of Constantine is counted, again accurately, from his initial proclamation in the west.

Malalas 13.7–8, pp. 320–21 Bonn, s.a. 330 (Jeffery and others, p. 175).

Chronicon Paschale, pp. 529–30
Bonn, s.a. 330
(Whitby and Whitby, pp. 17–18).

In the year 301 from the Ascension to heaven of the Lord and the twenty-fifth year of his reign, Constantine the most pious, father of Constantine II Augustus and Constantius and Constans Caesars, after building a very great, illustrious, and blessed city, and honouring it with a senate, named it Constantinople, on the 5th day before the Ides of May [11 May], on the second day of the week, in the third Indiction, and proclaimed that the city, formerly named Byzantium, be called second Rome. He was first to celebrate a chariot-racing contest, wearing for the first time a diadem of pearls and other precious stones.

---

33. Not strictly true, but Constantine's use of the diadem, familiar from his coins, is interesting as harking back to Hellenistic parallels; Lars Ramskold and Noel Lenski, 'Constantine's Dedication Medallions and the Maintenance of Civic Tradition', *Numismatische Zeitschrift* 10 (2012), pp. 31–58, at 42–3.

(Malalas)	(*Chronicon Paschale*)
He also celebrated a great festival on 11th May-Artemisios in the year 378 according to the era of Antioch the Great, ordering by his sacred decree that on that day the festival of the Anniversary of his city should be celebrated. On the same day, 11th May, he ordered that the public bath, the Zeuxippon, should be opened near the hippodrome and the Regia and the palace. He had another statue made of himself in gilded wood, bearing in its right hand the Tychē of the city, itself gilded, which he called Anthousa. He ordered that on the same day as the anniversary race-meeting this wooden statue should be brought in, escorted by the soldiers wearing cloak and boots, all holding candles; the carriage should march around the turning post and reach the pit oppose the imperial *kathisma*, and the emperor of the time should rise and make obeisance as he gazed at this statue of Constantine and the Tychē of the city. This custom has been maintained up to the present day.	And he made a great festival, and commanded by his sacred decree that the Anniversary of his city be celebrated on the same day, and that on the 11th of the same month Artemisios, the public bath Zeuxippon be opened, which was near the Hippodrome and the Regia of the palace. He made for himself another gilded monument of wood, bearing in its right hand the Tychē of the city, itself also gilded, and commanded that on the same day of the anniversary chariot races, the same monument of wood should enter, escorted by the soldiers in mantles and slippers, all holding white candles; the carriage should proceed around the further turning post and come to the arena opposite to the imperial box; and the emperor of the day should rise and do obeisance to the monument of the same emperor Constantine and this Tychē of the city.

Malalas continues with a notice on the establishment of distributions of bread to the citizens of Constantinople (13.9, pp. 322–23 Bonn, s.a. 330):

> The most sacred emperor Constantine, on the completion of his consulship, distributed largesse in Constantinople to the Byzantines, in the form of reed tokens for perpetual daily bread distribution. He called the loaves 'palatine' because they were given out in the palace. He set aside wine, meat and garments with each loaf and assigned revenues for them from his own resources; he called the loaves 'politikoi'.

The consulship can only be that of 329, from which it would follow that the institution of the bread distributions, like the consecration of the city itself, belongs to 330; *Chron. Pasch.*, however, gives a more exact and better date, 8 May 332;

> In the time of these consuls [Pacatianus and Hilarianus], bread began to
> be disbursed to the citizens of Constantinople, from 18 May.[34]

The first of Malalas' explanations for the naming of the loaves is at variance from our other information, the loaves being distributed not at the palace but at *gradus*, 'steps', or distribution points throughout the city, where lists of the qualified recipients were kept and the bakeries were registered.[35] It is from this procedure that the bread was known at Rome as *panis gradilis*, 'step-bread', otherwise *panis* (or *annona*) *civica*, as in Malalas' second explanation, the term *politikoi*, 'citizens' bread', echoing that used at Rome. 'Palatine' is probably an error of Malalas, possibly deriving from confusion or mistaken inference between the terms *palatinoi* and *politikoi*. It is conceivable that the distributions were introduced in two phases, the first being centred on the palace and the second on the *gradus* as they were organized and as the city expanded, and that their definition changed accordingly.

With all the wealth of information that they contain, these texts of Malalas and *Chron. Pasch.* raise a number of questions that will concern us in the later chapters of this study, but merit some remarks at this point. The first question relates to the nature of the new building that had already taken place in the city, in particular the extent to which its elements were based on or adapted from Severan prototypes, or were new designs of Constantine's planners. In the former category are included the Hippodrome, the adjacent Baths of Zeuxippos, opened for public use on the day of the consecration, and in the latter part of the imperial palace known as the Regia—probably, as at Antioch, the colonnaded avenues leading from the city to the palace precinct (Fig. 2.4)—together of course with the palace itself. These elements need to be seen with the infrastructure necessary for them to function. A hippodrome requires stabling, fodder, and veterinary services for its highly-bred horses, accommodation for its teams of jockeys and attendants, and facilities for training and practice—at Rome the circus and its associated activities gave their character to an entire city region[36]—while a public bath requires a water supply and resources for heating and the disposal of waste, not to mention the artistic embellishment, customer comforts, and general elegance that one expects in such an institution. A palace requires a maintenance staff of

---

34. *Chronicon Paschale*, p. 531 Bonn; Whitby and Whitby, p. 19 with note.

35. Below, Chapter 10, pp. 196–8; there were 117 *gradus* by the early fifth century.

36. The entry for Regio IX (Circus Flaminius) in the *Notitia* of the city of Rome reads 'Stabula numero IIII, factionum VI' (ed. Nordh, p. 86). Damasus, bishop of Rome, later established a church of St. Lawrence near the theatre of Pompey, also known as St. Lawrence 'in Prasino', sc. the Green faction; Matthews, *The Roman Empire of Ammianus*, p. 422. This is of course a different issue from that of the distribution of the faction supporters (*dēmoi*) in the city; see Alan Cameron's *Circus Factions* (1976).

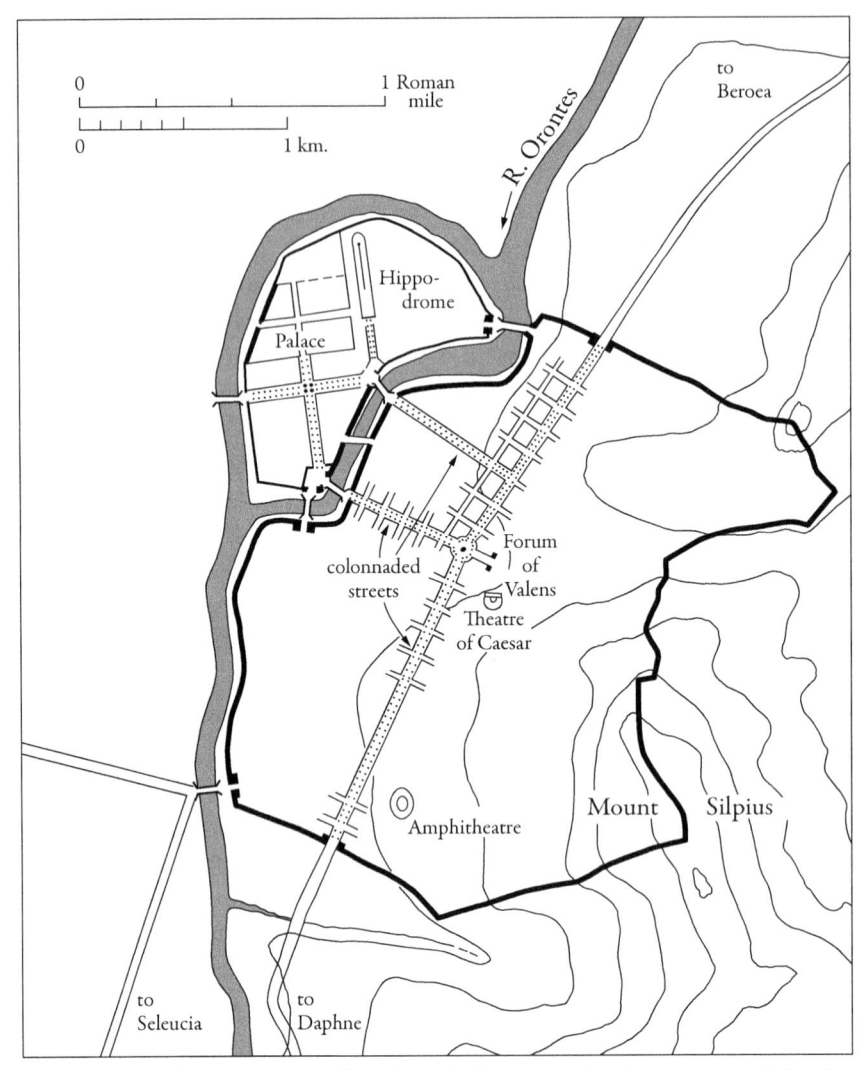

FIG. 2.4 Fourth-century Antioch; colonnaded streets and palace precinct. Other features of the city—amphitheatre, hippodrome adjoining the palace—are also relevant to the configuration of Constantinople. G. Downey, *A History of Antioch*, fig. 11, and P. Petit, *Libanius et la vie municipale à Antioche*, p. 127; J. F. Matthews, *The Roman Empire of Ammianus*, p. 73.

thousands, especially if some of the great offices of state were installed in its precincts. Between November 324 and May 330, how much of the newly founded city was built? To what extent were Constantine's planners able to take advantage of what was there before? There is also an immediate question of population and manpower. The church historian Socrates (2.13) gave the number of beneficiaries of the bread distributions mentioned by Malalas and *Chronicon Paschale* as 80,000, which has often been taken as a later projection rather than an enumeration of their original recipients. We should however remember the numbers of early inhabitants who were involved in building the city as they became residents of it and also, no doubt, supporters of the chariot-racing in the newly commissioned Hippodrome. Eunapius referred to the acclamations uttered by the people in the time of Constantine, if the grain-ships were unable to make harbour and bread ran short.[37] His complaint that the new population of the city was unable even to pronounce the emperor's name correctly may be better explained by their being Greek-speakers who found the emperor's name hard to pronounce than by his claim of inherent stupidity. They came from Greek cities around Byzantium and further afield to become residents of the new city and must have included many construction workers and contractors who had come to build it. There is also the imperial administration itself, which even in this earlier part of the fourth century must have numbered in thousands. From its earliest days, Constantinople was a largely bilingual city.[38]

We have to consider the physical and human implications of the work to be undertaken in the city and its administration—the procurement, transportation, and delivery of building materials, and the recruitment, accommodation, payment, and provisioning of thousands of workers and officials. The construction industry must always have had a migratory character, as contractors followed the opportunities and workers the employment wherever they were available, obviously with substantial movements of population (think of the Irish labourers employed in canal and railway construction in nineteenth-century England, or the settlements of building workers found in the vicinity of some ancient Egyptian cities).[39] The accommodation and servicing of such a population was a major economic undertaking. It was by no means the first time this had happened, of course; city building was common enough, but rarely on such a scale and over such a short period of time. Where did all these people live? What was their diet? (One can imagine the effects on the famous fishing industry of Byzantium.) How were their garbage and waste disposed of? They must have required a constant activity in iron- and woodworking for the replacement of their tools and equipment, craftsmen to make and repair carts and carriages, linen fabrics for their clothing and bedding. We may also ask how many of these workers became part of the permanent population of the city, as they saw in it an indefinite future of building and maintenance work—at which point we also have to consider their families, and the services in a retail trade in food, clothing, and consumer durables that they required.

---

37. Pp. 15, 217.

38. G. Dagron, 'Aux origines de la civilisation byzantine', *Revue Historique* ccxli (1969), pp. 23–56 is excellent, but we must add the common people of the city.

39. See below, p. 90f., on the district of the city known as Kainopolis.

All this may be self-evident, but it is part of the story, and it is worth pausing on the scale and expense of it. In Diocletian's *Edict on Maximum Prices* of 303, the wages of certain categories of building worker had been set at 50 or 60 rising to 75 or 150 denarii per day with sustenance. Among those specified in chapter VII of the Edict are builders in stone, cabinet-makers, carpenters, lime-burners, marble-workers, makers of wall-mosaics and tessellated floors, wall-painters and painters of pictures—the costs of some more specialized skills, and those for land and sea transport being listed in other parts of the Edict. The range of skills is more comprehensively listed in a law of 337 transmitted both in the Theodosian Code and in the *Codex Justinianus*, offering exemption from public services to those craftsmen, specified in an attached schedule, whose freedom from these duties should encourage them to pass on their skills to their sons. The schedule, which happens to be of western provenance (the law is addressed to the prefect of Rome), is presented here with slight editing, to bring out the skills of most interest in the building and enhancement of a city:[40]

Architects	Gilders	Iron-workers
Painters	Plasterers	Makers of *tessellae*
Statuaries	Silversmiths	Water technicians
Marble-workers	Coppersmiths	Goldsmiths
Panelled ceiling-makers	Foundrymen	Glassmakers
Stone-cutters	Carpenters	Plumbers
Masons	Portrait-sculptors	Wagon-builders (Wain-wrights)
Construction workers	Smiths	Sculptors
Woodcarvers	Staircase builders	Whitewashers
Mosaicists	Joiners	

We can hardly begin to imagine the financial cost of the works that were undertaken at Constantinople, but just to illustrate the orders of magnitude, to employ a single worker listed in the Prices Edict at a maximum wage of 50 denarii per day (plus food) for a working year of 250 days would have cost a total of 12,500 denarii at 303 rates of pay—the equivalent at that time of 12.5 gold *solidi* struck at seventy-two coins to the pound.[41] The cost of employing 10,000 workers at the

---

40. *CTh* 13.4.2 = *CJust* 10.66.1 (2 August 337), with the observations of Mommsen, ad loc., on the order of the entries, which are to be read down and not across the columns. If correctly dated, the law would be one of those addressed in his name by Constantine's successors after his death on 22 May, as claimed by Eusebius, *On the Life of Constantine* 4.67.

41. For the equivalence of 1,000 denarii and 1 solidus, see Simon Corcoran, *The Empire of the Tetrarchs* (1996), p. 226. The same relationship between the base metal and the gold coinage, allowing for a recalibration of the former, still holds in the early 320s (576 Licinian *nummi* to the gold *aureus*); John Matthews, *The Journey of Theophanes* (2006), p. 96.

lowest of these rates of pay for a total of ten years (12.5 × 10 × 10,000) would come out as 1,250,000 solidi, or just over 17,360 pounds of gold.[42] This is an immense sum, and only a fraction of what would be involved. It takes no account of transport costs, the employment of specialist workers (such as those listed above) at higher rates of pay, or monetary inflation in the quarter-century since 303, which had seen the price of gold quintupled by the early 320s, the base coin being revalued in accordance. The sums of money can be compared with those claimed to have been spent by Augustus in the *Res Gestae* (2,400,000,000 sesterces, the equivalent of 60,000,000 denarii of that time) or the fabulous sum propounded by Vespasian for the restoration of Rome after the civil wars of 68–70 (40,000,000,000 sesterces). The figure claimed by Augustus can be converted into the formal wealth requirement of 2,400 senators if that requirement were set at the million sesterces required by public law, or 600 senators if one considers the much larger sum, say 10 million, required to live and spend like a senator; we are speaking of the equivalent of the capital wealth of the entire senatorial order. Comparing the still lavish recorded incomes of some senators in the early fifth century, of the order of 1,500 to 4,000 pounds of gold plus one-third in the value of market produce from their estates, we are clearly in that rarefied realm of public expenditure known as imperial largesse—a good moment to remind ourselves of Constantine's reputation for both avarice and generosity, and the scale of the imperial patrimony as accumulated over centuries. We may add yet a further consideration, the scale of the minting activity, both in precious metals and in bronze coin, that must have been undertaken to serve this working population, first at Nicomedia and then at Constantine's new *moneta* established near the Golden Gate (p. 94).

A second and rather different set of questions relates to the religious character of the ceremonies recorded by Malalas and *Chronicon Paschale*. This is the emperor whose conversion to Christianity had already made a mark in the western provinces, who in these same years wrote a letter to the provincials of the east, in which he praised the Christian god as the author of his victories, beginning 'from the remotest shores of the British ocean', and whose engagement with the bishops at the council of Nicaea in 325 had revealed the depth of his commitment to his new religion.[43] Yet, even though they wrote centuries after the event, at a time when Christian ritual was an accepted feature of imperial protocol, there is no mention in either text of the High Masses, Te Deums, or Christian acclamations of later descriptions. The ceremonies as we have just read them make no reference to Christian, but seem to have conformed to modes of celebration appropriate to

---

42. Suetonius (*Life of Claudius* 20) notes that Claudius' attempt to drain the Fucine Lake near Rome occupied a labour force of 30,000 for eleven years.

43. Eusebius, *On the Life of Constantine* 2.28; above, Chapter 1, p. 7.

the occasion—circus races, the inauguration of baths, a great procession, displays of reverence for the Tychē of the city, and no Christian element nor clergyman in sight. Later sources that claim a procession starting at S. Sophia are rendered irrelevant by the fact that the Great Church was not yet built. It is worth adding, though there are some difficulties with it, the claim that the philosopher Sopatros—the same man, who according to Eunapius was executed for 'chaining the winds' that brought the grain-ships to Constantinople—had been a friend and adviser of Constantine, both at Nicomedia and in the devising of the consecration ceremonies of the new city. The difficulty is that the source that makes this claim, the sixth-century antiquarian John the Lydian, associates with Sopatros the 'hierophant Praetextatus', who, assuming his identification as the western senator and religious expert Vettius Agorius Praetextatus, was far too young at the time to have played any such role.[44] The case for Sopatros, if he can be detached from Praetextatus, is however a strong one; there must have been some sort of working party or advisory group to devise the consecration ceremonies, and Sopatros would be a qualified member of it. His fall to the machinations of the praetorian prefect Ablabius would reflect the ascendancy of a Christian faction at court in the years after the consecration of the city.

Leaving this aside, the signs of Constantine's intentions appear everywhere, expressing different aspects of the ideological construction initiated for the new city.[45] Like Rome, Constantinople was to be 'honoured with a senate'. It was to have a new senate-house in a new Forum built by Constantine, and a proconsul to govern it, corresponding to the old-established prefecture of Rome; only these two cities had individual governors rather than falling under the general administration of provinces. Shrines of the Tychai of Rome and Constantinople were put up in symmetrical positions in the Tetrastoon, the Severan forum now remodelled as the Augusteum,[46] and Constantinople's 'mystical name' associated with her Tychē, Anthousa, was a translation into Greek of that of Rome, Flora. Probably at a later time, the city was divided, like Rome, into the Fourteen

---

44. *PLRE* I, pp. 722, s. Praetextatus and 846, s. Sopater 1. T. D. Barnes, *Constantine and Eusebius* (1981), p. 383, n. 144 calls it a 'ludicrous story', which may be true as relating to Praetextatus, but not necessarily to Sopatros, for whom the alleged role seems far from unlikely.

45. See A. Alföldi, *The Conversion of Constantine and Pagan Rome* (1948), pp. 112ff. for a summary of the ideological parallels that follow—with reservations below, p. 42.

46. Below, Chapter 6, pp. 103–5. I would add the remarkable, most thoroughly documented article, one of a series, by Lars Ramskold, 'Coins and Medallions Struck for the Inauguration of Constantinople, 11 May, 330', *Niš and Byzantium* 9 (2011), pp. 125–58, tracing the consolidation of reverse types in the bronze coinages into images and symbols representing the parallel states of the two cities. Not all the issues can be dated to 330 precisely, the idea of the two cities having a prolonged and useful life. I find these and other articles by the same author posted on Academia.edu.

Regions that are the subject of this book; it possessed its Golden Milestone from which all roads were measured, its Circus Maximus, and a 'Capitolium'; what these things were like and what they meant in the configuration of the city will be discussed later. We should add Constantine's mausoleum, completed in time to receive the emperor's remains in 337. Situated at one of its highest points by a main road out of it, the mausoleum was a cardinal marker of Constantine's city. In certain respects, it resembles the configuration of the mausoleum of the Tetrarch Galerius at Thessalonica, a monument that Constantine must have seen often as he prepared his campaign against Licinius.[47] It stood in a precinct just off the main road into the city (the via Egnatia), connected to it by a double colonnade (Fig. 2.5). Constantine's lacked the triumphal arch that graced that of Galerius at the junction of via Egnatia and colonnade, but otherwise is laid out in a very similar pattern, designed to have the same impact upon one entering the city.

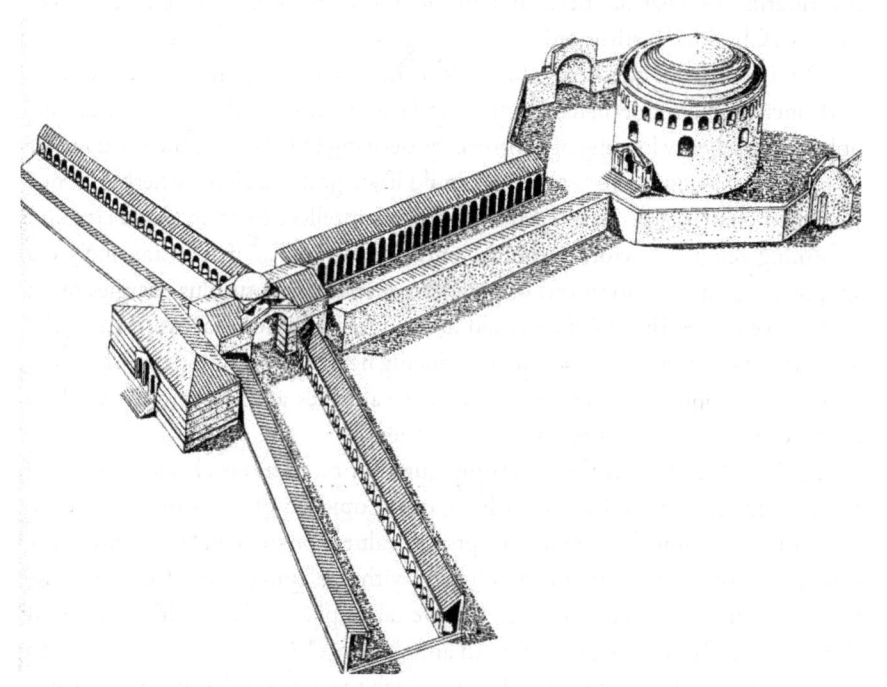

FIG. 2.5 Mausoleum of Galerius Arch and mausoleum of Galerius at Thessalonica; schematic reconstruction. The general configuration of the mausoleum, an enclosed precinct beside a main road into the city resembles that of Constantine at Constantinople (Chapter 9).

---

47. M. Johnson, *The Roman Imperial Mausoleum in Late Antiquity* (2009), pp. 119–29— though I do not believe that the mausoleum was used from the beginning as a church. See the discussion, with the work of Ken Dark and Ferudun Özgümüş, in Chapter 9 below, pp. 177–9.

It is also worth comment that both mausolea (and that of Diocletian at Split) finished up as churches, though by very different routes. Some of these innovations may have appeared under Constantine's successors, but others are attested very quickly, and were calculated to promote the idea of a Constantinople as a new Rome, an idea inseparable from his intentions in founding his city.

The question now arises, to what extent, as Constantinople replaced the old capital as the seat of imperial power, the emperor envisioned the city as representing something different in the minds of men—as the vehicle of an ideology stemming from his adoption of a new religion. Constantine never thought of his religion as a matter of private conscience alone; on the contrary, he was convinced that it was his duty to promote it (and to rectify its shortcomings), as the one to whom the Deity had in his wisdom committed the governance of the Roman empire. What role did Constantine intend his city to play in public policy, as a contribution to what has been thought of as a re-creation of the entire Roman state as a Christian institution?

This is a difficult question, which affects the premises upon which historians, both ancient and modern, have understood the meaning of the city. Constantinople carries a heavy loading of controversy, deriving in part from the portrayal of its founder as a restless reformer who could leave nothing alone, whether or not it needed change. 'He diverted his prodigious intellect by founding a city and reforming religions', wrote a fourth-century observer, as if Constantine were simply using these innovations of policy to entertain the surplus energies of an over-active mind. This observer could have added, as others do, overturning the army and the civil administration, introducing new taxes, and re-establishing the currency by robbing the provinces of their valuables and the temples of their treasures, which he also used to enrich his friends.[48]

Behind all this lurks the unsettling question of religious change: Constantine's acceptance of Christianity, which, in the opinion of his critics, led him to overturn everything familiar and of proven value. For some of these critics, the foundation of Constantinople was linked with the conversion of Constantine through events that were supposed to have taken place at Rome during his visit there in 326, to celebrate the twentieth anniversary of his reign. They advanced a narrative of the conversion, according to which the emperor became a Christian, not as the result of personal experiences during his rise to power in the early years but later, and for quite different reasons. His motive, it was alleged, was to win

---

48. Aurelius Victor, *De Caesaribus* 41.12: 'condenda urbe formandisque religionibus ingentem animum avocavit'; cf. Ammianus Marcellinus 16.8.12, 21.10.8 (the opinion of Julian after his elevation to the purple); Zosimus 2.33ff.

absolution for great crimes committed against his family—the recent execution of his eldest son Crispus Caesar, followed shortly afterwards by the death of his second wife Fausta, Crispus' stepmother, in suspicious circumstances; she died by scalding or suffocation in an over-heated bath-house, an accident which the emperor could easily be thought to have contrived and would be hard to investigate. No one knows, and few ever knew just what had happened, or what were the emperor's motives or even the extent of his responsibility, in either case. They were among those 'arcana imperii', as Tacitus would have said, those 'secrets of empire', of which the truth would never be divulged. According to this version of the facts, however, it was to gain forgiveness for these great sins when pagan priests refused to offer it, that Constantine, advised in a dream, adopted Christianity. The emperor is then alleged to have made his conversion public by refusing to take part in a traditional ceremony on the Capitol, after which he left Rome in disfavour with senate and people and resorted to the new capital city he would build on the Bosporus. There, he would be able to live and to indulge his taste for luxury, undisturbed by hostile public opinion, but it was not how the visit to Rome was meant to end.

The story is part of a critique of Constantine's character and policies that underlies a number of fourth-century and later sources. The fifth-century church historian Sozomen assigned it to certain 'Hellenes', by whom he meant the pagan historian Eunapius, and its elements can also be found in the satirical *Caesars* of Eunapius' contemporary Julian the Apostate.[49] Julian's story is well enough known, but worth repeating, both for entertainment value and as evidence for the critique of Constantine that was developed by hostile observers. It tells how a contest, what Greeks called an *agon*, was held before the gods of Olympus, in which the competitors, drawn from the race of the Caesars, strove to convince the gods which was the best of them. After the winner was declared, the philosopher emperor Marcus Aurelius, the contestants looked around among the gods and goddesses to find one of similar character to themselves, to whom they could attach themselves as a sort of divine mentor. So Marcus Aurelius took himself to Zeus and Kronos, Octavian to Apollo, and Trajan to that other eastern warmonger Alexander. Julius Caesar (not an emperor, but the founder of the line of Caesars, and a god at least as authentic as was Alexander the Great) wandered around until Ares and Aphrodite invited him to join them. Constantine could see no god that fitted his own way of life, until he saw Luxury (Τρυφή), who dressed him up in fine raiment and made him look beautiful (just like a late

49. Sozomen, *Hist. Eccl.* 1.5.1–5; Zosimus 2.29 (from Eunapius, above, p. 22).

Roman emperor, one might say) and took him off to Extravagance (Ἀσωτία). There he also found Jesus, who went around with Extravagance and is found making the following startling proclamation:

> Any seducer, any murderer, any sacrilegious or vile person, let him take heart and approach! With this water I will wash him and declare him cleansed at once. And even if he should commit these same sins again, let him but beat his breast and smite his head and I will cleanse him again!

To him, Julian concludes, Constantine came most gladly, escorting his sons from the assembly of the gods. Nevertheless, the avenging spirits punished them all for their impiety and exacted the penalty for the murder of their kindred, until Zeus allowed them to breathe again for the sake of their forbears Claudius and Constantius.[50]

Julian carries us forward to the carnage of his relatives that followed the death of Constantine, and to the civil wars of his sons, but the essential elements of his complaint are the same as in Eunapius and the other sources cited above. Constantine's reign is defined by luxury, extravagance, and domestic bloodletting, all connected by his adherence to a religion that would forgive him, even for a second time, for anything that he did (Julian, brought up as a Christian, allows himself a dig at the heretical practice of re-baptism). It gets to the heart of the pagan objection to Christianity: the virtue of the individual, and the reward of salvation that he might hope to accrue from it, was a matter of right behaviour, sustained piety, and laborious cleansing of the soul. It was not to be obtained by the instant gift of forgiveness of crimes, however great. Murder of one's kindred! The avenging deities were not so easily shaken off.

The story told by the pagans is easy enough to dismantle, partly on the basis of a better knowledge of the earliest years of Constantine's reign than was available to its authors. We can see, as they almost certainly could not, the origins of Constantine's conversion as early as 310, with his experience in a shrine of Apollo in Gaul, and trace its evolution through the campaign against Maxentius and later (above, Chapter 1, pp. 4–9). The emperor's Christianity is clear in pronouncements of the western years preceding the defeat of Licinius, while even the

---

50. Julian, *Caesars*, p. 336B (ed. Loeb, Vol. II), pp. 412–13. For Claudius (Gothicus) and Constantius the father of Constantine, see above, Chapter 1, pp. 2–6; on the death and succession of Constantine, see Richard W. Burgess, 'The Summer of Blood', *DOP* 62 (2008), pp. 5–51, and below, pp. 229–31. Julian alludes to the circumstances in *Letter to the Athenians*, pp. 270C–271B and in mythic form *To Heraclius the Cynic*, pp. 227C–234C (ed. Loeb, Vol. II), pp. 248–51 and 130–49.

council of Nicaea, where the emperor's Christian beliefs were plainly on show, preceded the date for the conversion alleged by these critics.[51] Constantinople was dedicated eighteen months before Constantine's visit to Rome, while at the time of the dedication his son Constantius joined his older brother Constantinus and their half-brother Crispus in the rank of Caesar. This was all with the clear intention to establish an imperial college, with Crispus as the senior member of the next generation. The emperor's plans for his new city were not conceived in the light of a visit to Rome that had not yet taken place, or of a dynastic crisis that had not yet happened. A part of Sozomen's argument against the Hellenes worth special note, is that Constantine's conversion must have preceded the death of Crispus, because the latter's name occurs with his father's in the protocols of laws favouring Christianity. This simple, decisive observation was made possible by an event of Sozomen's own time, the publication of the Theodosian Code, in which for the first time the legislation of fourth-and early fifth-century emperors was set out under topics and in chronological order. Sozomen, a lawyer at Constantinople who may have been acquainted with work on the Code as it advanced towards publication, is the first writer to have made use of that now irreplaceable text for the purpose of historical reconstruction.[52]

So the story was false, but there was a purpose to it, for it enabled Constantine's critics to show how, freed from the moral constraints of the old religion, the emperor used his new one to provide cover for his moral wickedness, and to legitimize his unrestrained character. The new city becomes the stage for Constantine's prodigal self-indulgence—a spendthrift home of luxury, in which he and his successors allowed themselves to forget the Roman virtues of discipline and parsimony, and their soldiers to grow soft in the ease of urban life.

Modern historians too have seen Constantinople as a sort of *tabula rasa*, a place in which the emperor could both indulge his taste for prodigality and luxurious living, and escape the pagan past in a Christian city looking to the future—for critics like Eunapius and Julian, these were two faces of the same coin. We find Constantinople portrayed as a distinctively Christian city, as a city, in the words of one writer, 'full of splendid churches and deconsecrated statues, where the fountains and public buildings reflected Christian, not traditional art', and where the evidence declares the explicitly Christian character of the foundation. Others

---

51. That this version of events can be assumed is largely thanks to the famous paper by N. H. Baynes, 'Constantine the Great and the Christian Church', *Proceedings of the British Academy* 15 (1929), pp. 341–442; reissued with a preface by Henry Chadwick (1972).

52. See John Matthews, *Laying Down the Law* (2000), pp. 51–52.

have thought that Constantine would be freed in his new city from the pressures exercised by the stubbornly pagan aristocracy of Rome.[53] This argument, encouraged perhaps by a tendency to assume Rome as the vantage point for everything, takes too much for granted. Part of the Roman aristocracy, members of a decreasing minority, did over the course of the fourth century emerge as a sort of 'pagan opposition' (that is to say, a movement of dissenting traditionalists, more or less united among themselves), but not yet, nor as part of an inevitable process. Nor would Constantine necessarily have expected this outcome—perhaps rather the opposite. He had been to Rome three times and would be acquainted with the Roman families who followed him into Christianity; given the obvious benefits to themselves, why should the rest not follow their example?

The notion of Constantinople as a city already in the time of Constantine full of splendid churches raises interesting questions to be discussed later (below, Chapter 9, pp. 172–82). The churches themselves are not easy to find—a good moment, perhaps, to note the observations of Gilbert Dagron and Cyril Mango, that a more forthcoming place to look for Constantinian churches is the Holy Land, and even old Rome itself.[54] In the Holy Land, four great basilicas were already seen by a visitor of 333, the so-called Pilgrim of Bordeaux. They were at Jerusalem (at the Holy Sepulchre and on the Mount of Olives), Bethlehem, and Mambre.[55] If the Holy Land was uniquely privileged by its direct connection with the historical origins of Christianity, Rome too was a special case, with its martyr-shrines reaching back into its Christian past, and imperial properties apt for conversion into churches (Fig. 2.6). Compared with such magisterial pretensions, Constantinople had no claim to be a 'holy city', whether from its own short history or from its past as Byzantium. It had no established Christian tradition, no record of involvement in the Great Persecution, no martyrs whose stories were told and deaths commemorated within the Christian community. The city did claim a martyr-saint, Mocius, to whom a memorial church was built just outside the Constantinian walls, but he is a shadowy character, whose entry in *The Prosopography of the Later Roman Empire* displays, like a suspect sporting record, the

53. Barnes, *Constantine and Eusebius*, p. 222; see too R. Browning, *The Emperor Julian* (1975), p. 27; Alföldi, *The Conversion of Constantine and Pagan Rome*, p. 110.

54. Dagron, *Naissance d'une Capitale*, pp. 388–409; Mango, *Le développement urbain de Constantinople*, pp. 35–36.

55. E. D. Hunt, *Holy Land Pilgrimage in the Later Roman Empire, AD 312–460* (1982). For the 'Pilgrim of Bordeaux' (*Itinerarium Burdigalense*, in *CCL* 175, pp. 15–20), see John Matthews, 'The Cultural Landscape of the Bordeaux Itinerary', in *Roman Perspectives* (2010), pp. 181–200, at 192–93.

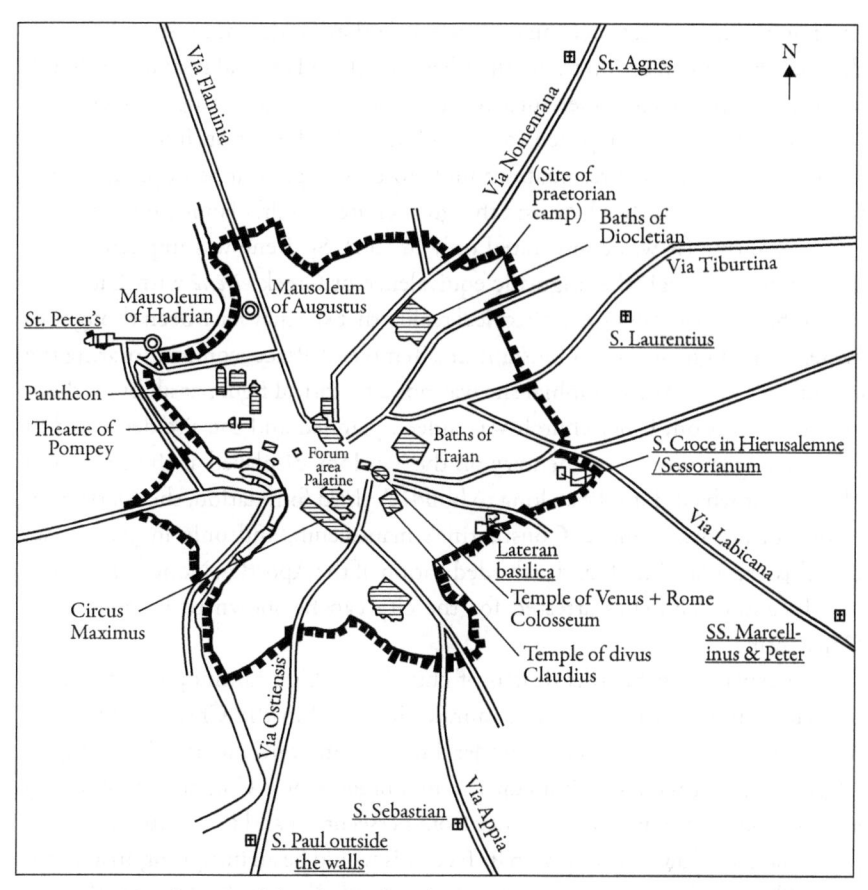

FIG. 2.6 Distribution of churches in fourth-century Rome. The map shows the location of the churches of the Constantinian era at the periphery of the city. R. Krautheimer, *Three Christian Capitals: Topography & Politics* (1983), p. 6.

panoply of asterisks and exclamation marks indicating the dubious nature of the historical details foisted onto him, and who does not appear at all in a standard reference work like *The Oxford Dictionary of the Christian Church*.[56] In providing Constantinople with a tradition of martyrdom that it otherwise lacked, the church may have played a role in Constantine's ideological conception of his new

---

56. An extant *Passio* of Mocius, supposedly martyred at Amphipolis at a very strange date ('the fourth year of Diocletian', sc. 287/8), is a work of pure fiction; 'apparently historically worthless', in Barnes' words (*Constantine and Eusebius*, p. 383, n. 140). Despite this half-hearted rejection, in a spirited addition to the hagiographical tradition Barnes can suggest that Mocius was 'perhaps known to Constantine in his youth' (p. 222)! See *PLRE* I, *!Mocius!* (p. 604), and for the saint's parents and other fictitious details, *!Euphrates!* (p. 299) and *!Eustathia!* (p. 310).

city, but its remote location in an undeveloped urban landscape must have limited the impact of any tradition than might have developed around it, and the church seems very early to have fallen into disrepair (below, Chapter 9, pp. 173–5).

Within the city, as opposed to beyond its walls, there is St. Irene, known as 'the old church' and so presumably built before its neighbour St. Sophia, though we do not know exactly when; and the 'great church' itself, planned but not built by Constantine (it was consecrated only in 360). St. Irene was imported from Thessalonica, though the linguistic equivalence of Greek *eirēnē* with Latin *pax* was perhaps as relevant as any historical reality that she may have been thought to possess; we might see it as Constantine's Temple of Peace, commemorating the end of civil war.[57] As for Sophia, she was not a historical figure at all but a theological abstraction; if her church was indeed planned and the site dedicated in 326, she might form a commentary on the 'wisdom' displayed at the council of Nicaea; but why did it take so long to build? A third foundation, the Martyrium Apostolorum, was built as Constantine's mausoleum, and only in 370 consecrated as a regular church under the dedication of the Apostles. None of the other fourth-century churches attested for the city can be shown to be as early as Constantine.

The explanation for this dearth of churches at Constantinople may simply be that there was little to commemorate there within the Christian tradition itself—no heroic tales of courage under duress, no martyrs' memorials, no imperial properties in which to implant the monuments of a Christian community eager to commemorate its emergence from persecution and its receipt of the emperor's favour. However simple on its face, this would be an intriguing answer, for it would imply that, for all his personal support of Christianity, Constantine did not think of it in the abstract as the vehicle of a new conception of state; its commemoration belonged within its own traditions, and not to any broader conception of statehood that was not yet attached to it.

The manner in which the identity of Constantinople was defined through its role as a Christian city, and at what point this began to happen, raises complicated questions with no easy answers. It should however be clear that Constantine's new capital should be seen in terms of its own advantages and not as the consequence of a rejection of Rome—as if he was ever going to reside in a city long understood to be too far from the frontiers to be an effective base for the work of an emperor. It is true that none of Constantine's three visits to Rome lasted for more than a few weeks, but it was by now uncommon for an emperor to make them at all, and Constantine's choice of 'Roman imagery' in his presentation

57. Alföldi, *The Conversion of Constantine and Pagan Rome*, p. 114, connects with the Augustan Ara Pacis, but this does not seem apt. A better parallel might be Vespasian's Templum Pacis.

of Constantinople is more an imitation of the old capital than a rejection of it. As for Constantinople as a Christian capital of the Roman empire, that is more true as a projection into the future than as a description of the fourth-century city. In this earlier period, as we will see in the following chapters, it was not churches but grand colonnades, commemorative columns, public squares, baths, and places of entertainment that would claim the attention of the visitor. Before we come to this, however, we need to address the character of the sources on the history of Constantinople and to lift the veil of legend and fantasy that later writers have placed between its true history and the modern observer.

3

Sources and Materials

THE FIRST PROBLEM before us as we address the earliest phases of the development of Constantinople is that, just because of the spectacular success of the city, they are hidden below many layers of later accretion. This is as true of the literary evidence as it is of its physical remains, as Byzantine writers, interested in the origins of their city and conscious of the need to rival the foundation stories of Rome, supplemented whatever historical information was available to them by legend and invention. To appreciate this, one only needs to pick up the fascinating collection of texts edited by Th. Preger under the title 'Writers on the Origins of Constantinople' (*Scriptores originum Constantinopolitanarum*), published in two instalments with continuous pagination in 1901 and 1907, now invaluably translated (with text and notes) by an authority on the topography of the city, Albrecht Berger.[1] These texts, alternatively referred to as *Patria* or *Patria Constantinopoleos*, present many challenges of interpretation, for we find in them all sorts of fictions and fables—erudite and implausible as they may be—but containing details that, if any of them turned out to be true, would be of great value to the historian of the city. The stories are often equipped with etymological and aetiological explanations resembling a parody of scholarship, and have little bearing on the subject-matter of this book. An example that is so connected is the statement that the location known as the 'Augoustion' (Augusteion or Augusteum, one of the most familiar features of the city), was previously known as 'Goustion' (from Latin *gustare*, 'to taste'), in allusion to the nearby food market. The notion is easily discounted (had anyone not heard of the Augusteion?), though it has the merit of mentioning the food market that was there when the interpretation was devised—unless it too was imagined to support the invented etymology.[2] No less entertaining is the explanation given of the location known

---

1. Th. Preger, *Scriptores Originum Constantinopolitanarum* (ed. Teubner 1901 and 1907; repr. in 1 vol., 1989); Albrecht Berger, *Accounts of Medieval Constantinople: The* Patria (*Dumbarton Oaks Medieval Library* 24, 2013).

2. *Patria* 2.15 (Preger, p. 158; Berger, pp. 57–59). See on what may have been a popular misunderstanding of the time (and on the confusion in the sources) Denis Feissel, 'Tribune et colonnes impériales à l'Augusteion de Constantinople', in *Constantinople réelle et imaginaire: autour de l'oeuvre de Gilbert Dagron* (Travaux et Mémoires 22/1 (2018)), at pp. 145–50.

From Byzantium to Constantinople: An Urban History. John Matthews, Oxford University Press.
© Oxford University Press 2024. DOI: 10.1093/oso/9780197585498.003.0003

as Gastria, 'The Pots', on the southern side of the city, so named by the empress Helena, we are told, when she brought in the relics of the True Cross by the gate of Psamatheia and planted there in flowerpots the lilies, cinnamon, ginger, basil, roses, marjoram, and balsam she had found growing by the precious relic, naming after them the monastery to which she eventually retired.[3] The story is false on every possible level (the gate of Psamatheia did not even exist in Constantine's day, its site being far outside the circuit of his city). Of sterner material is the claim that the surface area of the forum of Constantine matched that covered by the emperor's camp (*korté*) when he first came from Rome, the two semi-circular facing porticoes representing the stables surrounding the camp, while the rays emanating from the head of the statue of Apollo/Helios on the column of Constantine were made of nails from the crucifixion, 'shining like Helios on the citizens'.[4] If nothing else, it is an effective evocation of the configuration of the forum and a sidelight on the statue that surmounted the column of Constantine; an identification or affinity with Apollo as Helios that would well fit the self-representation of the emperor that we saw in Chapter 1 (pp. 6–11). Other claims might be distortions or embellishments of truth rather than outright fantasies. What of the three polished stone images of storks made by 'a man from Tyana, by name Apollonius' (the famous philosopher-magician of the late first century), which kept the city free of those birds, who had acquired the troublesome habit of dropping venomous snakes into the public cisterns and onto citizens as they walked in the streets? While the story locates Apollonius many centuries before his actual lifetime and misrepresents his profession, its author also says that the images were still extant in his own time (the sixth century), and that they did, through some magical power, keep storks out of the city and prevent snakes raining down from the sky. The last detail of this story could probably be authenticated.[5]

Some stories offer serious opportunities for exploring the early topography of the city as it could still be seen in later times. An anecdote in the text known as

3. *Patria* 3.4 (Preger, p. 215; Berger, pp. 141–43); Janin, *Constantinople Byzantine*, pp. 353–54 (Gastria), cf. 355–56 (Hélénianae), with V. Tiftixoglu, 'Die Helenianai nebst einigen anderen Besitzungen in Vorfeld des frühen Konstantinopel', in H.-G. Beck (ed.), *Studien zur Frühgeschichte Konstantinopels* (1973), pp. 49–83.

4. *Patria* 2.15; cf. 17 (Preger, pp. 158–59; Berger, pp. 57–58); 2.45 (Preger, p. 174; Berger, pp. 78–81). The word translated here as 'camp' is said to be an Iranian word for an item of clothing; perhaps equivalent to the Latin *procinctus*. According to *Patria* 3.11 ('Buildings'), the circular shape of the forum was to imitate the Ocean.

5. Apollonius and the storks: Hesychius, *Patria* 23 (Preger, p. 11; Berger, p. 15; on the author see below, p. 49); C. Mango, 'Antique Statuary and the Byzantine Beholder', *DOP* 17 (1963), pp. 53–75, at 68.

Parasteis syntomoi chronikai or 'Brief Historical Expositions', also contained in the *Patria*, tells how one Theodorus took a friend, a minor official called Himerius, to visit the place known as 'Kynegion'—the old Roman amphitheatre—to look at the statues there. One of the statues was declared by Himerius to be that of the builder of the Kynegion, upon which Theodorus replied that 'the builder's name was Maximian and the architect's Aristides'. No sooner had he said this than the statue toppled over and killed Himerius on the spot.[6] Theodorus was thrown into a panic. Having first attempted to dump his friend's body in 'the place where they throw the convicts', he then sought asylum in the Great Church of S. Sophia; there were no witnesses and he feared the charge of murder that did in fact follow. He was held innocent upon oath, at which point a text of the 'prophet Demosthenes' was produced by a philosopher, declaring that the statue was fated someday to kill a person of rank. In another version, the philosopher claimed that he had found beneath the statue a relief image of the man who would be killed. 'Consider these things truly', the story ends, addressing Philokalos, the real or fictitious person who had asked to hear it, 'and pray that you do not fall into temptation, and take care when you look at old statues, especially pagan ones!' The intervention of the statue was a delayed act of vengeance by a resentful and still dangerous culture.

Before dismissing the whole thing as a fable, we should note that it claims to be based on a first-hand account of the episode given by Theodorus to Philokalos, that it gives Himerius' title of *chartularius*, and that it purports to name the builder and the architect of the Kynegion; perhaps Theodorus had read, or misread, an inscription at the place. There may well have been tottering statues to be seen and inscriptions to be read in the disused structure, where the two men had gone with mules and attendants who had stayed outside and so were not witnesses of the accident. To require their mode of transport, the place must have been in what was by now an out-of-the-way location, a conclusion supported by the remark, in this and other texts, that it was where the bodies of executed criminals were dumped, and by what is known of the location of the amphitheatre (Chapter 6, pp. 85f., 101f.). There are surely usable items of authentic fact in all of this, but their recovery requires of the historian a peculiarly challenging combination of doubt and optimism, as could well be said of the *Scriptores* as a whole.

Before using the diverse texts of the *Patria* for historical enquiry, we need to gain some understanding of their origin and character. This too presents a

---

6. The story is told at *Parastaseis* 27–28 (*Patria* 2.24; Preger, p. 163; Berger, p. 65); translated with commentary by Averil Cameron and Judith Herrin, *Constantinople in the Early Eighth Century: The 'Parasteis Syntomoi Chronikai'* (1984), pp. 89–91 and 201–4; Mango, 'Antique Statuary', pp. 60–61.

challenge, for the texts are of widely different dates and authorship and exist in variant traditions, while on the other hand the interconnections between them often mean that they have to be interpreted in relation to each other.

We can however begin with a known character, the first of the texts (Preger, pp. 1–16; Berger, pp. 2–23) being the *Patria* ascribed to the *vir illustris* Hesychius. Something is known about this man, whose work has already arisen in Chapter 2 of this study (pp. 21f.). Born at Miletus, the son of an advocate also called Hesychius (a Hellenization of the well-known Latin *cognomen* Placidus) and a mother called Philosophia, he died sometime after 582.[7] Described by Byzantine sources as a 'pagan historian'—a writer in the Classical tradition, who, if he was a Christian, did not allow this to intrude on his manner of discourse—Hesychius wrote a world history in six parts, from the Assyrian king Bel to the death of the emperor Anastasius in 518. An addition covering the reigns of Justin and Justinian would take it down to 565. The history is lost except for later citations, but it seems to be a summary of Hesychius' description of the history of Byzantium as far as its re-foundation by Constantine that is preserved as this section of the *Patria*. The passage has already entered into play in connection with Septimius Severus' war against Pescennius Niger and his change of mind when, having first punished Byzantium by dismantling its walls and making it subject to the authority of Heraclea, he restored the city to its former status and built for it baths (the Zeuxippon) and a hippodrome (above, p. 22).

Both the details in that passage, and the absence of any hint of a Christian attitude in the text, would be consistent with the statement that Hesychius wrote in the Classical fashion. Describing how the city was named Constantinopolis and beautified by Constantine, he correctly locates both the Constantinian and the earlier walls of Byzantium, in relation to the 'Troadensian porticos' and the forum of Constantine respectively.[8] Again correctly, he describes Constantine's erecting of a statue of his mother Helena on a column in the Augusteion, the building of the semi-circular colonnades of the forum of Constantine and the column of the emperor that stood in it, the new senate-house in the same forum with its statues, and the imperial palace. Hesychius is in error in attributing the city's main aqueduct (the one still visible) to Constantine, though he is accurate for a later date, in saying that the city derived its water from sources near the town of Bizye, and his statement that Constantine built houses for the senators who

---

7. *PLRE* II, p. 555 (Hesychios 14), with Anthony Kaldellis, 'The Works and Days of Hesychios the Illoustrious of Miletos', *Greek, Roman, and Byzantine Studies* 45 (2005), pp. 381–403, and the new text produced by Kaldellis for the continuation of Jacoby's *Fragmente der Griechische Historiker*; Hesychios is no. 390, and this (the main extant fragment), is fr. 7.

8. Hesychios 39–42 (Preger, pp. 16–18 and 135; Berger, pp. 22–25).

followed him from Rome is a simplification much elaborated by later writers. People (senators and others) did come to live at Constantinople, and houses were built for them (Chapters 10–11).

The second text, the so-called *Parastaseis Syntomoi Chronikai*, or 'Brief Historical Expositions' as Cyril Mango styled them, has already been mentioned for the story of Himerius and the Kynegion. It is a substantial compilation of notes on monuments and statues in the city, dating from sometime in the eighth century.[9] The value of the work is inconsistent, but amid all the fantasy and distortion contained in it, there are passages that insist on being considered for the historical record. Its repertory of the ancient statuary that was still to be seen around the city in the eighth century is extremely valuable as an indication of what was there in the earlier period, when we think of the many circumstances that could have led to its destruction. One feature in particular is of interest. Among the scores of statues of emperors and empresses, gods and heroes, wild beasts and exotic creatures described, only a very small proportion has any Christian connotation.[10] Christian statuary, wherever it existed, was not to be found in the streets of Constantinople.

The third text, or rather accumulation of texts, in the *Patria* begins by repeating Hesychius' account as far as the Severi, but from the time of Constantine diverges from it, with the general effect of greatly, and by largely fictitious statements, exaggerating that emperor's role in the development of the city. A second section, compiled not earlier than the tenth century, is devoted to statues, and a third to buildings. A brief fourth section concerns the church of S. Sophia, based in part on an earlier text, which it also expands from other sources.[11]

The value of these texts lies not so much in their historical explanations, which are based more on antiquarian reconstruction than authentic information, as in their descriptions of buildings and monuments of an earlier period that still existed at their time of writing—even a fictional narrative may yield information about the physical setting in which it is placed. The same opportunities arise from descriptions of the processions that took place in the streets and public spaces of Constantinople. The most notable are found in the *De caeremoniis* of the

---

9. Translation and commentary by Averil Cameron and Judith Herrin (above, n. 6). The early eighth-century dating proposed by them has been questioned in favour of a date later in the century, but that does not affect its use in the present context. For the suggested English title, see Mango (n. 6 above), p. 60, commenting also on the 'very low intellectual level' of the book.

10. The repertory is set out at Cameron and Herrin (n. 6 above), pp. 48–51; below, Chapter 11 (p. 216).

11. To trace these texts, some of which are repetitious and exist in variant versions, around the pages of Preger and Berger is a work of research not undertaken here. Berger's invaluable translation does not offer a concordance of passages.

tenth-century emperor Constantine Porphyrogenitus, where we find numerous indications of the city plan laid out by his fourth-century predecessor, as processions wend their way past landmarks that had not changed in centuries.[12]

Other literary and sub-literary texts that are available to us are less idiosyncratic and closer in time than the *Patria*, and present more familiar problems of interpretation. From the time of Justinian (and especially with statuary, a main preoccupation of later texts, in mind), we should note the collection of epigrams by Christodorus of Thebes that comprises the entire second book of the Byzantine anthology known as the *Anthologia Palatina*. There is more here than meets the eye, if the editorial *lemma* attached to the collection is correct in referring it to the Classical statuary that still stood in the Zeuxippon baths at the time of their destruction in the time of Justinian (below, p. 85). Other poetic texts also may contribute to our understanding of the cultural identity of the city, notably the epigrams by different authors appearing in the Palatine Anthology, with *lemmata* that are often thought inauthentic but which, if genuine, may be extremely helpful. The best-known of these epigrammatists, the Alexandrian poet Palladas, is subject to differences of opinion, based on the recent publication of a papyrus anthology of poems supposedly written by him and claimed to be of early fourth-century date, as to whether he wrote in the time of Theodosius and his successor (the traditional and in my opinion still the best interpretation) or Constantine, and whether the city to which he refers as the site of a sustained Christian campaign against the gods and their artefacts was Constantinople or Alexandria (in my opinion, the latter).[13]

Our resources among written texts also include the chronographers, of whom the sixth-century *Chronicle* of John Malalas and the derivative *Chronicon Paschale* were deployed in the previous chapter for their information on the ceremonies used at the consecration of Constantinople. These writers have more to say on the development of the city in the period that concerns us, as does the Latin *Chronicle* of Count Marcellinus, written in the time of Justinian. These works present the difficulties that that they derived from multiple sources of unknown value and are of their nature episodic, but all include notices referring to the monuments

---

12. Mango, *Développement Urbain*, pp. 28, 31; see too John F. Haldon, *Constantine Porphyrogenitus: Three Treatises on Imperial Military Expeditions* (1990), pp. 136–51, with notes at 259ff.

13. The earlier date is supported in articles by Kevin W. Wilkinson, following his publication of the papyrus archive in *New Epigrams of Palladas: A Fragmentary Papyrus Codex (P.Ct.YBR inv. 4000)* (2012); see his 'Palladas and the Age of Constantine', *JRS* 99 (2009), pp. 36–60; 'Palladas and the Foundation of Constantinople', *JRS* 100 (2010), pp. 179–94; 'More Evidence for the Date of Palladas' and Πρύτανις and Cognates in Documentary Papyri and Greek Literature', *ZPE* 196 (2015), pp. 67–71 and 88–93. See however the criticisms of, among others, L. Benelli, 'Osservazioni sul P.Ct.YBR Inv. 4000', *ZPE* 193 (2015), pp. 53–63, and 'The Age of Palladas', *Mnemosyne* 69 (2016), pp. 978–1007.

of the city, to historical events that took place in its streets, and to the activities of its people.[14] So too do traditional historical texts, such as Zosimus, who had occasion to narrate events taking place in the city, as well as giving one of the fullest descriptions that we possess of the building programme of Constantine in relation to its Severan antecedents. Zosimus is particularly valuable for his connection with the lost history of the late fourth- and early fifth-century Eunapius, extending (not without bias, as we have seen) from the physical to the ideological aspects of the policies of Constantine. A particular episode narrated by Ammianus Marcellinus reveals important features of the city as it stood in the mid-360s and, in a vivid description, takes us into its streets with glimpses of its people.[15] Last but not least, imperial legislation, collected in the *Codex Theodosianus* compiled at Constantinople between 429 and its publication there late in 437, has much to say about the development of the city and the conditions of life there— food supplies and population, public and private building, water and housing, intellectual life and educational facilities, the financial and other obligations laid upon the senatorial class of the city.

A novel source of information that becomes available only very late in the history of Constantinople but contains much of value for the earlier period is the visual evidence of manuscript and printed maps, satisfying a growing interest among Europeans in what were for them exotic parts of the world and promoting the Classical and Christian origins of a city now in the hands of a non-Christian power.[16] These maps, half-way between panoramic, pictorial views of the city and topographic plans in the modern sense, appear in versions derived from two main sources.

The first and earlier of these sources consists of manuscript versions of a plan of Constantinople prepared to accompany copies of the geographer Christopher Buondelmonti's treatise *Liber Insularum Archipelagi*, completed around 1420 and

---

14. *Chron. Pasch.*, Whitby and Whitby (1989); Elizabeth Jeffries, Michael Jeffries, Roger Scott, et al., *The Chronicle of John Malalas* (1986), with *Studies in John Malalas* (1990); Brian Croke, *Count Marcellinus and His Chronicle* (2001), esp. ch. 4, 'Marcellinus and Constantinople'. See below, Chapter 11.

15. Amm. Marc. 26.6–7; below, Chapter 11 (pp. 232f.).

16. On this endlessly fascinating material see above all Ian R. Manners, 'Constructing the Image of a City: The Representation of Constantinople in Christopher Buondelmonti's *Liber Insularum Archipelagi*', *Annals of the Association of American Geographers* 87 (1997), pp. 72–102, the Chicago exhibition catalogue also by Manners, *European Cartographers and the Ottoman World 1500–1750: Maps from the Collection of O. J. Sopranos* (2007), esp. 'Mapping the City: *Civitates Orbis Terrarum*', at pp. 67–78; and Arne Effenberger, 'Konstantinopel/ Istanbul—die frühen bildlichen Zeugnisse', in Falko Daim (ed.), *Die byzantinischen Häfen Konstantinopels: Byzanz zwischen Orient und Okzident* 4 (2016), pp. 19–31 (Buondelmonti, pp. 19–24, Vavassore, pp. 25–28).

surviving in many copies of the fifteenth century.[17] Descendants of the Buondelmonti plan continue to show the city as it was before the Ottoman conquest, with variations of detail and annotations that might possibly reflect additional first-hand knowledge among early users, or differing selections of material from the archetypes.

Buondelmonti's map offers a basic N/S orientation, in which the city is shown as viewed from the south, looking from the Propontis northwards towards Pera (Galata) with the Bosporus descending from the north-east corner and the Golden Horn as an inlet from it (Fig. 3.1). The fortifications are clearly shown, though with some confusion relating to the moat protecting the land walls. This seems to be understood as an inlet of the sea, with the corollary that the Propontis itself is misrepresented; the opposing coastline in the south and south-eastern quadrant of the map is very dimly understood. Within the walls only basic elements of the old city, such as churches, are shown, and, until late in the series of copies, there is little interest in the Ottoman architecture that was beginning to appear. No attempt is made to suggest the economic and commercial life of the city, though the location of the harbours, at least on the Propontis shore, is indicated. Given the angle of vision of the plan, the northern shore of the city and Golden Horn are less clearly shown. Only occasionally is there any attempt to suggest the pattern of domestic occupation of the urban space, and if a road system is shown at all it is rudimentary. A feature of all versions of the map is however the commemorative columns of emperors, the relative positions of which give some sense of the articulation of the city, and, in one version of the map, a gate of the Constantinian city surviving into the fifteenth century.

The second map source is the printed panorama of the city, first published as a woodcut by Giovanni Andreas di Vavassore in around 1535 and widely copied thereafter from metal plates in a somewhat modernized style, most notably in the six-volume *Civitates Orbis Terrarum*, published by Georg Braun and Frans Hogenberg at Cologne between 1572 and 1617. The plates used in this publication, passed on to successive printers, were apparently used and reused until they were worn out. With assorted decorative embellishments, this is by far the most familiar image of the city in the first century after the Ottoman conquest. It is best appreciated in the original woodcut rather than in the derivative versions printed from metal plates, though these are impressively loyal to the original version and in some cases preserve finer detail.[18]

In the Vavassore panorama (Fig. 3.2), the city is viewed from the east looking into the peninsula, with Galata to the right. In contrast with the Buondelmonti

17. Including a presentation copy of Ptolemy's *Geography* made for the king of Naples *c.*1456; Manners, *European Cartographers*, p. 77 with fig. 39.

18. Manners, 'Constructing the Image', pp. 92ff.; and Manners, *European Cartographers*, pp. 57–70.

FIG. 3.1 The Buondelmonti Map. Biblioteca Nazionale Marciana, Venice (Ms cod. Marc. lat. xiv 25 = 4595, p. 123); Helen C. Evans (ed.) *Byzantium, Faith and Power (1961–1557)*, Metropolitan Museum of Art, New York; Yale University Press, New Haven and London (2004), Plate 246 and p. 401.

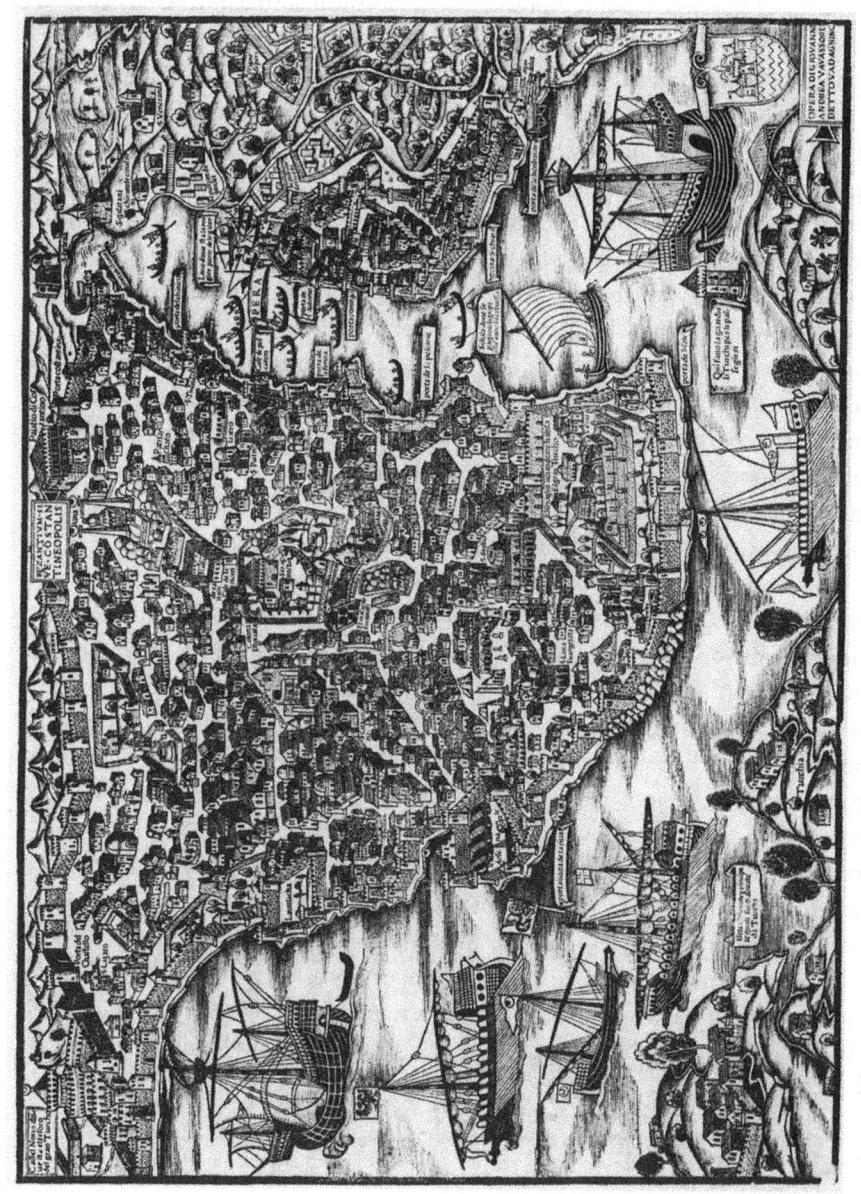

FIG. 3.2 The Vavassore panorama. Woodcut version of c.1535. Germanisches National Museum, Nürnberg.

series, the Ottoman city is clearly seen. The foreground is dominated by the new Seraglio (Topkapı) and its walls. The old Seraglio is in the middle distance, and beyond it the mosque of Mehmet the Conqueror, built at a high point of the city on the site of the church of the Apostles, originally the mausoleum of Constantine and his family. The great Süleymaniye mosque complex, begun in 1550 after the appearance of the original version of the Vavassore panorama, does not appear in its later versions, a tribute to the faithfulness to their archetype of these later printings. Like the Buondelmonti versions, the Vavassore map shows the ruins of the hippodrome and the columns of the emperors. Unlike its predecessor, it indicates the harbours of the northern and the shipyards of Galata as well as the Propontis shoreline of the main city, and with added pictorial detail gives a lively impression of maritime activity; the boats operating as ferries in the upper Golden Horn are an especially vivid touch.[19] An attempt is made to indicate the density of habitation within the city walls, although, as in the case of the Buondelmonti versions, there is no observable correlation with any road plan. A significant distortion in the panorama is that the space allowed for the area between the lost Constantinian walls is proportionately insufficient, but this is a feature shared by a famous Ottoman city plan of the same period.[20] It is understandable, given the nearly complete disappearance of the walls of Constantine by the sixteenth century.

The Vavassore map can however offer useful information, as well as make a very striking visual impression, when viewed in close detail. For instance, it defines the location of the column (and so the forum) of Theodosius by placing it within the walls of the Old Seraglio (Fig. 8.2). Its image of the harbour of Julian on the Propontis shore shows the two basins, one of them a shipyard, into which the harbour may have been divided, and the location of the harbour of Theodosius, recently the subject of spectacular excavations, is clearly identifiable in the gardens that came to occupy its silted bed. The indication of the harbours on the northern shore and the shipyards of Galata is mentioned above. These and other such details will be explored in later chapters of this study.

Finally among visual resources for the early history of Constantinople are the drawings of the narrative frieze of the column of Arcadius, set up in the forum of that emperor in 402, with the addition of a statue of Arcadius on its summit in 421. The column was dismantled as insecure in 1715, but not before it had been

---

19. As Arne Effenberg (n. 16 above, p. 28) observes with a nice touch of humour, Vavassore the Venetian has depicted the boats in the shape of gondolas, with the Golden Horn as a sort of Grand Canal.

20. Manners, *European Cartographers*, p. 70 and fig. 36. The source is Matrakçi Nasuh's *Book of Stages*, an account of Süleyman the Magnificent's march against Iran and Iraq in 1534–35, recently published in facsimile by Nurhan Atasoy; see the illustrated review by Tim Stanley in *Cornucopia* 55 (2017), pp. 35–43. The panorama of Istanbul is at p. 37 (Galata at 36), with detail of the hippodrome at p. 35.

drawn by visiting artists, especially in a partial version now in Paris, and in that donated to the library of Trinity College, Cambridge, by E. H. Freshfield, who had inherited the drawings and published them with commentary in the journal *Archaeologia* of 1921/2.[21] The Freshfield drawings were made by an unknown artist for Stefan Gerlach, who was in Istanbul as chaplain to an envoy of Maximilian II to the Ottoman court in 1572 and for a second time in 1574–78. Their general accuracy becomes more and more evident as one studies them, and there is a control in the quality of other drawings in the Freshfield dossier, including the still-extant base of the obelisk of Theodosius. In its narrative of the events shown on the frieze, the Arcadius column shows a number of images of the fourth-century city as functioning elements in the urban landscape (below, Chapter 8, Figs. 8.7–11). They are shown by kind permission of the Librarian and Fellows of Trinity College, from a digital record with an extremely high level of resolution.

Apart from the Buondelmonti and Vavassore panoramas and the column of Arcadius, and some other physical relics (more than one might expect) that leave traces above ground, our material evidence for the earlier city is as elusive as the literary, for the obvious reason that the building levels of fourth-century Constantinople lie deep below the modern city, with all that lies between them in the life of a teeming metropolis; the ground levels of the Augusteum and of the forum of Constantine, for instance, are between 2.0 and 2.5 metres under the present surface, as also seems to be true of the depth of the fourth-century church of the Apostles below the floor of the Fatih mosque. The surface of the Mesē was 2 metres below the present-day Divanyolu.[22] It is commonplace in urban archaeology to see a successful city rising upon its own ruins, or rather upon its very foundations. Our awareness of this legendary 'underground city' of Constantinople is currently being vastly enhanced through the initiatives of Ferudun Özgümüş in exploring it,[23] and this is a good moment also to mention the extraordinary

---

21. E. H. Freshfield, 'Notes on a Vellum Album Containing Some Original Sketches of Public Buildings and Monuments, Drawn by a German Artist Who Visited Constantinople in 1574', *Archaeologia* 22 (1922), pp. 87–104 with plates XV–XXIII. On the full content of the dossier (including drawings of a brown and a black rhinoceros from the Sultan's menagerie), see Cyril Mango, 'The Freshfield Album', in 'Constantinopolitana', *Jahrbuch des Deutschen Archäologischen Instituts* 80 (1965), pp. 305–6; repr. in *Variorum* (1993), ch. 2.

22. An intense and informative survey of the history and present state of archaeology at Istanbul is given by Ken Dark, in chs 1–2 of Dark and Ferudun Özgümüş, *Constantinople: Archaeology of a Byzantine Megalopolis* (2013). The examples and measurements of the depth of fourth-century Constantinople below ground level are given by Dark, p. 18; for the forum of Constantine, cf. Mango, 'The Porphyry Column', in 'Constantinopolitana', pp. 306–13. Compare the photographs of the Milion at Müller-Wiener, *Bildlexikon*, pp. 216–18. On the church of the Apostles, below, Chapter 9 (pp. 177–9).

23. Ferudun Özgümüş' contribution to this research was featured in NPR's feature "All Things Considered" of 23 July 2021 (https://www.kazu.org/npr-news/npr-news/2021-07-23/beneath-istanbul-archaeologists-explore-an-ancient-citys-byzantine-basements), in which he

survey of the water system of Constantinople by Jim Crow and colleagues, and the excavations of the harbour of Theodosius enforced, and also made possible, by the development of a transportation exchange at Yenikapı.[24]

A sixteenth-century visitor to Constantinople, the French antiquarian and diplomat Petrus Gyllius, known to us as Pierre Gilles, had occasion to discover for himself this transformation of late antique Constantinople into an underground city. Gilles was inspecting a group of seven Corinthian columns still to be seen in his day on the south-western side of S. Sophia (the side adjacent to the Augusteum), when he fell into the foundations of walls among which they stood. He had the presence of mind (and possibly the intention) to measure the depth below ground level of the base and shaft of the columns, which he determined to be six feet—quite close to the measurements given above. The height of the entire column, pedestal, capital, and all (he could not see the building platform on which they stood), he estimated as 46.5 feet. The columns stood just over 20 feet apart and each had a circumference of 18 feet—a diameter of more than 5.5 feet. The figures give some impression of the architectural grandeur of the early Byzantine city.

Pierre Gilles is described by Cyril Mango as the founder of the scholarly study of Constantinople, which does no more than justice to his contribution.[25] His visit to the city, arising from the diplomatic connections between King François I and Süleyman the Magnificent, lasted from 1544 to 1548, when he embarked on an eventful period of service in the Ottoman army in its campaign against Persia. He returned to the capital in 1550. A century since the capture of Constantinople by the Turks, much more of the ancient city was still visible than could be seen even a short time later. In his book, *The Antiquities of Constantinople*, published posthumously in Latin in 1561 and in an English translation in 1729, Gilles shows us Byzantine Constantinople literally disappearing before his eyes.[26] He watched workmen removing the pillars at the southern end of the hippodrome (the *sphendonè*), which we can still see on contemporary images of the

---

was credited with the discovery of three hundred sites lying under the present city. In the same program Kerim Altug, archaeologist and architectural historian with the Istanbul Metropolitan Municipality, was reported to have catalogued 158 cisterns and to be convinced that there were thousands.

24. Both projects described briefly at Dark and Özgümüş, pp. 9–10; Chapter 8 below (pp. 125–34).

25. In his Introduction to the volume of papers, *Constantinople and Its Hinterland* (ed. Mango and G. Dagron, 1995), p. 1.

26. Pierre Gilles, *De Topographia Constantinopoleos* (*The Antiquities of Constantinople, Based on the Translation by John Ball*); 2nd edn with new introduction and bibliography by Ronald Musto (1988). The episode described in the preceding paragraph is at *Antiquities* 2.18 (Musto, p. 104).

structure—they appear on all the visual sources described above and in Panvinio's famous engraving of 1580—and describes how the columns were squared off for paving an Ottoman bath-house, while the carved capitals, pedestals, and entablatures were roughed out for use in everyday building.[27] He wrote of a great fire in the Grand Bazaar that had revealed the fine commercial buildings hidden behind the merchants' stalls, as well as a 'nymphaeum' with forty-five pillars and a brick roof. An important thoroughfare of Constantine's city can still be traced through the Bazaar (Chapter 6 below, pp. 114f.), and it is likely that Gilles was looking at a relic of the Roman and Byzantine city; the 'nymphaeum' was no doubt a Byzantine cistern.[28] One of Gilles' most famous descriptions is of his discovery of the huge reservoir now known as the 'Cistern of the Basilica' because it occupied the emplacement of an earlier basilica, and one of his most eloquent is of the great equestrian statue of Justinian, one of the Seven Wonders of the City in Byzantine texts, being broken up for the foundries.[29] Justinian's leg, says Gilles, exceeded the author's own height and his nose was more than 9 inches long! He did not venture in public view to measure the legs of Justinian's horse, but found one of the hoofs to be 9 inches in height. By the time its sad fate overtook it, Justinian's statue was a thousand years old—still more, if it was a reused statue of Theodosius or Arcadius.[30] It is a strange thought that, recycled into cannon, it might have been used by the Ottoman forces to defend the Acropolis against the Venetian attack of 1687, during which the Parthenon was blown up.

Gilles laments the state of affairs, blaming both the Muslim Ottomans for their uncaring destruction of the ancient city and the ignorance of their Greek Christian subjects in their indifference to their vanishing antiquities.[31] Yet, at the same time as he presents this picture of neglect, he offers what may be our best chance of recovering the physical character of the fourth- and early fifth-century city. Relying on 'an ancient manuscript written over one thousand years ago by a gentleman more noble by his birth than his writings', Gilles constructed a survey

---

27. *Antiquities* 2.13 (Musto, pp. 83–84).

28. *Antiquities* 1.10 (Musto, pp. 30–31).

29. *Antiquities* 2.20 (Musto, pp. 11–12), 2.17 (pp. 97–98). On the 'Seven Wonders' of Byzantium see esp. G. Downey, 'Constantine the Rhodian: His Life and Writings', in K. Weitzmann (ed.), *Late Classical and Mediaeval Studies in Honor of Albert Mathias Friend, Jr.* (1955), pp. 212–21.

30. On the attribution of the statue to Theodosius see Ian Manners' article of 1997, p. 86, citing Mango, *Art Bulletin* 41 (1959), pp. 351–56. Malalas, s.a. 542, states however that it was originally a statue of Arcadius from the Forum Tauri (sc. of Theodosius); Elizabeth Jeffreys et al., *The Chronicle of John Malalas*, p. 287; below, Chapter 8 (pp. 144f., 150f.).

31. *Antiquities* 2.1 (pp. 51–52). Gilles' complaints are echoed by Ken Dark, in Dark and Özgümüş (n. 22 above), pp. 7–10.

of the city that is still the primary guide to its configuration in this early period. The manuscript is the text now known as the *Notitia urbis Constantinopolitanae*, a regional inventory of the city dedicated to the emperor Theodosius II.[32] In its few pages, the text identifies more buildings and amenities in more parts of the city than are known from any other source and identifies its resources in a way that permits at least a provisional description of the population of the city and its distribution through the urban area. The bureaucratic remoteness of the text is free from the distortions and fantasies that affect so many of our sources, and it is contemporaneous with the later part of the period that it covers. It is without any doubt the single most important source for the early history of the city of Constantine. Of the anonymous gentleman who wrote it nothing is known, unless we infer from some indications in his preface—he is at leisure, he admires the city and is very proud of it, has access to documentary information, and can presume to dedicate his work to the emperor—that he is a retired member of the administrative office of the urban prefect of Constantinople. Whatever his background, he shares with his discoverer Pierre Gilles the honour of having founded the modern study of the city.

It is to the *Notitia* that we now turn, beginning with an introduction and translation of the text. This is followed in Chapter 5 by a region-by-region description of the topography of the city based on the *Notitia*, and in Chapters 6–9 by a survey of its historical development based on the information that it provides, followed in Chapter 10 by a discussion of its housing resources and the distribution of its population. Lastly (Chapter 11), other sources are brought into play to support a more intimate portrait of the city of the fourth and early fifth centuries—the human action, as it were, within the stage setting provided by the *Notitia*.

---

32. Gilles does not say how or when he 'accidentally fell upon' this text, the manuscript tradition of which is entirely western; by the time that Gilles wrote, there were several versions of it. A translation was included as an appendix in Ball's edition of Gilles, but not in the 1988 reprint.

4

Notitia Urbis Constantinopolitanae

4.1 Introduction

The *Notitia urbis Constantinopolitanae* is one of a dossier of texts of a broadly technical and administrative nature, transmitted by fifteenth- and sixteenth-century copyists from a lost Carolingian manuscript once in the Cathedral Library of Speyer.[1] Several of the documents are illustrated, either in combination with the written text or as a frontispiece to it. Among the fully illustrated texts the most notable are the late fourth- to early fifth- century *Notitia Dignitatum*, with nearly a hundred illustrations to accompany the court and provincial offices of eastern and western empires with their insignia, registers of military units with their shield devices, and other symbols of power; and the so-called *Anonymus de rebus bellicis*, with illustrations to clarify the descriptions of the military and other inventions offered for the emperor's consideration. The *Notitia* of Constantinople is among the texts that possess an illustration only as a frontis-piece (Fig. 4.1). The picture, appearing in only one copy of the Speyer manuscript though others preserve the space for it, shows the city on its peninsula, portrayed in the 'modernizing' style in which the images are transmitted, but representing authentic details, namely the great church of S. Sophia, the equestrian statue of Justinian whose last days were witnessed by Pierre Gilles, and a representation of the spiral staircase, named Kochlias after the Greek word for a snail, that communicated between the palace and the hippodrome (Procopius, *Wars* 1.24.42).

The dossier also contains an illustration that once served as frontispiece to a similar text relating to the city of Rome. It shows a seated figure with the caption 'The city of Rome, once desolate, now restored to a greater glory in the most Holy Empire' (*Urbs quae aliquando desolata nunc clariosior piissimo imperio*

---

1. O. Seeck (ed.), in *Notitia Dignitatum* (1876), pp. 228–43. See on the history of these texts L. D. Reynolds (ed.), *Texts and Transmission: A Survey of the Latin Classics* (1983), pp. 253–57 (M. D. Reeve), with the title of the text adopted here; more detailed, E. A. Thompson, *A Roman Reformer and Inventor: Being a New Text of the Treatise* De Rebus Bellicis *with a Translation and Introduction* (1952), pp. 6–17. The substance of this and the following chapter is very close to what appeared as ch. 4 of Lucy Grig and Gavin Kelly (eds), *Two Romes* (2012). I am grateful for permission to include this material here.

From Byzantium to Constantinople: An Urban History. John Matthews, Oxford University Press.
© Oxford University Press 2024. DOI: 10.1093/oso/9780197585498.003.0004

FIG. 4.1 The city of Constantinople in the *Notitia*. Manuscript of 1436, Oxford, Bodleian Library, canon misc. 378.

restaurata), referring no doubt to a Carolingian restoration of the city—a description that must go back to the exemplar of the extant manuscripts. The text that once followed the illustration, corresponding to that for Constantinople, is lost, though similar documents in the form of regional catalogues of cities are extant for the city of Rome and, in summary form and by a very indirect route, Alexandria.[2] Like its Roman counterparts, the *Notitia* of the city of Constantinople is a

2. A. Nordh (ed.), *Libellus de Regionibus Urbis Romae* (1949); see esp. G. Hermansen, 'The Population of Ancient Rome: The Regionaries', *Historia* 27 (1978), pp. 129–68; cf. P. M. Fraser, 'A Syriac *Notitia Urbis Alexandrinae*', *Journal of Egyptian Archaeology* 37 (1951), pp. 103–8; considered in respect of Antioch by J. H. W. G. Liebeschuetz, *Antioch: City and Imperial Administration in the Later Roman Empire* (1972), pp. 95–96. See further below, Chapter 10 (pp. 210f.).

list of the physical and administrative resources of the city, arranged under the Fourteen Regions into which it was divided and, at the end of the text, a *Collectio civitatis* drawing together the contents of the separate regions. In a feature not found in the extant Roman examples, each region is prefaced by a brief topographical description. The most recent monuments are palaces, houses, and baths named after members of the Theodosian dynasty, namely the Augustae Galla Placidia (who held this rank from 421 or 425 until her death in 450), Theodosius II's sister Pulcheria (Augusta from 414 to 453), his wife Eudocia (Augusta from 423 to 443 though living on in exile to 460), and the 'nobilissimae' Marina (403–49) and Arcadia (400–44). The range of dates defined by these references is narrowed by the fact that the writer does not acknowledge the renaming of the 'Constantinian' baths of Region X after Theodosius II, which took place upon their long-delayed completion in 427.[3] These indications are consistent with other elements in the text. Its dedicatory preface describes Theodosius as having by his care brought the city to 'such a pitch of perfection as could not be surpassed' (*ita virtus et cura decoravit, ut eius perfectioni, quamvis sit quispiam diligens, nihil possit adiungere*), and in its summary at the end mentions the 'double line of walls' by which the city was guarded (*duplici muro acies turrium extensa custodit*). This clearly means the outer wall begun by Theodosius II and repaired or rebuilt at various later times; a law of 4 April 413 preserved in the Theodosian Code refers to the construction of a new wall 'for the protection of the most splendid city' and delegates the upkeep of its towers to the owners of the land on which they stood.[4]

Despite this mention of the later walls in the preface, the configuration of the city laid out in the text of the *Notitia* is that of an earlier period. The most concise proof of this is in a note at the very end of the text, when the 'length' of the city (its east-west measurement) is given as 14,075 Roman feet, from the Porta Aurea to the sea at the eastern end of the promontory. This measurement can only be from the Constantinian wall, from which point it is quite accurate.[5] The Porta Aurea itself, the original Golden Gate, is the first of the monuments listed under

---

3. *Chron. Pasch.*, s.a.; Whitby and Whitby, p. 70.

4. *CTh* 15.1.51, 'ad munitionem splendidissimae urbis'. The classic study is A. van Millingen, *Byzantine Constantinople: The Walls of the City and Adjoining Historical Sites* (1899). Later works were performed by the praetorian prefects Cyrus in 439–41 (*PLRE* II, p. 338, Cyrus 7), Constantinus in 447 (*PLRE* II, p. 317, Constantinus 22), and Pusaeus in 465 (*PLRE* II, p. 930). See P. Speck, 'Der Mauerbau in 60 Tagen. Zum Datum der Errichtung der Landmauer von Konstantinopel mit einem Anhang über die Datierung der Notitia urbis Konstantinopolitanae', in H.-G. Beck, *Studien zur Frühgeschichte Konstantinopels* (1973), pp. 135–78—using the *Notitia* itself as an argument for the dating of the walls. The crucial point is that, whatever the dating of the Theodosian walls, the city described by the *Notitia* pre-dates their construction.

5. As pointed out by Van Millingen, pp. 16–18 and 30–33; below, p. 121. The corresponding north-south measurement of 6,150 feet is very close to accurate for a line drawn through the forum of Theodosius.

the Twelfth Region, which is described, in the topographical sketch of the region preceding its list of amenities, as 'ennobled by the lofty grandeur of the walls' (*quam moenium sublimior decorat ornatus*). We should also note the omission of the church of St. Mocius, which may have a Constantinian origin and certainly existed by the end of the fourth century; it is omitted because it was outside the Constantinian wall and did not belong to any of the city regions (Chapter 9 below, pp. 173–5).

The explanation of the contradiction between the preface, which mentions the Theodosian walls, and the text of the *Notitia*, which takes no notice of them, could lie within the text itself, if it were a cumulative document subject to revision from time to time, always in danger of not being up to date in one way or another. Documentary lists—the *Notitia dignitatum* is an example—are not always updated consistently and in their revision may leave traces of an earlier situation that is still a part of what can be seen. It may be that the compiler, working with a fourth-century configuration of the city based on fourteen regions located (with the special exceptions of Regions XIII and XIV) within the Constantinian walls, was unable to do more than formally acknowledge those of Theodosius, which lie outside the text, beyond the limits of the fourth-century city. It is possible, too, that at the time he compiled his text, the Theodosian walls were seen as an outer defence of the entire urban area, with, as yet, relatively little development (or juridical definition) in the space between this circuit and its predecessor.[6] Only later were the Theodosian walls seen as the primary defence of the city; and only then that the name of the Golden Gate, its main ceremonial entrance, migrated to where its remains are now seen, at the southern end of the later wall. Such sources as *Chronicon Paschale* and Hesychius show that the 'old', or 'Troadensian' walls of the Constantinian period were still visible, at least in parts, after those of Theodosius were built. As we saw in Chapter 3 (p. 52), some versions of Buondelmonti's manuscript panorama of the city suggest that the Constantinian Golden Gate, labelled 'porta antiquissima pulchra', was extant as late as the fifteenth century.[7]

In the translation of the *Notitia* that follows, I retain the Latin text of the topographical introductions to the regions; this is laid out by clauses not to evoke a new style of poetry but to make clear how these sometimes awkward descriptions are articulated, and to facilitate their co-ordination with the schematic plans of the regions shown in Chapter 5. Aware that they are arbitrary

---

6. Mango, *Développement urbain*, pp. 49–50.

7. *Chron. Pasch.*, s.a. 451 ('Troadesian walls'; cf. Hesychius 1.43), 459 (cistern of Aspar near the 'old wall'); Whitby and Whitby, pp. 81, 85, and Chapter 6 below (p. 120); for Buondelmonti, Mango, *Développement urbain*, pp. 35–36, and above, pp. 118–20.

distinctions, I follow the transmitted text in showing where numbers are written out either in words or in Latin numerals. The translation follows the text in making the important distinction between *gradus*, 'steps' from which bread distributions were made, and *scalae*, quaysides or embarkation points for ferries. Even though it is hard to imagine that they are significant, it also reproduces the different ways in which the *Notitia* describes the *porticus*, or colonnades of the city. In Region I they are defined as 'continuous' (*perpetuae*), in Regions II–VII as 'grand' (*magnae*), and in Regions VIII–XIV as 'greater' (*maiores*). It may be that the number of colonnades, however they are styled, is connected with the number of main roads in the city, as distinct from the local 'streets or alleys' (*vici sive angiportus*) listed simply as 'vici' in all entries after Region II (though for some reason not counted in Region XIII), and clearly connected with the five *vicomagistri* listed (with the one exception mentioned below) for each region; Cassius Dio's word for the *vicomagistri* of Augustan Rome, στενωπάρχοι (55.8.8), derives from στενωπός, the Greek equivalent of *angiportus*.

It is well understood that in its generic (and original) meaning,[8] the Latin term *vicus* indicates a gathering of houses to form a neighbourhood, rather than a street in the more restricted sense of a thoroughfare narrower than a road (estimated, perhaps, by the level of wheeled transport they could accommodate).[9] Cassius Dio's Greek equivalent and the alternative term *angiportus* given by the *Notitia*, draw attention to the narrowness of streets rather than to their residential character, but the two are of course connected, if only because an *angiportus* will, with regulation as to width and projecting balconies,[10] contain residences appropriate for its narrowness, as opposed to the more substantial, free-standing houses and mansions to be found in colonnaded avenues. The *Notitia* takes in this order the three definitions *vicus*, residence (*domus*), and colonnade, after which are private baths, public and private bakeries, and *gradus* (on all this see Chapter 10 below).

Beyond a general understanding of the role of *vici* in the social and administrative structure of the city, it does not seem possible to use the figures given by the *Notitia* as evidence for this structure at Constantinople. The sixty-five

---

8. Sc. the Greek οἶκος (and its Sanskrit predecessor), just as 'vicinus' is a neighbour and a vicinity is a neighbourhood. The term is also used for a 'place' in general, and for a settled community, even quite a large one, possessing its own institutions within the territory of a larger city, like Bedriacum, between Verona and Cremona (Tacitus, *Histories* 2.22).

9. Salvatore Cosentino, 'Domus, vici e demografia nella *Notitia Urbis Constantinopolitanae*: alcune osservazioni', in I. Baldini and C. Sfameni (eds), *Atti del Covegno Internazionale del Centro Interuniversitario di Studi Abitative Tardoantica nel Mediterraneo* (2018), pp. 1–6, suggesting the Italian translation 'rione', a district or quarter.

10. Chapter 10, nn. 13–14; a law of Zeno writes of *angiportus* as 10 or 12 feet in width.

vicomagistri are equally distributed, five among each of thirteen regions; Region XIV was excluded from this mode of organization, in deference, no doubt, to its character as a sort of royal enclave under the direct purview of the emperor (Chapter 5, p. 95f.). The missing number of *vici sive angiportus* in Region XIII cannot be supplied from the grand total in the *Collectio Civitatis*, where the total of 322 is accurate for the other thirteen regions. On the other hand, there are fourteen *vernaculi* or public slaves for the entire city, from which it can be concluded that Region XIV possessed one like the others, and the number of *collegiati* listed in the grand total, 560, only reaches this total if thirty-seven *collegiati* are, as we would expect, assumed for Region XIV.

These figures are very different from those found at Rome, most obviously in the proportions of *vici* and *vicomagistri*. According to the testimony of Pliny there were in the later first century 265 *vici*, each one apparently with four *magistri* to give a total of more than 1,000 *magistri*, while a famous inscription gives a total of 262 *magistri* for the five regions of the city mentioned on it.[11] These figures are broadly consistent, and, allowing for increase over time, not so very far out of line with those given in the Roman catalogues, of 424 *vici* and 672 *vicomagistri*. On any calculation, however, they are many times those recorded for Constantinople, with its five *vicomagistri* for each of the thirteen regions that possessed them; nor can the total *vici sive angiportus* of Constantinople be mapped upon the numbers of *vici* recorded for Rome, a very much larger city. Perhaps we should conclude that the 322 *vici* at Constantinople are indeed streets and alleys counted individually, while the 265 and 424 *vici* at Rome are groups of streets forming local districts or quarters. The discrepancies reflect the different situations of the two cities—Constantinople a new foundation only a hundred years old, built on an enlarged site with a new administration, Rome an ancient metropolis with the accumulations of centuries in its streets.[12]

Other omissions and discrepancies are relatively few. The figure for private baths in Region X can be provisionally supplied from the grand total given in the *Collectio Civitatis* at the end of the text. The total of twenty public bakeries given in the grand total is not quite consistent with the sum of the separate regions, which gives twenty-one, and the number of private bakeries, listed in the grand total as 120, when taken region by region only reaches 113. Public baths (*thermae*)

---

11. *Hist. nat.* 3.5.66; cf. Suetonius, *Augustus* 30.1 and Cassius Dio 55.8.6–7; *ILS* 6073; for discussion, O. F. Robinson, *Ancient Rome: City Planning and Administration* (1992), pp. 11–12; Cl. Nicolet, *Space, Geography and Politics in the Early Roman Empire* (Eng. transl., 1991), pp. 195–97; L. Haselberger, *Mapping Augustan Rome, Journal of Roman Archaeology*, supplementary series, 50 (2002), p. 215.

12. It is perhaps worth adding that the religious duties of the *vicomagistri* at Rome, again evolving over centuries, were not replicated in the new capital.

are given in the grand total as eight, but nine are found under the separate regions. An especially interesting discrepancy is in the number of churches (see Chapter 9, pp. 173, 181). They are given in the grand total as fourteen, but only twelve can be found in the entries for the regions. Seven of these churches occur in just three regions (II, VII, IX), and six regions (I, III, V, VI, VIII, XII) have no church listed. Certain important items that appear in the grand total but are not listed under the individual regions, such as the 'Colossus' in the hippodrome and the 'golden tetrapylon' in the Augusteum, are noted below (p. 165f.).

I use the broadly defined term 'residence' for the *Notitia's* 'domus' for the somewhat opposite reasons that it includes the mansions of the imperial family and nobility that appear under this term, and because of the possibility or likelihood that in the matter of housing conditions in the city, the term takes account of apartment blocks (*insulae*) as well as free-standing homes.

4.2 Translation

The City of Constantinople, New Rome

It is often the case that men of learning, inspired according to the measure of their intellect by a restless desire for the unknown, apply their inquiring minds at one time to the customs of foreign peoples, at another to the secrets of the earth, lest, to the detriment of general knowledge, anything should remain unknown; for they think it a mark of indolence if anything that exists in the world of men should lie hidden from them. While such men of learning grasp the measure of the lands in miles, the seas in stades, the heavens by conjecture, I considered it ignorant and neglectful, free as I am from every worldly duty, that knowledge of the city of Constantinople, which is a training ground for life itself, should lie hidden. This city, surpassing the praise won by its founder, did the virtuous care of the invincible emperor Theodosius, rendering spotless and new the face of antiquity, so enhance that nothing could be added to its perfection, be a man never so diligent. And so, after careful inspection of all its quarters, and after reviewing the numbers of the associations of men who serve it, I have set my pen to a faithful account of every detail within the confines of a register or list; so that the attention of the admirer, instructed in all its monuments and filled with astonishment at the fullness of such great felicity, may confess that for this city no praise or devotion is adequate.[13]

---

13. Citing this last sentence, P. M. Fraser, *Journal of Egyptian Archaeology* 37 (1951), p. 108 (above, n. 2), writes of the *Notitia* as 'manifestly' a 'literary descriptive piece', to which one can reply that the author was entitled to praise his city and emperor in the bureaucratic, even departmental language that he was used to. Note too, on the Roman inventories (n. 2 above),

Prima regio
longa situ
plana in angustum producitur
a palatii inferiore parte contra theatrum maius euntibus,
dextro latere declivis in mare descendit,
regiis nobiliumque domiciliis clara.

The first region reaches out in length before those leaving the lower part of the palace in the direction of the great theatre.[14] It is on level ground and becomes progressively narrower, while on its right flank it descends downhill to the sea. It is distinguished by the residences of the royal family and the nobility.

Contained in it are:

the aforesaid great palace;
lusorium;
palace of Placidia;
residence (*domus*) of Placidia Augusta;
residence of the most noble Marina;
baths of Arcadius;[15]
streets or alleys, twenty-nine;
residences (*domus*), one hundred and eighteen;
continuous colonnades, two;
private baths, fifteen;
public bakeries, four;
private bakeries, fifteen;
steps (*gradus*), 4;
one curator, with responsibility for the whole region.[16]
one public slave (*vernaculus*), who serves the general needs of the region and is its messenger;
twenty-five *collegiati* appointed from among the various guilds (*collegia*), whose duty is to bring assistance in cases of fire;
five *vicomagistri*, to whom is entrusted the night watch of the city.

R. Behrwald, *Die Stadt als Museum? Die Wahrnehmung der Monumente Roms in der Spätantike* (2009).

14. This is the amphitheatre of Region II.

15. Throughout the text, the great public baths are listed earlier and separately from the much larger number of private baths.

16. The definitions of duties set out in this and the following three entries apply to all the regions and are not repeated in the text.

Secunda regio
ab initio theatri minoris
post aequalitatem sui latenter molli sublevata clivo,
mox ad mare praecipitiis abrupta descendit.

The second region, starting from the little theatre rises from level ground in a gentle, almost imperceptible ascent, then suddenly falls in steep cliffs to the sea.

Contained in it are:

great church;
old church;
senate-house;
tribunal [speakers' platform],[17] built with porphyry steps;
baths of Zeuxippus;
theatre;
amphitheatre;
streets or alleys, thirty-four;
residences, ninety-eight;
grand colonnades, four;
private baths, thirteen;
private bakeries, four;
steps (*gradus*), 4;
one curator;
one public slave;
collegiati, thirty-five;
five *vicomagistri*.

Tertia regio
plana quidem in superiore parte,
utpote in ea circi spatio largius explicato,
sed ab eius extrema parte nimis prono clivo
mare usque descendit.

The third region is level in its upper part, in that it holds there the broad expanse of the Circus, from the far end of which it descends in a very steep gradient to the sea.

Contained in it are:

the aforesaid Circus Maximus;
residence of Pulcheria Augusta;

---

17. Corrected from my mistranslation of 2012; Denis Feissel, 'Tribune et colonnes impériales à l'Augusteion de Constantinople', in *Constantinople réelle et imaginaire: Autour de l'oeuvre de Gilbert Dagron* (Travaux et Mémoires 22/1 (2018)), at pp. 126–28.

new harbour;

semi-circular colonnade, which from the resemblance in its construction is called by the Greek name Sigma;

tribunal of the forum of Constantine;

streets, seven;

residences, ninety-four;

grand colonnades, five;

private baths, eleven;

private bakeries, nine;

[steps,…];

one curator;

one public slave;

collegiati, twenty-one;

five *vicomagistri*.

Regio quarta
a miliario aureo
collibus dextra laevaque surgentibus
ad planitiem usque valle ducente perducitur.

The fourth region begins from the golden milestone, and with hills rising to right and left, follows the valley to level ground.

Contained in it are:

the aforesaid golden milestone;

Augusteum;

basilica;

nymphaeum;

colonnade of Fanio;

marble galley, in commemoration of the naval victory;

church or martyrium of S. Menas;

stadium;

quay (*scala*) of Timasius;

streets, 35;

residences, three hundred and seventy-five;

grand colonnades, four;

private baths, seven;

private bakeries, five;

steps, seven;

one curator;

one public slave;

collegiati, 40;

five *vicomagistri*.

Regionis quintae
non modica pars in obliquioribus posita locis
planitie excipiente producitur;
in qua necessaria civitatis aedificia continentur.

Of the fifth region, a considerable part lies on hillsides which give way to level ground. In this region are contained the buildings that supply the city with its necessities.

Contained in it are:

baths of Honorius;
cistern of Theodosius;
prytaneum;
baths of Eudocia;
strategium, containing the forum of Theodosius and square Theban obelisk;
olive-oil warehouses;
nymphaeum;
Troadensian warehouses;
warehouses of Valens;
warehouses of Constantius;
Portus Prosphorianus;
Chalcedon quay (*scala*);
streets, twenty-three;
residences, one hundred and eight-four;
grand colonnades, 7;
private baths, eleven;
public bakeries, seven;
private bakeries, two;
steps, nine;
food markets, two;
one curator;
one public slave;
collegiati, forty;
five *vicomagistri*.

Regio sexta,
brevi peracta planitie,
reliqua in devexo consistit;
a foro namque Constantini scalam usque
sive traiectum Sycenum porrigitur spatiis suis.

The sixth region after a short stretch of level ground lies for the rest downhill. Its area extends from the forum of Constantine as far as the quay and ferry crossing to Sycae.

Contained in it are:

porphyry column of Constantine;
senate-house in the same place;
shipyard;
harbour;
Sycae quay (*scala*);
streets, twenty-two;
residences, four hundred and eighty-four;
grand colonnade, one;
private baths, nine;
public bakery, one;
private bakeries, seventeen;
steps, seventeen;
one curator;
collegiati, forty-nine;
five *vicomagistri*.

Regio septima,
in conparatione superioris planior,
quamvis et ipsa circa lateris sui extremitatem
habeatur in mare declivior.
Haec a parte dextera columnae Constantini usque ad forum Theodosii
continuis extensa porticibus
et de latere aliis quoque pari ratione porrectis,
usque ad mare velut se ipsam inclinat et ita deducitur.

The seventh region is more level in comparison with the preceding, although it too falls away to the sea at the furthest point of its flank. This region runs with continuous colonnades from the right-hand side of the column of Constantine up to the forum of Theodosius, with other colonnades extending similarly to the side. The whole region descends to the sea and there comes to an end.

Contained in it are:

three churches: namely, Irene, Anastasia, and S. Paul;
column of Theodosius, with internal staircase leading to the top;
two great equestrian statues;
part of the aforementioned forum;
baths of Carosa;
streets, eight-five;
residences, seven hundred and eleven;
grand colonnades, six;
private baths, 11;

private bakeries, 12;
steps, 16;
one curator;
one public slave;
collegiati, eighty;
five *vicomagistri*.

Octava regio
ex parte tauri,
nulla maris vicinitate contermina;
angustior magis quam lata spatia sua in longitudinem producta conpensat.

The eighth region, beginning from the bull, at no point touches the sea. It is somewhat narrow rather than wide in shape but compensates for this by its extension in length.

Contained in it are:

part of the forum of Constantine;
left-hand colonnade, as far as the bull;
basilica of Theodosius;
Capitolium;
streets, twenty-one;
residences, one hundred and eight;
greater colonnades, five;
private baths, ten;
private bakeries, five;
steps, 5;
food markets, two;
one curator;
one public slave;
collegiati, 17;
five *vicomagistri*.

Regio nona
prona omnis et in notum deflexa
extensi<s> maris litoribus terminatur.

The ninth region lies entirely downhill, falling away in a southerly direction and ending in a long reach of the sea-shore.

Contained in it are:

two churches: Caenopolis and Homonoea;
Alexandrian warehouse;
residence of the most noble Arcadia;
baths of Anastasia;

warehouse of Theodosius;
streets, 16;
residences, one hundred and sixteen;
greater colonnades, two;
private baths, 16;
private bakeries, 15;
public bakeries, 4;
steps, 4;
one curator;
one public slave;
collegiati, thirty-eight;
five *vicomagistri*.

Regio decima
in aliud civitatis latus versa,
a nona regione platea magna velut fluvio interveniente dividitur.
Est vero tractu planior
nec usquam praeter maritima loca inaequalis,
longitudini eius latitudine non cedente.

The tenth region lies over to the other side of the city, being separated from the ninth region[18] by a wide road that is like a river flowing between them. Its surface is quite level and nowhere hilly except for the parts by the sea. It is as wide as it is long.

Contained in it are:

church or martyrium of S. Acacius;
baths of Constantine;
residence of Placidia Augusta;
residence of Eudocia Augusta;
residence of the most noble Arcadia;
greater nymphaeum;
streets, twenty;
residences, six hundred and thirty-six;
greater colonnades, six;
private baths, <22>;
public bakeries, two;
private bakeries, sixteen;
steps, 12;
one curator;
one public slave;

18. See below, Chapter 5 (p. 93) for the textual issue raised at this point.

collegiati, ninety;
five *vicomagistri*.

Regio undecima
spatio diffusa liberiore,
nulla parte mari sociatur;
est vero eius extensio tam plana, quam etiam collibus inaequalis.

The eleventh region is rather large in extent, and nowhere touches the sea. Its area is partly level, partly hilly and uneven.

Contained in it are:

martyrium of the Apostles;
palace of Flaccilla;
residence of Pulcheria Augusta;
brazen ox;
cistern of Arcadius;
cistern of Modestus;
streets, 8;
residences, five hundred and three;
greater colonnades, four;
private baths, fourteen;
public bakery, one;
private bakeries, three;
steps, seven;
one curator;
one public slave;
collegiati, thirty-seven;
five *vicomagistri*.

Regio duodecima
portam a civitate petentibus in longum plana omnis consistit,
sed latere sinistro mollioribus clivis deducta
maris confinio terminatur;
quam moenium sublimior decorat ornatus.

The twelfth region is entirely level as it extends before those approaching the gate from inside the city, but on the left side it descends in gentle slopes and terminates at the sea. This region is enhanced by the lofty splendour of the city walls.

Contained in it are:

golden gate;
Troadensian colonnades;

forum of Theodosius;
column of the same (*itidem*),[19] with internal staircase;
mint;
harbour of Theodosius;
streets, eleven;
residences, three hundred and sixty-three;
greater colonnades, three;
private baths, five;
private bakeries, five;
steps, 9;
one curator;
one public slave;
seventeen *collegiati*;
five *vicomagistri*.

Tertiadecima regio Sycena est,
quae sinu maris angusto divisa societatem urbis navigiis frequentibus promeretur;
tota lateri montis adfixa praeter unius plateae tractum,
quam subiacentium eidem monti litorum tantum praestat aequalitas.

The thirteenth region comprises Sycae, which is separated by a narrow inlet of the sea but maintains its connections to the city by frequent ferries. The entire region clings to the side of a mountain except for the course of a single main street, space for which is barely provided by the level ground of the sea-shores lying under the aforesaid mountain.

Contained in it are:

church;
baths of Honorius;
forum of Honorius;
theatre;
docks;
residences, four hundred and thirty-one;
greater colonnade, one;
private baths, five;
public bakery, one;
private bakeries, four;

---

19. Both forum and column are attributed to Theodosius (II), although the episodes portrayed on the column belong to the early years of Arcadius, and the forum was begun in his reign; see Chapter 8 (pp. 149–61). The harbour is of the first Theodosius.

steps, 8;
one curator;
one public slave;
collegiati, 34;
five *vicomagistri*.

Regio sane licet in urbis quartadecima numeretur parte,
tamen quia spatio interiecto divisa est,
muro proprio vallata alterius quodammodo speciem civitatis ostendit.
Est vero progressis a porta modicum situ planum,
dextro autem latere in clivum surgente
usque ad medium fere plateae spatium nimis pronum;
unde mare usque mediocris haec, quae civitatis continet partem, explicatur aequalitas.

The region that makes up the fourteenth part of the city is so counted, despite the fact that it is separated from it by some distance lying between them and is protected by a wall of its own, in a certain manner presenting the appearance of a separate town. To those advancing from the city gate, the ground is level for a certain distance, but then with a hillside rising to the right it descends very steeply to a distance of about half-way along on the road. From this point as far as the sea there then extends a modest level area, which contains (this) part of the city.[20]

Contained in it are:

church;
palace;
nymphaeum;
baths;
theatre;
lusorium;
bridge on wooden piles;
streets, eleven;
residences, one hundred and sixty-seven;
greater colonnades, two;
private baths, five;
public bakery, one;
private bakery, one;

---

20. See Chapter 5 below (pp. 95–6) for the location of Region XIV.

steps, five;
[one public slave];
[*collegiati*, thirty-seven].[21]

Now that we know it in its separate parts, it seems appropriate also to describe the configuration of the city taken in its entirety, to make clear the unique glory of its magnificence, the product of the labour of the human hand, supported also by the collaboration of the elements and the happy gifts of nature. For here indeed, by the consideration of divine providence for the homesteads of so many men of future ages, a spacious tract of land extending in length to form a promontory, facing the outlet of the Pontic Sea, offering harbours in the recesses of its shores, elongated in shape, is securely defended by the sea flowing on all sides; and the one space left open by the encircling sea is guarded by a double wall with an extended array of towers. Bounded by these, the city contains in itself all those things mentioned individually, which, the more firmly to establish the record of them, I will now gather together in summary.

There are contained in the city of Constantinople:

palaces, five;
churches, fourteen;
sacred residences of the Augustae, six;
most noble residences, three;
baths, eight;
basilicas, two;
forums, four;
senate-houses, two;
warehouses, five;
theatres, two;
lusoria, 2;
harbours, four;
circus, one;
cisterns, four;
nymphaea, 4;
streets, three hundred and twenty-two;
residences, four thousand, three hundred and eighty-eight;
colonnades, fifty-two;
private baths, one hundred and fifty-three;

---

21. No *curator* or *vicomagistri* are given for the fourteenth region. The public slave (*vernaculus*) and *collegiati* are inferred from the grand totals in the *Collectio Civitatis*.

public bakeries, twenty;

private bakeries, one hundred and twenty;

steps (*gradus*), one hundred and seventeen;

food markets, five;

curators, thirteen;

public slaves, fourteen;

collegiati, five hundred and sixty;

vicomagistri, sixty-five;

porphyry column;

columns with internal stairs, two;

Colossus;

golden tetrapylon;

Augusteum;

Capitolium;

mint;

maritime steps (*scalae*), three.

The overall length of the city from the golden gate in a straight line as far as the sea-shore is fourteen thousand and seventy-five feet, and its breadth is six thousand, one hundred and fifty feet.

5

The Fourteen Regions

IT IS NOT certain whether it was Constantine or a successor who conceived the idea of organising his city under the Fourteen Regions described in the *Notitia*. Cyril Mango offered arguments for Theodosius I as their originator, and there is no reason to object to this, the idea of a New Rome, part of the Constantinian conception of the city, being applied progressively over time.[1] It was for instance not until the time of Constantius, with the promotion of its governor to *praefectus* and its senate to the rank of *clarissimus*, that the institutional status of the new city was made equal to that of Rome. At whatever time they were introduced, the Regions were laid out to conform to the primary features of the Constantinian city plan, but it is as important to recognize the past history as well as the future development of the urban space that was so defined. Constantinople was not designed on a blank sheet of paper. If the forum of Constantine, lying just outside the Severan city, was a focal point of his new city, in other ways it is evident that his planners exploited an urban design that was there already.

As is apparent when its text is overlaid upon a ground plan of the city (Figs 5.1–3 below), the *Notitia* bears in many places the imprint of the past, from its origins as a Greek colony to the developments of the Severan period. Region I, the palace area, adjoined the hippodrome, which composed a large part of Region III and ran up to the Zeuxippon and Augusteum in Region IV; these two, if not the hippodrome itself, were originally Severan foundations, the Augusteum, as we have seen, being a reconfiguration of the Severan colonnaded forum, or Tetrastoon.[2] In these south-eastern sectors of the promontory (leaving aside the ancient Greek city on its northern coast), Constantine's projects fit naturally into an urban framework established for Byzantium in the Severan period. It is

---

1. 'Le Mystère de la XIVe Région de Constantinople', *Mélanges Gilbert Dagron* (Travaux et Mémoires 14, 2002), p. 455; at some time after 381 Regium ceased to have an independent bishop, which might mark its absorption into the Constantinopolitan urban framework presented in the *Notitia*.

2. Above, Chapter 2 (p. 36), with further discussion in Chapter 6 (pp. 103–5); Mango, *The Brazen House: A Study of the Vestibule of the Imperial Palace at Constantinople* (1959), pp. 42–47.

From Byzantium to Constantinople: An Urban History. John Matthews, Oxford University Press.
© Oxford University Press 2024. DOI: 10.1093/oso/9780197585498.003.0005

further west, in the newly developed territory outside the Severan city, that Constantine's enterprise takes form as a new creation. Beginning from the Severan city gate, as many as four Regions took their bearings from the new forum of Constantine that lay just beyond it, and these Regions and several others were bounded by the main thoroughfares laid out for the new city. The most important of these was the great colonnaded avenue known as Mesē or Central Avenue, which linked its cardinal points. Beginning at the Augusteum, and running along the Severan colonnades to the old city gate, the avenue led on through the forum of Constantine and the future site of the forum of Theodosius, and some distance after this divided. Its southern branch led to the Golden Gate in the wall of Constantine, its northern extension past the mausoleum of that emperor, keeping the mausoleum to its right, and advancing to the successor of the Thracian gate seen by Cassius Dio.[3] The basic configuration of the city, in the shape of a rotated letter Y widening into the peninsula, can be understood in relation to these points of reference.[4]

Within this framework, the twelve intramural Regions were laid out in an orderly pattern running from the eastern end of the promontory to the Constantinian wall, with two Regions (XIII and XIV) located outside them. Regions I–XII can be plotted as two bands of Regions running westwards along the Propontis and Golden Horn respectively, expanding into a row of three Regions running from north-east to south-west inside the city wall. The only serious question as to the location of the intramural Regions has concerned Regions VII and VIII, but this is easily resolved to leave Region VII facing the Golden Horn to the north and VIII facing the Propontis to the south.

The following survey takes the intramural Regions in three groups (I–VI, VII–IX, X–XII), followed by the two extramural Regions. It is the purpose of the survey only to locate the Regions and describe their basic character. The only advantage claimed over earlier descriptions, is that it is offered in close conjunction with the text of the *Notitia*, and incorporates the topographical introductions to the Regions, as well as of the institutions listed under them.[5] The outline plans that

---

3. The Mesē, properly speaking, ran from the Golden Milestone to its point of separation into northerly and southerly branches, beyond which it ceased in any meaningful sense to follow a 'middle' course through the city. On many maps, the southern branch of the road is marked 'Mesē', which may reflect Byzantine usage.

4. The configuration is well described by Sarah Bassett, *The Urban Image of Late Antique Constantinople* (2004), pp. 22ff.

5. See ch. 4 of Janin's *Constantinople Byzantine*, 'Les Régions Urbaines'; Cyril Mango's *Le Développement Urbain de Constantinople*; and especially A. Berger, 'Regionen und Straßen im frühen Konstantinopel', *Istanbuler Mitteilungen* 47 (1997), pp. 349–414. In the last of these, a German translation and commentary on the *Notitia*, the text is split up into the more general

accompany the descriptions of the Regions are a schematic attempt to display this correlation of the *Notitia* with the ground plan of the city. Taken in the three groups mentioned, they use the *Notitia* to show (1) the basic configuration of the city within the walls of Constantine; (2) (shown in italics) the topographical introductions to the Regions of the city; (3) the physical resources listed under the Regions, approximating the position of these, whether individually or in groups, wherever possible; (4) directional arrows showing the relations between different features of the Regions, and places where the *Notitia* itself indicates movement within or between Regions (for example the location of the amphitheatre in Region II, as reached from Region I). The commentaries on each Region are intended merely to establish or refine matters of topography in relation to the information offered by the *Notitia*; historical arguments on questions of urban development are left to Chapters 6–9 below, and the question of housing to Chapter 10.

5.1 Regions I–VI

Region I (Janin, p. 49; Berger, pp. 357–58; Fig. 5.1), beginning in the triangular wedge of land between the hippodrome and the Propontis shore, runs from the 'lower part' of the palace towards the north-east, with the acropolis of Byzantium rising before it to the left, and the coast of the promontory to the right. Between acropolis and sea, the Region advanced in a narrowing configuration towards the 'greater theatre' (*theatrum maius*), which was itself not in this Region but is listed, as an amphitheatre, under Region II.[6] Not all the locations of the Region's amenities are exactly known, but that of the great palace itself (the first entry in the entire document), is an established point of reference.[7] Like the palaces of Thessalonica and Antioch (and, in its later periods, Rome) it adjoined the hippodrome, to which it was connected by a corridor leading directly from the palace to the imperial box (*kathisma*). From here the emperor could view the races, give audience and meet the

---

discussion of the regions and is not set out as a list, which is important in understanding it. I have however taken constant and appreciative note of Berger's descriptions of the Regions, as of Janin's study and of Pierre Gilles' *Antiquities of Constantinople*.

6. The identification of the greater theatre as the amphitheatre of Constantinople is important for the topography of Regions I and II. I find it hard to believe (with Berger, p. 359) that the 'theatrum minus' of the *Notitia* can be the amphitheatre (nn. 11, 15 below).

7. Berger, p. 358. The Palatium Placidianum was connected with a daughter of Valentinian I who died in 394 and the Domus Placidiae Augustae with Galla Placidia, Theodosius' daughter by his second wife. Its location is shown to be near the (later) church of SS. Sergius and Bacchus by its use as the lodging of papal legates, located near that church. 'Nobilissima Marina' was a sister of Theodosius II. For the Arcadianae, overlooking the Propontis shore, see Procopius, *Buildings* 1.11.1f.

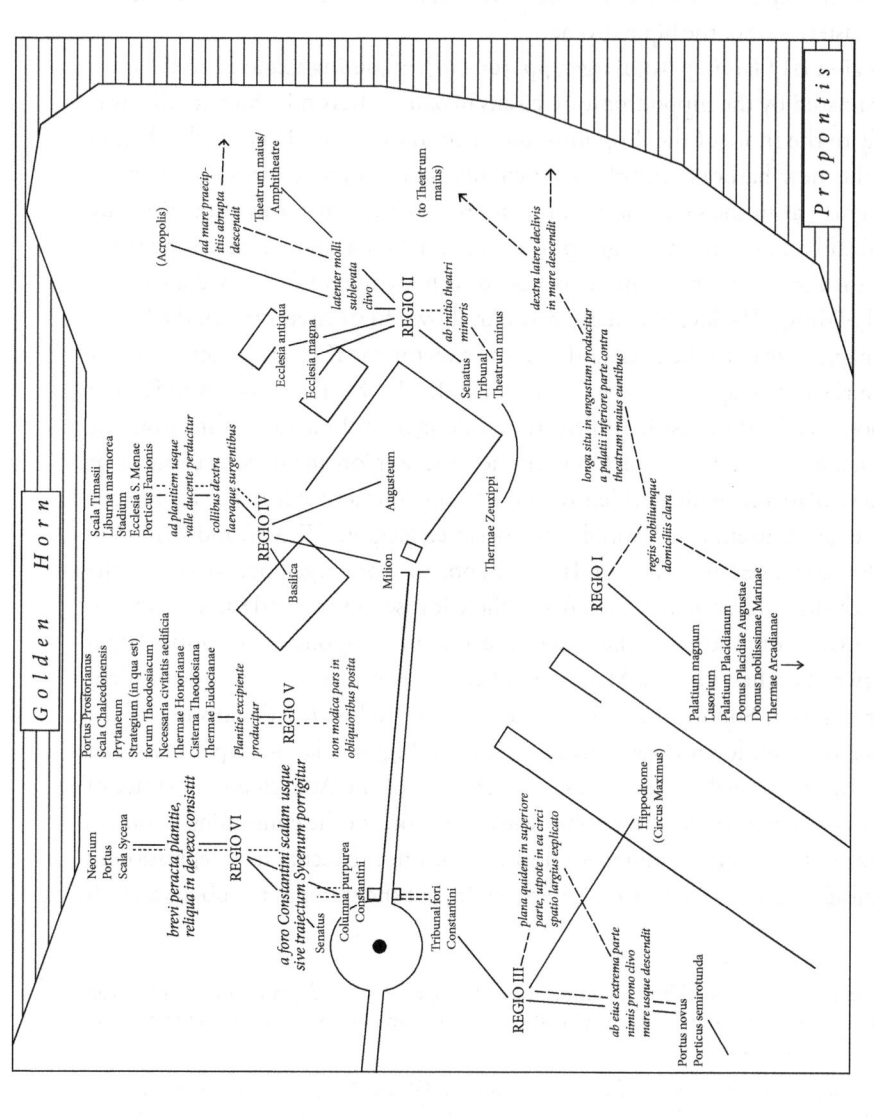

FIG. 5.1 The intramural Regions of Constantinople: Regions I–VI. This and the following two figures apply the information of the *Notitia* to a schematic groundplan of the city. Roman characters and solid lines indicate the lists of amenities in the Regions. Italics and broken lines show connections with the topographical introductions of the Regions. Especially notable in Regions I–VI are the locations of the theatre and amphitheatre, and the inclusion of the Augusteum in Region IV, with its surrounding institutions in Region II.

assembled people; on the pedestal of the obelisk of Theodosius, which still stands in its original location in the hippodrome, the emperor and his supporters are shown in just this attitude, in the very place where they assumed it (Fig. 9.1a and b). Region I has here a precise if somewhat theoretical boundary, for the hippodrome itself was assigned to Region III. The border between Regions I and III thus ran along the south-eastern side of the hippodrome.

Region III (Janin, p. 50; Berger, pp. 360–61), adjoining Region I to the west, is dominated by the hippodrome or 'circus maximus', beyond which it falls away steeply to the shore of the Propontis. Included in this coastal part of the Region were the 'new harbour' and the semi-circular portico known from its shape as the Sigma (from the Greek letter in its more archaic form); these amenities are described by Zosimus as the gift of the emperor Julian, though given the time-scale it is obvious that another emperor (or other emperors) also had a hand in their building.[8] The location of the harbour, shown in its later form on the Vavassore map, survives to the present day in the street name Kadırgalimanı, or 'galley harbour', which may represent its northern limit.[9] To the north, the Third Region was bounded by the Mesē in its first stretch along the colonnade leading from the Augusteum to the forum of Constantine. The Region included a tribunal or speakers' platform, which evidently stood on the southern side of the forum, but not the forum itself, which was divided between Regions VI, VII, and VIII.[10]

The starting-point of Region II (Janin, pp. 49–50; Berger, pp. 358–60) is the 'lesser theatre' (*theatrum minus*), from where it rose in the 'gentle ascent' known to thousands of tourists, to the area of the ancient acropolis. Its amenities begin with two churches, Ecclesia Magna, and Ecclesia Antiqua. Their axiomatic iden-tifications as S. Sophia and S. Irene means, if we follow the description of the *Notitia*, that the 'lesser theatre' from which the Region takes its departure stood below them, somewhere to the east or north-east of the Augusteum. No trace of the theatre survives; like the amphitheatre it was one of the continuing resources of Graeco-Roman Byzantium. An imprint was once detected in a depression in the hillside below the kitchens of the Seraglio, but the status of the observation is

---

8. Zosimus 3.11.3; as noted by his commentator François Paschoud (and others), Julian can hardly have initiated and built a new harbour and portico in a six-month stay in the city (below, Chapter 7, pp. 125–30).

9. See Mango, *Développement urbain*, pp. 38–39, and Gilles, *Antiquities* 2.15 (p. 92), for the name Caterga Limena or 'Port of the Three-Decked Galleys'; below, Chapter 7 (pp. 127–9).

10. It is suggested (by Berger, p. 361, and others) that the Domus Pulcheriae Augustae listed under this region may be the confiscated mansion of the *praepositus sacri cubiculi* Antiochus, partially excavated in the 1960s between the north-western side of the hippodrome and the Mesē and still visible as incorporated in the (also ruined) church of St. Euphemia; *PLRE* II, p. 102 (Antiochus 5); Müller-Wiener, *Bildlexikon*, pp. 122–25. This would be a further indica-tion of the date of composition of the *Notitia*.

uncertain, and the *Notitia* shows that the theatre stood to the south of this location. The depression, if it is not a natural feature, might rather be a trace of the amphitheatre, to which might be attributed the remains of seating discovered in 1959.[11]

Region II also contained a senate-house and tribunal, to be distinguished from the later foundations in the forum of Constantine.[12] The location of the senate-house is known, since accounts of the Nika Riot of 532 refer to it as facing the church of St. Sophia, with reference to the danger it suffered from the conflagration; it must then have stood not far from that church, on the eastern side of the Augusteum.[13] With that side of the Augusteum so occupied, it would be obvious, even if nothing else were known about it, that the bath complex known as the Zeuxippon extended on its southern side, in the space between the Augusteum and the northern end of the hippodrome (in Region III) and the palace (in Region I). The extent and character of the Zeuxippon are shown by the eighty statues of Greek and Roman gods, heroes, and literary eminences it still contained in the time of the sixth-century poet Christodorus, whose poem on the subject constitutes the entire second book of the *Anthologia Palatina*.[14] To include all these amenities, Region II must have wrapped itself around the southern, eastern, and northern sides of the Augusteum, the listed monuments being located on these three sides while the Augusteum itself was in Region IV.

As well as the *theatrum minus* already mentioned, Region II also contained the *theatrum maius*, or amphitheatre. The location of this structure was in the northerly part of the Region, since the narrowing Region I, as we saw, extended *towards* it as it followed the coast below the acropolis. The amphitheatre must then have stood below the acropolis to the east, somewhere below the kitchens of the Topkapı Palace.[15] This location is confirmed in a law in the Theodosian Code,

---

11. Günter Martiny, 'The Great Theatre, Byzantium', *Antiquity* 12 (1938), pp. 89–93; Berger, p. 359.

12. See the article of Denis Feissel, 'Tribune et colonnes impériales à l'Augusteion de Constantinople', in *Constantinople réelle et imaginaire: autour de l'oeuvre de Gilbert Dagron* (Travaux et Mémoires 22/1 (2018)).

13. Procopius, *Buildings* 1.2.1 (in archaizing language); 'Before the senate house (*bouleutērion*) [there was] a sort of market-place (*agora*), which the people of Byzantium call Augustaion'; cf. *Chron. Pasch.*, s.a. 621 (Whitby and Whitby, p. 117), 'the Senate-house by the Augustaion, as it is called' (to distinguish it from the senate-house in Constantine's forum). I suggest in Chapters 6 and 10 that it was the meeting-place (*bouleutērion*) of the *curia* of Byzantium under the Severan development of the city.

14. C. Mango, 'Antique Statuary and the Byzantine Beholder', *DOP* 17 (1963), p. 57.

15. See above, n. 11. The sources work if the 'lesser theatre' of the *Notitia* is the Classical theatre, and the 'greater theatre' is the amphitheatre of Region II. Otherwise known as Cynegion (Greek Κυνήγιον), an arena for *venationes*, one of the most important uses of large amphitheatres in the later period, its location by the sea to the east of the acropolis is confirmed by the

forbidding lime-burning along the shore of the promontory 'between the amphitheatre and the harbour of Julian'; the kilns are to be removed in order to main-
tain the environmental health (*salubritas*) of the city and of the imperial palace,
which lay between them.[16]

Region IV (Janin, p. 51; Berger, pp. 361–62) is easily identified as following
the valley running northward from the Augusteum to the Golden Horn, with the
acropolis (sc. Topkapı) to the right.[17] The Region also contained the Miliarium or
Milion, the 'golden milestone' from which departed the Mesē and the road
system springing from it; the reference to a 'golden tetrapylon' in the *Collectio
Civitatis* at the end of the document defines the architectural form of this structure as a quadriform arch. On the western (more precisely north-western) side of
the Augusteum stood a basilica with precinct, the location and orientation of
which are now marked by the so-called cistern of the basilica (Yerebatan Sarayi);
if we may compare the architectural ensemble of forum, basilica, and colonnade
found at Severan Lepcis Magna, we might ask whether the basilica too was an
original foundation of that period.[18] Of the other items listed under Region IV,
the marble warship (*liburna*) commemorating a naval victory no doubt overlooked the sea,[19] while the Scala Timasii, named after a general of Theodosius I,
was a set of steps forming a quay, one of three such 'scalae' mentioned by the
Notitia. The *stadium*, a survival from the ancient Greek city, was located near to the
sea below the northern slopes of the acropolis, where Justinian built guest-houses.[20]

The three Regions V–VII form a sequence along the northern side of the peninsula. All are bounded by the Golden Horn, with the Mesē as their southern
limit. With Region V (Janin, pp. 51–52; Berger, pp. 362–64), the character of the
city changes and we enter a commercial district; here, as the *Notitia* says, were
situated the buildings that provided the city with its necessities. No fewer than
four *horrea* (warehouses or granaries) are listed, as well as two sets of public baths
of the Theodosian dynasty, named (or renamed) after Honorius and Eudocia

---

existence of a gate named after it; Gilles, *Antiquities* 4.4 (a very clear description); see above,
Chapter 3 (p. 48) for an episode recorded there. Berger, pp. 353, 390, puts the amphitheatre
'nach der Notitia' just above the site of S. Irene, but this seems untenable.

16. *CTh* 14.6.5 (4 October 419) to Aetius, city prefect of Constantinople.

17. Cf. Mango, *Développement urbain*, p. 19 for the importance of this road (a processional
route from the hippodrome to the strategium).

18. Below, Chapter 6 (p. 105).

19. Alan Cameron and Jacqueline Long, *Barbarians and Politics at the Court of Arcadius*
(1993), p. 238 with n. 170, connect the 'liburna' with the defeat of Fravitta by Gainas in 400,
but it may possibly have commemorated Constantine's victorious sea-battle against Licinius.

20. Procopius, *De aedificiis* 1.11.27.

respectively.[21] The Region also contained a *prytaneum*, whose name suggests that it too was a part of the ancient Greek city, and an important area also known by its Greek name, the *strategium*. If these were the names for the old council-house and agora of Greek Byzantium (Chapter 6, pp. 99–100), we can see how far the expansion of the Roman period has drawn the city's centre of gravity away from its ancient site. The name of the harbour listed in this Region, *prosphorianus* ('import harbour'), suggests that it was the commercial harbour of the Greek city, adjacent to the military dockyard and harbour (*neorium* and *portus*) of Region VI.[22] Region V also included the crossing to Chalcedon and the continuation into Asia Minor of the highway from the west to Constantinople.

Moving into Region VI (Janin, p. 52; Berger, pp. 364–65) we find the dock-yard and military harbour just mentioned. Both *neorium* and *portus*, as is clear from Cassius Dio's account of the Severan siege of Byzantium, were enclosed by the pre-Constantinian walls of the city.[23] Another maritime facility was the *scala Sycena*, from where, then as now, sailed the ferries that connected the main city with Region XIII (Sycae). At its southern limit at the Mesē, Region VI included the part of the forum of Constantine containing the porphyry column of the emperor and his new senate building, which therefore stood on the northern side of the forum, with the column at its centre. This gives us a firm point of reference, for Constantine's column still stands in its original location, an emblematic sight in present-day Istanbul. An image of it, with indications of its location at the end of the double colonnades from the Augusteum, appears on the early fifth-century column of Arcadius (cf. Fig. 6.9 and Chapter 8, p. 154).

Of those so far described, Regions II, IV (in part), V, and VI cover the Greek and Graeco-Roman city of Byzantium as it had developed on and around the an-cient acropolis, behind the harbours and commercial facilities of the Golden Horn. The remaining portions of Regions II and IV follow the development of the city to the south of the acropolis and, with the part of Region III occupied by the hippo-drome and the part of Region I advancing up the coast towards the amphitheatre, reflect its expansion during the Roman period. Byzantium now surrounded the acropolis, with a decisive contribution of the Severan period to the south of it.

---

21. On the *thermae Honorianae* see Chapter 8 below (p. 148). The absence from the *Notitia* of the famous 'baths of Achilles' in this region might be explained by their being renamed after Eudocia after her marriage to Theodosius in 421 (Berger, p. 363).

22. Gilles, *Antiquities* 3.1, discusses the variant 'Bosphorianus' as an obvious corruption of the true form of the name. For the interpretation of these installations as the commercial and military harbours of early Byzantium, see Mango, *Développement Urbain*, pp. 14–15.

23. Above, Chapter 2 (pp. 18f.); Cassius Dio 75.10.5, referring to the 'harbours' of the city; Zosimus 2.30.3. The *neorion* is shown by Janin on his Map I (cf. Berger, p. 365) at present-day Bahçekapı, where there was a city gate named after it; cf. Gilles, *Antiquities*, 1.20.

5.2 Regions VII–IX

Continuing westward from Region VI, we cross the hypothetical line of the Roman walls of Byzantium, which no doubt provided the limit between Regions VI and VII; even if the walls did not still exist (and it is unlikely that there was no trace of them), their course would provide as natural a line of division as earlier of defence. From this point, the series of largely commercial Regions that began in Regions V and VI continues into Region VII (Janin, pp. 52–53; Berger, pp. 365–67; Fig. 5.2), one of the two intramural Regions whose locations have been questioned. The matter is easily resolved, once we grasp the point of view from which the *Notitia* presents the situation. Region VII extends from the right of the column of Constantine towards the forum of Theodosius, and is defined by the colonnade running between the two on the northern side of the street; Region VIII contains the corresponding left-hand colonnade. Since the organization of the Regions as a whole is viewed from east to west and Region VII is explicitly described from this point of view, it is clear that this Region is to the north of the Mese and reaches to the Golden Horn.[24] It includes the column of Theodosius that stood in his forum (in its northern part, evidently), and part of the forum itself, as well as two equestrian statues (his sons Arcadius and Honorius).

The *Notitia* also mentions the colonnaded streets that led off the Mese at right angles towards the Golden Horn. This is important for our conception of the street plan of Constantinople, particularly since the *Notitia* lists six colonnades under Region VII. Depending on how one counts colonnades (singly or in pairs), this indicates that at least three main streets led northwards from this stretch of the Mese.[25] A particularly interesting feature is the presence of three churches, of SS. Irene, Anastasia, and Paul (the fourth-century bishop of the name), in what, from its general character and from the number of residences listed for it, seems to have been a heavily populated working-class area. This will be helpful information when we consider the social distribution of the population of Constantinople in Chapter 9.[26]

---

24. The question is settled by the first three entries in Region VIII, where the east-west orientation is clear: 'Partem fori Constantini; *porticum sinistram taurum usque*; basilicam Theodosianam'; Region VIII is to the *left* of the Mese as one faces the statue of the bull that gave to the forum of Theodosius its alternative name, Forum Tauri.

25. Including the right-hand portico of the Mese itself under the total of the six porticoes. The five others might then indicate three other streets, one of them forming the boundary of the region, so with only one portico counted under it (2, 2, 1). Berger, pp. 366 and 397, seems to exclude the Mese from the count and produces four streets, the outer two forming boundaries between regions (so 1, 2, 2, 1), but to exclude the Mese from the count seems to me unnatural.

26. See Berger, pp. 365–66 and 397 for the locations of these churches.

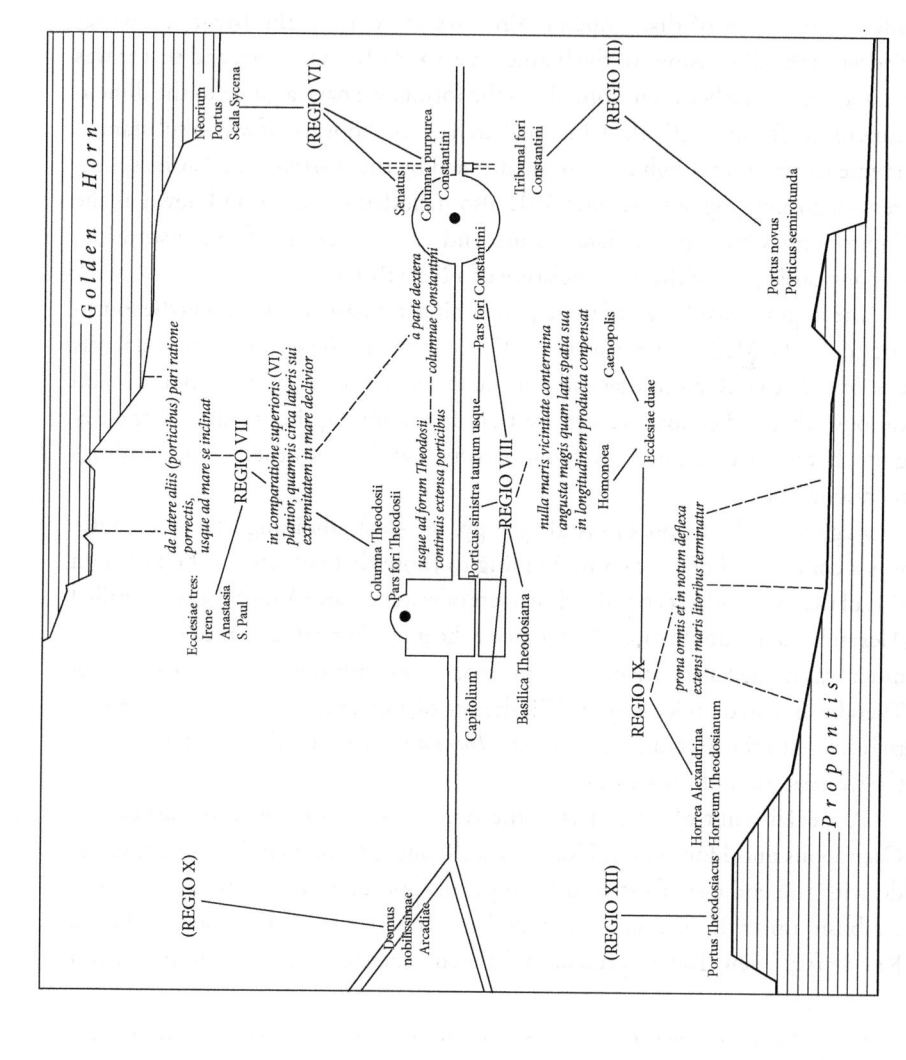

FIG. 5.2 The intramural Regions of Constantinople: Regions VII–IX.

Golden Horn

Propontis

(REGIO X)

Domus nobilissimae Arcadiae

(REGIO XII)

Portus Theodosiacus Horreum Theodosianum

Horrea Alexandrina

REGIO IX

prona omnis et in notum deflexa extensi maris litoribus terminatur

Homonoea

Caenopolis

Ecclesiae duae

nulla maris vicinitate conterminna angusta magis quam lata spatia sua in longitudinem producta compensat

Basilica Theodosiana

REGIO VIII

Porticus sinistra taurum usque

Capitolium

Columna Theodosii Pars fori Theodosii

usque ad forum Theodosii continuis extensa porticibus

Ecclesiae tres: Irene Anastasia S. Paul

REGIO VII

de latere aliis (porticibus) pari ratione porrectis, usque ad mare se inclinat

in comparatione superioris (VI) planior, quamvis circa lateris sui extremitatem in mare declivior

a parte dextera — — — *columnae Constantini*

Pars fori Constantini

Neorium Portus Scala Sycena

(REGIO VI)

Senatus Columna purpurea Constantini

Tribunal fori Constantini

(REGIO III)

Portus novus Porticus semirotunda

We now return, on the other side of the Mesē, to two Regions on the southern shore of the promontory, balancing the series we have seen to the north. Region VIII (Janin, p. 54; Berger, pp. 367–68) is one of the four Regions that took their starting point from the forum of Constantine. As we just saw, it faced Region VII across the Mesē, from the forum of Constantine as far as that of Theodosius. It also included the basilica of Theodosius, which therefore stood on the southern side of the forum of that emperor. Since we know from the Byzantine writer Kedrenos the dimensions of the basilica (240 × 84 Roman feet), and that it was built alongside rather than frontally to the forum, we have a guide to the dimensions of the forum itself. The triumphal arch of Theodosius, of which substantial fragments remain though it is not mentioned by the *Notitia*, stood at its southwestern corner (Fig. 8.1). Region VIII also included the location known as the Capitolium; whatever the date, nature and exact location of this institution, it is obviously part of the nomenclature of a New Rome.

The Region was elongated in shape, running in a narrow strip along the southern side of the Mesē from the forum of Constantine to the Capitolium, and it was one of only two Regions that did not touch the sea at any point. From this and various other indications we can see that it was among the smallest of the Regions, but it still contained two food-markets as well as the other public buildings mentioned here.[27]

Region IX (Janin, pp. 54–55; Berger, pp. 368–69), adjoining VIII to its south, was a commercial district corresponding to those that we saw on the northern side of the peninsula. It contained two sets of warehouses. One of them was called Alexandrina, no doubt after the source of the grain imported to the city, and the other was named after Theodosius, in association with the large new harbour of Theodosius listed under Region XII, the site of a spectacular recent excavation;[28] to be close to the harbour, the *horreum Theodosianum* would be located towards the western limit of the Region.

A special point of interest is in the two churches attributed to Region IX, Caenopolis and Homonoea. Homonoea ('Concord') perhaps has something to do with the endlessly frustrated attempts of Constantine and his successors to establish unity in the eastern churches. The name of Caenopolis (Greek Καινόπολις, 'New Town') presents a different question; the Region in which it

---

27. It would fit the configuration of the Region implied by the *Notitia* if one of the markets were at the location of the later Amastrianum.

28. For a description and photographs of the work in progress, see Mark Rose and Şengül Aydingün, 'Under Istanbul', *Archaeology* (July/August 2007), pp. 34–40; Chapter 7 below (pp. 128, 146). I owe thanks for the tour of the excavations (and preliminary lunch), given me by their director Metin Gokcay, and to Scott Redford of Koç University, for his help in bringing it about.

stands is deeply embedded within the city of Constantine, and Caenopolis was in that context not a 'New Town' at all. Two possibilities come to mind. Caenopolis may be an existing name reflecting earlier settlement beyond the walls of Graeco-Roman Byzantium.[29] This does not seem very plausible, however (in relation to which neighbouring city if not Constantinople does the place acquire this name?), and another suggestion seems worth consideration. Perhaps 'Kainopolis', located close to the area of Constantinian building operations south and to the west of the Augusteum (palace, hippodrome and Zeuxippon, forum of Constantine) might have been a settlement of the actual builders of Constantinople, who must have numbered in the thousands, included craftsmen as well as unskilled labourers, and all needed somewhere to live. It would be a city of workmen similar to what is shown near Egyptian Thebes, or the 'store cities' of Pithom and Rameses, said in Exodus to have been built by the Israelites for Pharaoh; it was from Rameses that the Israelites took their departure from Egypt (Exod. 1:11, 12:37).[30] The people who built these cities would live there while they did so. It could be that, in a neat anticipation of the New Rome, Kainopolis was informally or colloquially called this before Constantinople itself was formally consecrated.

5.3 Regions X–XII

As we move west towards the Constantinian walls, the peninsula widens, and the last three intramural Regions form a sequence following the course of the walls in a south-westerly and southerly arc (Fig. 5.3). There is little distinctive about the way they are characterized in the *Notitia*, and they lie apart from the administrative and commercial parts of the city that we have seen so far. Other indications suggest that they were later and less intensively developed than the more central Regions; they are also larger, and have interesting numbers of streets and houses, to be discussed in Chapter 10 (pp. 205–8).

Beginning in the north, Region X (Janin, p. 55; Berger, pp. 369–70) is described as a spacious Region, relatively flat except where it fell away to the sea.

---

29. See also Berger, p. 368, for this view of Kainopolis. An alternative is that the name indicates building land won from the sea, but the location of the two churches (Berger, pp. 368–69, 397) is against this; they are too far to the north. The episode described at *Chron. Pasch.*, s.a. 407 (Whitby and Whitby, p. 61), when roof tiles from the basilica of Theodosius blew down to Kainopolis in a storm, also suggests not too great a distance between them. Janin's Map I locates the district at the 40–50 m contour level.

30. According to a later legend, told to the Christian pilgrim Egeria, but not in Exodus, the Egyptians burned down Rameses before they set off after the Israelites; *Itinerarium Egeriae* 8.5 (trans. J. Wilkinson, *Egeria's Travels* (1971), p. 102)—not historical evidence but it assumes that the Israelites had been living in the city as they built it.

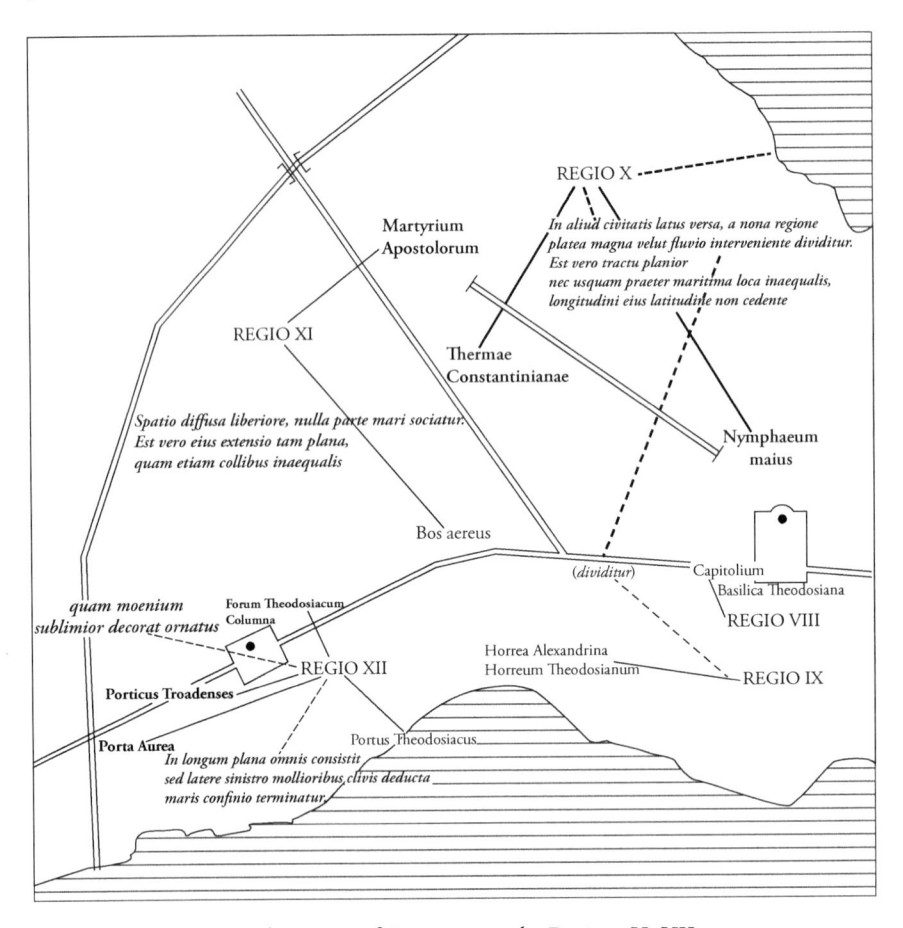

REGIO X

Martyrium
Apostolorum

*In aliud civitatis latus versa, a nona regione
platea magna velut fluvio interveniente dividitur.
Est vero tractu planior
nec usquam praeter maritima loca inaequalis,
longitudini eius latitudine non cedente*

REGIO XI

Thermae
Constantinianae

*Spatio diffusa liberiore, nulla parte mari sociatur.
Est vero eius extensio tam plana,
quam etiam collibus inaequalis*

Nymphaeum
maius

Bos aereus

(*dividitur*)   Capitolium
                       Basilica Theodosiana
                       REGIO VIII

quam moenium   Forum Theodosiacum
sublimior decorat ornatus   Columna

Horrea Alexandrina
Horreum Theodosianum

Porticus Troadenses   REGIO XII   REGIO IX

Porta Aurea   Portus Theodosiacus
        *In longum plana omnis consistit,
        sed latere sinistro mollioribus clivis deducta
        maris confinio terminatur*

FIG. 5.3 The intramural Regions of Constantinople: Regions X–XII.

It contained a church of S. Acacius, baths and three imperial mansions, and a large nymphaeum or water-basin; this is no doubt connected with the spectacular aqueduct attributed to the emperor Valens that fed into it, and the other provisions made by him for an enhanced water-supply (below, Chapter 7, pp. 130–4). The story of the Constantinian baths listed under this Region is a complicated one, the essence of which is that, even if he might have begun them, the baths were considered a foundation not of Constantine but of his successor Constantius (and they were not completed until many years even after his time).[31] Since we

---

31. Eusebius, *Life of Constantine* 4.59, claims that Constantine built baths near his mausoleum, but whether these baths have anything to do with the 'Constantinianae' of the *Notitia* is unclear (Berger, p. 370, distinguishes them). See further Chapter 7 n. 2.

know from descriptions of imperial processions that the baths stood on the right-hand side of the northern branch of the Mesē to one leaving the city, as also, further out, did the church of the Apostles, the boundary between Regions X and XI must have veered northward beyond the baths and crossed the road, to allow the church to belong to Region XI.

According to the text of the *Notitia*, Region X was separated from Region IX by a wide avenue, presumably the Mesē, which divided them 'like a river' (*platea magna velut fluvio dividitur*). There is a difficulty about such a boundary between Regions X and IX, in that the elongated Region VIII, stretching from the forum of Constantine to that of Theodosius and on to the Capitolium, seems to lie between them. The solution adopted by Berger is to suppose either that the compiler of the *Notitia* made an error, and should have written that Region X was divided 'as if by a river' from Region VIII (and not IX), or that the text has been corrupted to the same effect.[32] This is not a desirable solution if there is a reasonable alternative, which in this case would be that the Capitolium lay not as far west as it is often placed but much nearer to the basilica of Theodosius; there are in fact other advantages in this (p. 90). The text could then stand with regional limits amended to allow Regions IX and X to have a significant common boundary.

Region XI (Janin, pp. 55–56; Berger, pp. 370–72), which is also noted as unusually spacious as well as one of only two Regions to be landlocked, contained palaces of Theodosius I's wife Aelia Flaccilla and Theodosius II's sister Pulcheria, two water-cisterns, and the martyrium of the Apostles. This very important monument, whether in its original form as the mausoleum of Constantine or as the church of the Apostles that it later became, was one of the cardinal points of the city. Lying in the site now occupied by the mosque of Mehmet the Conqueror, it stood, at just over 60 metres above sea level, at one of the two highest points of the city within the Constantinian wall. The Region also contained a 'brazen ox', marking the location of the later Bous, or Forum Bovis.[33] This confirms the great extension of Region XI, as it reached down from the heights of the church of the Apostles as far as the southern branch of the Mesē.

The last of the intramural Regions, Region XII (Janin, p. 56; Berger, pp. 372–73), lying in the south-west corner of the city, is rather distinctively introduced as 'glorified by the lofty splendour of the city walls'; *quam moenium sublimior decorat ornatus*. It is not clear why this Region in particular should be so honoured, since the walls formed the limits of all three Regions X–XII; except that

---

32. Berger, p. 368 ('Die einzig mögliche Erklärung . . .').

33. If 'Bous' was in fact a forum; Marlia Mundell Mango, 'The Commercial Map of Constantinople', *DOP* 54 (2000), pp. 189–207, at p. 192.

Region XII also includes in an emphatic position—the entry begins with it—the Porta Aurea or Golden Gate. This is another cardinal point of Constantine's city, the entry from the west along the re-aligned route from Regium (see below). Region XII also included another forum of Theodosius, completed under the second emperor of that name and better known to us as the forum of Arcadius, who had begun its construction in 402/3 (below, Chapter 8, pp. 149–61).[34] Placed between the Golden Gate and the forum of Arcadius are the 'porticus Troadenses', also mentioned by Hesychius and other sources (Chapter 3, p. 49). It is not clear whether these colonnades ran all the way from the Golden Gate to the division of the Mesē at the Philadelphion; we might see them from the point of view of one entering the city, as an architectural extension of the Golden Gate itself. There were also in this Region the extremely important new harbour of Theodosius and its associated warehouses, and the mint. This was an institution of the time of Constantine, who very soon began to strike coin in the city and certainly intended to go on doing so.[35] Given the physical movements and value of the materials involved in the striking and distribution of coin, a situation by the city walls and the most heavily supervised main gate would offer obvious attractions.

5.4 Regions XIII–XIV

These, in broad outlines to be traced in more detail later, are the mainland or intra-urban Regions of Constantinople. Two remain, of which Region XIII, 'Sycena' (Janin, pp. 56–57; Berger, p. 373), covers the settlement across the Golden Horn at Sycae (Galata). The introduction to this Region mentioned the 'frequent ferries' that connected it with the main part of the city; we saw that Region VI contained the Scala Sycena from which the crossing began. Region XIII was crammed in up the hillside, and possessed a single main road running along the more level land by the shore; visitors will appreciate the accuracy of this

---

34. The date is given by Theophanes' *Chronicle*; *Chron. Pasch.*, s.a. 422 records the placing of a statue of Arcadius (who had died in 408) on the summit; Whitby and Whitby, p. 69.

35. It has been suggested on the basis of coin types that Constantine initiated the celebrations of the thirtieth anniversary of his reign, as he had the twentieth before his visit to Rome, in the old capital of Nicomedia; see P. M. Bruun, in *RIC* 7 (1966), at pp. 15 (an 'exceptionally rich *vota* series' of *solidi* minted at Nicomedia), 57 n. 3, 74–75, 628ff. (nos. 175–80). However, *Chronicon Paschale* is explicit in giving the location of the *tricennalia* as Constantinople (Whitby and Whitby, p. 20 (25 July 335)). According to Lars Ramskold, 'Coins and Medallions Struck for the Inauguration of Constantinople, 11 May 330', *Niš and Byzantium* 9 (2011), pp. 126–29, the Constantinople mint opened in 326.

description. It contained a church and theatre—the latter recalling the earlier existence of Sycae as a separate community—and shipyards.[36]

If Region XIII is an anomaly, Region XIV (Janin, pp. 57–58; Berger, pp. 374–75) is still more so, for while not, like XIII, lying over the water it was separated from the main city, and possessed its own wall and gate. We seem to have an urban community outside the city of Constantine but incorporated with it. Like Region XIII, it had a church and theatre, a palace, and a 'lusorium', or sports field, and there was a wooden bridge built on piles.

Historians have generally located Region XIV in the district north of the city later known as Blachernae. These interpretations have been challenged in typically concise and forceful papers—though with different results, acknowledged with a nice touch of humour—by Cyril Mango. Mango had first argued that, since the *Notitia* mentions in its preface the 'double line of walls' by which the city was defended, the point from which the separation of Region XIV was measured must be the Theodosian walls. These came right up to Blachernae, which could not then have been described as a separate community in relation to them.[37] Region XIV would therefore have to be located farther to the north of the Constantinian city. Mango pointed to two locations, the suburb of Eyüp or the more distant location of Silâhtaraga at the head of the Golden Horn, in both of which places a bridge existed at one time or another. In the latter case, this would be only to cross the river Barbyses, which one hesitates to think of as a major landmark, and in a later addendum to his paper Mango allowed that this location, which he initially thought of as the more likely of his suggestions, was 'perhaps too distant to be identified as the XIVth Region'.[38]

The description of the *Notitia* given in the introduction to Chapter 4 above (pp. 63f.), calls into question the basic assumption of Mango's interpretation of the point of separation of Region XIV from the main city. It is true that the preface to the *Notitia* mentions the double fortifications of Constantinople, but as we saw, this does not express the perspectives of the text itself. The twelve intra-urban Regions are there conceived and shown as lying within the walls of Constantine, and were clearly laid out before the Theodosian walls were built. Taking the wall of Constantine rather than that of Theodosius as the point from

---

36. The theatre was restored by Justinian, when, in another recognition of its quasi-independent status, Sycae was renamed Justinianopolis (*Chron. Pasch.*, 618.16; Whitby and Whitby, p. 110; Berger, p. 373).

37. C. Mango, 'The Fourteenth Region of Constantinople', first published 1986, reprinted in his *Studies on Constantinople* (1993), ch. 7. Berger, p. 374, supported Blachernae, but in relation to Silâhtaraga, not Eyüp.

38. Mango, 'The Fourteenth Region', addendum (at end of volume), p. 6.

which the separation of Region XIV is measured, Blachernae or somewhere near it comes back into play as the more likely candidate.[39]

This was not, however, Mango's last word on the subject, and he has recently offered a new solution, paradoxical perhaps, but more convincing than either of these alternatives. Region XIV is now located at the settlement of Rhegion— Regium in Latin texts, the source of occasional confusion with the southern Italian city of Reggio di Calabria.[40] At 12 Roman miles from Constantinople, this seems at first sight rather far from the city, but outweighing this objection is the substance of the entry in the *Notitia*. Region XIV has a palace and a 'lusorium', otherwise found in combination in Region I, as well as a city wall, theatre, nymphaeum, baths, and a church. Like Sycae, the place was a separate urban community but, unlike it, also an imperial residence. Furthermore Regium, with the coastal lagoons between it and Constantinople, is the most likely location for a bridge built on wooden piles, crossing a large, shallow body of water; it is difficult to imagine such a structure as crossing the deeper waters and rockier shores of the Golden Horn.[41] The development of Regium and the construction of its bridge are implied already in 333 by the Pilgrim of Bordeaux, who entered the city by this route.[42] This happens to be the first attestation of a direct route between Regium and Constantinople, which had earlier been approached by a more northerly route by way of the imperial residence at Melanthias and entering the city by the Thracian gate. Though separated from it by half a day's journey, Regium was an integral part of the city and reflects a newly developed coastal approach to it. The military suburb of Hebdomon (the 'seventh milestone') lay between the two.

The *Notitia* is not a complete record of the city, and it contains inconsistencies. It is in the *Collectio Civitatis* and not in the main text of the *Notitia* that the

---

39. I earlier thought of it as the location of Region XIV, taking the topographical introduction in the *Notitia* to indicate, not Blachernae precisely, but the district of Balat in the valley descending to the sea to its south. The case for Blachernae is revived by Martin Hurbanič, 'The Topography of the 14th Region of Constantinople: A Critical Reexamination', in S. Turlej and others (eds), *Byzantina et Slavica: Studies in Honour of Maciej Salamon* (2019), pp. 129–37. Hurbanič is correct in identifying the point of departure from the city as the wall of Constantine and not Theodosius, but does not consider the institutional (above, n. 1) and textual arguments for Rhegion.

40. 'Le Mystère de la XIVe Région de Constantinople', pp. 449–55. For the confusion with Reggio di Calabria, already noted by Gothofredus in his commentary on the Theodosian Code, see my *Western Aristocracies and Imperial Court* (1975), p. 178 n. 2.

41. Its description in the *Notitia*, 'pons sublicius sive ligneus', invites comparison with the Pons Sublicius at Rome, but there can have been little resemblance; E. M. Steinby (ed.), *Lexikon Topographicum Urbis Romae* IV (1999), pp. 112–13 (Coarelli).

42. *Itinerarium Burdigalense* 570.7–8 (*CCL* 175, p. 8).

Miliarium Aureum of the Augusteum is described as a 'golden tetrapylon', revealing the architectural form of this important structure. The *Collectio Civitatis* also mentions a significant monument that is absent from the main text. This is the 'Colossus', the stone-built obelisk, 32 metres high, still to be seen on the *spina* of the hippodrome and identified from a dedicatory inscription of Constantine Porphyrogenitus, comparing the structure with the Colossus of Rhodes.[43] There is no mention of the famous obelisk of Theodosius with its bilingual verse inscription recording its erection by the urban prefect in the space of thirty days, with a pictorial depiction of the technique employed,[44] nor of the bronze tetrapylon that stood at an important crossroad, half-way between the forum of Constantine and that of Theodosius (below, p. 114 with Figs. 6.7–8). The *Notitia* does not mention the arch of Theodosius that formed the ceremonial entrance to his forum (Fig. 8.1), though it lists the column and equestrian statues that stood there (Figs 8.2–3), and the statue of the bull that gave to the forum its alternative name of Forum Tauri. Nothing is said of the so-called 'Gothic column' below the northern slopes of the acropolis, still a neglected feature of the Classical remains of the city.[45]

Also missing is any recognition of the aesthetic exuberance of the city. The columns of Theodosius and Arcadius are noted for the internal staircases that led to their summit, not for the sculptured decoration that led Vavassore's and other later images to identify them by the phrase, 'colonna istoriata'; nor is there any reference to the statue of Constantine placed on top of his famous column—an interesting omission, since the statue, showing Constantine in the guise of Apollo as Sun-God, was somewhat controversial. Yet the imagery suited the early self-presentation of Constantine, and by the early fifth century was probably taken for granted as an acceptable portrayal of an emperor in an idiom familiar to all.

Despite these and other omissions, which will call for discussion in the following chapters, the *Notitia* is a unique, and uniquely well-focused source for

---

43. Janin, *Constantinople Byzantine*, pp. 192–93 (with the text of the inscription).

44. *ILS* 821; below, Chapter 9, Figs. 9.1–2.

45. It is unclear whether it is a monument of Claudius II 'Gothicus' or some other, or what might be its original date. The epigraphic formula 'Fortunae reduci ob devictos Gothos' (given in Greek by John the Lydian) seems to require an emperor who led a campaign from the city against the Goths and returned safely. This would fit Constantine's Gothic victory of 332 or the first, successful campaign of Valens in 367–69, possibly even that of Theodosius of 382. The inscr. is *ILS* 820 (*CIL* 3.733), where it is assigned to Constantine's campaign of 332; Müller-Wiener, *Bildlexikon*, p. 53, John Freely and Ahmet S. Çakmak, *Byzantine Monuments of Istanbul* (2004), pp. 19–21. According to John the Lydian, the column was originally surmounted by a statue of Tychē, according to a fourteenth-century source, by a statue of the founder of Byzantium, Byzas the Megarian. The evidence does not favour the interpretation offered by K. W. Wilkinson, *JRS* 100 (2010), at pp. 183–85.

the development of Constantinople in the first century of its existence. Not only this, but behind the lists of the resources of the Constantinian and later periods are significant traces of the antecedent Graeco-Roman city, confirming the impression that it was both an ancient and a very important urban centre long before Constantine put his hand to it. Any city will present to the eye a combination of past and present, and the *Notitia* is not just a list of the contemporary resources of the city, as if it had no previous history; it captures a developing urban landscape at a particular moment in time. The aim of the next group of chapters is to apply the information provided by the *Notitia* to the story of urban development at Constantinople from its Greek and Roman origins through the time of Constantine and his successors to the early reign of Theodosius II, under whom the compiler wrote.

6

Urban Development (1)

BYZANTIUM TO CONSTANTINOPLE

6.1 The Graeco-Roman City

THE *NOTITIA URBIS Constantinopolitanae* shows us a city as it stood at the moment when its lists were compiled; but the lists are cumulative, and reach back into the past at the same time as they document its present. Especially when transferred to a ground plan of the city, the *Notitia* makes clear the extent of its debt to the Graeco-Roman past. It has much to say about the earlier city as Constantine discovered it—an ancient and significant Greek city in an important commercial and strategic location, profiting from the wider horizons and economic resources of the Roman empire and, in the early third century, from imperial favour.

In order to track more closely the development of the city, in what follows the Regions will be presented in a slightly different grouping from that observed in the previous chapter, beginning with Regions IV–VI, which form a continuous sequence along the northern side of the peninsula, and cover the part of the peninsula occupied by the Greek colony of the seventh century BCE and its Greek successors, and by the Roman city that followed in the first two centuries of the empire. The location of the settlement offered sheltered anchorage within the Golden Horn, with some difficulty of access if a north wind joined the flow of the Bosporus and impeded access from the south, though this had not deterred Greek colonial expeditions into the Black Sea, nor an extensive Athenian trade in grain with the Crimea. Experienced navigators could use the quieter waters and back-currents of the Bosporus to make their way northwards, while the Bosporus, and the Golden Horn itself, yielded a spectacular harvest of fish, the famous tunny-fish (*pelamydēs*) mentioned by Strabo (p. 17).

The traces of the Greek city are preserved in named institutions in these Regions. Region V contained a prytaneum (*prytaneion*), and an area also known by its Greek name, strategium (*stratēgion*). Taken together, these were the names for the council-house and *agora* of the Greek city, the latter after its chief magistrates, the *stratēgoi*, as the place where they had accommodation and conducted their

From Byzantium to Constantinople: An Urban History. John Matthews, Oxford University Press.
© Oxford University Press 2024. DOI: 10.1093/oso/9780197585498.003.0006

official duties.[1] These duties included but were not limited to military affairs; in an archaic or Classical Greek city with a citizen army a large part of public business, in the conduct of levies, the keeping of records of eligibility for service in the army and navy, and of those liable for the building and maintenance of fleets (what in a modern state would count as taxation) had to do with military activity and its organization. The strategium was an expansive tract of land, because a forum of Theodosius was later built within its limits; it was perhaps because of this that a part of the area, not incorporated in the new forum but still functioning as a public space, was known as the lesser strategium.[2] The name of the harbour listed in Region V, Prosphorianus (*prosphorianos*, 'import harbour'), suggests that it was the commercial harbour of the Greek city, adjacent to the military dockyard and harbour (*neōrion* and *portus*) of Region VI.[3] Another ancient Greek survival in the same region was the stadium (*stadion*), located by the sea north of the acropolis.[4]

Moving west into Region VI, we come to the dockyard and military harbour (*neōrion*) just mentioned. Dockyard and both harbours, as we can see from Cassius Dio's account of the Severan siege of Byzantium, were enclosed by the Roman walls of the city, as, no doubt, by those of the Greek period.[5] The later continuation of the commercial character of this maritime district by the Golden Horn is marked by the comment in the introduction of the *Notitia* to Region V, that here were situated the facilities that provided the fourth-century city with its necessities, listing no fewer than four *horrea* (warehouses or granaries). Region V also included the ferry crossing to Sycae and, in the Roman period, the continuation into Asia Minor of the main highway from the west.

These parts of the Greek city of Byzantium stood below the precipitous northern slopes of the acropolis described by the *Notitia* in its introduction to

---

1. That is, two *stratēgoi*, the *stratēgion* being their 'Amstlocal'; *RE* 3 (1899), col. 1144 (Kubitschek). These were the executive magistrates, the eponymous magistrate at Byzantium being styled *hieromnamon*. For this and other aspects of the civil administration, Thomas Russell, *Byzantium and the Bosporus*, §6.2 at pp. 224–25. The form *stratēgoi* is an Ionicization of the Doric *stratāgoi*, the dialect of the founding city of Megara.

2. Cyril Mango, *DOP* 54 (2000), pp. 177–78 with his appendix, 'The Situation of the Strategion', at pp. 187–88; Marlia Mundell Mango, 'The Commercial Map of Constantinople', pp. 189–207, at 198. The strategion or its immediate environs must also have been the location of the so-called 'Gothic column', discussed at Chapter 5, n. 45.

3. Chapter 5, nn. 22–3.

4. Procopius, *Buildings* 1.11.27: 'very close to the sea, in the place called the *stadion* (for in ancient times, I suppose, it was given over to games of some kind).'

5. Chapter 2 above (p. 18f.), with Cassius Dio 75.10.5, referring to the 'harbours' of the city; Zosimus 2.30.3; Chapter 5, n. 22.

Region IV, normal access to the acropolis being by way of the gentler ascent to the south. The city must have extended in this direction along the valley to the west of the acropolis and, perhaps to a lesser extent, along the coastal tract to the east. Two of Byzantium's most conspicuous ancient monuments help to define this process of expansion. As we saw in Chapter 5 (p. 84), the *Notitia* begins its topographical guide to Region II with the 'little theatre', from which the ascent to the acropolis begins, and then lists its two churches, the 'great' and the 'old church', respectively S. Sophia and S. Irene. It follows from a combination of these notices, that the theatre stood near the churches, at the lower end of the ascent to the Acropolis. Since it is natural to think of the theatre as Greek foundation, we may assume that the city had extended round the acropolis to the level ground at its southern end, by a road leading through Gülhane Park and past the site of the archaeological museum. Region II, the acropolis itself, also contained some of the most important ancient temples of Byzantium, whose fate we shall read about later. The *Notitia* has nothing to say about these now superannuated monuments, but they were a conspicuous feature of the earlier city.

In the Roman period, one would guess in the second or early third century, Byzantium also acquired an amphitheatre or 'great theatre' (*theatrum maius*). A similar convergence of indications as in the case of the theatre defines its position. Like the theatre, the amphitheatre is listed under Region II, its location being indicated in the topographical introduction to Region I (see Chapter 5 and Fig. 5.1), as in in the northern part of the narrowing stretch of land between the seashore and the eastern slopes of the acropolis, somewhere below the Topkapı kitchens. Other evidence supports this view, notably an early fifth-century law forbidding lime-burning along the shore of the promontory 'between the amphitheatre and the harbour of Julian', a tract of land including the imperial palace.[6] The amphitheatre, a Roman building no doubt later than the theatre, was most readily accessible from the city around the north-eastern corner of the peninsula. It is possible that the eastern flank of the acropolis was developed later than the western, and that the amphitheatre was built in what was still a relatively undeveloped part of the peninsula. In a much later period, it is presented as a derelict (and dangerous) structure in a neglected part of the city (above, p. 48).

The possession by Byzantium of such an amenity as an amphitheatre is only at first sight surprising. There were other cities of the Greek east, especially those which were in contact with the culture of the west or were leading cities of their provinces, that had acquired one; Syracuse in Sicily, Achaean Corinth, Herodian Caesarea, Pergamum in Asia Minor, and Syrian Antioch are examples, all of them capital cities of their provinces or (the case of Pergamum) with

---

6. *CTh* 14.6.5 (4 October 419); above, p. 85f.

pretensions to be such.[7] Byzantium presents a still clearer case, for as we saw in Chapter 2 (p. 18), its provincial affiliations were rather special. The city belonged to the Asiatic province of Bithynia-Pontus and possessed influence and lands in Asia, but it stood in Europe, and sustained a relationship with the lower Danubian regions (and their armies) through the military roads connecting them with the east. It is a perspective that not only tells us something about an amphitheatre, but makes even clearer the attractions of the site to Constantine; it lay at the eastern end, both of the roads leading from Italy and the west through the Balkans, and of the military highway through the Danube basin.

Later sources refer to the theatre and amphitheatre as built by Severus, or else to his having added stoas to them.[8] If a choice is called for between these alternatives, the second is the more likely. Byzantium would already possess its theatre, and to add a stoa or colonnade to an existing structure was a common form of urban munificence. Whatever their date of origin, both theatre and amphitheatre of Constantinople were still in use in the time of Justinian, the latter for hunting-displays (*venationes*) rather than the gladiatorial combats of an earlier era (the same was true of Rome).[9] And where else did Theodora learn her art or her father produce the wild-beast shows for which he was responsible as bear-keeper (*ursarius*) of the Green faction?

The *Notitia* is silent on what must have been a conspicuous feature of the Classical city, the acropolis itself and the temples of the gods that stood there. By its time of composition the temples, those of Apollo, Artemis, and Aphrodite, had been decommissioned and converted to other uses, chosen to make fun of the gods who had occupied them; they have no place in a description of a fifth-century Christian city. Although he is said to have deprived them of their financial support, it is not claimed in the sources that Constantine physically destroyed the temples of Byzantium. This came later, in the time of Theodosius.[10] We must imagine the temples, into whatever state of neglect they fell, overlooking the landscape as they always had, as time went on falling victim to the lime kilns

---

7. Berger, p. 360, is mistaken in claiming that Corinth was the only Greek city with an amphitheatre. Apart from the examples given above, an admittedly unexpected case is Berenice in Cyrenaica; *IGR* 1.1024, line 27. See too Josephus, *Ant. Iud.* 15.341 (Caesarea); perhaps more doubtful, 15.268 (Jerusalem), 17.161 (Jericho).

8. Martiny, *Antiquity* 12 (1938), p. 90, gives the sources on this aspect (*Chronicon Paschale* and the Souda).

9. As shown in the classic study by A. Chastagnol, *Le Sénat sous le règne d'Odoacre: recherches sur l'épigraphie du Colisée au Ve siècle* (*Antiquitas*, Reihe 3, Band 3; Bonn, 1966). For the deserted κυνήγιον of later times, see the anecdote reported in Chapter 2 above (p. 48).

10. Below, pp. 182–4. On this matter of dating I note my disagreement with the articles of Kevin Wilkinson, in *JRS* 99 (2009), pp. 36–60 and 100 (2010), pp. 179–94.

emitting their smoke along the coastline below, and surrendering their finely dressed stone for use as building materials and the manufacture of cement.

6.2 *The Severan Period*

It was argued earlier, that claims made by our sources of the restoration and enhancement of Byzantium by the Severan emperors are in all essentials authentic, and this is assumed in what follows, noting that they provided the conditions for and framework of those of Constantine. The Severan developments, which can be seen most clearly in the *Notitia* entries for Regions II and IV, consolidated the encirclement of the acropolis. As they did so they changed the focus of the city and gave it a new monumental zone to the south of the acropolis, corresponding in the present-day city to the open space between the church of S. Sophia and the hippodrome (Fig. 6.1). We might call this the 'new city' of the Severans, taking its departure from the 'old city' of Byzantium on its original site by the Golden Horn.

The central feature of this development was the four-sided *agora* (or forum) known as the Tetrastoon from the colonnades (*stoai*) that surrounded it on all sides; remodelled, it was the precursor of the Augusteum listed by the *Notitia* under Region IV, and will often be most conveniently referred to by this name.[11]

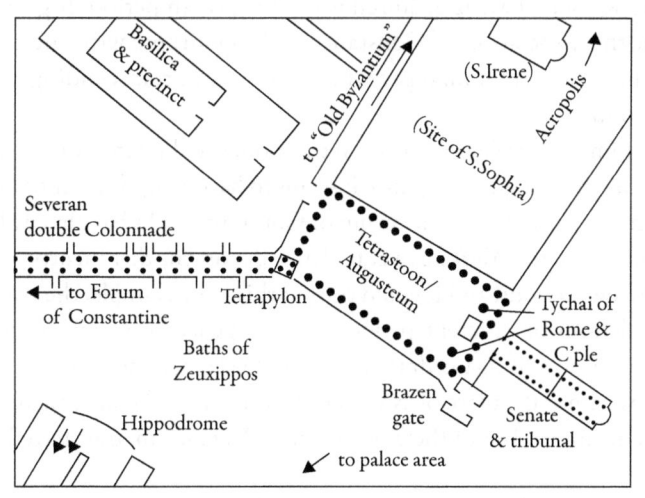

FIG. 6.1 The civic center of Constantinople: Tetrastoon and Augusteum.

---

11. Müller-Wiener, *Bildlexikon*, pp. 248–49 (Tetrastoon/Augusteion), 51–52 (Zeuxippon), 64–71 (hippodrome).

From the western corner of the Tetrastoon a double-colonnaded street led to the main gate in the evidently rebuilt city wall—reflecting, no doubt, the grant of colonial status to Byzantium.

Given the attribution of the Tetrastoon and its colonnades to the Severan emperors, it is natural to look to this period also for at least some of the other civic institutions recorded there by the *Notitia*. Both Zeuxippon and hippodrome were claimed by Hesychius and Malalas (with *Chronicon Paschale*) to have been left unfinished by the Severans and to have been completed and dedicated rather than built *ab initio* by Constantine. There is no reason why the Zeuxippon should not have been initiated by Severus or Caracalla (we have only to think of the latter's baths at Rome), and third-century economic conditions might explain why it was left unfinished. The hippodrome presents a more complex case. It is true that archaeological investigation of the surviving structure has not shown a building period earlier than the time of Constantine,[12] but this might be because of the scale of the fourth-century reconstruction. If there was a Severan hippodrome similar to that built, for example at Lepcis Magna under the Antonines,[13] then its enlargement to the scale and function demanded by Constantine must have involved extensive rebuilding (which would have to be done very rapidly if it was to be ready for the consecration of Constantinople in 330). Lepcis Magna was one of many cities that possessed a circus or hippodrome, and there is no inherent reason why Byzantium should not be among them, having acquired it in the Severan period. It goes without saying that the association of Constantine's hippodrome with the palace and its role in imperial ceremonial gave it an importance transcending that of the earlier period.

Another important feature of the Tetrastoon, listed by the *Notitia* under the rubric *senatus*, raises a question, since it seems to have a duplicate entry in Region VI, in the northern sector of the forum of Constantine. As has already been emphasized, however, the *Notitia* is a cumulative document that incorporates elements of different periods, and it could be that this is an example, the two 'senates' being foundations of different periods that happened to survive concurrently. This possibility would again draw us to the Severan period, if the *senatus* of Region IV were not the place of assembly of the re-created senatorial order of the entire eastern empire, but of the city council of Byzantium, transferred from the

12. C. Mango, 'Septime Sévère et Byzance', *Comptes Rendus de l'Académie des Inscriptions et Belles-Lettres* (2003), pp. 593–608.

13. The dedication was in 162, as the culmination of an earlier period of development; G. di Vita-Evrard, 'Les dédicaces de l'amphithéâtre et du cirque de Lepcis', *Libya Antiqua* 2 (1965), pp. 29–37; Mattingly, p. 120 (noting John Humphreys' suggestion that the circus may have existed in an earlier version before its date of dedication).

ancient Greek city to the Severan civic centre, where it may have replaced the *prytaneion*, a survival of the old city listed under Region V. Procopius, in a moment of pedantic antiquarianism, calls it a council-house, or *bouleutērion*.[14] Given its location near to the palace, it might have acquired a broader function, as the city council of Byzantium merged into a newly established eastern senate. It was perhaps then that was added the tribunal with porphyry steps that stood before it, another feature replicated in the forum of Constantine (though on the opposite side of the forum from the senate building); from here public announcements would be made, speeches made and imperial missives be read, judgements given by those in authority.[15]

Above the tetrapylon and behind the north-west corner of the Augusteum is listed a basilica, its location and orientation marked to this day by the so-called cistern of the basilica (Yerebatan Sarayi), constructed in its precinct in the time of Justinian. The basilica, which is referred to in a number of fourth-century sources, for example as the location of the fourth-century law school, is not usually considered as a part of the Severan development, but it is not out of the question that this was so.[16] It would form as integral a part of the Severan Tetrastoon as it was of the Constantinian Augusteum. If the Severan developers had been so thoroughgoing in moving the city's monumental centre as to provide a new forum, senate-house and tribunal, monumental colonnade, and city gate, they could well have thought of adding a basilica as part of an integral urban design. In this as in other ways, we may compare the architectural ensemble found at Severan Lepcis Magna (Figs 6.1–2). Constantine's basilica at Trier, which is obviously connected with that city's role as a capital city, is actually not as large as the basilica at Lepcis Magna, while his famous basilica on the Sacred Way at Rome is a re-making of one of Maxentius. The dimensions of the Byzantium basilica are not known, since those of the cistern that replaced it (138 × 64.6 m) are those of the entire precinct and not just the building.[17]

---

14. Above, p. 85 n. 13 Mango, *Développement Urbain*, p. 26 queries the function of 'un second bâtiment du Sénat', but that is to assume that both buildings were of Constantinian origin. The problem dissolves if this were not the second but the first *senatus*, of Severan date, itself succeeding the Greek *prytaneion* of Region V.

15. I was mistaken in my 2012 translation of this word as it occurs in Region IV; the *tribunal* is a speaker's platform for addressing the people, not a court-house, see Denis Feissel, 'Tribune et colonnes impériales à l'Augusteion de Constantinople', in *Constantinople réelle et imaginaire: Autour de l'oeuvre de Gilbert Dagron* (Travaux et Mémoires 22/1, 2018), at pp. 121–28.

16. Müller-Wiener, *Bildlexikon*, pp. 283–85, skirts the possibility that the basilica has an earlier origin, for which the Severan development of Byzantium would be the likeliest context.

17. The Lepcis basilica measurements are 85 × 48 m, the Constantinian basilica at Trier 67 × 27.5 m. For the basilica at Rome, L. Richardson, Jr, *A New Topographical Dictionary of Ancient Rome* (1992), pp. 51–52.

It is nowhere stated that Septimius Severus or any third-century successor rebuilt the walls demolished after Severus' capture of the city. If however it is true
that the city acquired colonial status under Caracalla, it can hardly have been left
without them; and no source records that Byzantium had trouble with the invad-
ing Goths and Heruli in the middle years of the third century. The implication is
that the walls were rebuilt; like their fourth-century successors, these barbarians
would avoid attacking a strongly fortified city. We may draw the same conclusion
from the fact that Constantine himself was ready to besiege Byzantium to over-
throw Licinius before his rival fell back upon Chalcedon. Licinius took this
course of action because Byzantium was not big enough to contain the numbers
of men in his following, not because it was unfortified; while the decisive military
action, clearly declaring Constantine's advantage, was a sea battle, not a siege. The
defences of Byzantium were not put to the test on that occasion, as they had been
by Severus' generals in 193.

Taking this display of monumental urbanism for what it was, an outburst of
imperial munificence to a favoured city, there is nothing untoward in it. A striking and well-documented comparison (not to mention archaeological access to a
deserted site), both for its Severan background and for its combination of
architectural elements, is Tripolitanian Lepcis Magna (Figs 6.2–3). Severus'
contribution to his city of origin is so described in the words of its most recent
historian, David Mattingly:[18]

(1) a broad and lavishly ornamented colonnaded street running along the
west bank of the wadi Lebda and connecting the harbour with the *de-
cumanus*. The presence of the Hadrianic baths (aligned off the normal
grid in order to catch the sun on its south-facing hot rooms) necessitated
a kink in the road and this junction was marked by a massive nymphaeum
facing an exhedra across a small piazza; (2) an enormous new forum and
basilica complex situated on the north side of the colonnaded street,
covering no less than seven or eight of the original *insulae*. Created in an
irregular quadrilateral of 142/123 × 82/92 m., the forum was dominated
by a colossal temple at its southwest end, with the basilica placed perpen-
dicularly across the northeast side of the forum; (3) a quadriform arch at
the main road junction, decorated with reliefs portraying the Severan
family; (4) a major remodeling of the harbour basin, etc.

18. David Mattingly, *Tripolitania* (1994), pp. 120–22; see too J. B. Ward-Perkins, 'Severan Art
and Architecture at Leptis Magna', *JRS* 38 (1948), pp. 59–80.

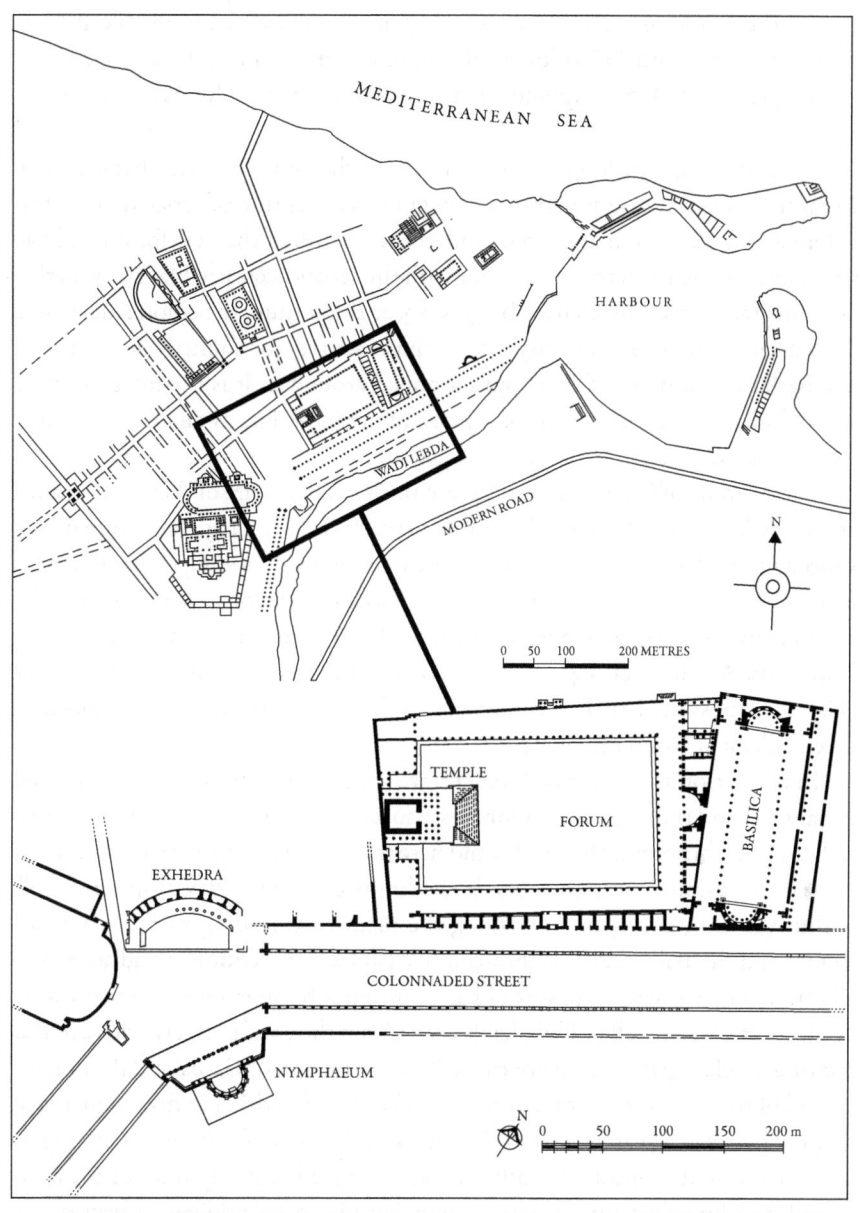

FIG. 6.2 and 6.3 Severan civic development at Lepcis Magna. D. E. L. Haynes, *The Antiquities of Tripolitania* (1956, rep. 1959), opposite p. 71; D. Mattingly, *Tripolitania* (1994), pp. 116–22, at 121; J. B. Ward-Perkins, *The Severan Buildings of Lepcis Magna* (1993).

The whole enterprise was marked by an "immense" use of marble and exotic stone, with 112 columns of Aswan granite in the basilica and new temple, and 400–500 cippolino marble columns in the colonnaded street.

It is a parade of architectural magnificence with the same elements that we see at Byzantium, in each case as part of an integrated conception of urban design. The colonnade at Lepcis ran along the south-eastern flank of the new forum and basilica, linking the modernized harbour with the second-century Hadrianic baths, and integrating the whole ensemble. Just so, at Byzantium, the colonnade linked Tetrastoon with the Severan city gate, with the senate- (or council-)house, tribunal, basilica, and baths of Zeuxippus grouped around it. It is the integration of the architectural elements in a conception of urban design, as much as the elements in themselves, that invites the comparison.

The example of Lepcis is not unique in the Roman empire of that time—more especially in the east, where colonnaded main streets are a regular feature of advanced urban design. A prime example is the colonnade running through Jerusalem (colonized by Hadrian as Aelia Capitolina), as shown on a mosaic map of the sixth century (cf. Fig 6.5), but other late Hellenistic and Roman cities, such as Damascus, Antioch (cf. Fig. 2.4), Gerasa, and the well-known case of Palmyra (Fig. 6.4), possessed such a colonnade, and show its function in connecting diverse elements of an urban plan.

In pursuit of its urban development, we should also consider the suburbs of Byzantium and the nearby communities associated with it. The influence of cities did not stop abruptly at their walls, and here too we might expect to find traces of the earlier period—locations outside the limits of Severan Byzantium that fell within the Constantinian city. Along the main road leading to the city from Thrace and the Balkans, the eighth-century *Parastaseis* mentions an advance fortification, or *proteichisma* (a sort of barbican) built by an emperor named Carus at the location later called Philadelphion.[19] Given the confusion elsewhere in the *Parastaseis* relating to an emperor called 'Severus the son of Carus' and the unlikelihood of the actual emperor Carus having built such a thing in his fragmentary reign of just over a year, it is natural to think of the *proteichisma* as originating in an earlier period. It must evidently have stood outside the city walls of the time in order to be called this, and so cannot have been an original institution of the Constantinian period. We saw earlier (p. 90f.) that the district known as Caenopolis, 'New City', may also precede Constantine's city or at least should be

19. *Parastaseis* 56 (on this source see Chapter 3, pp. 48, 50); Averil Cameron and Judith Herrin, pp. 130–31 with their note at 244. For 'Severus son of Carus' (Caracalla the son of Severus?), *Parastaseis* 37 (Cameron and Herrin, pp. 98–101 with 212–13); for the Philadelphion, below, Chapter 7 (p. 134).

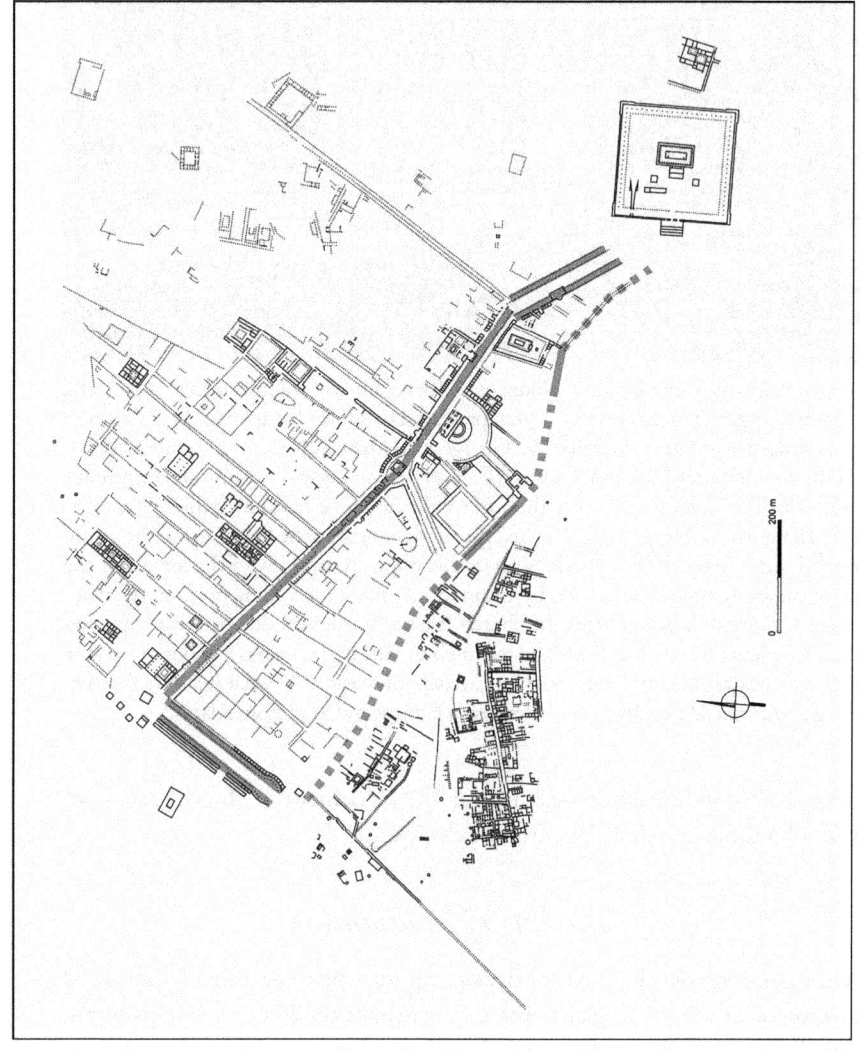

FIG. 6.4 Palmyra: central area and Grand Colonnade. The plan shows how the colonnade helps to co-ordinate the elements of urban design as it approaches the temple of Bel at its far end, and provides a defining sense of movement in the city.

200 m

0

FIG. 6.5 Madaba map; the Grand Colonnade at Jerusalem. This famous image is part of a large mosaic, originally measuring 21 × 7m., preserved in somewhat damaged condition in the apse of the sixth-century church of St. George at Madaba in Jordan. Its centerpiece is a plan of the contemporary city of Jerusalem (*hagia polis Ierousa[lem]*), the most conspicuous feature of which is a colonnaded street, the *cardo* of the Roman city, running through the city from the Damascus or Neapolis (sc. Nablus) gate in the north to the Sion Gate in the south. In a central location on the colonnade (seen upside down in this view of the mosaic) is the church of the Holy Sepulchre as built by Constantine; the steps leading up from the main street into a courtyard, beyond this the church itself with the rotunda over the supposed burial place of Jesus, all much as described by Eusebius. The entire map is laid out in the apse of the church exactly in conformity with the actual orientations of what it shows. M. Avi-Yonah, *The Madaba Mosaic Map* (Jerusalem, 1954); image by OUP from Alamy.

considered separately from it—perhaps as the settlement of the thousands of workers who came in to build Constantine's city.

6.3 The City of Constantine

The Constantinian development of Byzantium took place against a background of the growth of the existing city, and of the expansion and renovations of the Severan dynasty. It was from here that Constantine's programme took its departure, the emperor's planners making inventive use of what was already there.[20] In order to 'anchor' his city in its predecessors, Constantine had little to do but run his road system from the heart of the Severan city by setting the Miliarium

---

20. Bauer, pp. 148–67 (Augusteion), 167–87 (forum of Constantine). In the Nika Riot of 532, among much else the fire destroyed 'the two great colonnades which extended as far as the market place (*agora*) which bears the name of Constantine' (Procopius, *Wars* 1.24.9); Fig. 6.6.

(or Milion) at the south-western corner of the Augusteum. From this point the Severan colonnade led directly to his city gate, which, in a brilliantly inventive stroke, was reversed in orientation to form a transition from Severan Byzantium into the forum of Constantine, opening a perspective from one city into the other. Hadrian had done something similar at Athens, in building a gate leading from the 'city of Theseus' on one side, to the new 'city of Hadrian' on the other, and there is a more exact parallel in the Numidian city of Cuicul (Djémila), where the gate of the old city became a monumental entrance to a new forum that lay outside it. There is a difference, in that Cuicul had begun to spread away from its colonial site of the early second century, the new forum expressing a shift in the physical economy of the city that had already taken place; it was as a matter of deliberate urban planning that the same development was initiated at Constantinople. The building of sequential forums, marking successive stages in economic development, is a commonly found feature of Roman urban planning; Lepcis Magna shows it, as, of course, did Rome, and we will find it at Constantinople, as the city expanded to the west, the only direction open to it.

Of the total of fifty-two 'grand colonnades' enumerated by the *Notitia* for the entire city, only three are given names, one of them the *porticus Fanionis* in Region IV.[21] It seems likely that this was the main street (recorded as a processional route in the sixth century) leading northwards from the Milion to the harbours and other institutions of Graeco-Roman Byzantium by the Golden Horn.[22] If so, the *porticus Fanionis* will also have been part of the monumental development of the city before the Constantinian foundation; once the Severan Tetrastoon was built, shifting the social and political focus of the city to the south, there must have been such a thoroughfare, awaiting only its embellishment with colonnades if it did not have them already, running along the western flank of the acropolis to the 'old city' of Byzantium.

The Milion, named in both introduction and text of Region IV as 'golden milestone' (*miliarium aureum*), appears in the *Collectio Civitatis* under the designation 'tetrapylon aureum', a description that reveals its physical character. A tetrapylon or quadriform arch, a well-known element in Hellenistic and Roman urban architecture, is a gateway or arch with four openings, used to articulate urban thoroughfares at crossroads. They could be elaborate structures with complex architectural functions, for example in harmonizing streets that did not quite align (as at Lepcis and Palmyra), or in integrating different types of urban space. This was the case with the *tetrapylon aureum*, three of its four passages opening, respectively, to the north onto the thoroughfare to the Golden Horn and old city just described, to the east onto the Augusteum and the public

---

21. The others are the *porticus semirotunda* known as 'Sigma' in Region III and the *porticus Troadenses* of Region XII.

22. Mango, *Développement Urbain*, p. 19.

buildings on the far side of it, and to the south onto the hippodrome and Zeuxippon. The fourth passage opened onto the double-colonnaded avenue leading to the forum of Constantine. Whether or not the Tetrastoon was, like the colonnade, of Severan origin, the addition of the Golden Milestone, marking the beginning of the road system connecting the city with the provinces of the Roman empire both western and eastern, gave it a new function. With its echo of imperial Rome, this is clearly a Constantinian innovation.[23]

Passing the along the double colonnade and through the site of the old Severan city gate, we come to the forum of Constantine and the new city beyond it. The forum was entered at each end through gateways of Proconnesian marble[24] and was circular or oval in shape, with facing curved colonnades, and the column of Constantine at its centre. On its northern and southern sides respectively, Constantine repeated two of the structures already existing at the Tetrastoon, namely senate-house and tribunal; the presence of these duplicated institutions is one indication that the *Notitia* is dealing with an earlier city, onto which that of Constantine was grafted. The new senate-house has a special importance, in pointing to Constantine's further plans for the senate of the New Rome. In moving from the old *bouleutērion* in the second region to a new senate-house in the sixth, the city council of Byzantium entered into a radically enhanced role as the senate of the eastern Roman empire. In the process it changed its identity, as it took in new senators from all over the eastern empire and from within the imperial administration—at the same time, no doubt, shedding those members of the old city council who were unequal to the challenges of their new situation. In a much longer time frame, the same process of transformation, new senators replacing old as the senate acquired a changed role under imperial government, had affected the senate of old Rome also. At Rome the process is measured in centuries, at Constantinople it took place in little more than a generation. Already under Constantius the senate and city administration of the new capital were given a status and duties matching those at Rome, even though its senators were much less wealthy than their western counterparts.[25]

With the guidance of its cardinal points, it is not difficult to map out the further elements of the Constantinian urban plan, especially if we bear in mind that monuments of a later period whose position is known were accommodated in the framework laid out by Constantine's planners (Fig. 6.6).[26]

---

23. For the Miliarium Aureum in the Roman forum, erected by Augustus in 20 BCE as the symbolic centre of the Roman empire and its road system, see F. Coarelli, *Rome and Environs: An Archaeological Guide* (2007), p. 64.

24. Proconnesus was an island in the Propontis, about 100 km from Constantinople (see Fig. 2.2); the marble could be transported directly by sea.

25. On the senate and senators of Constantinople, see further Chapter 11 (pp. 221–3).

26. For what follows see esp. Mango, *Développement Urbain*, pp. 27ff.

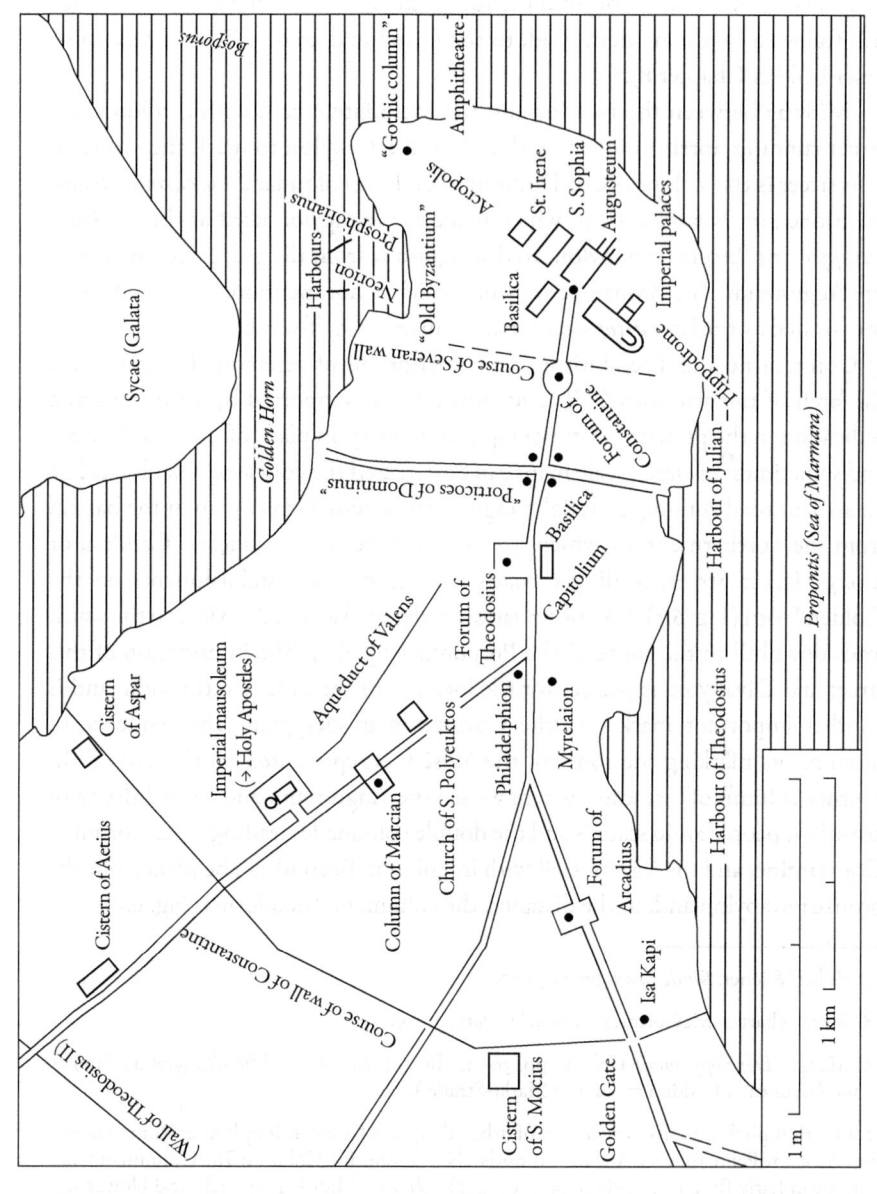

FIG. 6.6 Fourth-century Constantinople.

Following the Mesē from its origin at the Tetrapylon, its line along the present-day Divanyolu was confirmed by the discovery of the drainage system underlying it, and the column of Constantine, which stood in the centre of his forum, is a clear marker of its route. Beyond the forum the road continued in a direct line, still followed by the modern road, to the forum and arch of Theodosius, to be described (in Chapter 8).[27]

Midway between the two forums, the Mesē intersected with a colonnaded street running north to south, with a second tetrapylon to mark the crossing. This street is the 'colonnade of Domninus' or 'long colonnade' (*makros embolos*) mentioned in Byzantine texts, which name the tetrapylon itself as the *chalkoun tetrapylon* or 'bronze tetrapylon', to distinguish it from the golden tetrapylon in the Augusteum. The Bronze Tetrapylon, which is not mentioned in the *Notitia*, was located by the later *artopoleion* (bakers' market), half-way between the forums of Constantine and Theodosius; some descriptions of ceremonial routes call it the 'arch of the artopoleia'.[28] The identification is supported by an unexpected indication in the present-day topography of the city. In plans of the grand bazaar and sometimes on larger-scale maps can be detected the course of what looks like an ancient road running at a slight angle to the internal street plan of the bazaar, from the northern end of which it emerges to become Uzunçarşı Caddesi, or 'Long-Market Street', leading towards the commercial establishments on the Golden Horn (Fig. 6.7).[29] A continuation of the road across the Mesē to the south leads downhill to the shore of the Propontis (Fig. 6.8). The intersection of this street and Divanyolu is perfect for the location of the bronze tetrapylon, and is another important marker in the Constantinian city plan. The sequence of monuments marking the route of the Mesē was represented on the early fifth-century column of Arcadius, where we see the Augusteum and its vicinity with crowds of people amid statues and the double colonnades leading to the forum of Constantine, and the forum itself with its column. Beyond can be picked out the bronze tetrapylon and, in the distance, the column of Theodosius (Fig. 6.9).[30]

---

27. Müller-Wiener, *Bildlexikon*, pp. 269–70.

28. See the chart at McCormick, *Eternal Victory*, p. 219.

29. Mango, *Développement Urbain*, pp. 30–31; Berger, *Istanbuler Mitteilungen* 47 (1997), p. 396 (Uzunçarşı Caddesi = 'Langer-Markt-Straße').

30. On triumphal columns as an aspect of urban design, at Constantinople as at Rome, see esp. the articles by Pelin Yoncaci-Arslan, 'Towards a New Honorific Column: The Column of Constantine in Early Byzantine Urban Landscape (1)', *METU* (Middle East Technical University) *Journal of the Faculty of Architecture* 33.1 (2016), pp. 121–45, and 'Registrars of Urban Movement in Constantinople; Monumental Columns of the Mese', *Annual of Istanbul Studies* 7 (2018), pp. 7–29.

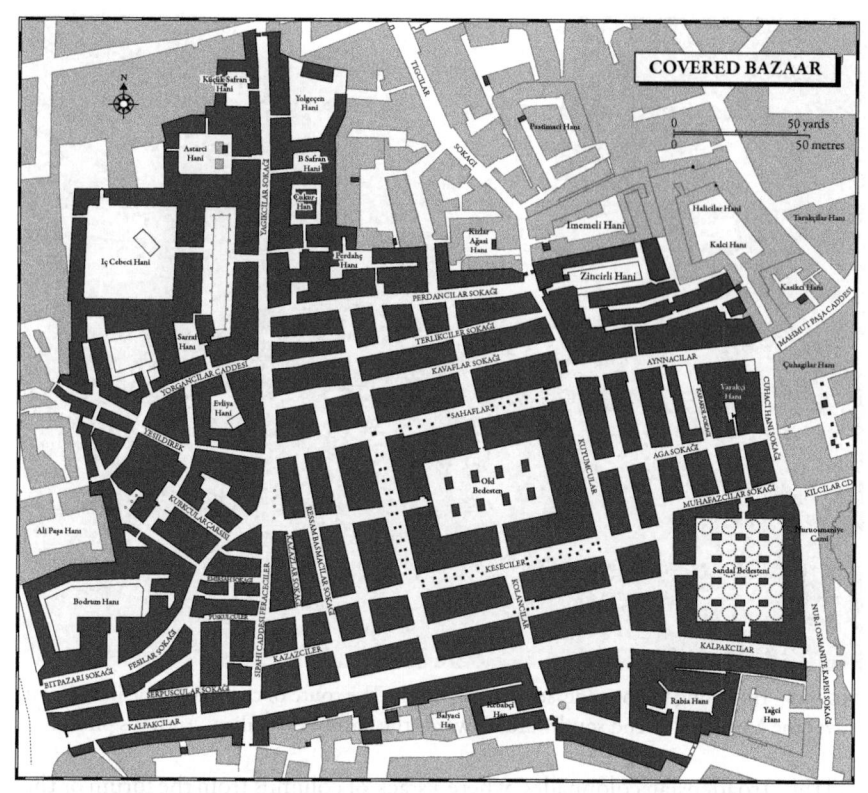

FIG. 6.7 The 'Long Colonnade' in the Grand Bazaar. The route of the colonnade runs at a different angle from the rectangular pattern of galleries aligned with the Old Bezestan at the centre of the Bazaar. To the north the colonnade, under the name Uzunçarşi Caddesi, or 'Long-Market Street' runs to the shoreline of the Golden Horn, while to the south it crosses the Mesé, here Yeniçeriler Caddesi, at the location of the Bronze Tetrapylon, before continuing south to the Propontis shore at the harbor of Julian.

Resuming its progress from the forum of Constantine to the west, the Mesē ran in a direct line to the later site of the forum and arch of Theodosius. At some point beyond this, the road, so far an undivided thoroughfare separating the regions to north and south, divided into two branches, of which the southerly branch is easily followed. After first descending to the highway exchange at Aksaray, where its course is lost, it emerges to veer left along the course of a road shown on city plans (and clearly visible on Google Earth) as Cerrahpaşa Caddesi, continuing as Mustafa Paşa Caddesi. Passing the base of the column of Arcadius on its right-hand side (pp. 151–3 below), this road has long been understood to represent the southern extension of the Mesē. It approaches the Constantinian Golden Gate through what the *Notitia* and Hesychius as well as *Chronicon Paschale*

FIG. 6.8 The 'Long Colonnade' seen to the south. The route of the colonnade just after it leaves the Mesē to descend southwards towards the harbour of Julian. Author's photo.

call the 'Troadensian colonnades', where a stack of columns from the forum or the colonnades used to be seen in a little plot of land by the side of the road.[31]

Lacking such precise markers in the modern street plans, the northern division of the Mesē is less easy to trace. Its general course is however clear. The least abrupt reconstruction would place the division of the Mesē into two branches somewhere near the Lâleli ('Tulip') mosque, 500 metres west of the forum of Theodosius; this then would be the site of the Philadelphion, at the meeting of the three roads, that is to say the undivided Mesē and its two branches, described by a much later source (Chapter 7 below, p. 137). The road must have passed the fifth-century column of Marcian and forum,[32] and along the south-western side of the building terrace bearing the mausoleum of Constantine, later church of the Apostles, on the site and with the alignment of the Fatih mosque.

---

31. Mango, *Développement Urbain*, p. 27 n. 32 (seen in 1982). The same observation was made by Ferudun Özgümüs as he guided me past the site in November 2007. Hesychius (above, p. 49) stated that Constantine 'moved the [Severan] walls outwards to the so-called Troadisian portico' (cf. *Notitia*, Region XII, following 'porta aurea').

32. Below, n. 44. It is likely too that it passed not far from the fifth- and sixth-century church of St. Polyeuktos (that is to say, the location of the church took advantage of it).

FIG. 6.9 The Forum of Constantine, in sixteenth-century drawings of the column of Arcadius. The forum is recognized by its circular shape and surrounding colonnades, with the column of Constantine surmounted by a standing image of the emperor (cf. Fig. 2.3). The double roofs of the Severan colonnades leading from the Augusteum enter the forum at the top. The three figures seen beyond the forum, and at the extreme right-hand hand edge of the image seem to stand on pedestal bases indicating that they are statue groups. Below them is the tetrapylon marking the intersection of the Mesē with the Portico of Dominus or 'Long Colonnade', and in the distance behind this the column of Theodosius. Outside the forum, in what must be a typical urban scene a pair of men is filling up pitchers carried by a third person with water from an underground cistern; above them is the portrayal of a mythological scene perhaps representing the battle of Ulysses' men with Scylla and Charybdis referred to by a contemporary poet (*Epigr. Bob.* 51, 'In Scyllam Constantinopolitanam in circo'). See further Figs. 8.7–9 below. E. H. Freshfield, 'Notes on a Vellum Album', etc., *Archaeologia* 22 (1922), pp. 87–104. Reproduced with kind permission of the Master and Fellows of Trinity College, Cambridge.

The form and position of the mausoleum, in a prominent position just inside the city by a main road into it, mirrored those of the mausoleum of Galerius at Thessalonica, which Constantine must have seen several times, as he had those of Augustus and Hadrian at Rome.[33]

---

33. Mango, *Développement Urbain*, p. 30; and 'Constantine's Mausoleum and the Translation of Relics', *Byzantinische Zeitschrift* 83 (1990), pp. 51–62, reprinted in *Studies on Constantinople* (1993), ch. 5; below, Chapter 9 (pp. 177–9) on the nature and evolution of the site. The mausoleum

The trajectory of the road beyond the Constantinian walls is indicated by the fifth-century cistern of Aetius, which it skirted on the southern side. It left the Theodosian city by the so-called Hadrianople gate in the wall of Theodosius, corresponding to the Charisius gate in the wall of Constantine.

As was noted earlier, the divided Mesē is the key to the spatial structure of Constantinople, forming what has been called the 'armature' of the city as a sort of capital letter Y rotated 90° anti-clockwise, linking the Augusteum with the forum of Constantine and providing boundaries for regions lying on the southern and northern sides of the peninsula and then, in southern and northern branches, integrating the Golden Gate and imperial mausoleum as cardinal points in the urban plan.

The armature extended its reach to the routes into the city, in the first place a road coming in by the coastal route from Regium and entering by the Golden Gate. As we saw (p. 96), the first mention of this route is by the Pilgrim of Bordeaux travelling to Constantinople in 333; it is presumed that it was a new road, approaching the city by way of a bridge or causeway, the 'pons sublicius' recorded by the *Notitia*, carrying it over the coastal lagoons between Regium and Constantinople and passing through what developed as the garrison city of Hebdomon (the 'seventh milestone'), about half-way between them.[34] An older road approached from the northwest by way of the imperial residence at Melanthias. This was the road connecting with the Thracian hinterland of Constantinople and with the military zones of the lower Danube; it was that taken by the emperor Valens as he left Constantinople to face the Goths on the battlefield of Hadrianople in 378.[35] It should be added that according to Procopius (*Buildings* 4.8.4–9), as late as the time of Justinian and until that emperor relaid it with dressed stone, the direct road to Regium was uneven and liable to flooding in bad weather.

Contrasting with the internal articulation of Constantine's city, the line of his defensive wall, possibly his first planning decision after taking the city from Licinius, is anything but certain, though its general alignment is not difficult to determine. There is a widely recognized clue to their southern sector in the name of a ruined mosque, previously a church, known as Isa Kapı Mescidi, 'mosque of the gate of Jesus'. The mosque occupies a corner plot on the continuation of

---

of Augustus stood in an analogous position in relation to the via Flaminia—outside the Servian but inside the Aurelian walls. Constantine's mausoleum was outside the Severan walls of Byzantium but inside his own.

34. The effect was to continue to the city the old via Egnatia, which had reached only as far as the river Hebrus (Maritza), with an extension to Perinthus and a sea crossing to Pylae connecting with Nicaea (Fig. 2.2). For Melanthias see Fig. 2.3.

35. Amm. Marc. 31.11.1, 12.1.

Cerrahpaşa as Mustafa Paşa Caddesi, and its name is also preserved in the street name Esakapı Sokagi that comes from the north (and appears on a nearby bus stop). It has long been supposed that 'Isa Kapı' preserves the memory of a now vanished monumental gateway, which, given its location beyond the column and forum of Arcadius on the southern branch of the Mesē, is to be identified as the great gate of Constantine known as Porta Aurea.[36] The conclusion is supported by the presence on some versions of the Buondelmonti map of a structure shown to the west of the column of Arcadius, with the caption 'antiquissima pulchra porta' (Fig. 6.10), and by a letter of 1411 by the Byzantine writer Manuel

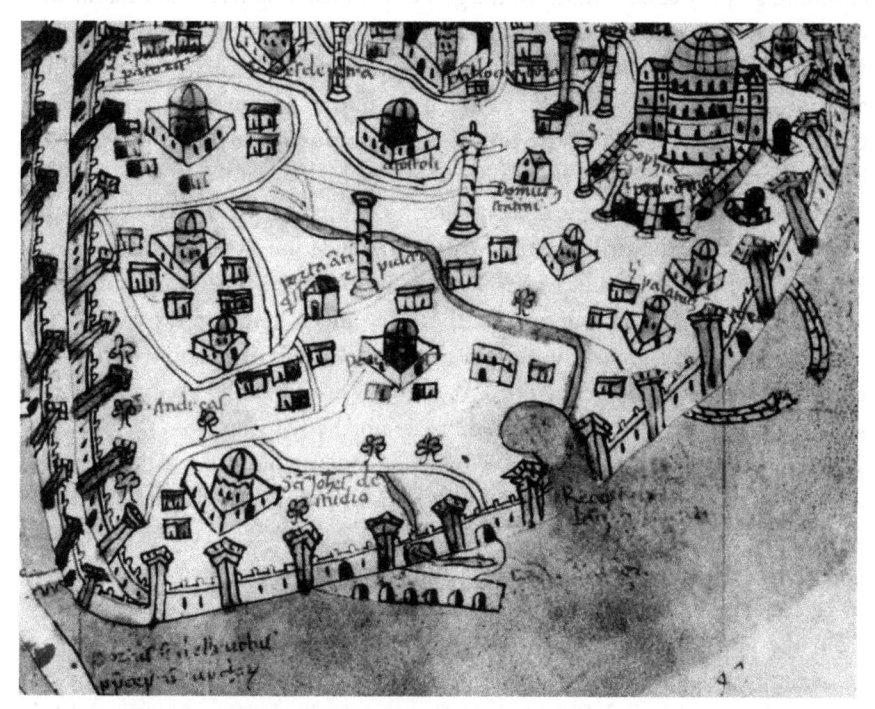

FIG. 6.10 The city gate ('Porta Aurea') in the Buondelmonti map. The gate, with the caption 'porta antiquissima pulchra', is shown in relation to the columns of Theodosius and Arcadius with the river Lykos running between them, issuing in error into the harbour of Julian. An unconnected lesser watercourse, which should actually be the Lykos, enters the former harbor of Theodosius, leaving a little pool that does not reach the sea. This may be the artist's way of indicating the silting of the harbor.

36. Mango, *Développement Urbain*, p. 25; illustrated at John Freely and Ahmet S. Cakmak, *Byzantine Monuments of Istanbul*, pp. 290–92; Müller-Wiener, *Bildlexikon*, pp. 118–19, cf. Berger, p. 37 (the identification is already in Mamboury's guide of 1925); cf. K. R. Dark and Ferudun Özgümüş, *Constantinople: Archaeology of a Byzantine Megalopolis* (2013), pp. 28–30, with reference to the letter of Manuel Chrysoloras. The mosque itself is now again in use; Dark and Özgümüş, p. 29.

Chrysoloras that seems to refer to it. His words, 'a high gate built of great marble blocks with a portico above it', are an apt description of a two-storied Roman gateway. The location is convincing in itself, and for what it implies of the course of the Constantinian wall, which would descend to the Propontis at a point just before the coastline veers southwards. At this point, the location of the wall defines itself. To bring it to the sea beyond this point would add substantially to the length of the wall to be built (and defended) with no territorial advantage.

Northwards from Isa Kapı, the wall would follow the line of Esakapı Sokagi, continuing by the eastern limits of the gardens of Hekimoğlu Ali Paşa Camii and the cistern of Mocius, then crossing the grounds of a hospital in the erstwhile Lykos valley, before turning in a north-easterly direction above the Fatih mosque and advancing to the Golden Horn along the line of Aksemsettin/Yavuz Selim Caddesi. A wall approaching the Golden Horn on this alignment would reach it, by the shortest route, at a strategically opportune high point.[37]

An essential element in this reconstruction of the Constantine city wall is the impression left by the structure on the topography of the city in the period after it had passed out of use but was still visible in some places; it did not just disappear when the Theodosian wall was built but merged into an expanding city landscape. Just as it skirted the eastern side of the cistern of Mocius (running to the east of the extramural church from which the cistern took its name), we may similarly identify the course of the wall in its northerly sector from the position and orientation of the cistern of Aspar, the construction of which began in 459.[38] We can suppose that the cistern was built just outside, probably adjacent to the old wall and sharing its orientation.[39] Even if the wall as a physical entity is lost to us, we have a number of indicators of its course, between which points of reference it remains speculative: namely, its end-points as inferred above from the position of the Golden Gate close to Isa Kapi, and the alignment of sections of the wall with the cisterns of Mocius and Aspar. These five indicators, with a reading of the mind of Constantine's planners (we may think

37. For this hypothetical course, see Dark and Özgümüş, *Archaeology of a Byzantine Megalopolis*, p. 30. The street names are for convenience in using a modern plan of the city. There is in the garden of Hekimoğlu Ali Paşa Camia a row of in situ columns; Dark and Özgümüş, site no. 67 with colour plate 14.

38. *Chron. Pasch.*, s.a.: a 'very large cistern near the old wall'; Whitby and Whitby, p. 85; cf. above, Chapter 4, n. 9.

39. Dark and Özgümüş, pp. 28, 30, etc. The cisterns are described at Crow, Bardill, and Bayliss, *The Water Supply of Byzantine Constantinople*, pp. 128–32. Müller-Wiener's map references are B/C6/7 (Mocius) and D3/4 (Aspar). For the church of S. Mocius, see Chapter 9 below (pp. 173–5), with discussion of its possible location in Dark and Özgümüş, p. 43.

ourselves back to the famous procession of November 324), are sufficient to justify entering that emperor's wall on the plan of the city with more confidence than is often attempted. It is not surprising if so prominent a feature should leave an impression on a later city plan, even as it went out of use and was dismantled or adapted for other purposes.

In a brief note at the very end of the *Notitia*, the east-west measurement of the city from the Golden Gate in a straight line (*directa linea*) to the shore is given as 14,075 Roman feet, with a north-south measurement across the peninsula of 6,150 Roman feet. The measurements are written out in words, reducing the chances of a corruption in the figures (it is possible that an earlier phase in the transmission of the *Notitia* was written in Roman numerals). Now the Roman foot is given as 11.65 inches, or 0.97 of the English foot. This yields a west-east dimension for the city of 13,653 English feet, or 4,551 yards; which converts to a measurement of 4,369 metres. This is a slight overestimate of the distance from Isa Kapı to the eastern limit of the city at the present-day lighthouse, the actual distance being exactly 4,000 metres. However, the lighthouse is not quite the easternmost point of the peninsula, and a measurement taken to any point further north, say to Mangana, or any deviation from a perfectly straight line, yields a figure extremely close to that given by the *Notitia*. The north-south measurement of 6,150 Roman feet is accurate for a line drawn through Beyazit, the site of the forum of Theodosius, which seems a natural place to make such a measurement at the time of writing of the *Notitia*. It is a monument to the importance of the forum as a main focal point of the city—and, of course, to the city's development towards and beyond it after the time of Constantine.

This may be as much as we can expect to discover from the street plan of the modern city.[40] Plans of Roman cities do survive in unexpected circumstances (the road through the grand bazaar is an example), but before we search for Constantinople in the streets of Istanbul, we must take account of the programmes of urban development pursued in the later and post-Byzantine period, especially in the great age of Ottoman building. As is well known, a mosque is aligned towards Mecca, which in Istanbul requires an orientation to the south-east. It so happens that the orientations of the hippodrome and imperial palace, the mausoleum of Constantine (later the church of the Holy Apostles) and St. Sophia are already in that direction or at right angles to it, with the result that the Sultan Ahmet mosque (the Blue Mosque) could be built onto the foundations of the imperial palace, the Faith mosque raised upon the footings of the Holy Apostles and St. Sophia transformed into a mosque without posing problems of orientation.

---

40. The reconstructions of Berger, 'Regionen und Strassen', pp. 387ff. are absorbing but hypothetical, and to my mind over-schematic.

The same was not true elsewhere, where the Beyazit and Lâleli mosques and the Suleymaniye complex were all built on the same south-east orientation as each other, which has nothing to do with any Roman plan.[41] As opportunities arose to modernize the street plans around the mosques, the new roads in these districts were often aligned with the mosques (as is particularly clear around the Fatih mosque and the Suleymaniye). The result in some parts of the city is a Roman-style plan that is unconnected with that of with ancient Constantinople; what looks like an overall design is really just the similar orientations of mosques and the streets around them in different parts of the city.

Later, the developments of the nineteenth century moved towards a Classical model, in expressing a deliberate aim to assimilate the city to a western European model of urban planning. The reformers took advantage of the fires that afflicted the crowded alleys and wooden buildings covering the greater part of the city, in order to redesign it after a modern fashion.[42] Development has continued, and plans of the city from the nineteenth century, like those of Mamboury's guide book of 1925, show a street plan that has little in common with that of the present-day, still less the ancient city.[43]

Yet, the nineteenth-century and modern planners may have achieved the interesting feat of recreating the urban design of Constantine, based on a struc-ture of main avenues diverging along the widening peninsula—the 'armature' described above. Its focal point was the branching of the Mesē west of the forum of Theodosius. To the south, the continuation of the Mesē followed Cerrahpaşa Caddesi to the Porta Aurea, while its northern extension ran past the future column of Marcian, skirting Constantine's mausoleum and leading out towards the Charisius or Hadrianople gate; all this we have seen.[44] An intermediate road between the two branches might correspond to Millet (Turgut-Özal) Caddesi,

---

41. This is not to say that the later buildings bear no relation at all to the Roman and Byzantine city. The Beyazit mosque overlooks an open space corresponding to the forum of Theodosius while being on an orientation quite different from it, while Lâleli may stand at the division of the Mesē on the site of the Philadelphion. For the Faith mosque and the Holy Apostles, see Chapter 9 below (pp. 177–9).

42. See the fascinating book by Zeynep Çelik, *The Remaking of Istanbul: Portrait of an Otto-man City in the Nineteenth Century* (1986), chs 2–3.

43. Çelik, p. 5 (map of 1840); E. Mamboury, *Constantinople: Tourist's Guide* (1925).

44. Müller-Wiener, *Bildlexikon*, pp. 54–56. The column is an example of the mutability of the urban landscape; cf. Mamboury, p. 289: 'a few years ago [it] stood in a private garden, but as a result of the fire of the Tchirchir quarter in 1908 and the subsequent replanning of these parts, it now stands at a cross roads.' The private garden may represent the forum in which the column stood, but the modern street plan is no guide to its original configuration. For the forum, *ILS* 824 (reading 'forumque' for 'torumque' in line 2, an obvious correction), and Bauer, pp. 213–15; the column is briefly referred to by Gilles, *Antiquities* 4.2 (ed. Musto, p. 184).

following the course of the Lykos river (now disappeared) to the wall of Constantine and beyond it to the Topkapı gate in its Theodosian successor. Between these diverging main routes, the streets would be laid out in rectangular or trapezoidal sectors widening into the broader part of the peninsula.[45] It is the natural way to handle the site while respecting Classical principles of urban planning, even though it is incidental, or rather a common response to geographical constraints, that from their very different standpoints, Constantine's planners and the nineteenth-century modernizers of Istanbul came to similar results.

---

45. A. Berger, 'Streets and Public Squares in Constantinople', *DOP* 54 (2000), pp. 161–72, offers what to me seems like an unduly schematic reconstruction of the more detailed street pattern; see Ken Dark, 'Houses, Streets and Shops in Byzantine Constantinople from the Fifth to the Twelfth Centuries', *Journal of Medieval History* 30 (2004), pp. 83–107.

7

Urban Development (2)

THE SUCCESSORS OF CONSTANTINE

THE FUTURE EMPEROR Julian, who was born there, said in an oration to Constantine's successor Constantius, that Constantine had in less than ten years built a city 'as far surpassing all others as it is itself lesser than Rome'—a nice turn of words, though it is very doubtful whether Constantinople yet enjoyed the size or status of Carthage, Antioch, or Ephesus, let alone Egyptian Alexandria. Later in the same speech, he assigns to Constantius the completion of a city wall 'that was then only begun'.

Julian captures both the scale and the limitations of Constantine's achievement.[1] We must be careful to put this in context. Apart from the uncompleted city walls, the actual building work of Constantine, impressive though it is, was limited to the remodelling of the Tetrastoon and its appurtenances, the creation of a new forum just outside the Severan city, the building of his mausoleum at one of the highest points of the site, the establishment of the road plan, or 'armature' of the city and the laying out of a new route to the imperial residence at Regium. Other projects conceived by Constantine though left to his successors to accomplish included the completion of the 'great church' of St. Sophia, planned in 326 though dedicated only in 360, and the 'Thermae Constantinianae' of the *Notitia* (Tenth Region), which are taken to be the same as the massive bathing establishment near the church of the Apostles, known from other sources as 'Constantianae'.[2] The construction of these baths, begun in April 345 according to *Chronicon Paschale*, proceeded very slowly. In a speech delivered, probably, in 357, the orator Themistius

---

1. Julian, *Or.* 1, 8B–C, 41B; ed. Loeb, vol. 1, pp. 20, 104. For what follows, in addition to works already cited, see Nick Henck, 'Constantius ὁ Φιλοκτίστης', *DOP* 55 (2001), pp. 279–304, esp. 284–93.

2. G. Prinzing and P. Speck, 'Fünf Lokalitäten in Konstantinopel', in H.-G. Beck, *Studien zur Frühgeschichte Konstantinopels* (1973), at pp. 179–81. These great baths are distinct from those mentioned by Eusebius (*On the Life of Constantine* 4.58–60) among the amenities provided by Constantine for the precinct of his mausoleum (Berger, p. 369). The passage of Eusebius is carefully translated by Cyril Mango in his 'Constantine's Mausoleum and the Translation of Relics', *Byzantinische Zeitschrift* 83 (1990), pp. 51–62, p. 55 (= *Studies on Constantinople* (1993), ch. 5).

From Byzantium to Constantinople: An Urban History. John Matthews, Oxford University Press.
© Oxford University Press 2024. DOI: 10.1093/oso/9780197585498.003.0007

could only refer to the ground plan and prospective beauty of the foundation. In a case that should be of interest to archaeologists, Ammianus Marcellinus happens to mention the use of building materials for the baths brought in from the dismantled walls of Chalcedon, hence after 365 when that city fell to a siege, and the baths were not inaugurated until 427 in the time of Theodosius II, after whom they were re-named.[3] Their location in the Tenth Region presumes access to an upgraded water supply, which entered the city on this line (below, p. 131). Since Themistius also mentioned the search for new sources of water, it may be that this was a cause of the delay in completion. In this still undeveloped part of the city it would not matter so much if even a large area remained a building site for so long.

An immediate challenge was to provide for the expanding economic needs of the new city. The most notable early contribution is assigned to Julian, though it is evident that the creation of a major new harbour cannot have been both planned and achieved during Julian's short reign, still less during the sixth months from late 361 to early summer 362 which were all the time he spent in the city as emperor.[4] Whether Julian dedicated a project begun by his predecessors, or initiated one completed after his time, his name was attached to the new facility. It is the 'new harbour' listed by the *Notitia* under the Third Region, where it is mentioned (as also by Zosimus) with a colonnade called 'Sigma' after its resemblance to the Greek letter. A possible view of the ensemble is that the Sigma was a curved colonnade following the quayside; if so, it would resemble the first-century harbour at Ostia built by Claudius (Fig. 7.1). The location of the harbour below the hippodrome is indicated in the introduction to the Third Region in the *Notitia*, and is not difficult to find; it is marked by a deviation of the sea-walls, by the trace of a harbour mole on older plans of the city, and by the name Kadurgalimanı, 'Galley Harbour' (*Caterga Limena* in Pierre Gille's description) that is still attached to the district, especially to a curved parade overlooking what is now a park with fountains. Vavassore's panorama shows the locations both of Julian's harbour and that of Theodosius beyond it (Fig. 7.2).[5]

---

3. Henck, pp. 285–86; *Chron. Pasch.*, 534 ('Constantianae'), 580–81 ('Constantinianae') (Whitby and Whitby, pp. 25–26, 70); Themistius, *Or.* 4.58b–c; Amm. Marc. 31.1.4, cf. 26.8.2. The failure of the *Notitia* to rename the baths might be an indication of the dating of the document (above, p. 63).

4. Zosimus 3.11.3, with Paschoud's commentary, ed. Budé, I, pp. 98–99. The harbour was modernized by Justin II and named Sophiae or Sophiana after that emperor's wife.

5. See esp. Mango, *Développement urbain*, p. 39; Müller-Wiener, *Bildlexikon*, pp. 62–63. Mango's estimate of the added capacity of the harbour of Julian is 1,000 metres harbour frontage, with moorings for around 125 merchant vessels—an over-estimate, if any of the ships were on the scale of the dedicated grain-ships from Alexandria (see below, on the harbour of Theodosius, p. 146). A comparison with Lepcis adduces the latter's frontage of 1,200 metres, with capacity for 155 ships. That of Ephesus may have approached 2,000 metres.

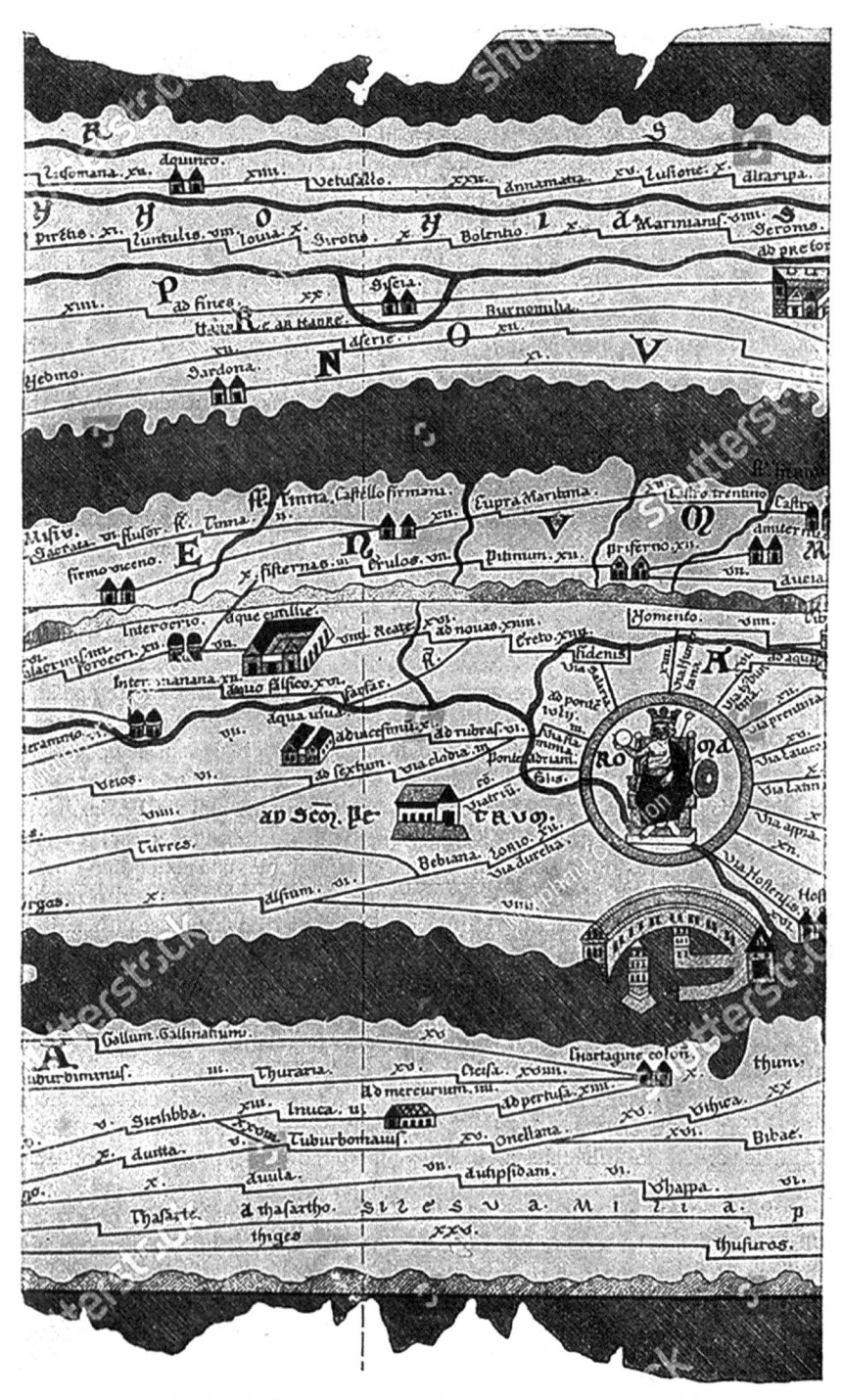

FIG. 7.1 The Claudian harbour at Ostia in the Peutinger Map. Though he never saw it, the semi-circular colonnade enclosing the harbor might be a model for the colonnade in the shape of a Greek letter *sigma* attributed to Julian's harbour at Constantinople. Konrad Miller, *Die Peutingersche Tafel* (1887); image, OUP from Shutterstock.

FIG. 7.2 The Propontis shore in the Vavassore panorama. Acknowledgement as for Fig. 3.2 above.

The latter has through silting of the river Lykos been transformed into gardens, while that of Julian, or its late Byzantine successor the Kontoskalion, is portrayed as still in use as a harbour and shipbuilding dock ('arsenale'). Vavassore's image may already recall an earlier period, for Pierre Gilles had in the same years described the harbour as 'almost demolished and enclosed by a wall', with women washing their linen in what was left of it. Some people had seen

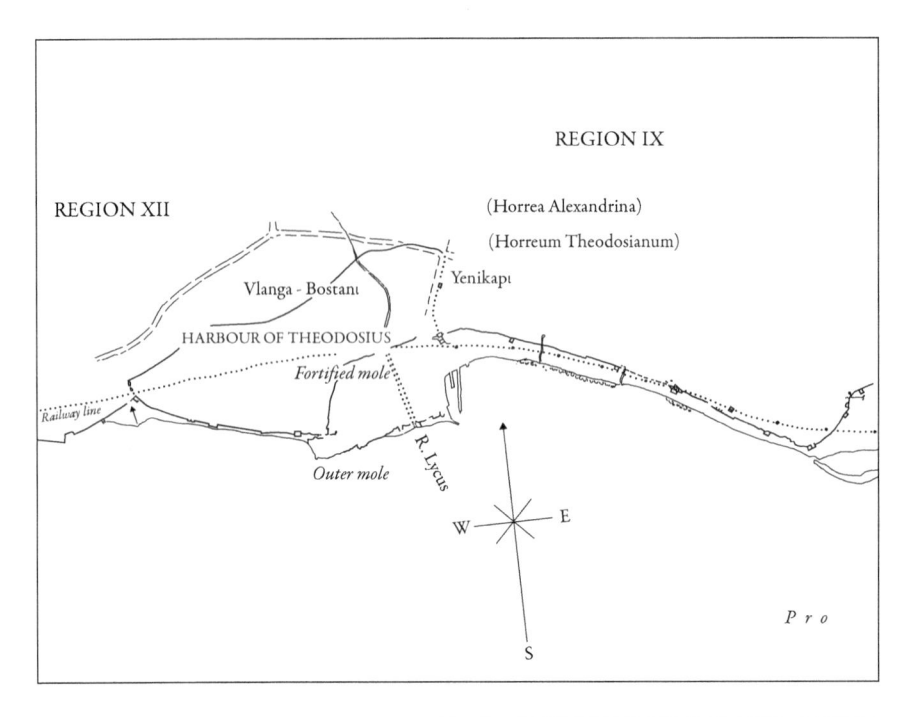

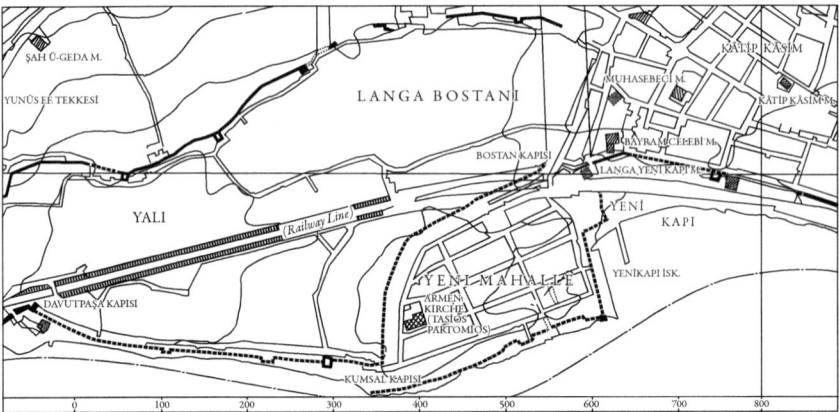

FIG. 7.3 The Propontis shore and harbours of Constantinople. Adapted from the map provided by Arthur Henderson for A. van Millingen's *Byzantine Constantinople: the Walls of the city and adjoining historical sites*, published in 1899; for the corresponding street plans, Müller-Wiener, *Bildlexikon* (1977), pp. 60–3. The map incorporates the surveys made for the building of the railway line along the coast and round the end of the peninsular to Sirkeci station. It is shown in a transposed N/S orientation, with revised captions. Some features, such as harbour moles, may be developments later than the fourth and fifth centuries. As Mango points out (*Développement urbain*, p. 38), harbours need to be dredged and cleaned out, enlarged and modernised, in the course of which they may acquire different and multiple names. On the Propontis coast there are two major harbours, those of Julian (aka Sophia, Kontoskalion) and Theodosius (aka Eleutherios).

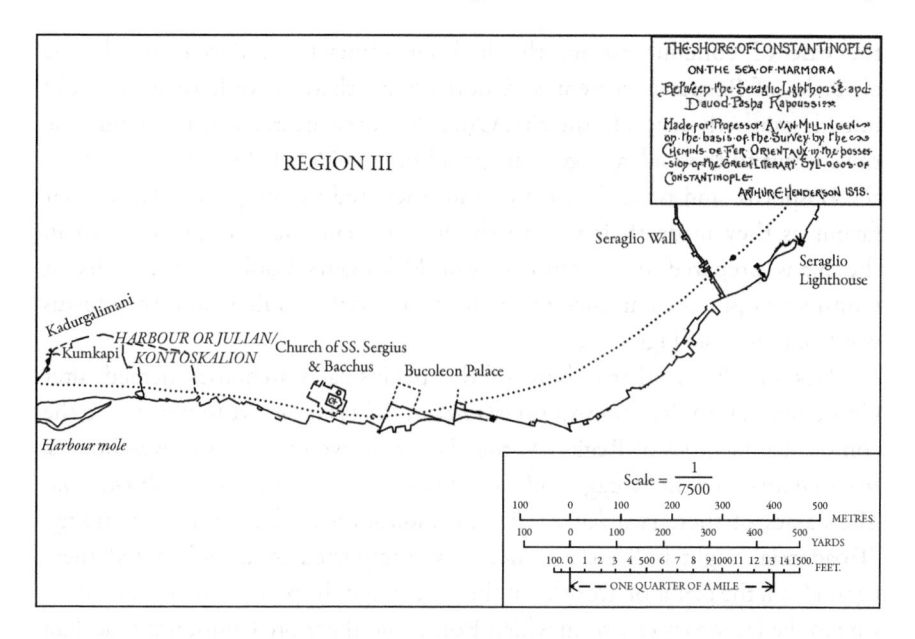

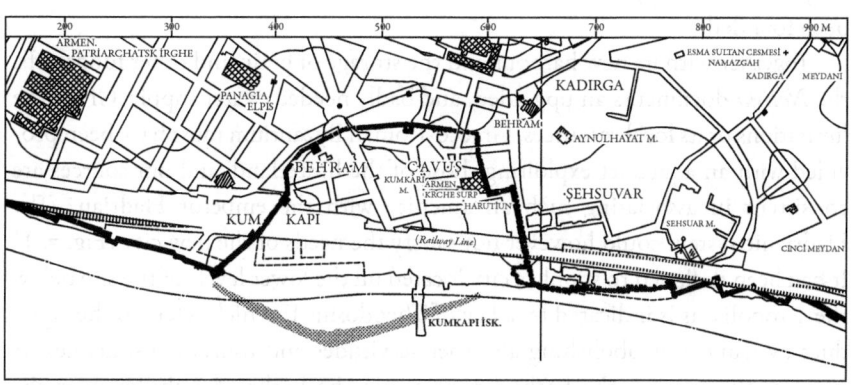

FIG. 7.4 The Propontis shore and its installations in van Millingen (2).

the wrecks of Ottoman galleys that had sunk there.[6] If the original harbour indeed had the two sections shown on the Vavassore panorama, it might have repeated the pattern seen in the old Byzantine city, with the dockyard and commercial harbour listed separately in the *Notitia* and mentioned in Dio's account of Severus' siege of the city. Julian's harbour provided ready access to high-consuming institutions like the hippodrome and palace as well as following the development of the city along the shores of the Propontis, and established a close connection with the administration as the ships were built and maintained, as it were, under the emperor's eye. From the point of view of

---

6. *Antiquities* 2.15 (ed. Musto, p. 92).

the ease of communication, the harbour somewhat relieved the double obstacles of Bosporus current and north wind that, as we have seen, could impede southerly access to the city. Once they drew near, navigators could use the current to their advantage as it spread more widely below the entrance to the Bosporus, and treat the north wind, sheltered by the peninsula, in their favour as they made their way to the harbour entrance. As can be seen in the plans prepared to accompany van Millingen's book on the walls of Constantinople, the entrance to the harbours both of Julian and Theodosius was from the east (Figs 7.3–4).

Back on the northern shore of the peninsula, warehouses named after Constantius and Valens (*horrea Constantiaca, Valentiniaca*) are found among the commercial facilities of Region V, together with two other sets of warehouses, *horrea olearia* for the storage and clearance of olive oil, and *horrea Troadensia*. The names of these two *horrea* give no indication of their time of building. 'Troadensia' might indicate a source of the imported foodstuffs stored there (grain from the plains of Troy?), but the name might be purely ornamental, referring to the legendary city from which Rome, and therefore Constantinople, had been founded.

Together with its new harbour and the storage of grain and other foodstuffs, the *Notitia* documents an upgraded, and badly needed, water supply. Given the limitations of its local resources, Graeco-Roman Byzantium must have been provided with an aqueduct exploiting those of the hinterland, and our sources are consistent in associating such an amenity with the emperor Hadrian.[7] The Hadrianic system could however not satisfy the needs of the new city (Fig. 7.5).[8] It had been designed to supply a city located on the lower levels of the site below the acropolis, as is indicated by a law of Theodosius II which refers to the aqueduct by name and, abolishing all other servitudes and usurpations, defines its users as the people, the baths (mentioning the baths of Achilles near the strategion) and the imperial palace.[9] The aqueduct followed the contours on the northern side of the promontory, with branches to the Augusteum, imperial palace, and Zeuxippon, all establishments on the lower level. It cannot have carried water to the higher levels of the Constantinian and later city; at elevations of

---

7. Mango, *Développement Urbain*, p. 20.

8. See on this question Cyril Mango, 'The Water Supply of Constantinople', in Mango and G. Dagron with G. Greatrex (eds), *Constantinople and Its Hinterland* (1995), pp. 9–18, and above all the transformative work of James Crow, Jonathan Bardill, and Richard Bayliss, *The Water Supply of Byzantine Constantinople* (*Journal of Roman Studies* Monograph 11, 2008); see pp. 118–21 (aqueduct) and 127 (*nymphaeum*).

9. *Cod. Just.* 11.42.6 (439/41); Crow, Bardill, and Bayliss, appendix I, pp. 115 and 227 (though the law is of Theodosius II, not Theodosius I).

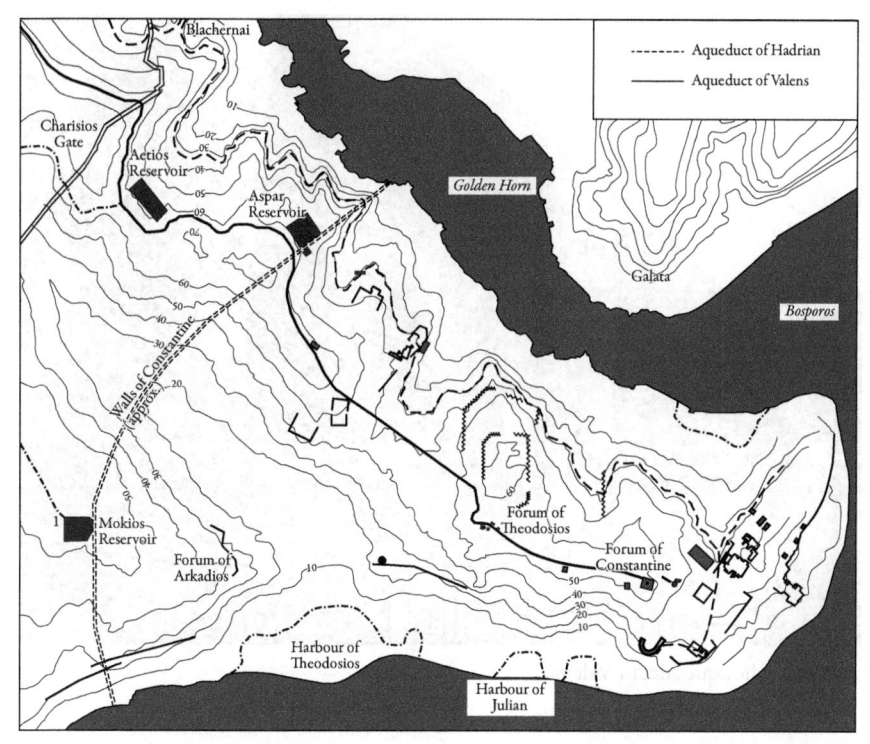

FIG. 7.5 The water supply of Constantinople; aqueducts and cisterns. The known or projected lines of the Hadrianic and fourth-century aqueducts show how they entered the city at different respective elevations, maintained by the aqueduct of Valens to accommodate the higher levels of urban development. Only major public cisterns are shown; there were very many others. Adapted from James Crow, Jonathan Bardill, Richard Bayliss, *The Water Supply of Byzantine Constantinople*, Map 12 with Chapter 5.

50 metres, the forums both of Constantine and Theodosius are higher than the ancient acropolis.

The more elevated system that was needed to satisfy these needs is attested by the massive aqueduct spanning, at an elevation of nearly 60 metres, the valley between what are conventionally (though not in the fourth century) known as the fourth and third hills of Constantinople (Fig. 7.6). The aqueduct, of which the elevated section is only the most spectacular element of a complex system that originates far out in the countryside, brought water into Constantinople along a contour just to the north of the Charisius or Hadrianople gate in the later Theodosian wall, and delivered it to a water-basin (*nymphaeum maius*), listed by the *Notitia* under the Tenth Region. This 'greater nymphaeum' is clearly the *hydreion megiston*, the Greek equivalent of the Latin term, described by the church historian Socrates as built near the projected site of the forum of Theodosius by

FIG. 7.6 The aqueduct of Valens.

the urban prefect Clearchus, hence in 372/3.[10] Since the relevant part of the forum of Theodosius was in Region VII, to be adjacent to it the nymphaeum must have been located at the eastern extremity of Region X. It was the central distribution point for the water delivered by the aqueduct, as important a feature of the economic life of the city as was the Mesē for the movement of traffic within it.

Raised aqueducts served a double function, the utilitarian and more obvious one of delivering water in sufficient quantities for the use of the population, but also doing so from a high elevation, generating the gravity-fed pressure needed to distribute the water throughout the urban area and provide the power for its public fountains. If we find it surprising that the *Notitia* makes no specific mention of the elevated aqueduct, this may be a consequence of our perspectives in seeing the great structure separately from the system of which it formed part. A contemporary observer, Gregory of Nazianzus, refers to the 'underground and aerial' course of the water—a description that could be applied to many a Roman aqueduct, in which the combination of tunnel and raised channel was commonplace;

10. *Hist. Eccl.* 4.8; Mango, 'Water Supply', p. 14; Crow, Bardill, and Bayliss, p. 127; *PLRE* I, Clearchus 1 (pp. 211–12). Jerome's *Chronicle* dates the aqueduct (that is to say its inauguration) to 373, underlining its importance: 'a quo [sc. Clearcho] necessaria et diu expectata votis aqua civitati inducitur'.

the Pont du Gard in southern France is a well-known (and beautifully engineered) example.[11] From the point of view of the *Notitia*, the 'nymphaeum maius' was the defining element.

With its combination of economic and aesthetic purposes, a nymphaeum, not only a distribution point but a decorative ensemble of flowing water, fountains, and statuary, should be differentiated from a plain cistern, intended for the storage, and not the display, of water; cisterns, examples of which can be seen all over the Mediterranean area, were utilitarian objects and look like it. The *Notitia* lists only one cistern from this period, named after Domitius Modestus, a long-serving praetorian and urban prefect of Valens. Located in Region XI, the cistern of Modestus stood at a still higher point than the elevated aqueduct; we might think of it as the head reservoir of the new system, providing a steady flow of water to the great aqueduct and from there to the nymphaeum and subsidiary distribution points in the city. This is the first of the major urban reservoirs of Constantinople to be attested; others, and many private ones, were added later.[12]

In response to the work of the reign of Valens, orators spoke of a city that, dying of thirst before, was now plentifully supplied with water and, with the great aqueduct itself, of a nymphaeum established by the emperor's urban prefect and a cistern by his praetorian prefect, and they were not exaggerating.[13] As in the case of the harbour of Julian, however, we must be looking at the result of a longer programme of planning and surveying than can be attributed to the work of any one emperor (a programme no less complex and skilful than the modern archaeological research that has revealed it); we have seen that the construction in the Tenth Region of the massive 'Constantinianae' baths already anticipates an improved water supply in that part of the city, and that Jerome writes of the provision of water made possible by the aqueduct of Valens and Clearchus as something 'needed and long prayed for' (above, n. 10)—long, too, we may suspect, in

---

11. Gregory of Nazianzus, *Or.* 33.6 (*PG* 36.221C); the same image is used by Themistius, *Or.* 13.168a–b, trans. Simon Swain, *Themistius and Valens: Orations 6–13*, TTH 78 (2021), p. 336; Mango, *Développement Urbain*, p. 41; Crow, Bardill, and Bayliss, *Water Supply*, p. 14. The Pont du Gard delivered water to Nîmes from a distance of 50 km and a descent over that distance of 17 m; a grade of 0.00034%. The grade of the Constantinople aqueduct system is calculated at 0.7 m per km (0.0007%).

12. Janin, *Constantinople Byzantine*, pp. 206–15 lists six open and fifty-one covered cisterns from various periods; Mango, 'Water Supply', p. 15, refers to a total of 'close to 100'. The tally of publicly built cisterns fails to do justice to the private installations in the palaces and great houses. E. Mamboury in his guidebook entered twenty-two cisterns of various periods, several of them discovered by himself in the early years of the twentieth century. The discussion is placed on a new level by the work of Crow, Bardill, and Bayliss; on cisterns, pp. 125–55, with a concordance at 144ff. (170 cisterns in the areas covered by them).

13. Themistius, *Or.* 13.167d; Mango, *Développement Urbain*, p. 41.

the building. We might even think of the post-Constantinian development of Constantinople as a question of 'waiting for its water'. And this need continued. In the course of its development into the great metropolis of future centuries, the demands of Constantinople for water produced the most complex system of delivery and storage known from anywhere in the Roman world.

As the great aqueduct shows, the author of the *Notitia* did not include every monument or landmark that we would expect him to; it was enough for him to mention the cistern and nymphaeum that serviced the great structure. Passing from utilitarian to monumental, another absent landmark of which he must have been aware (it occurs neither in its regional catalogue nor in the *Collectio Civitatis* at the end of the text) is the Philadelphion. The omission is deserving of note because, as we saw in the description of processional routes (Chapter 3, p. 50f.), it was an important landmark, marking the division of the Mesē into its southern and northern branches.[14] We saw earlier (p. 108), the claim of the *Parastaseis* that the Philadelphion was once the site of a defensive outwork built by the emperor Carus, which would serve a marker of the expansion of the city at that time. A further, special reason for interest is the connection of the Philadelphion with one of the most familiar visual images of late Roman political life, the porphyry statues of imperial figures known as the 'Tetrarchs', taken as plunder in the Venetian sack of Constantinople in 1204 and now seen in a prominent position at the corner of St. Mark's cathedral—not far from the beautiful gilded horses that also came to Venice at this time (Fig. 7.7 and below, p. 169f.). The provenance of the figures at Constantinople and even their origin within the city were confirmed when, in an extraordinary archaeological *coup*, the missing left foot of one of them was found in explorations of the Byzantine church and later mosque known as Myrelaion (Bodrum Camii), a city block south of the Mesē just beyond the forum of Theodosius. The Myrelaion itself is not the site of the Philadelphion, but it is not far away, and we can easily imagine that the foot, broken off in the looting and reused as masonry ballast, may have wandered this short distance from its original location.

There is however a complication, for an under-appreciated problem with the identification of the figures as Tetrarchs is that they are from the wrong city. Those emperors (Diocletian, Maximian, Galerius, and Constantius the father of Constantine), antedate by a whole generation the foundation of Constantinople,

---

14. Müller-Wiener, *Bildlexikon*, pp. 266–67, with bibliography to the mid-1960s and an unconvincing reconstruction by P. Verzone, 'I due gruppi in porfido di S Marco in Venezia ed il Philadelphion di Constantinopoli', *Palladio* 1 (1958), pp. 8–14; Mango, *Développement urbain*, pp. 28–30.

FIG. 7.7 The 'Venice Tetrarchs'.

and its predecessor was not a city with which they had any serious connection.[15] They can hardly have been displayed at Byzantium before the foundation of Constantinople and it is unlikely that they would be made there at any later time; Constantine would have little reason, once his power was established, to commemorate the Tetrarchs. Who then are these imperial figures, and what were they doing at Constantinople?

That they are indeed emperors is implied by the material of which they are made, the porphyry stone, a rare Egyptian granite, being an imperial monopoly.

15. A passing visit of Diocletian (with Galerius?) to Byzantium on 10 November 294 has its own interest but does not count as such (Barnes, *New Empire*, p. 54).

A familiar example of its use is the great sarcophagus of Constantine's mother Helena from her burial place at the church of SS. Marcellinus and Peter by the via Labicana near Rome (now in the Vatican Museum). One might add the array of unfigured porphyry sarcophagi recovered from the imperial burial place at the Holy Apostles and now displayed in front of the Istanbul archaeological museum. The Venice figures can hardly be called naturalistic, but they are individually characterized, and it seems clear from the distinctions of age shown within the pairs of emperors and the differentiations in their individual features, that they are intended to represent four individuals shown in two sets of matching gestures. It would require a perverse ingenuity to argue that they are other than the Tetrarchs.

A second, often unnoticed feature, which may however help towards a solution, is that the Venice representations, sculptured in high relief but not in the round, are not free-standing statues. They have clearly been broken from a larger monument, on which, from the point of view of size and configuration, it is hard to see them as the major element, rather than as supporting figures in a larger presentation.

At this point two paragraphs in the later text known as *Parastaseis* (above, pp. 48, 59) have something to contribute, in describing the sculptural elements that characterized the Philadelphion. The paragraphs are mildly contradictory in their interpretations, but the differences are not significant; their authors are clearly describing the same pieces, even though they did not have certain knowledge of their identity.

The first text is brief and oblique, saying only that the sculptures at the Philadelphion commemorated the brotherly love of the sons of Constantine the Great, greeting each other at Constantinople after their father's death.[16] Not that they actually did meet in that place, the text correctly explains (the sons of Constantine never met after their father's death in 337, and their relations with each other after that moment were more murderous than familial), but that is where the meeting was commemorated. Given the poetic license allowed to propaganda, such a meeting need not have taken place for it to have been imagined and pictured, but this could only have been after the reduction of the number of Constantine's sons from three to two by Constans' elimination of his brother Constantine II in 340.

---

16. *Parastaseis* 48, 50; Preger, pp. 177–78; Berger, pp. 83–85; above, p. 50n. on the date of the *Parastaseis*. Among the items of evidence set out by Janin, p. 410; *Anthologia Palatina* 9. 799–810 records the building and/or repair of a mouseion and the placing there of a portrait of the emperor by a learned Christian named Mousélios, in poems written 'On the porphyry column in the Philadelphion'. Possibly this was the Musellius who was *praepositus sacri cubiculi* in 414, in which case the emperor in question would be Theodosius II; *PLRE* II, Musellius 1 (p. 768).

In the second paragraph of the *Parastaseis*, it is Constantine himself who is said to have used the monument (without saying that he built it) to commemorate his sons. In the words of the *Parastaseis*:

[Constantine] made statues of his sons next to that porphyry column, showing them seated on a throne. He made relief pictures of his deeds on that column, and Latin inscriptions which indicate the final days. The column stands opposite his two sons who are seated on a throne, and *the others who are embracing each other.*[17]

One can imagine various ways in which a porphyry column engraved with scenes of imperial achievement and inscribed Latin texts, seated statues of emperors, and others greeting each other can have been arranged. Whatever the identity of the figures seated on the throne, the sons 'who are embracing each other' look very much like the sculptures that we have, with the two seated figures forming the central features of the monument. These must in turn be the same as the seated figures, also made of porphyry, known in the Middle Ages as the 'honest judges', of which a description is given in a very late source (later even than the sack of Constantinople in which the extant statues were taken from the city), Manuel Chrysaloras (*c*.1350–1415).[18] The 'judges' sat on thrones at the junction of three roads between the sculptured columns of Theodosius and Arcadius; that is to say, at the divergence of the Mesē into its two branches, exactly where our evidence places the Philadelphion. It seems clear that we are looking at descriptions of the same monument, comprising the reliefs that we have, with other, seated figures, and a porphyry column with Latin inscriptions.

We should remember our earlier conclusion that, granted the differentiations of age between the two pairs of figures, their gestures and the distinctions in their features, we are looking at four persons shown in two pairs, each pair with one elder and one younger participant, who can hardly be other than the Tetrarchs. If so, it also becomes clear that we have been looking at the wrong city as their place of origin. The Tetrarchs had no connection with Byzantium before its re-foundation as Constantinople, and they are unlikely to have been commemorated there after it; Constantine had no motive to do so. The differentiations of age preclude the claim that they showed the sons of Constantine embracing each

---

17. *PLRE* II, Musellius 1 50 (Berger, p. 85). The reference to the 'final days' is a characteristic misreading of a Latin inscription that was no longer understood, while the claim that Constantine placed on the column a gilded and bejewelled image of the cross, in accordance with the cruciform figure he had seen in the sky, is an obvious anachronism.

18. Mango, *Développement Urbain*, p. 29 describes these statues from the medieval accounts, noting their location between the columns of Theodosius and Arcadius.

other (they would then have been shown as coeval), while there is no historical moment at which Constantine himself, if he were to be the older figure in each group, would be shown embracing just two rather than a greater number of sons. It should be added, that if the older of the two figures in each group were to be identified with Constantine, its features are unlike any other portrayals that we know of that emperor.

These difficulties make it appropriate to ask whether the statue group, and the monument of which it formed part, were brought in from somewhere else, acquiring in the process a newly adapted meaning. Constantinople had an insatiable appetite for imported works of art, and, as can be seen from their role as Venetian plunder, these were prize pieces; it is not so surprising that among their many descriptions, the *Parastaseis* should describe a work of art that we happen to possess. Attention is at once drawn to Diocletian's capital of Nicomedia, a city so built up by the generosity of previous emperors, in the words of Ammianus Marcellinus (22.9.3), that it resembled a region of the Eternal City herself; all of which lay in ruins after a major earthquake in 358, followed by an aftershock in 362 that destroyed much of what was left standing (Amm. Marc. 17.7.1, 22.13.5); after which it lapsed as an imperial capital city. Perhaps it was then that the Tetrarchs found a new home at Constantinople.

A possible setting for their transfer might lie in events of less than eighteen months after the second catastrophe at Nicomedia, when, on 26 February 364, in nearby Nicaea, the officer Valentinian was chosen as emperor to succeed Jovian. Leaving Nicaea, Valentinian entered Nicomedia on 1 March and from there proceeded to Constantinople, where on 28 March he took his younger brother Valens as his colleague. It was an outstanding moment of fraternal affection, acknowledged as such at the time. 'Most excellent imperator', said an outspoken senior general when the matter was being discussed, 'if you love your family you have a brother, but if you love the state, consider carefully whom you should choose!' (Amm. Marc. 26.4.1). Valentinian hid his annoyance and chose his brother. After spending the rest of the year at Constantinople, the brothers went to Sirmium, where they divided the empire, its administration, and its army, Valentinian taking the western provinces as his portion, and Valens the east, where he established his power after the defeat of the usurper Procopius.[19]

It is hard to think of a more apposite moment for a proclamation of brotherly love between emperors, and this may be the origin of the Philadelphion, the statues of the Tetrarchs from Nicomedia being given a new identity

---

19. As described in Ammianus Marcellinus Book 26; *The Roman Empire of Ammianus*, pp. 188ff. See below, Chapter 11 (p. 232f.).

as Valentinian and his brother at Constantinople, arranged to show not four, but two emperors in duplicate images in different parts of the monument, and other statues appearing as the enthroned 'honest judges' described by Manuel Chrysaloras. The joint rule of Valentinian and Valens, commemorated by a display of statuary originally intended to portray the Tetrarchs, seems an apt interpretation of the name of the Philadelphion. If so, the monument is another marker in the enlargement of the city from its Constantinian core to the developments of the Theodosian period. As the same time, it is worth adding that all these developments fall within the urban design laid out by Constantine, and should be considered within the framework of the intentions of the founder of the city.

A city expanding like Constantinople in the fourth century will make clear its needs for a developing infrastructure, without special regard for the government of the time. Its needs are inherent in its growth. We have seen this in the case of the harbour of Julian, whose transitory six months in the city were clearly not enough to accommodate the planning, building, and completion of the harbour named after him. The city's needs for an expanding harbour capacity will have become clear on their own account and in their context; there were city as well as resident imperial administrations, and the armies of men, architects and designers and building workers active in the city for the past thirty years, to whom the city's needs were of concern. This is not to imply that an emperor would have no interest in its development—of all the opportunities available to them, monumental building and urban development were matters to which emperors paid particular attention. Constantine's personal interest is obvious, from the day he marked out the new city's walls to the design of his mausoleum, and it would be strange if Constantius, whose fascination with the monumental grandeur of Rome is a guiding theme of Ammianus' description of his visit there in 356, came back with no ideas for the new Rome. If we were to search for the date of foundation of the Capitolium, listed by the *Notitia* in the Eighth Region, we might do worse than think of this emperor and context. Constantius' concern for his city is clear from the programme of legislation that he set in hand upon his return from the west—not to forget that it was this emperor under whom the great church of S. Sophia was dedicated, and who initiated the transformation of the mausoleum of the imperial family into the church of the Holy Apostles (Chapter 9 below, pp. 175–9).

We must also consider the physical and economic infrastructure required to sustain the city as it expanded to the higher ground on which its later developments rested. Here we encounter the massive aqueduct attributed to the emperor Valens, together with the cistern and nymphaeum connected with the names of his praetorian and urban prefects—adding the extensive surveying and building works outside the city to locate and channel the water sources to feed the system. As we have seen, Jerome, who will have seen the works in the first few years of their existence (he was in Constantinople in 381), described them as necessary and long desired, with Gregory of Nazianzus extolling the wonders of their construction (p. 132f.). As with the harbour of Julian, it is the emperor together with his officials who deserve the credit for the consummation of works which in their scale and complexity must have taken many years to accomplish—not to forget the expense. It is no accident that, after the massive losses somewhat ironically achieved by the austere Julian on his Persian campaign, both Valentinian in the west and, through his father-in-law Petronius, Valens in the east, were known for their parsimony and strict exaction, some said extortion, of taxes.

It is on the great aqueduct and its appurtenances that the monumental developments of the Theodosian period depended. Soaring aqueducts, wherever they are found (which is everywhere), are the most imposing monuments that we have to the Romans' skills in technology and construction, and in the careful management of a territory. As we admire their technical accomplishment, we should also acknowledge the quality of urban life that their utilitarian splendour made possible.

8

Urban Development (3)

THE THEODOSIAN AGE

THE DEVELOPMENTS JUST described extended the physical resources of Constantinople without changing the focus of its public life, which was still concentrated upon the eastern sectors of the city. The harbour of Julian lay below the hippodrome at no great distance from the forum of Constantine, while the 'makros embolos' linking the Mesē with the Golden Horn and the Propontis was not far beyond it; the great baths in Region X, whether correctly known as 'Constantinianae' or 'Constantianae', were not yet finished, and still in a somewhat isolated location. The aqueduct of Valens and its associated works, however, perhaps also the building of the Philadelphion, signalled an expansion of economic and social activity, and this pattern of development advanced further in the time of Theodosius, when the spread of urban activity west of the forum of Constantine produced a greater integration of the entire urban area and a significant shift of focus.[1] The key to this development was the forum of Theodosius, welcomed in a speech delivered by Themistius, in a series of lively images contrasting the city left behind by Constantine with the one now extended by Theodosius, and documenting the steady march westwards of the city and the growing integration of its parts:

> No longer is the vacant ground in the city more extensive than that occupied by buildings; nor do we cultivate more land within our walls than we occupy; the beauty of the city is no longer scattered over it in patches, but covers its whole area, like a robe embroidered to the very fringe. The city gleams with gold and porphyry. It has a new Forum, named after the emperor; it owns baths, porticoes, gymnasia; and its former extremity is

---

1. On this period of development Berger, 'Regionen und Strassen', pp. 402–9; and esp. Brian Croke, 'Reinventing Constantinople: Theodosius I's Imprint on the Imperial City', in MacGill, Sogno, and Watts (eds), *From the Tetrarchs to the Theodosians* (2010), pp. 141–64; also Chapter 11 below.

From Byzantium to Constantinople: An Urban History. John Matthews, Oxford University Press.
© Oxford University Press 2024. DOI: 10.1093/oso/9780197585498.003.0008

now its centre. Were Constantine to see the capital he founded he would behold a glorious and splendid scene, not a bare and empty void.[2]

The *Notitia*, a sort of administrative commentary on Themistius' eloquence, documents this process of urban development as it drew the city out to the walls of Constantine and shifted its economic centre to the west—a progression measured by the sequence of forums (Severus to Constantine to Theodosius to Arcadius) strung along the Mesē as it made its way to the Golden Gate. The development also tended to concentrate the economic activity and high population levels of the city on its southern side.

Inaugurated in 393 with an equestrian statue of the emperor added in the following year, the forum of Theodosius was constructed in a level area along the Mesē, about 600 metres west of the forum of Constantine. Combined with the physically extant evidence, the *Notitia* allows us to locate the forum and determine its configuration.[3] Its southern limit is shown by the continuing drainage channels running under a triumphal arch in its south-western corner, of which substantial remains exist on the southern side of Yeniçeriler Caddesi as it continues Divanyolu through Beyazit Square, itself representing the open space of the forum (Fig. 8.1).

The main part of the Theodosian forum was assigned to Region VII, which as we have seen faced Region VIII across the colonnades of the Mesē. In this northern section of the forum was erected a column of Theodosius, later styled 'Colonna Istoriata' for the spiral sculptures of which slight fragments remain. Its location in the northern part of the forum is confirmed by Vavassore's panorama, of which the detail shown below puts the column inside the walls of the Old Seraglio (Fig. 8.2).[4]

On the south side of the forum, as is shown by its attribution to Region VIII, stood a new basilica, and on that side too was the statue of a bull that gave to the forum its alternative name of Forum Tauri. According to the Byzantine writer Kedrenos, the dimensions of the basilica (which was destroyed by fire in 465), were 240 × 84 Roman feet, which, since we also know that it was built alongside rather than facing the forum, is a guide to the dimensions of the forum itself.[5]

---

2. Themistius, *Or.* 18; cited at van Millingen, p. 42. It was through Beyazit, the location of the forum of Theodosius, that the north-south measurement of the city was given; above, p. 121.

3. Müller-Wiener, *Bildlexikon*, pp. 258–65 (plan at p. 261); and Bauer, *Stadt, Platz und Denkmal*, pp. 187–203, with speculative reconstructions. For the date of inauguration and the equestrian statue, *Chron. Pasch.*, s.a. 393 and 394 (Whitby and Whitby, p. 55).

4. Mango, *Développement Urbain*, p. 45; Berger, pp. 148ff.

5. Berger, p.167 n. 95; Janin, *Constantinople Byzantine*, p. 176; Müller-Wiener, *Bildlexikon*, pp. 258–60. However, estimates of the dimensions of the basilica as *c.*80 × 28 m are over-generous, given that the Roman foot measures 11.65 inches (97 per cent of the English foot), and that the metre is 39.37 inches (109 per cent of the English yard of 36 inches). On these calculations, the length of the basilica is closer to 70 than 80 metres.

FIG. 8.1 Remains of the Arch of Theodosius. The relics frame the exit of the Mesē from the south-west corner of the Forum of Theodosius. The structure consisted of a central gateway between two pairs of columns, with smaller openings (as seen here) to either side. The curious pattern on the columns has been much discussed, and is generally taken to suggest a lopped tree trunk (rather than tears or peacock feathers); John Freely and Ahmet Cakmak, *Byzantine Monuments of Istanbul*, pp. 43–4, with reconstruction from Müller-Wiener, *Bildlexikon*, p. 263. Author's photograph.

We should imagine the Mesē as passing through the forum along the flank of the new basilica, and continuing beyond it through the arch of Theodosius, with the column of Theodosius dominating the forum on the right-hand, northern side.

The *Notitia* also mentions two 'magnos equites', equestrian statues, which, being listed under Region VII, must also have stood in the northern sector of the forum. Since we know that the equestrian statue of Theodosius mentioned earlier stood on top of his column, it is natural to think of them Theodosius' sons Arcadius and Honorius.[6] From the position of the monuments in the forum, the statue and column of Theodosius must have faced south, with his sons' statues placed on each side of the column, on what appear from their descriptions in the *Patria* to be matching quadruple arches (*tetrapyla*).[7]

---

6. As described at *Patria* 2.47 (from the *Parastaseis*; Preger, p. 176; Müller-Wiener, *Bildlexikon*, p. 262; Berger, pp. 82–83); the *Notitia* implies the same, placing the 'equites magnos duo' immediately after the column. I think it unlikely that the two statues were placed on the arches postulated by Mango at eastern and western entrances to the forum; their attribution to Region VII locates them with the column in the open space of the forum.

7. Mango, *Développement Urbain*, p. 44 n. 40.

An unexpected source of information on these statues may be the drawing of an imperial horseman that appears in a fifteenth-century manuscript once at Istanbul but now in the Library of the University of Budapest (Fig. 8.3). The drawing, in which the mounted figure holds an orb surmounted by a cross in his left hand and makes a gesture of address with his right, is thought to represent the famous equestrian statue of Justinian placed on a column erected in the Augusteion in 543 and described in detail by Procopius (*Buildings* 1.2.5–12). The discrepancy in the headgear, which Procopius describes as a crested helmet 'that gives the impression that the head moves up and down', but in the sketch more resembles a plumed tiara, may be explained by the replacement of the original headgear by a repaired or substitute version, after it fell off in the early ninth century and was restored to its place by an intrepid steeplejack. According to

FIG. 8.2 The column of Theodosius ('Colona Istoriata'). The column is seen in its position inside the wall of the Old Seraglio in a detail of the Vavassore panorama of Constantinople. Shown for clarity of detail from a metal copy of the original woodcut. Acknowledgement as for Fig. 3.2.

John Malalas, however, writing in the sixth century, the statue of Justinian was originally one of Arcadius that, as we have just noted, had stood on a pedestal in the forum of Taurus (or Theodosius). It cannot be the statue of Theodosius himself that surmounted his column, since that was still in place in the tenth century, but it is quite possible that the statue of his elder son was removed for its new purpose. An interpretation of the words on the flank of the horse, 'fon[s] gloriae perennis Theodosii', might be that they were added to the statue sometime after Arcadius' succession in 395, to celebrate the glory either of the first Theodosius, the emperor's father, or of the second, his son, who succeeded him in 408. After centuries in its new location, the statue was removed by Mehmet II and broken up to make cannon. It is the statue, understood by him to be of Justinian, of which Pierre Gilles saw the imposing remains in the 1550s, while it awaited its delivery to the foundries (above, p. 59).[8] What happened to its companion piece in the Theodosian forum, the statue of Honorius, we have no idea. There was no particular incentive for the house of Theodosius to keep it there for long.

Of the four forums listed by the *Notitia* for the entire city (a fifth was in the detached Region XIII at Sycae), the two not so far described were a forum of Theodosius located in the strategion in Region V, and the forum and column of Arcadius, listed as *forum Theodosiacum* in Region XII. The second of these is discussed below. The forum in the strategion, as much a remodelling of the strategion as a new construction, was an enhancement of the existing commercial district, in which is also noted a 'Theodosian cistern'. The Theban obelisk which according to the *Notitia* was erected in this forum may have been that seen by Pierre Gilles near the houses of the Sultan's glassworkers, where it was purchased by a Venetian nobleman and sent to Venice.[9]

Two other forum areas between those of Theodosius I and Arcadius, the Forum Bovis and the so-called Amastrianum, are not mentioned in the *Notitia* and must have come into being later. The *Notitia* does however list the 'brazen ox' (*bos aereus*) that gave its name to the later Forum Bovis. In doing so it documents the extension of the Eleventh Region, under which the ox is listed, as far as the southern branch of the Mesē. To be listed in Region XI, the ox must have stood on the northern side of the road, in the same way that we can tell that the statue of the bull in the forum of Theodosius must have stood to the south of the Mesē to be listed in Region VIII, with the column of Theodosius in the northern part of the forum.

---

8. See the articles of 1959 and 1991 reprinted in C. Mango, *Studies on Constantinople* (1993), chs 10 and 11. The notice of Malalas is at *Chron.* 18.94, s.a. 534; Elizabeth Jeffreys et al., *The Chronicle of John Malalas*, p. 287.

9. *Antiquities* 2.11 (ed. Musto, pp. 76–77). Gilles apparently saw the obelisk erected (or re-erected?) near the glaziers' houses and later on its side, when he measured it at 30 feet.

Under Region IX is listed a Theodosian warehouse (*horreum Theodosianum*), associated no doubt with the 'Theodosian harbour' of the adjacent Region XII, constructed by dredging out and enlarging the area of alluvial deposit left over time by the river Lykos. Like that of Julian, the harbour of Theodosius leaves its mark in the outline of the city, from which we can see that it may have added up to 1,500 metres to the available quayside capacity (Fig. 7.3).[10] Both harbour and warehouse reflect the needs of an increasing population for imported produce, also attested by the undoubtedly contemporary *horrea Alexandrina*, located in the same Ninth Region as the Theodosian warehouse.

The new installations were part of an extensive commercial development in this hitherto distant part of the city, and brought its harbour resources to the fullest extent that was ever achieved; nothing was added to them even in the periods of urban growth in the fifth and later centuries.[11] This lack of further development is in a way surprising, if for example we compare the total capacity of the three harbour areas, estimated as 1,500 metres of quayside in the old harbours on the Golden Horn, 1,000 metres in the harbour of Julian, and now 1,500 metres in the harbour of Theodosius, a total of 4,000 metres of moorings accommodating, on an optimistic estimate, around five hundred ships, with the 1,200 metres of quayside in the Severan harbour at Lepcis Magna.[12] It is possible that the harbour of Lepcis is an example of over-investment for reasons of prestige (though Lepcis was a great trading city, and the signs of wear and tear of mooring ropes on the quayside show use over a long period of time). A more proportionate comparison might be the 2,000 metres of harbour frontage at Ephesus, a city whose population may, in this period, approximate to that of Constantinople. Seen in this context, and allowing for the need to accommodate military as well as commercial vessels, the harbour of Theodosius may indicate some anticipation of the future needs of the city.

We must allow for adaptability in the management of harbours, and the understanding of local conditions. Every city is its own special case, and it is not

---

10. Müller-Wiener, *Bildlexikon*, pp. 60–61; Mango, *Développment Urbain*, pp. 39–40. For an introduction to the excavations, see Mark Rose and Şengül Aydingün, 'Under Istanbul', *Archaeology* (July/August 2007), pp. 34–40; and for detailed discussion, Andreas Külzer, 'Der Theodosioshafen in Yenikapı, Istanbul: ein Hafengelände im Wandel der Zeit', in Falko Daim (ed.), *Die byzantinischen Hafen Konstantinopels: Byzanz zwischen Orient und Okzident* 4 (2016), pp. 35–50. The quayside capacity is a rough calculation from the outline of the harbour.

11. Mango, p. 40; above, Chapter 7 with plans (p. 128f.).

12. The estimate of Mango, p. 38, of five hundred vessels in harbour at one time, of the 3,600 vessels needed to supply the city with grain, is approximate and only meant to indicate orders of magnitude. It may be that an average of beam of 8 m is an under-estimate of the size of the ships, and that more space needs to be allowed to manoeuvre the vessels into position at the quayside.

easy to convert the physical capacity of harbours into the type of traffic that used them. We should however compare an estimated requirement of around 8 metres to provide mooring for a regular merchant ship, to the much larger vessels that are on record, especially the massive ships used to bring grain from Alexandria. The most famous of them, the ship described by Lucian as blown off its course from Alexandria to Rome into the harbour at Piraeus where it became a magnet for sightseers, is said to have had a beam equivalent to almost 15 metres.[13] Not all the ships that berthed in the harbours of Constantinople will have been of this order of magnitude, but some were, if the Horrea Alexandrina just mentioned are any guide to their origin. Nor of course were all seagoing ships ever in harbour at the same time (how long did it take to turn a ship around and have it at sea again?), and the arrival of the grain-ships from Alexandria was predictable by the season; their arrival could be anticipated and preparations made. The majority of ships that came into the harbours were no doubt an assortment of vessels of various sizes and all sorts of destinations and points of origin.

To give some impression of the scale of operations, in Diocletian's *Edict on Maximum Prices* from more than twenty years before the foundation of Constantinople, the costs of transport of cargoes by sea are given between a number of major harbours in east and west. Including Byzantium, an important harbour before it ever became an imperial capital, and Nicomedia because Byzantium inherited its position, the list of harbours is as follows (it is assumed that the specified routes were in both directions):

Alexandria to Nicomedia and Byzantium;
Oriens (the diocese) to Byzantium;
Nicomedia to Rome, Ephesus, Thessalonica, Achaia, Salona, Pamphylia, Phoenice, Africa;
Byzantium to Rome, Trapezus, Amastris, Sinope, Tomi.

It is what the Roman equivalent of an international shipping harbour looked like.[14] It is of course also likely that Constantinople was able to service its suburban and detached areas, like Sycae, Regium, and the military establishment at Hebdomon, from satellite ports in the Bosporus and Propontis (as we saw in

---

13. Lionel Casson, *Ships and Seamanship in the Ancient World* (1971), pp. 186–89. More typical is the 7/10 m beam accepted by Mango from J. Rougé, *Recherches sur l'Organisation de Commerce Maritime en Mediterranée sous l'Empire Romain* (1966), pp. 69–71.

14. The list of harbours is compiled from §XXXV in the edition of M. Giacchero, *Edictum Diocletiani et Collegarum de pretiis rerum venalium* (Genoa, 1974), with the additional fragment from Aphrodisias published by Joyce Reynolds and Charlotte Roueché, *Aphrodisias in Late Antiquity* (1989), pp. 393–97.

Chapter 3, the fishing industry was distributed among many smaller ports along the Bosporus). As in the case of the harbour of Julian, the location of the harbour of Theodosius at some distance from the southern exit of the Bosporus must have helped to alleviate the difficulties sometimes experienced by ships approaching Constantinople from the south.

Tracing the development of the city through the *Notitia*, we have reached the walls of Constantine and the limit of what is covered by the text. The walls are acknowledged for their grandeur in the topographical introduction to Region XII, the first entry of which is the Golden Gate of Constantine and the second, between the Golden Gate and the forum of Arcadius, the colonnades known as *porticus Troadenses*, which presumably linked them. We do not specifically know whether the colonnades extended the whole length of the southern extension of the Mesē to its division at the Philadelphion, but it is likely that they did so.[15]

Other amenities from the Theodosian period include public bathing establishments named after members of the dynasty; the *thermae Arcadianae* in Region I, and two sets of baths, *Honorianae* and *Eudocianae*, in the densely populated Region V. Unless it was simply renamed then, the last of these cannot have preceded the marriage of Licinia Eudocia to Theodosius II in 421, while the *Honorianae*, as we know from a law of 412, were being enhanced by an avenue of colonnades, on land acquired by exchange for property elsewhere in the city; the baths may have been started under Theodosius I and named in honour of his son, or by Arcadius and named after his brother at a time when the name of Honorius was held in regard at the eastern court.[16] There were also *thermae Honorianae* together with a *forum Honorianum* in Region XIII (Sycae), and a cistern of Arcadius in Region XI, out by the city wall; these too could have been named in the later years of Theodosius I, when Arcadius and Honorius were heirs-apparent, or at certain times after their joint succession in 395.

Although the *Notitia* lists four cisterns in the grand total of the *Collectio Civitatis*, only three are named in the text itself: the cisterns of Modestus in Region XI, of Theodosius in Region V, and of Arcadius just mentioned as in Region XI. Which, if any, of the known cisterns of Constantinople accounts for the missing item is not clear—some of the most famous, such as those of Aspar and St. Mocius outside the Constantinian walls, and the 'cistern of the basilica' at the Augusteum, belong to a later period. A possible candidate is a cistern constructed in

---

15. Hesychius connects the Troadensian colonnades with the wall of Constantine; above, Chapter 3 (p. 49). The only connection with the *horrea Troadensia* of Region V is the recurrence of the Troad in the nomenclature of the new Rome.

16. *CTh* 15.1.51. The law concerns the exchange of real estate between the baths and the ancient basilica, presumably the one near the Augusteum (p. 86). The marriage of Eudocia and Theodosius was on 7 June 421; K. G. Holum, *Theodosian Empresses* (1982), p. 115.

407 under the pavement of the forum of Constantine, according to an entry in the sixth-century *Chronicle* of Marcellinus which is well informed on Constantinople. A second candidate, the immense open cistern of Aetius, completed, again according to Marcellinus, in 421, cannot be the missing item in the *Notitia* since it is outside the city walls of Constantine. This cistern, otherwise connected with Theodosius II's sister Pulcheria, was an important facility, its inauguration being attended by the emperor as a great public occasion. With a depth of 15 metres and a surface area of 244 × 84 metres (an immense capacity), the basin has more than enough room for the football stadium that it now houses.[17]

The development of the water regime, an essential element in the sustained growth of the city, can be described in terms of an increase of supply by the enhancement of existing sources, the exploitation of more distant sources, and an increase of storage facilities in the form of cisterns. This picture is that of the *Notitia* as well as of the modern research mentioned earlier (p. 133n.), and conforms to the broader account presented here of the development of the city; a design of Constantine filled out by his first successors, and only expanding in the later fourth century to fill the entire area within his city walls. The harbour named after Julian is a sign of the expanding needs of the city, without taking its physical development beyond the Constantinian framework, but this was to change in the succeeding years, with the building of the forum of Theodosius, and the establishment of the harbour of Theodosius, to the west of that of Julian. This expansion of the commercial configuration of the city was matched by an enlargement of its food management resources in the form of new *horrea* for the storage and distribution of grain and other imported foodstuffs. All of this development, recorded by the *Notitia*, was within the framework established for the city by Constantine.

The third forum listed under the name of Theodosius is what is generally known as the forum of Arcadius with its column, of which the base, still in situ, helped to identify Cerrahpaşa Caddesi as the southern extension of the Mesē (above p. 115f.).[18] The base, pictured here in its present condition (Fig. 8.4), stands on the north side of Cerrahpaşa Caddesi in the untidy little square, formerly the Slave-Girl Market, which is all that is left of the forum. From a house abutting its northern side it is still possible to enter the hollow base of the column to see the first steps of the internal staircase that led to the top, and the column was covered by a spiral frieze, suggested

---

17. *Chron. Pasch.*, s.a. 421; cf. Whitby and Whitby, p. 68; there is some confusion arising from there being two names for the same cistern. The cistern is marked on plans of Istanbul as a sporting field. According to Janin, p. 204 (published in 1964), the conversion took place in 1962.

18. Müller-Wiener, *Bildlexikon*, pp. 250–53, with street and 2-metre contour plan at 251 (Abb. 284); Franz Alto Bauer, *Stadt, Platz und Denkmal*, pp. 203–12 and Abb. 67. The lower right-hand corner of Müller-Wiener's plan shows the western extremity of the harbour of Theodosius. The location of the forum, which stands at 42 m, was known as Xerolophos, 'Dry Ridge'.

FIG. 8.3 Drawing of an imperial horseman. The drawing, from a fifteenth-century manuscript formerly held in the Seraglio Library at Istanbul and from 1877 at Budapest, is thought to represent the equestrian statue of Justinian placed on a column erected on the southern side of the Augusteum in 543 and described in detail by Procopius (*Buildings* 1.2.5–12). According to Malalas, the statue was originally one of Arcadius that had previously stood on a pedestal in the Forum of Taurus (or Theodosius), and this is supported by the reference to 'two large equestrian statues', presumed to be the sons of Theodosius I, Arcadius and Honorius, that stood in the forum at the time of the *Notitia*. It cannot be the statue of Theodosius himself that stood on his column in the Forum Tauri, since that was still in place in the tenth century. A possible interpretation of the words on the flank of the horse, 'fon[s] perennis gloriae Theodosii' ('source of the eternal glory of Theodosius')

both in Buondelmonti's plan of the city and in the Vavassore woodcut of a century later. The monument was erected in 402, shortly after the events portrayed on it, but the statue of Arcadius surmounting it was put in place only in 421, long after the death of its honorand in 408.[19] The Theodosius after whom the forum is named in the *Notitia* is of course Arcadius' successor Theodosius II (408–50). In Buondelmonti's plan, the column is placed in its correct position relative to the column of Theodosius at Beyazit and the Lykos valley, and, in some versions of the plan, to the Golden Gate ('porta antiquissima pulchra') of Constantine (p. 119). It is a cardinal point in the articulation of the city.

The column was dismantled as unsafe in 1715, but had earlier been drawn by visiting artists, especially in a partial version now in the Louvre, and in that given to the library of Trinity College, Cambridge, by E. H. Freshfield, who had inherited the drawings from his father and published them with commentary in the journal *Archaeologia* of 1921/2.[20] The drawings were made by an unknown artist for Stefan Gerlach, who was in Istanbul as chaplain to an envoy of Maximilian II to the Ottoman court in 1574. Their general accuracy becomes more evident as one studies them, and there is a control of their quality in drawings by the same artist of the still extant obelisk base of Theodosius in the hippodrome. The images shown here and elsewhere in this book are from an excellent new digital version made available by the kind permission of the Librarian and Fellows of Trinity College, Cambridge.

The western face of the column base, as shown in the Freshfield drawings (Fig. 8.6), reveals two important features of its northern side, the entrance

Continued

might be that they were added to the statue of Arcadius as the origin of the glory of Theodosius II. The statue was taken down by Mehmet II and broken up for the foundry. In the 1550's Pierre Gilles saw its fragments and reported that the leg of Justinian exceeded the author's own height, the nose was over nine inches long and one of the horse's hoofs nine inches in height. C. Mango, *Studies on Constantinople* (1993), Chapters X & XI (originally published 1991 and 1959).

---

19. The date of the column is given by Theophanes as 402/3; for the dedication of the statue, *Chron. Pasch.*, s.a. 421 (Whitby and Whitby, p. 69).

20. E. H. Freshfield, 'Notes on a Vellum Album Containing Some Original Sketches of Public Buildings and Monuments, Drawn by a German Artist Who Visited Constantinople in 1574', *Archaeologia* 22 (1922), pp. 87–104 with plates XV–XXIII. References are to aspect (east, south, west) and register (1–13) of the column. Müller-Wiener, *Bildlexikon*, p. 252 (Abb. 285), shows the western face of the base, with fragmentary traces of the sculptures; see Franz Alto Bauer, n. 18 above, and the classic treatments by Kollwitz and Becatti; also Alessandro Taddei, 'La Colonna di Arcadio a Constantinopoli. Profilo storico di un monumento attraverso le fonti documentali dale origine all'età moderna' (reference unavailable), pp. 38–102 with plates; pdf text available on Academia.edu.

FIG. 8.4 Base of Arcadius column viewed from the east. Author's photograph.

doorway to the spiral staircase, and the absence of decorative carving on this aspect of the base. The entrance was on its least frequented side, which was left unadorned at what we may call the back of the monument. The primacy of the opposite, southern face is confirmed by the drawing of the summit of this side of the column (Fig. 8.5). Here we see that the spiral staircase opens out onto a balcony (no doubt with balustrade), from which an observer could look down over

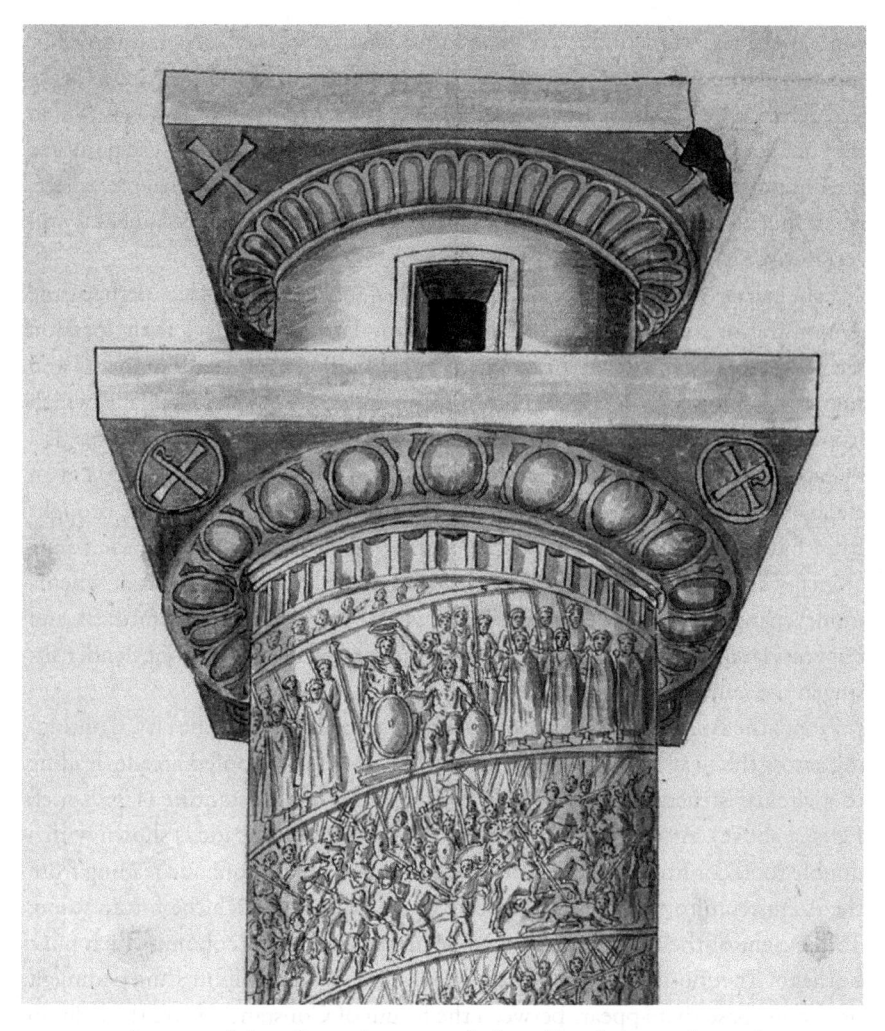

FIG. 8.5 Summit of Arcadius column, south face. The drawing shows the viewing platform overlooking the forum.

the forum and across the Mesē, with a view to the harbour of Theodosius and the Propontis. From the alignment of the column and its location on the north side of Cerrahpaşa Caddesi, we may conclude that it stood in the northern sector of the forum of Arcadius and faced south over it. The same was true of its precursor in the forum of Theodosius, where a position in the northern sector of the forum, indicated by its attribution to the Seventh Region, is confirmed by the panorama of Vavassore (Fig. 8.2 above).

As to the events narrated on the column, despite Freshfield's view, supported by J. B. Bury, that they concerned an episode of the 380s, there is now general agreement that the subject of the reliefs is the uprising in 399 of the Gothic general Gainas, who conducted some sort of coup d'état at Constantinople but was forced by popular demonstrations to leave the city, to be followed into Thrace and defeated by a Roman army under Fravitta.[21] The events and the way in which they are portrayed are highly interesting in themselves, but more to the point for present purposes is that, in narrating them, the reliefs provide a visual retrospective of fourth-century Constantinople even as a sort of pictorial commentary on certain aspects of the *Notitia*.

The narrative begins with an agitated scene in a public place, perhaps the demonstrations that forced Gainas' withdrawal from the city; their location seems to have been the Augusteum, to judge by the array of monuments and statues depicted (W1 > S1; Figs 8.7–8). The appearance of an elephant, which from the absence of any indication of a pedestal seems intended to be taken as a living creature and not a statue, is disconcerting, until we read in the *Patria* of an elephant who was a well-known figure in the city at precisely this time. Brought from India in the time of Theodosius and raised at Constantinople, the young animal was led into the hippodrome and on the way suffered an insult when a moneychanger for a joke hit him with a switch. The elephant remembered, and ten years later, when he was fully grown, encountered the same moneylender sitting in the same place as before, and killed him.[22]

From the Augusteum, the action moves westwards through the city. Continuing across the next two frames of the frieze (S1 > E1) is a roofed arcade, leading to a circular structure that can only be the forum of Constantine (Fig. 8.9; cf. Fig. 6.9 above). At its point of entry into the forum, the arcade is shown with a double roof, confirming its identification as the double colonnade leading from the Augusteum to the gates of the Severan city, beyond which the forum stood. To the right of the forum we see at some distance a further column which must be that of Theodosius; and if so, then the monument with columns and pediment on a stone base that appears between the forum of Constantine and the column of Theodosius should be the 'bronze tetrapylon' which stood at the intersection

21. J. H. W. G. Liebeschuetz, *Barbarians and Bishops: Army, Church and State in the Age of Arcadius and Chrysostom* (1990), appendix II at pp. 273–78 and plates 1–7—with bibliography, to which I would add Michael McCormick, *Eternal Victory: Triumphal Rulership in Late Antiquity, Byzantium and the Early Medieval West* (1986), pp. 49–50; Alan Cameron and Jacqueline Long, with Lee Sherry, *Barbarians and Politics at the Court of Arcadius* (1993), pp. 238, 247–48.

22. *Patria* 3 ('On Buildings'), 89; Preger, pp. 247–48; Berger, pp. 182–83. The *New York Times* Science Section, dated Tuesday 11 August 2020, carried a story of an Asian elephant named Mara, who when sold by one circus to another encountered her former trainer and killed him. After a miserable period in a zoo, the story ends happily in a wild-life refuge in Brazil.

FIG. 8.6 Base of Arcadius column from the west, showing the undecorated north face with doorway to the spiral staircase inside the column.

of the Mesē with the important cross-road later known as the 'long colonnade' or 'colonnade of Domninus' (p. 114).

If this reading is correct, this section of the frieze picks out the most conspicuous features of the Mesē from the Augusteum to the forum of Theodosius. After the division of the Mesē beyond the forum of Theodosius, Gainas must have followed the northern branch, since his way out of the city took him into Thrace. This seems to be the perspective assumed by the reliefs in the next register, which show Gainas leaving Constantinople behind a structure that must be intended as the city wall as he

FIG. 8.7 Arcadius column (W1); Popular agitation in the Augusteum.

FIG. 8.8 Arcadius column (S1); statues and monuments in the Augusteum. The (real) elephant, the figure of Victory and the mythological scene (cf. Figs. 6.9, 8.9) may allude to the nearby Hippodrome.

advances behind it (W2; Fig. 8.10). The row of double arches in the background may represent the aqueduct of Valens, reversing the actual topography of Constantinople so as not to omit so prominent a feature of it. Viewed from the north, as visualized in this scene, the aqueduct runs on the near side of the Mesē, not beyond it.

The other structures shown in this segment are described by Liebeschuetz as 'a two-towered gate, what looks like the narthex of a major church, and in the

FIG. 8.9 Arcadius column (E1); Augusteum, double colonnade and Forum of Constantine. Two men draw water from a cistern for a customer; on the mythological scene shown above this group see above and Fig. 6.9. To the right, bronze Tetrapylon (?) and, in the distance, the column of Theodosius.

background a two-storeyed or even three-storeyed colonnade' (p. 275). If the last of these is after all the aqueduct of Valens, the church might be one of the three churches mentioned by the *Notitia* in the Seventh Region. It does not have the characteristics of the mausoleum of Constantine, as converted in 370 to become the church of the Apostles.

We are next shown Gainas' departure from the city, with a figure of Victory hovering overhead in the compositional frame provided by a city gate, brandishing what looks like a wreath of victory (S2; Fig. 8.11); the figure whom she is addressing, presuming this to be Gainas, seems to be recoiling from the gesture. Another female figure, perhaps the Tychē of the city, seems to bar the gate to prevent his return—Victory and Tychē, it is an old combination! Gainas' status as a refugee is suggested by the presence of a child at his side; the Roman army that will defeat him makes it appearance at a later juncture of the narrative. The gate must be imagined as the so-called 'gate of Attalus' terminating the northern branch of the Mesē at the wall of Constantine. These events took place, and the frieze was designed, before the building of the land walls of Theodosius II, which form no part of the story; we are still looking at the framework of the Constantinian city. Only one element in the narrative of warfare that follows is relevant to topography, the image of a failed attempt to cross the Hellespont with men struggling in the

FIG. 8.10 Arcadius column (W2); Gainas and his followers in the city. Behind the departing Goths is a double tower with gateway, what appears to be a major church (perhaps one of those listed by the *Notitia* in Region VII), and in the background a long series of double arches perhaps representing the aqueduct of Valens.

water.[23] The *Notitia* lists a marble warship (*liburna*), which stood in the fourth region in commemoration of the sea-battle, possibly referring to this recent event. The images presented at Figs 8.12–13 (W5, 7) are representative of this phase of the narrative.

Turning our attention, finally, to the summit of the column, we see, on its southern and most prominent side, the crowning of Arcadius with a wreath of victory (S13; Fig. 8.14). As mentioned, the forum of Arcadius was established in 402/3, six years before the death of its honorand. We do not know how long it took to compose the frieze or to complete the column (they were intricate structures), but the statue on the summit was placed there only in 421, many years after Arcadius' death. The time-lag suggests an intriguing line of interpretation. The figure of Arcadius shown receiving the crown stands on a little pedestal—that is to say, he is a statue (as in the scenes in the Augusteum at the start of the narrative), in recognition of the fact that, with Arcadius dead these many years, the events shown on the frieze already belong to the past; one could hardly show Arcadius as a living emperor. Still more intriguing then, the figure of Arcadius with its pedestal is shown on the frieze just as the viewer of the southern aspect of

---

23. Better understood in the Louvre version of the reliefs than in the Freshfield drawings; E9, cf. Liebeschuetz, plate 3.1. Müller-Wiener, p. 250 Abb. 283, gives an overall view of the Louvre drawing of the column (late seventeenth century).

FIG. 8.11 Arcadius column (S2; Gainas leaves the city. He is escorted by a winged Victory; a female figure, possibly the Tychē of Constantinople, bars his return. Behind the procession are what look like armed soldiers supervising its exit.

FIG. 8.12 Arcadius column (W5); pastoral scene in Thrace. A herdsman tends his animals, and behind him are country folk in their huts or summer settlement (it does not look like a Gothic encampment, and the herdsman is facing in the opposite direction from the Goths).

FIG. 8.13 Arcadius column (W7); Goths and Romans. The Goths advance by the banks of a river (or the Hellespont), shadowed by a Roman fleet. In the top left-hand corner a shipbuilder is working on a new vessel.

FIG. 8.14 Arcadius column (S13); summit of the column (cf. Fig. 8.5 above). Arcadius stands on a pedestal (i.e. statue base) among courtiers and being crowned by Victory. Beside him, seated, is possibly his son Theodosius, under whom the statue surmounting the column was erected.

the column would see the actual statue standing above it. The frieze, which began with the early fourth-century monumental area of Constantinople, takes us through time to its most recent acquisition, the column of Arcadius itself and the late emperor's statue on its summit.[24]

---

24. On the uppermost register of the eastern side (E13) is another imperial figure, possibly Honorius, shown as sharing his colleague's victory and thereby asserting the unity of eastern and western imperial regimes. The scene is higher up the gradient of the spiral frieze than the crowning of Arcadius, but on the less prominent eastern face. It may not be an emperor at all, but (for example) the victorious Fravitta.

9

Other Monuments, Palaces, and Churches

IN CHAPTERS 6–8 the *Notitia urbis Constantinopolitanae* was used with other evidence to trace the development of the city, from the Archaic and Classical Greek city of Byzantium on the site chosen by its founders north of the acropolis, clustering around its harbours on the Golden Horn, through its expansion along both sides of the acropolis to the area south of it through the first centuries of the Roman empire, to the monumental development of the city under the Severi. A critical moment in the story was the city's forgiveness for its support of a usurper, followed by its promotion as a colony and the rebuilding of its walls—the walls that defended the city in the third century and faced Constantine in the campaign against Licinius that gave him command of a united empire. The impact of Constantine's victory was immediate and comprehensive. Within the enlarged framework of new walls planned immediately after the defeat of Licinius, the city of Constantine was set to grow into the capital city imagined by the emperor, though it rested with Constantine to achieve only the first stages of its growth. These involved the building of a new palace adjacent to a hippodrome and monumental baths that may have been left unfinished from the Severan period. Next to these were monumental developments certainly of Severan origin, including a forum or agora and colonnades leading to a city gate, beyond which Constantine established his own forum with his column and statue in the middle. Constantine's intention to have his city grow to its limit within the walls designed by him was made clear by the building of the Golden Gate as the main entrance to the city along a new road from Regium, and by the establishment of the imperial mausoleum in a relatively distant part of the urban area. The filling of this space as far as the new walls—the city described by the *Notitia*—was for his successors to achieve as the city grew into its role as the major capital city of the eastern empire, succeeding Nicomedia and, in due course, surpassing, though never, in this period, entirely replacing Antioch.[1]

---

1. See the observations of Sylvain Destephen cited above at Chapter 4, n. 25; esp. 'From Mobile Center to Constantinople: The Birth of Byzantine Imperial Government', *DOP* 73 (2019), pp. 9–23, with illuminating maps at pp. 15 and 18.

From Byzantium to Constantinople: An Urban History. John Matthews, Oxford University Press.
© Oxford University Press 2024. DOI: 10.1093/oso/9780197585498.003.0009

Along with its monumental development, we have also seen the westward movement in the economic focus of the city, through a sequence of monuments and forums strung out along the branches of its arterial roads, what was called above its 'armature'. The growth of the city as seen in its public monuments requires a corresponding development of its infrastructure. This took time. Only under Julian, whether or not he completed it, do we find a new harbour on the southern coast of the peninsula; until this time visitors to the city, its imports of food and materials and supplies for such institutions as the palace and hippodrome, needed to be brought into the harbours on the Golden Horn and transported across the peninsula—not a great distance, but unnecessary when there was sea on both sides. We have seen too an expansion of the water supply of the city as its needs increased, its building levels became more elevated and its economic activity moved further into the peninsula. The whole area of the Theodosian forum, from the later fourth century a focal point of the economic and social activity of the city, could not have functioned without the development of the water supply documented from the reign of Valens, one of the greatest achievements of its kind from anywhere in the Roman empire. We should add the building of a new harbour of Theodosius on the southern shore of the peninsula, with associated storehouses and granaries matching those by the old harbours on the Golden Horn. The sculptured frieze of the column of Arcadius, standing in the latest forum to be registered by the *Notitia*, offered a narrative overview of the city as it stood in the early fifth century.

For all of this, the evidence of the *Notitia* was of central importance, both in its own right and as offering a measured control of what we know from other sources, but there is still much to add, before we pass on to the question of housing in Chapter 10. The *Notitia* includes features that do not fall under the categories reviewed so far, and adds some major items, including significant monuments that appear in the *Collectio Civitatis* but not under the Regions to which they belonged. It also omits some that one would expect to have been included. All were part of the architectural, economic, and therefore human landscape that we should imagine for the city.

9.1 Colonnades, Arches and Gateways, Columns and Obelisks

Most immediately obvious in defining the character of the city (seeing it through the eyes of a visitor) are the fifty-two *porticus*, or grand colonnades, of the *Collectio Civitatis*, their numbers under individual regions ranging from one to seven colonnades.[2] These were clearly a prominent aspect of the city and must have done much to establish the visual impression that it made. The total number of colonnades as listed under the separate Regions can be made to match that in the *Collectio* on the assumption that the named 'porticus Fanionis' of Region IV and the 'porticus semirotunda' or 'Sigma' of Region III are not included in the totals of four and five colonnades respectively listed under these Regions. A problem with this assumption might be that neither the *porticus Fanionis* nor Sigma is separately listed in the *Collectio*; in these and one or two other cases where a colonnade is individually mentioned under a particular Region, we cannot be sure whether it is meant to be included either in the total given for that Region or in the grand total in the *Collectio*.[3] Given that these are only a few among the relatively large numbers we are dealing with, the uncertainty is not very serious, especially when we consider the more general problem that we are not even sure how colonnades were counted—whether the colonnades on each side of a street were counted separately, and whether a continuous colonnade might have been counted in separate sections as it left one Region and entered another.[4] Both seem likely assumptions. In the case of Regions VII and VIII, it seems obvious that the colonnades on each side of the Mesē between the forums of Constantine and Theodosius would be counted separately, and it is likely too that in other cases where a colonnaded street formed a boundary between Regions one side is counted under each Region.[5] This would account for the single colonnade listed under Region VI, if a colonnaded street formed the boundary with one of its neighbours. Such an explanation will not account for the single colonnade of Region XIII (Sycae), which has no neighbour. It seems likely that the *porticus maior* of this Region framed both sides of the single main street by which the Region is characterized, clinging to the only level ground available for it. This case is best treated as an exception.[6]

A further complication is that *porticus* did not only exist in the form of continuous colonnades along main avenues, but also to frame public spaces. The forum of Constantine contained two-storied colonnades on each side of its circular space, which was itself divided between three Regions (V–VII), with a

---

2. Marlia Mundell Mango, 'The Porticoed Street at Constantinople', in Nevra Necipoğlu, *Byzantine Constantinople: Monuments, Topography and Everyday Life* (2001), pp. 29–51, at 44ff.

3. Viz. 'porticus magna una' (Region VI); 'porticus Troadenses' (Region XII); see note 7.

4. Marlia Mundell Mango, at p. 45, assumes, I think correctly, that colonnades are counted separately on each side of a street, and as they passed from Region to Region.

5. '*porticus sinistra* Taurum usque' (Region VIII); cf. Region VII, introduction: '*a parte dextra* columnae Constantini usque ad forum Theodosii continuis extensa [sc. regio] porticibus.'

6. Region XIII, introduction: 'tota lateri montis adfixa praeter unius plateae tractum, quam subiacentium eidem monti litorum tantum praestat aequalitas.'

fourth Region (III) touching it. It is impossible to say how these colonnades were distributed between these Regions or how they were counted, and the same problem must occur elsewhere, for example in the forum of Theodosius, which is also divided between different Regions.[7]

It is probably best to use the fifty-two colonnades of the *Notitia* to create an impression of the city as a whole rather than as a tool of analysis of particular parts of it, though it may occasionally be possible to attempt this. An example may be Region VII just mentioned, where the topographical introduction mentions 'continuous colonnades' on the right-hand side of the Mesē from the forum of Constantine to that of Theodosius, with others running in a similar fashion along the roads striking out from the Mesē towards the Golden Horn.[8] If we subtract from the total of six grand colonnades listed under Region VII the right-hand portico of the Mesē, we are left with an odd number of colonnades, one of which might be accounted for by the boundary with Region VI. This leaves four porticos, which we can understand as flanking two main streets leaving the Mesē for the north in the manner described by the *Notitia*. There must have been such streets, and it seems safe to assume their existence in a plan of the city.

Among other architectural features, the *Collectio* correctly distinguishes the porphyry column of Constantine from the two columns, of Theodosius and Arcadius, that were constructed around an inner staircase giving access to the summit. Nothing is said, either in the main text of the *Notitia* or in the *Collectio*, of the 'column of the Goths' below the northern slopes of the acropolis, possibly because it was seen as a relatively ordinary monument of no particular interest (even though it may well have been of the Constantinian period).[9] It should however have a bearing on local topography, on the assumption that it stood in an open space, to be viewed by the public from the distance that such a monument requires. This might well be the strategion or part of it, which we have seen as a feature of the Greek city, later subdivided to form a secondary forum of Theodosius (I or II).

As we saw earlier, the *Notitia* lists under its different names the Golden Milestone otherwise known as the *tetrapylon aureum* in the Augusteum, but not the 'bronze tetrapylon' that was an important architectural feature marking a crossroads on the Mesē between the forums of Constantine and Theodosius (p. 114). Nor does it mention the arch of Theodosius that formed the western entrance to his forum, although it does list the column and equestrian statues that stood in the forum,

---

7. Note also the 'porticus Troadenses' of Region XII, leading along both sides of the Mesē from the golden gate at least as far as the forum of Arcadius. The region also included three 'grand colonnades', which could have surrounded the forum of Arcadius.

8. 'a parte dextera columnae Constantini usque ad forum Theodosii continuis extensa porticibus et *de latere aliis quoque pari ratione porrectis*'; Berger, 'Straße und Regionen', pp. 366, 397.

9. Chapter 5, n. 44.

and the statue of the bull that gave to the forum its alternative name. From the description in the *Notitia* and other sources, we can be sure that the column of Theodosius and the two equestrian statues stood in the northern part of the forum, and the bull on the southern side of the Mesē at its south-eastern entrance (p. 88). The *Notitia* thus leaves us to grasp the architectural character of the Mesē as it made its way through a series of monumental gateways marking the city's development to the west; from the Milion through the double colonnades to the eastern entrance to the forum of Constantine at the site of the old city gate, through the corresponding archway at the western end to the bronze tetrapylon and the arch of Theodosius, and on through the forum of Arcadius to the Golden Gate.

Perhaps surprisingly to us, the *Notitia* fails to mention the famous obelisk erected in the hippodrome by Theodosius' prefect of Constantinople, Proclus, whose inscription on the base of the obelisk records in both Latin and Greek versions how the obelisk was raised in the space of thirty days, with a picture to show how the job was done (Fig. 9.1).[10] We also see the emperor Theodosius and his court receiving submissive envoys of Goths and Persians, as if he had defeated peoples with whom he had at best made equivocal agreements, facing the assembled hippodrome crowds in exactly the same place as he was accustomed to in reality (Fig. 9.2).

Theodosian Constantinople shared with Augustan Rome a taste for obelisks. A 'square Theban obelisk' that stood in the forum of Theodosius in the strategion is mentioned as an integral part of the forum; as we saw earlier, it may have been the obelisk seen by Pierre Gilles lying on its side near the Golden Horn. The *Collectio* includes the forum in its count of four without separate mention of the obelisk, but it does list a significant monument of the type that does not appear in the main text. This is the 'Colossus', the built obelisk, 32 metres high, still to be seen on the *spina* of the hippodrome and identified on the basis of a dedicatory

FIG. 9.1 Base of obelisk of Theodosius, details of engineering. The scene indicates in schematic fashion the procedures by which the obelisk was raised on the *spina* of the Hippodrome.

10. Stefan Rebenich, 'Zum Theodosius obelisken in Konstantinopel', *Istanbuler Mitteilungen* 41 (1991), pp. 447–76 with plates 51–53. See too the articles on triumphal columns as urban markers by Pelin Yoncaci-Arslan, cited at Chapter 6, n. 30 above.

FIG. 9.2 The emperor faces the people; south-east face of Theodosius obelisk base. Originally a monument of Pharaoh Thutmose III, the obelisk was brought to Constantinople and for some time lay abandoned, until raised on the *spina* of the Hippodrome in 390 by the urban prefect Proclus, with an inscription celebrating his achievement and the illustration shown in Fig. 9.1 of how it was done. The obelisk broke during transportation and the extant part consists only of its upper portion, about two-thirds of its original height of around 60 metres. The sculptured faces show the emperor in various guises before his people assembled in the Hippodrome including, on the west face, envoys from Goths and Persians paying homage to Theodosius, who had made peace treaties with both peoples. The face shown here portrays Theodosius with his wife Galla and Arcadius and Honorius, his two sons by his first wife Aelia Flaccilla, presiding over circus races from the imperial *kathisma* with assembled courtiers and palace guard, the latter carrying the round shields that can be seen in the military insignia of the *Notitia Dignitatum*. Below them are high-ranking patrons of the games, possibly the senators of Constantinople; other faces of the base show what is more obviously intended to be the viewing public at large. The two standing figures could possibly be Proclus and his wife, shown inaugurating the games (Theodosius was absent in the west at this time). The scenes are portrayed in the very location in which they took place.

inscription of Constantine Porphyrogenitus on its eastern face, comparing the structure with the Colossus of Rhodes, and indicating that the work undertaken by him was one of restoration of a decayed monument. The present-day appearance of the obelisk is misleading, for what we see is the exposed core of a monument originally covered with bronze plaques, for which the fixing marks can still be seen. Given its naming by Constantine Porphyrogenitus, it seems reasonable to infer that this is the Colossus mentioned in the *Collectio*, but from what period before the composition of the *Notitia* the monument derives is impossible to say.[11]

---

11. Janin, *Constantinople Byzantine*, pp. 192–93 (with the text of the inscription).

Clad in its bronze plaques, it must have been a very splendid monument, adding greatly to the visual impact of the hippodrome and its appurtenances.

9.2 Gradus *and* Scalae

The *Notitia* includes three 'scalae'; the 'scala Timasii' of Region IV (Timasius was a famous general of Theodosius), and the *scalae* in Regions V and VI, located at the water crossings to Chalcedon and Sycae. Listed together in the *Collectio* as 'scalae maritimae', they were passenger quays or landing stages for the ferries that maintained the links between Constantinople and its Asiatic suburbs and neighbours. The general scene is vividly portrayed in the Vavassore panorama (Fig. 3.2 above).

Also listed in the *Collectio Civitatis* are 117 'gradus', or flights of steps, a total that can be made up for the separate Regions if a missing number of ten is assigned to Region III.[12] The term *gradus* has a special meaning in relation to the distributions of bread established by Constantine after the example of Rome, where the bread was given out from such steps and was hence known as 'panis gradilis' (p. 31).[13] In every case (except for the missing entry in Region III), both in the main text of the *Notitia* and in the *Collectio Civitatis*, the number of *gradus* immediately follows that of the public and private baths and bakeries and should be taken together with it. This information, and that contained in the *Notitia* about the number of houses and public and private baths and bakeries, are further discussed in Chapter 10 on the population of Constantinople.

Located by the *Notitia* in Region XII, between the forum and harbour of Theodosius and not far from the Golden Gate, is the imperial mint (*moneta*). Constantine did indeed begin minting at Constantinople as early as 326, in the later years of his reign sharing production with Nicomedia.[14] We do not know when the mint at Constantinople was built, nor exactly where it was, but it is enough to know that there was such a location to imagine the activity in and around it. Minting was an operation requiring specialized skills, some of them, as for example the engraving of dies, of an extremely advanced craftsmanship. There was a need for raw materials such as charcoal as well as the bullion from which the coin was made, and for their transportation. Mint-workers (*monetarii*) were among those, like linen-workers, bakers, and purple-dye fishers, whose services were

---

12. Seeck's edition (p. 232) inserts in the apparatus 'Gradus undecim' to conform with the *Collectio*, but my own count requires only ten.

13. A. Chastagnol, *La Préfecture urbaine à Rome sous le Bas-Empire* (1960), p. 315; cf. A. H. M. Jones, *The Later Roman Empire*, p. 696; 'Here too [sc. at Constantinople] the bread was issued from "steps", which according to the Notitia numbered 117', etc. The administrative evidence is set out at *CTh* 14.15–17.

14. See above, Chapter 5, n. 35.

required by the state and whose rights were curtailed by law (women both of higher status, and those tied to their place of origin, were forbidden to marry them).[15] The actual manufacture of the coin was as near to an industrial activity as one finds in the ancient world, with teams of workers, organized into *officinae* or production units, striking the coins one by one in huge numbers, for circulation in an increasingly centralized operation.

It is worth pausing for a moment on the indifference of the *Notitia* to the aesthetic as opposed to the organizational character of the city. There is no mention of what would surely have been their most obvious feature to contemporaries, that the columns of Theodosius and Arcadius were elaborately sculptured monuments recording the emperors' victories; it is only commented that one could climb up a staircase inside them. There is no hint that the column of Constantine was surmounted by a statue of the emperor, in a somewhat controversial posture, that of Apollo the Sun-God, that has caused endless discussion of the emperor's religious outlook. The *Notitia* does mention the statue of the bull that gave its name to the forum of Theodosius, and the 'brazen ox' that came to identify the so-called Forum Bovis, and there were the 'two great equestrian statues' to be seen in the forum of Theodosius (cf. Fig. 8.3). The latter, we have seen, were probably of the emperor's sons Arcadius and Honorius, the statue of Theodosius himself on the summit of the column not being mentioned; it was dedicated on 1 August 394, while the emperor was absent on a campaign in the west, from which he never returned.[16]

There is a great deal on which the *Notitia* has nothing to say. While appreciating its monumental development, we would never guess the sheer elegance of the city with its squares and colonnaded avenues, or the wealth and richness of the statuary to be seen in the streets of the city and in its public institutions; the lovely bronze *quadriga* horses now at the cathedral of S. Marco in Venice (more plunder from the sacking of Constantinople in 1204) may give some impression of what could be seen (Fig. 9.3). Famous both before and after their removal from Constantinople, the statues were shown in the imperial triumph of Napoleon at Paris in 1798, and returned to Venice in 1815. The workmanship, gold leaf hammered into the bronze, is characteristic of the fourth century; it is one of the skills of refined metalworkers mentioned in the law on craftsmen cited above.[17] We have reason to appreciate St. Jerome's joke on the rise to greatness of Constantinople through the 'nudity' of other cities—not only the influx of population to the detriment of other cities, but the importation of their Classical, that is to say

---

15. These rights are set out at *Codex Theodosianus* 10.2.

16. *Chron. Pasch.*, 565 (Whitby and Whitby, p. 55); Theodosius died at Milan on 17 January 395.

17. *CTh* 13.4.2; above, p. 34. On the techniques of workmanship used in the making of the horses, see the articles by various specialist authors in *The Horses of San Marco*, pp. 171–87.

FIG. 9.3 The gilded bronze *quadriga* taken from Constantinople in the Venetian sack of 1204 and now in the cathedral of S. Marco. John and Valerie Wilton-Ely (transl.; various authors), *The Horses of San Marco, Venice* (1977). Image from Wikimedia Commons, file: "Dolce sgardo bronzeo",jpg ("Il cavalli di bronzo all interno della Basilica di S. Marco") (Gianfranco Zanevello, 2017). The horses displayed on the outside balcony of S. Marco are copies of the originals.

their nude, statues of gods and heroes. If we are to believe the sixth-century poet Christodorus, the Zeuxippon was in the author's lifetime an amazing sculpture gallery of Greek and Roman gods, heroes, and literary luminaries, which casts a flood of light on the cultural ambience of Constantinople.[18] None of this was of concern to the author of the *Notitia*. His work is a list with only the most occasional elaboration, presenting to us an institutional and architectural shell, a sort of stage design into which we have to insert the cultural and aesthetic life of the city as well as the events that filled its streets (the column of Arcadius showed us a few of these); but as to what he does tell us, his information, in substance and in detail, is irreplaceable. A successful stage design will frame how a drama is performed.

9.3 Palaces and Great Houses

A further category of public or quasi-public buildings is that of the palaces and great houses of the imperial family (the *Notitia* lists no residence of any named

---

18. Above, pp. 51, 85. This tradition is the central concern of Sarah Bassett's *The Urban Image of Late Antique Constantinople*, focusing on the sculpture collections to be found there; see esp. ch. 2, 'Creating the Collection'.

private individual, though the presence of 'houses of the nobility' is indicated in the introduction to Region I). Following is a list of such establishments, with the Regions in which they are found, and with indications of the dates to which, or between which, they belong. There is a minor discrepancy in the number of palaces and residences listed in the text of the *Notitia* and those counted in the *Collectio Civitatis*. The *Collectio* mentions five palaces where only four are listed under the Regions, and six houses of the Augustae where only five are listed. The number of houses of 'nobilissimae' is consistent at three, though it is possible that one of them, the 'domus nobilissimae Arcadiae' listed under both the ninth and tenth Regions, was a single residence spanning with its gardens the borders of two Regions:

Region I	palatium magnum;
	palatium Placidianum (Augusta 421–50);
	domus Placidiae Augustae (Augusta 421–50);
	domus nobilissimae Marinae (403–49);
Region III	domus Pulcheriae Augustae (Augusta 414–53);
Region IX	domus nobilissimae Arcadiae (400–444) (cf. Region X?);
Region X	domus Augustae Placidiae;
	domus Augustae Eudociae (421–43/460);[19]
	domus nobilissimae Arcadiae (cf. Region IX?);
Region XI	palatium Flaccillianum (Augusta, d. 387);
	domus Augustae Pulcheriae;
Regio XIV	palatium.

The most immediately obvious characteristic of these attributions is their concentration on the dynasty of Theodosius. Apart from the special case of Constantine's 'great palace', only the *palatium Flaccillianum*, named after Theodosius' first wife Aelia Flaccilla, precedes the death of that emperor in 395. The others—palaces and residences of the Augustae Galla Placidia, Eudocia, and Pulcheria, and of the 'nobilissimae' Marina and Arcadia—are clustered in the second and third decades of the fifth century. What may be misleading in this is the likelihood that residences passed from generation to generation in the imperial family, being renamed as they did so. The palace and two *domus* of Galla Placidia are an example. The limits of time between her elevation as Augusta in 421 and the composition of the *Notitia* being so very narrow, these properties must already have existed under different names to be assigned for her use or ownership when she arrived as a refugee from the

---

19. Eudocia, wife of Theodosius II, became Augusta on her marriage in 421. She died in the Holy Land in 460, where she had lived in disgrace from 443; Holum, *Theodosian Empresses*, pp. 193–94.

west.[20] We cannot infer from their listing in the *Notitia* when these palaces were actually built.

No less noteworthy than their concentration in time is the distribution of these residences. Three are in Region I, where they formed part of the larger complex of the great palace. Another was in the adjacent Region III, where the residence of a great political figure of the period, the *praepositus sacri cubiculi* Antiochus, was also located, if it is correctly identified among the confusing structures between the hippodrome and the Mesē, partially excavated in 1964. The residence is perhaps to be identified with the 'domus Pulcheriae Augustae' of the *Notitia*, being taken into imperial possession on Antiochus' fall from favour in 421.[21]

In contrast, no residence of the imperial family is to be found in Region II (the old city of Byzantium), nor in the extension of the Graeco-Roman city on the northern and western sides of the acropolis (Region IV). Unsurprisingly, none is to be found in any of the commercial Regions overlooking the Golden Horn (Regions V–VII); members of the imperial family did not live among docks and warehouses. Three residences were located in the spacious and less heavily developed Region X, one of them, the 'domus nobilissimae Arcadiae', possibly extending into the adjacent Region IX, and two more in Region XI. This concentration of imperial residences in five of the fourteen Regions, with six residences in just two of them, should have something to say about the social and economic character of the Regions of the city, to which we will return in Chapter 10.

9.4 Churches

There is also the unexpectedly difficult question of churches. We earlier saw the claim that Constantine filled his new city with splendid churches and its streets with Christian and not Classical art, commenting briefly on the difficulty of finding the churches (above, Chapter 2, pp. 42–5). Conceding the priority we would expect by the early fifth century, the regional inventories of the *Notitia* begin with an entry 'ecclesia' in all but one of the cases where a church is listed for that Region; of the eight Regions that possessed one or more churches, only Region IV fails to begin like this, the 'church or martyrium of S. Menas' falling down the list into seventh position, between the 'marble *liburna* commemorating

---

20. The *Notitia Dignitatum* includes under the *dispositio* of the eastern *castrensis*, 'Curae palatiorum' and under his *officium*, 'Tabularium dominarum Augustarum' (*Not. Dig.; Or.* 17.8; cf. *Occ.* 15.9; 'tabularium dominae Augustae'). The symbols of the *castrensis* are presented as the precious metalware and furniture of the palaces.

21. R. Naumann, *Istanbuler Mitteilungen* 16 (1965), p. 145 (above, Chapter 5, n. 10); Müller-Wiener, *Bildlexikon*, pp. 122–25. The identification is supported by the connection of the location known as *ta Antiokhou* with the ruined church of S. Euphemia 'of the hippodrome'.

the sea battle' and the stadium. The reason for the delayed appearance of this church is not clear, for even if the martyrium were of recent foundation, it could have been put at the head of its Region in a list that included it. A different priority is observed in the *Collectio Civitatis*, where the first entry is reserved for the 'five palaces' of the emperor and his family.[22] Churches come next, after the palaces but before the houses of the Augustae and 'nobilissimae'—a neatly expressed sense of priorities. It would be interesting to know whether the compiler of the *Notitia* would have entered a church above the 'palatium magnum' in Region I (as he did for Region XIV), but he was not put to that test, since the First Region did not possess any.

As with palaces and other imperial residences, there is a discrepancy in the number of churches between that given in the *Collectio*, with its total of fourteen, and the twelve churches that are listed under the individual Regions.[23] To begin with an apparent anomaly, the *Notitia* makes no mention of an important foundation almost certainly to be assigned to Constantine, the extramural church of S. Mocius (Mōkios), whose name day, 11 May, is the same as that of the consecration of Constantinople. The significance of the coincidence is debated.[24] Whatever ceremonies of a more traditional kind were devised for this event, the choice of S. Mocius' name day would be significant, if we knew of its observance at this early date. However, no source makes the connection. Given the distinctly fictional identity of the saint, it seems as likely that the name-day of S. Mocius is a later invention deriving from that of the consecration of Constantinople as that it was chosen by Constantine for that purpose.

The reason for the absence of S. Mocius from the *Notitia* is a very simple one, and has nothing to do with its role in the ecclesiastical life of the city or its ideological character. Like martyr-churches elsewhere, it was a cemetery church located outside the city walls, and could be attributed to none of the Regions described by the *Notitia*.[25] It adds to our sense of Mocius' historical unreality, that the supposed martyr was commemorated in an extramural church—but one built two miles beyond the walls that would have been in existence at the time of his

---

22. As mentioned above, only four *palatia* are listed among the Regions.

23. For a discussion of the early churches of Constantinople in relation to the foundation of the city, see Dagron, *Naissance d'une Capitale*, pp. 388–409.

24. Barnes, *Constantine and Eusebius*, p. 222, makes much of the coincidence in his presentation of Constantinople as from the outset an expressly Christian city. The date of the consecration is given by Hesychius and the *Patria* (Preger, pp. 18, 143) as well as by Malalas and *Chronicon Paschale* (above, p. 29f.), but none of these sources, nor Eusebius' *Life of Constantine* nor any other text makes the connection. Dagron, *Naissance d'une Capitale*, ch. 1, at pp. 37–41, is indifferent: 'détail intéressant, mais dont il est difficile de rien inférer.'

25. Mango, *Développement Urbain*, p. 35; Dagron, *Naissance d'une Capitale*, p. 395. Despite Barnes, *Constantine and Eusebius*, p. 222, it was not a mile outside the walls of Constantine's city.

martyrdom. It is true that some of the martyr churches of Rome were built at burial sites some distance outside the city, but Rome was a very much larger place than Severan Byzantium. In this case it is almost as if someone, appointed to invent the location of a Christian martyr's burial, had the bad luck or judgement to choose the wrong set of walls, those of Constantine rather than Severus. And it is at least an awkward detail that according to the *Life* of S. Mocius, his actual martyrdom took place at Amphipolis, nearly 300 miles to the west of Byzantium.

The church has nevertheless a contribution to make to the urban history of Constantinople. Its first involvement in any recorded historical event is of the year 402, and a connection with Constantine is not directly claimed before the opening chapter (as it survives) of the eighth-century *Parastaseis* and another passage in the *Patria*.[26] According to these sources the church, built by Constantine in an area of pagan occupation on the site of a temple of Zeus (a contradiction of what is otherwise thought of as a funerary church in a necropolis), collapsed in the third consulship of Constantius, which was in 342—such an early date surely pushes the construction of the church back to the reign of Constantine, as well as attesting a poor standard of construction no doubt common in these early years of the growth of the city.[27] The church then passes from view until the time of Theodosius, when it was conceded for the use of Arian heretics, who repaired and used it for their services. After seven years in the hands of the Arians, the church collapsed again, killing many in the midst of their liturgy. This may be a refinement of the narrative intended to heighten the wickedness of Arians punished for their heresy; but if their occupation of the church was connected with Theodosius' law of 384 banning Arians and other heretics from the city of Constantinople (*CTh* 16.5.13), then the seven years in question would be 384–91, after which the church must again have been restored. An identical dispute enveloped Milan at just the same time in the controversy over the Basilica Portiana ('By-the-Gate') occupied by Arians after their expulsion from the city, when bishop Ambrose challenged the heretics' appropriation of an extramural church for their assembly.[28]

It might be thought that the concession of S. Mocius for the use of the Arian congregation at Constantinople would ill fit the peremptory tone both of this law and of a sequel of just four years later (*CTh* 16.5.15), but if the story is true, and the similar events at Milan support it, it would place the foundation of this church and its subsequent history well back into the fourth century, for most of

---

26. Sozomen 8.27; *Parastaseis*, ed. Cameron and Herrin, pp. 56–57 with notes at 167–68; cf. Preger, pp. 19 (from *Parastaseis*) and 208–9; Berger, pp. 128–29.

27. As alleged by Zosimus 2.32.

28. F. Homes Dudden, *The Life and Times of St. Ambrose* (1935), Vol. I, pp. 270–80.

which it was in disrepair. Far from being emblematic of Constantine's foundation of a Christian city, the church was never at the centre of the ecclesiastical life of the fourth-century city. This is not surprising if we consider how far it was situated from the areas of urban development of that time; we will see in the following chapter that the adjacent Regions X and XI were the latest of the intramural Regions to be developed. Subject to early structural failure and subsequent neglect, it was conceded for the use of a marginal heretic congregation and only after urban development had caught up with it did it enter into the regular ecclesiastical life of the city, to produce the great church described by Procopius in the time of Justinian (*Buildings* 1.4.27).[29]

This is to begin with a church that, for the reasons given, is not mentioned in the *Notitia*. Of those that are so mentioned, the foundations of S. Sophia and S. Irene, styled respectively the 'great' and the 'old church' (*ecclesia magna* and *ecclesia antiqua*), are first to claim attention, in their well-known locations on the lower slopes of the acropolis, just to the north of Constantine's Augusteum. A physical relation between the churches and the Augusteum, in what we might call an alliance between the civic and the religious dimensions of the new capital, was however not quickly established, for it is only S. Irene, the more distant from the new civic centre, that can be assigned, more or less by default, to Constantine. *Chronicon Paschale* places the consecration of S. Sophia under Constantine's successor, coinciding with a council of bishops that deposed Macedonius 'on account of his many personal faults' (and for his unwillingness to believe in the full divinity of the Holy Ghost) and replaced him by Eudoxius, who was consecrated on 27 January 360 in the presence of seventy-two bishops, whose names are registered.[30] The actual enthronement of Eudoxius will have taken place in the 'old church' of S. Irene, since the consecration of S. Sophia, on 15 February, was yet to follow—one had to avoid either aspect of a double impropriety, of a bishop's enthronement preceding the consecration of the church in which it was performed, or of the consecration of the church by one who was not yet bishop. The account of the inauguration of the church in *Chronicon Paschale* gives some indication of the glamour of the occasion:

> the emperor Constantius Augustus presented many dedications, great gold and silver treasures, and many gemmed and gold-threaded cloths for the holy altar; in addition also, for the doors of the church diverse golden curtains; and for the outer entrances varied gold-threaded ones;

---

29. The remains of the church, with all its pillars still standing, were seen by Gilles near the cistern of Mocius; *Antiquities* 4.8 (ed. Musto, p. 204).

30. *Chron. Pasch.*, s.a. 360, with Whitby and Whitby, pp. 34–35, citing (at n. 110) the reservations of G. Dagron on the date of the foundation.

so he lavishly bestowed many gifts at that time on the entire clergy, and on
the order of virgins and widows and on the hospices. For the sustenance
of these and of the beggars and orphans and prisoners, he added a grain
allocation of greater size than that which his father Constantine
had bestowed.

The same source adds the unexpected information that the consecration of
S. Sophia took place a little more than thirty-four years after Constantine had
laid its foundations. The time-frame would take us back to 325, very soon after the
dedication of the city, and before its formal consecration in 330. Why did the
completion of the church take so long, especially given the rapid pace of
Constantine's church building at Rome, Jerusalem, and in other places? It has
been suggested that the date of dedication might have been inspired by a later,
anachronistic desire to associate the foundation of the church with that of the
city, or conceivably through confusion with the foundation of the city itself.
Neither argument seems likely and would do nothing to explain the slow appearance of an iconic monument that should be at the heart of Constantine's understanding of the meaning of his new city. Unless there were problems arising from
the preparation of the site and from the demolition of whatever structures stood
behind the north-eastern facade of the Severan Tetrastoon as it was converted
into the Augusteum, the form of the church as a traditional basilica in the Roman
style—what some sources call a 'racecourse church' (*dromikē*) because of its resemblance to the plan of a hippodrome—should have presented no special difficulties in construction.[31] We are not looking at the mighty Justinianic structure
that stands there now, but at something much more modest and traditional in
design. Perhaps it was simply a matter of manpower and resources, bearing in
mind the scope of Constantine's other building in the city. Government is a
matter of priorities, choices have to be made, expenditures planned, and there
were just too many things to be done. It might have seemed more important to
complete the emperor's mausoleum than to build a new church beside the old one
of S. Irene, and there was always the latter to carry the liturgical burdens of the
bishop of Constantinople. The retrospective chronology offered by *Chronicon
Paschale* has however the interesting effect of placing the dedication of the site in
the year of the council of Nicaea and in the earliest days of Constantine's building
of his new city; perhaps the Council of Nicaea itself was the 'Holy Wisdom'

---

31. For the term *dromikē* to indicate the elongated basilical form, see for example the first
sentence of the treatise on the building of the church in the *Patria*; Preger, pp. 74, 214; Berger,
pp. 140–41, 230–31; Whitby and Whitby, pp. 59, 64. It was in the same form that the church
was rebuilt by Theodosius II after the fire of 404 under Arcadius.

commemorated by the dedication! The phrase could be understood of any doctrinal position that a later emperor happened to take.

During the period from 325 to the consecration of S. Sophia, while the 'great church' was an undeveloped building site, we should think of the 'old church' of S. Irene as the focus of the ceremonial Christianity of the court and city of Constantine. Both churches were planted in the monumental area of old Byzantium, where they acted as a counterpoise to the ancient temples and other public buildings on and around the acropolis, as well as eventually creating a setting for the ceremonial repertory that would develop in the public space in front of the imperial palace. These two churches, which were eventually administered as a single foundation, satisfied the political and ceremonial needs of the capital, and in the case of S. Sophia the philanthropic impulses of the government, rather than the congregational needs of its Christian population, who on the whole (see Chapter 10, pp. 201–8) did not live in this part of the city.

The history of the church of the Holy Apostles in Region XI ('Martyrium Apostolorum' in the *Notitia*) is still more complicated, for it was not built as a church at all, but as the mausoleum of Constantine and the imperial family. The monument stood on the elevated site now occupied by the Fatih mosque and probably on the very same emplacement of the mosque, by the northern branch of the Mesē as it approached the walls of Constantine through what was not yet a densely populated part of the city.[32] A public funerary monument in a now traditional pattern, the mausoleum had neither clergy nor provision for a congregation, nor were the memorials of the twelve Apostles that surrounded the body of Constantine the object of cult. The risks of ecclesiastical encroachment were however obvious. In his description of the double ceremonies devised for the interment of Constantine in 337 (p. 230), Eusebius of Caesarea could write as if the mausoleum were already a church, an ambiguity emphasized when, in 356, the remains of Timothy the follower of St. Paul and legendary first bishop of Ephesus, and in the following year of the apostles Luke and Andrew were brought to the city and, amid the singing of psalms and hymns, laid to rest there—obviously

---

32. On the site of the mausoleum and later church complex on the emplacement of the Faith mosque, see the revelatory studies of Ken Dark and Ferudun Özgümüş, 'New Evidence for the Byzantine Church of the Holy Apostles from Fatih Camii, Istanbul', *Oxford Journal of Archaeology* 21.4 (2002), pp. 393–413, and in *Constantinople: Archaeology of a Byzantine Megapolis* (Final Report on the Istanbul Rescue Archaeology Project; English language report by Ken Dark (2013)), pp. 83–96 with appendix 1 at 106–10; Müller-Wiener, *Bildlexikon*, pp. 405–11; Dagron, pp. 401–8 and Philip Grierson, 'Tombs and Obits of the Byzantine Emperors (337–1042)', *DOP* 16 (1962), pp. 21–29. The Turkish resistivity (GPR) survey of 1999, reported by Dark (2013), p. 95, seems to have detected the Justinianic rebuilding of the Holy Apostles at 1.25 m below the present floor level of the Fatih mosque, with an earlier building, which would be the fourth-century structure, at 2.5 m below this.

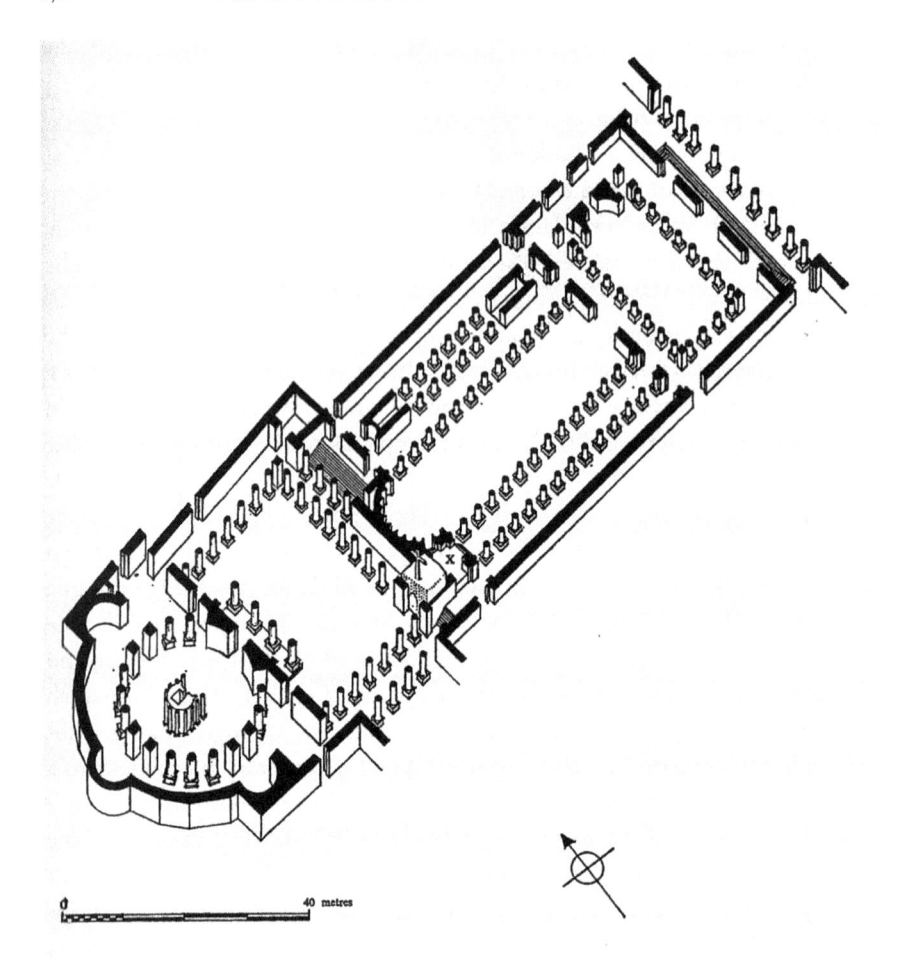

0   40 metres

FIG. 9.4 Reconstruction of Church of the Holy Sepulchre in Jerusalem. The church is shown as an architectural parallel to the Holy Apostles, as developed from the originally free-standing mausoleum of Constantine in the rotunda to the west, by the addition of a 'racecourse' basilica accessed across a colonnaded courtyard. Patria 3,1; Preger, p. 214, Berger, pp. 140f. The true alignment of the Apostles is at a 90° clockwise rotation of this image. John Wilkinson, *Egeria's Travels* (1971), p. 45.

in some relationship to the existing memorials of these evangelists.[33] Given these ecclesiastical tendencies, it was only a matter of time before the foundation was formally consecrated as a church, and this happened, after extensive rebuilding initiated by Constantius and continued by Valens, in 370; the date of consecration is given by *Chronicon Paschale* as 9 April.[34] The resulting complex of mausoleum

33. *Chron. Pasch.*, s.a. 356, 357; Whitby and Whitby, p. 33.

34. Whitby and Whitby, p. 48.

and basilica offered a similar pattern to the Holy Sepulchre at Jerusalem, the two elements facing each other across a colonnaded courtyard (Fig. 9.4). It could be the consecration of this church that inspired the Alexandrian poet Palladas to write of the discovery of 'twelve more recent gods' that enabled faithless women to forswear their previous oaths by the twelve Olympians.[35]

The Holy Apostles and S. Irene are the only churches assigned to Constantine by the fifth-century church historian Socrates, in a remark that, prematurely for the time of which he is writing, assumes the transformation of Constantine's mausoleum, and ignores the extramural church of S. Mocius. He would not have omitted this, if he thought it was part of the founding ideology of the new city.[36]

Regions VII and IX offer a very different picture from the image of public ceremonial presented so far. Region VII has the largest number of churches of any Region, namely the three churches of saints Irene (to be distinguished from the 'ecclesia antiqua' of Region II), Anastasia, and Paul (not the apostle, but a popular bishop of the mid-fourth century), and Region IX has the two churches of Homonoea and Caenopolis. Both Regions were densely populated areas associated with the harbours and other commercial facilities of Constantinople and in the latter case, as suggested above (p. 90f.), with the actual building of the city. We can well imagine that, with five churches between them, they catered for a large Christian community among the working people in this part of the city; here, as much as in the ruling circles of the political elite, is where the Christianization of Constantinople as a matter of popular belief rather than a projection of imperial ideology is to be found. The church of S. Paul in particular expresses the loyalty of the population to an aggressive leader whose prominence in theological causes earned him exile and an early death from the fearful Constantius. Until its absorption by S. Sophia, the 'ecclesia antiqua' of S. Irene was the episcopal seat of the city, the church where bishops were consecrated, but it was S. Paul's that was the focus of the support enjoyed by this bishop among the populace of Constantinople. Previously occupied by Macedonian heretics (followers of the deposed bishop mentioned above), it was dedicated in the name of Paul by the emperor Theodosius, bearing the skull of its former bishop in solemn procession through the city.[37]

These two Regions account for five of the twelve churches listed by the *Notitia* under the Regions of Constantinople. SS. Irene and Sophia in Region II

---

35. *Anthologia Palatina* 10.56, differing from the interpretation (and date) offered by K. W. Wilkinson, *JRS* 100 (2010), at pp. 189–91.

36. Socrates, *Hist. Eccl.* 1.16; Mango, *Développement Urbain*, p. 35; Dagron, *Naissance d'une Capitale*, pp. 392–93 (S. Irene).

37. Brian Croke, 'Reinventing Constantinople: Theodosius I's Imprint on the Imperial City', in *From the Tetrarchs to the Theodosians: Later Roman History and Culture, 284–450 CE* (2010), pp. 241–64, at p. 255.

account for two, the Martyrium Apostolorum for another and two more are found, without attributions, in the extramural Regions XIII and XIV. This leaves just two churches in the main part of the city, one in each of Regions IV and X. Both are described in the *Notitia* with the phrase 'ecclesia sive martyrium', with attributions respectively to saints Menas and Acacius. Like the unlisted S. Mocius, the designation of these churches as *martyria* reaches back to the ideological (that is to say, the imagined) origins of the Christian community in the persecutions of the early fourth century. Whether this gives to the churches themselves a very early origin is another matter. In Region IV the martyrium of S. Menas was known through historical events that affected it by the early fifth century, but it was not connected with Constantine until much later, and by unreliable sources. There were stories that the church was built into the remains of a temple of Poseidon, like that of S. Mocius into a temple of Zeus (or Heracles), but the validity of such claims is doubtful. If true they would make a Constantinian origin less rather than more likely, since this archaeological situation, of temples and other pre-Christian secular buildings converted into churches, is generally from a later period.[38]

The church of S. Acacius in Region X was dedicated to the third of the legendary martyr-saints of Byzantium. Procopius' description, much fuller than his fleeting reference to S. Mocius, is again of a Justinianic rebuilding over an earlier foundation. In the precinct of what Procopius calls this 'very large church' was the walnut or chestnut tree from which the saint was claimed to have been suspended, but this again takes us into the aura of pious fiction surrounding so many early saints, especially when it is also claimed that this saint was buried in the same place of his execution—not the usual Roman practice in criminal jurisdiction! Although no source connects it reliably with Constantine, it is one of the earliest known churches. In 359 the remains of Constantine were, amid public protest, transferred there to permit the building works that transformed his mausoleum into the martyrium of the Apostles—it was one of the complaints against the deposed Macedonius that he had allowed the remains of Constantine to be moved.[39] It no doubt owed its selection for this honour to the practical consideration of its proximity in a neighbouring Region.[40] It is worth adding that Region X,

---

38. Dagron, *Naissance d'une Capitale*, pp. 395–96; the case of S. Menas is the stronger of the two; cf. p. 376 n. 5. A spectacular instance is the building of the cathedral of Siracusa into the shell of a temple of Artemis. For the fate of three temples of Byzantium, see below, pp. 182–4.

39. Whitby and Whitby, pp. 34 n. 108, 48.

40. Procopius, *Buildings* 1.4.25–26; *Naissance d'une Capitale*, pp. 393–95, 405; Cyril Mango, 'Constantine's Mausoleum and the Translation of Relics', *Byzantinische Zeitschrift* 74 (1990), pp. 51–62 (reprinted in *Studies in Constantinople*, ch. 5). A fictional *Passion* of S. Acacius is in *Acta Sanctorum*, Mai II, pp. 762–66.

which contained it, was adjacent to and in some ways a continuation of the commercial Region VII with its three churches.

However significant the discrepancy in the number of churches, whether twelve as in the main text of the *Notitia* or fourteen as in the *Collectio Civitatis*, it does not seem a large number for a century's development of what historians have seen as a city founded as a Christian capital of the Roman empire and developed as such. As was noted in Chapter 2 (pp. 42–5), the number of authentically Constantinian foundations at Rome (not to mention Jerusalem) is far more impressive, both in number and in their grandeur and attested wealth (and for their speed of construction), than the modest list for Constantinople. Of the churches listed by the *Notitia*, only S. Irene and the Martyrium of the Apostles have a secure Constantinian origin—the latter in its original form as Constantine's mausoleum. S. Sophia, even if planned by Constantine, was dedicated by his successor many years later. Of the three martyrs' shrines of saints Mocius, Menas, and Acacius, the last is attested before the early fifth century only through the circumstances of its use as a depository for the remains of Constantine, and S. Mocius was marginal to the city, and in a poor state of repair. There is nothing against the idea that, after the examples he had seen and set at Rome, Constantine would have wished to establish martyrs' shrines at Constantinople also, even if the actual martyrs would have to be invented.[41] Such foundations may fall under Eusebius' partisan claim that Constantine consecrated new Rome to the 'God of the martyrs',[42] but we are not able to say whether any of the three martyrs' shrines listed by the *Notitia* was founded by him.

In considering the distribution of churches, it is also striking that according to the regional lists of the *Notitia*, six Regions (I, III, V–VI, VIII, XII) did not possess any church at all. Two missing churches might be indicated by the *Collectio Civitatis* at the end of the text—though they might equally have been found in Regions that already possessed one church or more. None is found in the palace area in Region I, although there must have been chapels in the palaces and great houses—the mansions of sympathizers are often found harbouring dissidents of various colours, and when the western pilgrim Egeria came to the city in the early 380s she remarked on the great numbers of martyr memorials she had visited. Many of these were no doubt private enterprises.[43] It is obvious that more was going on in the city than we happen to know about, and certainly more than is revealed by the *Notitia*, but it remains true that in the whole of Regions II–VI,

---

41. R. Ross Holloway, *Constantine and Rome* (2004), ch. 3.

42. *Life of Constantine* 3.48.2 (cited by Barnes, p. 383 n. 143).

43. *Itinerarium Egeriae* 23.9, trans. John Wilkinson (1971), p. 122; Croke (n. 35), p. 247.

the Graeco-Roman and Severan city onto which Constantinople was grafted, there are listed only the two ceremonial foundations, side by side in the Second Region. Of these, only S. Sophia imposed itself physically upon the public architecture of the Augusteum; and no other church of the fourth and early fifth centuries overlooked any of the main squares of Constantinople as they extended through the city. There was no church imposing its presence on any of the forums of Constantine, Theodosius, or Arcadius.

In other parts of the city, the distribution of churches reflects the presence of a substantial Christian populace, especially in those Regions where more than one is listed, but it is not easy to trace their influence as far back as the age of Constantine. Building no doubt on the Constantinian precedent, his successor Constantius had a much more extensive role in establishing the Christian credentials of the new city; which is only to say that, no more than Rome, was Constantinople built in a day. None of this is intended to belittle the tumultuous events of ecclesiastical history, ranging from aggressive populist bishops to great church councils, the importation of relics and the foundation of monasteries, that took place over the period from Constantine to Theodosius II (Chapter 11 below, p. 241f.); only to observe that the urban planning of this period was not primarily designed to accommodate them. The fourth-century city was not physically dominated by its churches, and the religious policies of Constantine were only one of the many strands of its meaning.

Of these other strands, it is not surprising that no temples are mentioned in the *Notitia*, for at the time of compilation they had long been decommissioned. Historical Byzantium had its temples, naturally—Artemis, Apollo and Aphrodite, Poseidon the sea-god (all of whose involvements with Troy as the predecessor of Constantinople went back to the *Iliad*); and there would certainly have been shrines of the legendary founder Byzas, Zeus, and of course the emperors, not to mention the Tychē of the city. Some temples were monumental in scale, to judge by the massive Medusa heads re-used as column bases in the sixth-century 'cistern of the basilica', and the scores of Classical capitals to be seen down there. Viewing the upturned Medusa heads can have a disorienting effect, and much has been made of the supposed insult, in what looks like a brutal contradiction of their original appearance (Fig. 9.5). On the other hand, one uses what one has, and these were convenient building materials, for use in a location that was to be roofed over, never open to the light of day. If the purpose was to humiliate them, their humiliation was borne in total darkness for a thousand years from the time of Justinian to their rediscovery by Pierre Gilles in the sixteenth century. The fate of the Medusa heads is what would now be called collateral damage in the Christianization of the Roman empire.

It is only towards the end of the fourth century, that we read of the decommissioning of the great temples of Artemis, Apollo, and Aphrodite on

FIG. 9.5 Medusa head in Cistern of the Basilica (Yerebatan Sarai).

the acropolis, and their transformation into everyday uses. According to John Malalas:

> The emperor Theodosius in that year pulled down the three temples in Constantinople on what was formerly known as the Acropolis. He made the temple of Helios [Apollo] into a courtyard surrounded with houses and donated it to the Great Church of Constantinople. This courtyard is known as the 'Courtyard of Helios' to the present day. The temple of

Artemis he made into a gaming room for dice players. The place is called
'The Temple' to the present day, and the street nearby is called 'The Fawn'
[Artemis was a famous huntress]. The temple of Aphrodite he made into a
carriage house for the praetorian prefect, and he built lodging houses close by,
and gave orders that penniless prostitutes could stay there free of charge.[44]

The same author had earlier written that not long before the end of his reign,
Constantine had deprived the same three temples of their revenues, which would
add up to a coherent policy, first of the disestablishment and later the destruction
of the pagan temples, with its stages spread over several decades.[45] All in all, it
does not look as if Constantinople the city was in any particular hurry to find its
identity as the Christian capital of the Roman empire. The conversion of the
three temples into the secular uses mentioned by Malalas was not far removed in
time from the destruction of the Serapeum at Alexandria, an act that is usually
seen as the end of one phase of the decline of paganism. Constantius' removal of
the dangerously popular bishop Paul is more or less contemporaneous with the
exile of the bishop of Rome Liberius, who had to be spirited out of the city because of the passion of his supporters among the people, 'qui eius amore flagrabat'
(Amm. Marc. 15.7.10).[46]

Constantine's slow start in giving to his city the panoply of churches that one
might expect was not because of any uncertainty in his or his successors' intentions. It is more that the city itself, lacking its own Christian traditions ready for
commemoration, did not provide a natural expression of a concept of the relations of church and state based on them. A city is not a *tabula rasa* on which a
new philosophy can be written as if on a blank page; it is a complex entity that
must find room for the traditions of the people who live in it. Anyone who,
having read Eusebius, comes to Constantinople expecting to find a Christian city
in all the applications of that term will be disappointed, just as one might have

---

44. Malalas, p. 345 Bonn (Elizabeth Jeffreys et al., p. 187), entered under the years 379/83.
Chron. Pasch., s.a. 379, adds 'when the glorious Constantine was emperor, he only closed the
temples and shrines of the Hellenes; Theodosius destroyed them'; Whitby and Whitby, p. 50.
Here too I part company from the two articles (with others) of Kevin Wilkinson, cited at
Chapter 3, n. 13. On the general issue, Catherine Nixey's *The Darkening Age: The Christian
Destruction of the Classical World* (2018) is notable for its rich documentation, and for its clear-
sighted understanding of how much these policies mattered to those who suffered from them.

45. Malalas, p. 324 Bonn (Jeffreys, p. 176). The date is uncertain but the entry immediately
precedes Constantine's death. Malalas identifies Artemis with the moon, one of the goddess's
traditional associations.

46. Amm. Marc. 15.7.10. Compare the popularity and violent death of George of Alexandria,
22.11.3–11.

been to find its consecration ceremonies rooted in the traditions of an older world and naked statues in its streets (again with acknowledgements to Jerome). Neither Julian in his speeches to Constantius, nor Themistius in his address to Theodosius, felt any need to mention churches. To the objection that, given his own beliefs and the conventions of the genre in which he spoke, Themistius at least is unlikely to have done so, it could be responded that even if Julian spoke as a still Christian member of the house of Constantine, he would have been confronted by a distinct dearth of material. Not churches but city walls, public squares and colonnades, aqueducts and cisterns, harbours and warehouses, bakeries and bath-houses, private housing extended to new parts of the city—it is this physical pattern of urban development in the Classical manner of which the *Notitia* best informs us. It is to the housing and population of Constantinople that we turn next.

10

Housing and Population

FOLLOWING THE TOPOGRAPHICAL introductions and lists of monuments discussed in the previous chapters, the *Notitia* gives for each Region of Constantinople information pertaining to the life of the population of the city—the public and private baths and bakeries, private houses, streets, and alleys that it contained, and among its administrative resources the numbers of *gradus* (distribution points for the bread dole) and *collegiati*, corporations of men deployed against fire and other urban hazards. The *Collectio Civitatis* at the end of the text gives grand totals of all the items listed—residences (*domus*) numbered in thousands, with streets, baths, and bakeries rising into the hundreds. The figures are a treasure trove of information, which, however difficult to interpret, it would be neglectful to pass over. The purpose of this chapter is to consider them as a guide to the population of the city and its living conditions, complementing the questions of physical development described so far.[1] Three cautions should be entered at the outset. First, the figures are not statistics with controlled parameters but are subject to all sorts of variable conditions, known and unknown; second, Roman numerals are extremely vulnerable to distortion in the transmission of a text; and third, although the figures are given Region by Region and suggest differences between them, the character of the city will have changed by gradual stages as one moved around it. The regions are administrative and not socio-economic boundaries, and the transitions between them were more gradual than the figures, taken by themselves would imply.

The numbers given by the *Notitia* under the categories most relevant to these issues are assembled in Table 10.1. Evident at a glance are some striking differences between regions. An extreme case is the contrast between the seven streets (*vici*, in full *vici sive angiportus*) and ninety-four houses (*domus*) of Region III and the

---

1. The chapter covers some of the same ground as Salvatore Cosentino, '*Domus, vici* e demografia nella *Notitia Urbis Constantinopolitanae*: alcune osservazioni' (above, Chapter 4, n. 9); Dimitris P. Drakoulis, 'The Functional Organization of Early Byzantine Constantinople According to the *Notitia Urbis Constantinopolitanae*', in P. Doukellis et al. (eds), *Openness: Historical and Philosophical Studies in Honour of Prof. Emeritus Vasiliki Papoulia* (2012), pp. 153–82; and the works of Albrecht Berger and others mentioned in earlier chapters.

From Byzantium to Constantinople: An Urban History. John Matthews, Oxford University Press.
© Oxford University Press 2024. DOI: 10.1093/oso/9780197585498.003.0010

Table 10.1 The population of Constantinople: the *Notitia* by Region

	I	II	III	IV	V	VI	VII	VIII	IX	X	XI	XII	XIII	XIV	Totals
Colonnades	2	4	5	1+4	7	1	6	5	2	6	4	2	1	2	52
Streets and alleys	29	34	7	35	23	22	85	2	16	20	8	11	—	11	322
Houses	118	98	94	375	184	484	711	108	116	636	503	363	431	167	4,388
[Houses ÷ streets	4.1	2.9	13.4	10.7	8.0	22.0	8.4	5.1	7.35	31.8	62.9	33.0	—	15.2]	
Public baths (*thermae*)	1	1	0	0	2	0	1	0	1	1	0	0	1	1	9(8)
Private baths	15	13	11	7	11	9	11	10	15	[22]	14	5	5	5	153
Public bakeries	4	0	0	0	7	1	0	0	4	2	1	0	1	1	21(20)
Private bakeries	15	4	9	5	2	17	12	5	15	16	3	5	4	1	113(120)
Gradus	4	4	[10]	7	9	17	16	5	4	12	7	9	8	5	117
Churches	0	2	0	1	0	0	3	0	2	1	1	0	1	1	12(14)
Collegiati	25	35	21	40	40	49	80	17	38	90	37	17	34	[37]	560

eighty-five *vici* and 711 *domus* of Region VII, and between the respective numbers of twenty-one and eighty *collegiati* for these two regions. Yet despite the wide numerical differences between them, the proportions are consistent. The ratio of houses to streets in each case (13.4 and 8.4 respectively) is in the same middle range among the regions as a whole, suggesting a similar pattern of occupation in two districts which, although not contiguous, were in the same central part of the city; both were part of the Constantinian expansion just beyond the limits of Severan Byzantium, and both were connected with areas of commercial activity. The higher numbers of streets, houses, and *collegiati* for Region VII may reflect a difference not only in size, which is not as extreme as the numbers imply, but in the physical character of these two regions.[2] One can see at once how this might be so, for apart from the harbour of Julian, Region III contained what the *Notitia* calls the 'vast expanse' of the hippodrome. This was not likely to catch fire in any normal circumstances, while outbreaks of disorder associated with the hippodrome would be checked by intervention from the nearby palace rather than by *collegiati*; nor should we forget the ancillary services required for the functioning of a hippodrome (above, p. 31), all of which reduced the stock of building land for houses. The pattern and density of occupation in these two regions were not dissimilar, but the presence of the hippodrome and its facilities meant that the proportion of Region III occupied by housing was less.

This may seem to be a satisfactory explanation of some of the differences in the figures for Regions III and VII, but it is arbitrary since there is no special reason to compare these two regions in particular, and other cases show additional complications. Why, for instance, should there be the eighty-five streets that we just saw for 711 houses and eighty *collegiati* in Region VII, with a ratio of 8.4 houses to streets, but only twenty streets for the 636 houses (with ninety *collegiati*) of the adjacent Region X, a ratio of 31.8 houses to streets and almost the same number of *collegiati*?[3] In Region XI, next in sequence after Region X, the figure of a mere eight streets for 503 houses—a ratio of 62.9 houses to streets with only thirty-seven *collegiati*—is a still more disconcerting example. To judge merely from the larger numbers of houses, Regions X and XI had more in common with each other than they had with other parts of the city. This is plausible, since they are outlying and spacious regions, lying just within the city

---

2. The large number of *gradus*, at seventeen for Region VII and ten for Region III, is also suggestive of a dense population, but the latter number, missing in the text, is an extrapolation from the total in the *Collectio Civitatis*.

3. For the present I translate *domus* as 'houses' but offer a more refined analysis below. In the translation of the *Notitia* above I prefer 'residences'. On *vici sive angiportus*, see Chapter 4 above (p. 65f.).

wall of Constantine, and may have shared features deriving from their relatively late development within the overall plan of the city. On the other hand, the discrepancies between their respective proportions of streets to houses (20:636 and 8:503) and of *collegiati* to houses (90:636 and 37:503) suggest that there were also features that they did not share. In its larger numbers both of houses and *collegiati* Region X has as much in common with Region VII, its neighbour on the other side (80:711), but very much smaller numbers of streets and alleys (twenty as against eighty-five). It may be, and geography might suggest, that Region X is at a point of transition between different patterns of development and contained great diversity within its own extensive boundaries, but it remains to be seen what these patterns were and how they worked out in practice.

The presence of such a mighty feature as the hippodrome is a warning that, apart from the differences of social character that we would expect to find between regions, there may also be physical features within them, man-made as well as natural, that will affect their housing capacity. This is not the only reason why the figures for particular regions may, if taken too rigidly, lead to false comparisons. As noted earlier, the residential patterns in the city and the transitions between them were more fluid than the formal division into regions will show; a pattern of occupation in one of them may result from the continuation into it, of a similar pattern in its neighbour. In what follows I take the regions in groups, looking for contrasts and similarities between the groups at large without seeking to include all of them under a single set of criteria, and without attempting too much detail in the conclusions that are drawn. We are helped in this more limited aim by our knowledge of the location of the regions, and by the fact that the descriptive introductions to the regions give a guide to their physical and social character.

10.1 Domus *and* insulae

In such a matter, we might expect help from a comparison between the *Notitia* and the regionary catalogues that, under the titles *Curiosum* and *Notitia*, survive from fourth-century Rome.[4] The general similarities between the documents,

---

4. A. Nordh, *Libellus de Regionibus Urbis Romae* (1949); see esp. G. Hermansen, 'The Population of Ancient Rome: The Regionaries', *Historia* 27 (1978), pp. 129–68; S. Cosentino, '*Domus, vici* e demografia' (n. 1 above); and esp. J. Arce, 'El inventario de Roma: Curiosum y Notitia', in W. V. Harris (ed.), *The Transformations of Urbs Roma in Late Antiquity, Journal of Roman Archaeology* 33 (1999), pp. 15–22. The MS history of the *Curiosum* and the *Notitia urbis Romae*, and the relations between them, is a complicated matter that need not be pursued here. Unexpected light is shed by the appearance of the so-called *Breviarium* appended to the regionaries, in Book 16 of the Syriac *Chronicle* of the sixth-century writer known as Pseudo-Zachariah Rhetor under the year 546, the capture of Rome by Totila; see the richly documented account

in the presentation of the two cities in their fourteen regions, the cumulative totals at the end of the documents, and so on, meet the eye. On the other hand, the differences too are conspicuous, both in the numbers that are given for the various amenities listed, and, in the case of domestic residences, the definitions in use. The last of these points raises an especially difficult issue.

The inventory of residential buildings given for the city of Rome is startling in its scale and diversity. It strikes the attention at once, that the number of houses (*domus*) given for Rome, at 1,790, is much smaller than that for Constantinople, at 4,388.[5] On the other hand the number of apartments or apartment blocks (*insulae*) at Rome, in excess of 46,000, is so large as to raise serious questions for attempts to use the figures to calculate the population of Rome.[6] Of the 1,790 Roman *domus* just nine, including such atypical examples as the imperial *domus Augustana* and *Tiberiana*, are named as of special note; of the *insulae* one only, the famous 'Insula Felicles' in Region IX—a building so large that Tertullian employed it as an evocation of heaven![7] The 'Insula Felicles', whatever its real name ('Felicula'?), must have exceeded the common height of such structures at three or four storeys, the ground floor often being used for commercial purposes. The Roman catalogues also list items, such as latrines, mills, libraries, and temples, that are not mentioned at all in the more summary *Notitia* of Constantinople, describing a more recent and much smaller city (and one in which temples need not be counted).[8]

Discussion of the figures for Rome must address the term *insula*, which in legal terms means a building not sharing party walls with its neighbours, but is often used for a special case of this situation, the multi-occupied tenement blocks familiar especially from Ostia but also known from physical remnants at Rome, where insulae were incorporated into later structures that still show their form.[9]

---

by Geoffrey Greatrex (ed.) and Robert R. Phenix and Cornelia B. Horn (trans.), *The Chronicle of Pseudo-Zachariah Rhetor* (TTH 55, 2011), at pp. 419–24 (with further literature on the regionaries).

5. See S. Cosentino, '*Domus, vici* e demografia', p. 2, with references including Dagron, *Naissance d'une capitale*, pp. 525–27.

6. Hermansen, pp. 146–54. See below on the question of *insulae*.

7. See T. D. Barnes, *Tertullian: A Historical and Literary Study* (1971), pp. 243–45, doubting whether Tertullian was ever in Rome (opinions will also differ as to whether he ever set eyes upon heaven). The summary of the *Notitia* and *Curiosum* that appears in the *Chronicle* of Pseudo-Zachariah lists 1797 (for 1790) 'houses of nobles', but the gloss is a later addition without authority.

8. A library at Constantinople is mentioned at *CTh* 14.9.2 (8 May 372).

9. James E. Packer, 'Housing and Population in Imperial Ostia and Rome', *JRS* 57 (1967), pp. 80–95 with plates.

On the basis of the number of *insulae* given by the *Notitia* of Rome, multiplied by a conjectured figure of forty occupants per *insula*, it was argued long ago by the Italian scholar Guido Calza that the population of Rome in the early fourth century came out at around 1,800,000, and that *insulae* covered 9,755,000 square metres, about 70 per cent of the 13,868,750 square metres contained by the Aurelian walls. Even though Calza later modified his estimate, as regards *insulae* his figures are much too high. They are based on arbitrary assumptions as to occupation levels within the *insulae* and are surely incorrect on the meaning of the term.[10] The most convincing way to correct the numbers is, with Gerkan and Packer, to interpret the term *insula* not as an entire apartment building but as a single apartment—a living unit in a multi-occupied building, as distinct from a *domus*, a single-family residence.[11]

As for the figures themselves, given their scale and precision it seems likely that they were assembled not by the actual counting of physical entities throughout the city, an unimaginably complex operation, but through the registration of properties for legal and administrative purposes such as taxation, the recording of entitlements, or distributions of food and wine. Whatever its basis, the distinction between the two types of accommodation is not made at all by the *Notitia* of Constantinople, where the number of 4,388 *domus* is much greater than the 1,790 listed for Rome, but no *insulae* are mentioned.[12] Their absence might in principle be explained in one of two ways: that none were built by the time of compilation of the *Notitia*; or that they did exist but the compiler took no notice of them, either omitting them altogether or including them in the total of 4,388 *domus*.

It seems impossible that there were no *insulae* at all. A law of Zeno of 474/499, clarifying a law of his predecessor Leo (457–74), envisages buildings 100 feet in

---

10. The calculations of Calza are reported in Platner and Ashby, *A Topographical Dictionary of Ancient Rome* (1926), p. 281, s. 'Insula'; cf. Hermansen, pp. 146–48. Calza's assumptions would entail 4,000 *apartment blocks* at the Forum Romanum alone, a conclusion rightly rejected by Packer, p. 83. His later estimate reduced the population to a notional 1,215,648. In favour of the interpretation offered here (which seems to me unanswerable), is cited G. R. Storey, 'Regionaries-Type Insulae 2: Architectural/Residential Units at Rome', *American Journal of Archaeology* 102 (2002), pp. 411–32; G. Greatrex, *The* Chronicle *of Pseudo-Zachariah Rhetor*, p. 421 n. 158.

11. Packer, p. 83. A *domus* might adjoin an *insula*, as at *Digest* 32.91.6, but here too the distinction is between single- and multi-occupation.

12. Hermansen, pp. 154–57; Cosentino, p. 2—noting that the term *vicus* encompasses the buildings to be found in them, subject to the planning regulations mentioned in the following note. This would admit without proving the presence of multi-occupied *insulae*. The number of *domus* given in the *Collectio Civitatis* agrees with the sum of those in the individual regions.

height.[13] This is higher than the Augustan limit of 60 or 70 feet, reduced again by Trajan to 60 feet, a limitation which, if not ignored in practice, would permit five storeys of reducing ceiling height as one ascends inside the building, with businesses on the ground floor and residential accommodation above. This is evidence from a much earlier period than concerns us here, but given the early growth of Constantinople and the incentives to live there, it is unlikely that no building speculator had shown up to construct multi-occupation blocks for new arrivals unable to afford individual houses, and to accommodate transient workers and newly established businesses. Yet the compiler of the *Notitia* could not have ignored *insulae* completely, had they been the dominant feature of the city landscape. The situation is unlike that at Rome, with large numbers of *insulae* appropriate for a bigger and more densely populated city. A comparison with Manhattan is more or less irresistible, for the unsatisfied appetite for housing leading to the construction of endless apartment blocks; there are rather few of what a Roman would call '*domus*' left in New York City. The housing stock at Constantinople must have been differently weighted from that of Rome, with a higher proportion of *domus* to *insulae*. It will be obvious that this imposes conditions on the size of the population that can be projected from the figures in the *Notitia*, while the physical appearance of the city will have been very different from that of Rome. Privately owned homes, even of some elegance, could certainly be built crowded up against each other[14] (as in the hillside terrace houses found at Ephesus), but they are distinct from apartment blocks.

That there were free-standing residences at Constantinople, from the greatest to the relatively humble, is self-evident. Region I of the *Notitia* contained 'the houses of the nobility', in addition to which there are listed throughout the document at least twelve palaces and residences of members of the imperial family (Chapter 8 above, pp. 170–2). Other aristocratic *domus* are known from references in the sources, from archaeology, and from the naming of quarters of Constantinople after prominent inhabitants of the city. Although this form of naming districts

---

13. *CJust* 8.10.12⁴, addressed to the prefect of Constantinople Adamantius, who held office within these years; trans. Bruce Frier (ed.), *The Codex of Justinian: A New Annotated Translation,* etc. (2016). The law shows concern for the preservation, not only of public rights such as the width of *angiportus* (10 ft) but of private benefits, such as sea views enjoyed by neighbours, and their privacy; windows 'for light' are not to be positioned less than 6 feet from the floor. See James Packer (n. 9 above); A. G. McKay, *Houses, Villas and Palaces in the Roman World* (1975), esp. ch. 4, 'Italian Multiple Dwellings'; O. F. Robinson, *Ancient Rome: City Planning and Administration* (1992), pp. 34–38, 'Building Regulations'.

14. But not up against public buildings. *CTh* 15.1.46, of 22 October 406, requires a space of 15 feet between them—more than the 10 feet required for the width of *angiportus* by the law of Zeno cited above.

became more common in later times, the properties of Theodosius' praetorian prefect Fl. Rufinus and of the same emperor's general Promotus are examples that originate in our period.[15]

Such great aristocratic residences are a special case, vastly different from the modest dwellings of the general (even well-to-do) population of the city. As for these residences, houses built by private individuals for their own use, fourth-century laws refer to them by way of establishing the qualifications of their residents to receive the bread dole; in using this incentive to encourage members of the administration to 'increase the magnitude of the city by their zeal for building', as a law of 393 puts it, the emperor was clearly thinking of family houses built by private initiative.[16] A law of Valens addressed to the prefect of the city Clearchus sets out the different categories of *domus* in terms of their access to the water supply of the city, recently enhanced by courtesy of this same Clearchus. The finest houses, possessing baths of the more elegant kind, are permitted to use a pipe of a two-inch diameter or even, 'if the dignity of the owner requires it', a maximum of 3 inches. Owners of less opulent houses, still with baths, may use a pipe of 1.5 inches, while the most modest residences (without their own baths, presumably) will be content with a pipe of a half-inch diameter.[17] A basic calculation will show the wide differences between these categories of residence. On the assumption of a standard rate of flow, a 3-inch pipe has rather more than twice the capacity of a 2-inch pipe, four times that of a 1.5-inch pipe, and thirty-six times the capacity of a half-inch pipe. We are making the acquaintance of the many inhabitants of Constantinople who, not possessing baths in their homes, frequented the more than 160 public and private baths of the city.

10.2 Public and Private Baths

Table 10.2 sets the same figures for houses and streets beside the numbers of public and private baths. The public baths (*thermae*) are those of Arcadius (Region I), Zeuxippos (II), Honorius and Eudocia (both in V), Carosa (VII), Anastasia (IX), Constantine (X), Honorius (XIII), and one unnamed (XIV). The total of nine *thermae* listed in the main text is greater by one than the grand

15. For τὰ Ῥουφίνου, see Janin, *Constantinople Byzantine*, p. 421; τὰ Προμότου, p. 417. See above, Chapter 5, n. 10, for the partly excavated mansion in Region III of the *praepositus* Antiochus.

16. *CTh* 14.17.11 (26 April 393): 'ut...aedificandi studio magnitudinem urbis augerent.' See Jones, *Later Roman Empire*, p. 689: 'In the Eastern capital there was, it would appear, a much larger middle class, consisting mainly of officials and lawyers and professional men, who lived in separate houses.'

17. *CTh* 15.2.3, again to Clearchus (15 June 372 or 373), probably misattributed to his urban prefecture in 382; above, p. 132.

Table 10.2 Public and private baths

	domus / vici	thermae	balneae privatae
I	118/29	1	15
II	98/34	1	13
III	94/7	0	11
IV	375/35	0	7
V	184/23	2	11
VI	484/22	0	9
VII	711/85	1	11
VIII	108/21	0	10
IX	116/16	1	15
X	636/20	1	[22?]
XI	503/8	0	14
XII	363/11	0	5
XIII	43/—	1	5
XIV	167/11	1	5
Total	4,388/322	9(8)	153

total given in the *Collectio Civitatis*, which may perhaps have omitted the un-named establishment of Region XIV. The disproportionately large number of private baths (*balneae privatae*) in Region X is an extrapolation from the grand total at the end of the *Notitia* and may be incorrect. On the other hand, there were many residents to serve in that region, and as we saw in Chapter 7, p. 131f., it lay on the contour line by which, from the time of Valens, water was brought into the city. It is possible that there was a proliferation of bathing establishments along this line, as entrepreneurs seized the opportunities provided by a much-improved water delivery system (and paid the city authorities for access to it).

The relatively late date of the foundation of public *thermae* has already been noted. Only two, named after Constantine's sister Anastasia and Constantine himself, in Regions IX and X respectively, are connected with the name of that emperor and his family. The Anastasian baths are referred to by Ammianus Marcellinus as the scene of an episode in the rebellion of Procopius in the year 365. We do not know when before this they were built, but if Ammianus was correct they preceded the reign of Valens, to which they are often attributed.[18] We have

---

18. 26.6.14: 'Anastasianas balneas…, a sorore Constantini cognominatas'. See Janin, *Constantinople Byzantine*, p. 216; Chapter 11 below (p. 232).

seen too that the so-called Constantinianae were begun only under Constantius and were not dedicated until 427. On the other hand, Constantine undoubtedly set his stamp on the baths of Zeuxippos, as he transformed the Severan Tetrastoon into the Augusteum and (unless he built it entire) upgraded the hippodrome. The date of the unnamed baths of Region XIV cannot be determined, but the others show a concentration on the later fourth and early fifth centuries; the baths of Valens' wife Carosa, then those of Arcadius and Honorius (two sets of the latter), which might be either Theodosian or post-Theodosian foundations. The baths of Theodosius II's wife Eudocia in Region V may be the same as the earlier baths of Achilles, if they were renamed in the empress's honour and later reverted to their original name; this is a possible explanation for the absence of the Achilles baths from the *Notitia*.[19] Apart from the presence of two establishments in Region V, which may respond to the physical toil undertaken in its harbour and warehouses, there is little to remark on the distribution of the public *thermae*. No part of the main city was very distant from one, and of the two extra-mural regions, XIII and XIV, each had its own set by the early fifth century.

Private *balneae* are found in all parts of the city. Of the fourteen regions, nine have ten or more sets of private baths. Two of those with smaller numbers, at five each, are the extra-mural Regions XIII and XIV, the latter being on any count one of the smallest regions and a special case because of its connections with the emperors, and one is Region XII, which has no public baths either, and has already been suggested to have developed later than its neighbours. Depending on the part of the region in which they lived, its inhabitants had access to the Anastasianae and to the fifteen sets of private baths in Region IX.

It is impossible to draw precise conclusions on the distribution of private baths, since they may vary greatly in size and the *Notitia* does not make this distinction. We must also allow for private facilities in the palace quarters and the mansions of the wealthy, not to mention the houses in the first two categories of those described in the law of Valens cited earlier (houses with baths, entitled to the use of water pipes of 3 and 1.5 inches diameter respectively). These will not have met the broader social, leisure, and business uses to which baths were put in an ancient city, but they will have eased the pressure on the publicly accessible facilities. With a minimum of five *balneae* in any one region and an average of more than ten per region, in addition to the nine public *thermae* distributed among eight regions, the city was well furnished with this essential facility. At the

---

19. Janin, *Constantinople Byzantine*, p. 216. The baths of Achilles (under this name) were burned down in 433 and re-opened in 443. At p. 220 Janin misreports the Eudocianae as 'Eudoxianae'.

same time, it is clear that Constantinople was still a very much smaller city than Rome. In the *Notitia* of the city of Rome, the number of public baths is given as eleven, but the number of private establishments at 830. The number of public baths at Rome may seem relatively modest, until we consider the question of scale. Even the great Zeuxippon can hardly have approached the vast extent of the baths of Caracalla or Diocletian. 'Baths as big as provinces', wrote Ammianus Marcellinus, to convey their impact on the emperor Constantius on the occasion of his visit to Rome in 357—perhaps also on himself, as he came to Rome to seek his literary fortune in the early 380s (16.10.14).

10.3 Public and Private Bakeries

In Table 10.3 the same figures for houses and streets are repeated beside those for public and private bakeries (*pistrinae*), adding the number of *gradus* in each region, since all three elements were interconnected; both the bakeries and the recipients of the dole were assigned to particular *gradus* for the distributions of bread. The *Notitia* recognizes the connection, invariably placing the number of *gradus* immediately after those of public and private bakeries. There are some discrepancies between the totals added up by region and those given in the *Collectio Civitatis* (shown in brackets), but they are not such as to undermine

Table 10.3 Houses and streets, bakeries, *gradus*

	domus / vici	pistrina publica	pistrina privata	gradus
I	118/29	4	15	4
II	98/34	0	4	4
III	94/7	0	9	[10?]
IV	375/35	0	5	7
V	184/23	7	2	9
VI	484/22	1	17	17
VII	711/ 85	0	12	16
VIII	108 /21	0	5	5
IX	116/16	4	15	4
X	636/20	2	16	12
XI	503/8	1	3	7
XII	363/11	0	5	9
XIII	431/—	1	4	8
XIV	167/11	1	1	5
Total	4,388/322	21 (20)	113 (120)	117

the broad inferences that may be made from the figures. The number of *gradus* for Region III, missing from the *Notitia*, is inferred from the *Collectio Civitatis*, and seems large in relation to the other figures for this region.

The distribution of bakeries was not simply a function of the division of the city into its regions. Recipients of the bread dole were obliged to receive it at the *gradus* to which they were assigned by residence and where their names were registered, but this need not be in their own region; the distributions were established before the regions, and the inhabitants of Constantinople were not obliged to buy their bread in the region in which they happened to live. It might be more convenient for inhabitants of Region XI, a large region with many houses but few bakeries, to buy their bread in the adjacent Region X, which has many, or for the inhabitants of Region XII, with only five bakeries, to buy it in nearby parts of Region IX, with fifteen. A literal insistence on the figures would mean little in face of the mobility of the people of Constantinople as they lived their daily lives. Nevertheless, the pull of locality is strong, and bread is a basic commodity. A family's bread would naturally be bought locally in most circumstances, some of it at market price to supplement the fixed-price public distributions. It is then striking to find as many as four public and fifteen private bakeries among the 'noble houses' of Region I. The population in this region, of people hidden away in the palaces and great houses, must have been deceptively numerous. At the same time the presence of only four *gradus* suggests a relatively small number of residents entitled to the dole, not surprising if they were in large part the dependants of the imperial and other great families who lived there.

Less surprising are the low numbers of four private (and no public bakeries) in Region II, if we bear in mind that this region largely consisted of the Graeco-Roman city with its acropolis, and possessed the second smallest number of houses of any of the regions (and only four *gradus*)—though it was still graced by a relatively large number of private baths, suggesting pleasant excursions to this historic part of the city. Region VIII, the smallest region, possessed only five private bakeries and the same number of *gradus*. The small numbers of bakeries in the much larger Regions XI and XII may strengthen the other indications that these Regions were relatively late to join the economic development of their neighbours, and the small numbers both of baths and bakeries in Region XIV are consistent with the special circumstances of that detached community, which, if correctly located at Regium (p. 95f.) was little more than an extended palace precinct.

At the other extreme are the large numbers, both of public and private *pistrinae* and of *gradus*, in the commercial areas of the city. Region V, the heart of this commercial activity on its northern side, shows by far the largest number of public bakeries (seven), and its neighbours to the west, VI, VII, and X, some of the largest numbers of private bakeries (seventeen, twelve, and sixteen); these

four adjacent regions have fifty-four *gradus* between them, confirming the high
population levels implied by the economic nature of these regions. Similarly, the
other main commercial district, Region IX to the south of the peninsula, shows
as many as four public and fifteen private bakeries, the low number of *gradus*, at
four, being consistent with the low number of houses (116) recorded for this
region. In the cases of Regions V and IX the large numbers of public bakeries may
also be connected with the granaries (*horrea*) recorded for these regions.

In general, and without taking account of the distinction between public and
private baths and bakeries, some of which were very large and some very small
(the Zeuxippon or Constantinianae cannot be treated like a modest street-corner
bath-house run by a private individual and his family), the numbers of these essential institutions are of the same order of magnitude: 153 baths (possibly too
high a figure), and anything between 133 and 141 bakeries, taking the highest and
lowest combinations from the numbers given in the *Notitia*. The average number
of each institution runs to about ten per region, with a set of baths for every
twenty-eight and a bakery for every thirty-one *domus*, in each case with a bath or
bakery almost for every second street.[20] These are crude numbers, for the regions
of Constantinople differed widely in their general character and in their rate of
development, and they are only intended to give a general impression of the provision of these services as they are documented by the *Notitia*.

It is also possible, as a matter of general observation supported by the *Notitia*,
to discern at least in outline the distribution of the population of Constantinople.
In the south-eastern corner of the promontory was the palace quarter and the
noble houses clustered around it. These contained a large population of servants
and attendants, relatively few of them qualifying for the bread dole and so requiring a correspondingly low number of *gradus* in relation to the large number of
bakeries. North of this quarter, and of the monumental development of the Augusteum, was the acropolis and the ancient city of Byzantium and the remains of
its old institutions, with a larger but still limited population. The Mesē was a
spine of economic as it was of monumental development to the west. On the
shores of the peninsula to north and south were the harbours and associated commercial installations, and it is here that we find high population levels implying
multi-occupation of apartment buildings. This pattern of occupation continues

---

20. A relevant sidelight on baths and bakeries (and on the diversity of senators' incomes) is the
legacy to the Roman church of the 'illustrious lady' Vestina, as recorded by the *Liber Pontifica-
lis*. It included 'a bath close to the basilica Liviana, near the temple of Mamurus, revenue 32
solidi; a house with a bath on the Clivus Salutis, revenue 77 solidi, 1 tremiss; the bakery called
Castoriani on the Vicus Longus, revenue 61 solidi, the bath on the Vicus Longus, called the
Temple, revenue 40 solidi, 3 siliquae', not to mention 'one quarter of the duties extracted at the
Porta Nomentana, revenue 22 solidi, 1 tremiss'; *Liber Pontificalis* 42.54; translated R. P. Davis
(TTH 6, rev. edn, 2000), pp. 33–34.

to the regions by the wall of Constantine, where it gives place to a higher proportion of individual housing in parts of the city that were developed later. This we shall see more closely in what follows.

10.4 The Population of Constantinople

We begin with a problem of definition raised earlier, relating to the word *domus*, of which the *Notitia* claims there were 4,388 in the city as a whole, with figures for the separate regions. Is the term an essentially juridical definition or is it a physical criterion? Does it mean, in Cyril Mango's words, a 'substantial house',[21] or does it have the more abstract sense of a residence or 'household' without reference to the form of accommodation, possibly defined by some qualification such as entitlement to the bread dole, such that *domus* comes in practice to be coterminous with a household? The notion that *domus* means the same thing at Constantinople as at Rome with its vast numbers of *insulae*, and that there were nearly three times as many *domus* at Constantinople as at Rome is clearly extremely problematic. A closer analysis is needed, which might begin by asking how the numbers should be distributed between free-standing houses and larger units of accommodation, and the occupation levels we can assume for each.

As we saw, the interpretation of *insula* in the *Notitia* and *Curiosum* of Rome as an entire apartment block led to distortion in our sense of the physical appearance of the city, and to greatly inflated estimate of population levels. It is better to suppose that the term denotes a living unit in a multi-occupied building, whether this was one of the three- to four-storied custom-built structures known from Rome and Ostia, or a subdivision of a more modest establishment, or even something as archaeologically indeterminate but commonplace as a private house with rooms to let. As for occupation levels, James Packer's estimate of four inhabitants per apartment seems a little too much like an image of the modern nuclear family, allowing insufficiently for the accumulation of relatives, and for the over-crowding endemic in a big city. Even individuals who came to Rome and lived in (presumably) rented accommodation, like Apuleius, Ammianus Marcellinus, Augustine, and even St. Paul, not to mention an observer like Juvenal (if he writes from personal experience), can be assumed to have been accompanied by friends and travelling companions; coming to Rome from the upper echelons of their local societies, to advance themselves in various ways and with connections in the city, such people did not travel or live alone. When one considers dependant relatives and, sometimes, the one or two servants that were attached to the families living in such apartments, and allows for the greater capacity of some apartments, a notional allowance of six occupants per *insula* does not seem too high.

---

21. *Byzantium: The Empire of the New Rome* (1980), p. 76; cf. A. H. M. Jones, n. 16 above.

As for *domus*, individual houses in the sense preserved by the *Notitia* of Rome, we are looking at occupation levels that varied widely, from family groups in their modest homes to the mansions of the senatorial and former equestrian classes, including many successful freedmen, with household staffs that might number in the hundreds.[22] The range of possibilities makes the whole question of an average level of occupation of the individual house very difficult to answer, but given a Roman upper class encompassing far great numbers than the traditional senatorial order, a large proportion of the 1790 *domus* listed by the Roman *Notitia* must have fallen into the category of extremely opulent establishments, with huge numbers of household staff.[23] A purely illustrative assumption of one hundred inhabitants per *domus* gives a total of 179,000 in this category, and on a reckoning of six occupants for each *insula*, the number of *insulae* listed by the Roman *Notitia* yields a population of 279,612 living in apartments. At 458,612 we are on the way to an overall population estimate approaching 1 million, not unlikely since we have not allowed for the huge staffs of the imperial palaces, visitors to the city, or the dispossessed who, according to Ammianus Marcellinus (14.6.5), made their homes in the arcades of the theatres, or the usual movement in and out of the city of people who lived around it but not within the bounds of its Fourteen Regions.

Another approach to the figure of 4,388 *domus* at Constantinople might lie in the relationship between *domus* and other elements of the urban infrastructure recorded in the *Notitia*, for example that between *domus* and *gradus*, as discussed above. Table 10.4 lists in two columns the seven lowest and the seven highest numbers of *domus* for each of the fourteen regions. The first number in each column is the number of *domus* arranged in rising order, the second is the number of *gradus*, and the third is the ratio between them.

It is interesting, though no doubt fortuitous, that there is a clear break between the numbers of *domus* in the respective columns; the lowest number in each column is roughly half the highest in that column, and the highest number in the first column (184) is about half the lowest number in the second (363). In each column the numbers of *gradus*, and therefore the ratio between *domus* and *gradus*, are consistent with the break in the numbers of houses; in only one case,

---

22. Compare Ammianus' description of senators dragging their households through the streets of Rome 'like ransacking armies' (14.6.16–17; cf. 28.4.18). In the partially preserved Testament of 'Dasumius' (*CIL* 6.10229; Bruns, *FIRA⁷*, no. 117), it is possible to detect the manumissions of at least fifteen household slaves (including 'contubernales'), and the original text must have contained many more. Such large-scale testamentary manumissions presume substantial slave *familiae*; see my 'A Last Will and Testament', *Roman Perspectives* (2010), pp. 111–56, esp. at 138–39 and 143–45.

23. A notorious case is the urban *familia* of four hundred urban slaves ('familia omnis quae sub eodem tecto mansitaverat') condemned to die 'vetere ex more' after the murder of their master, the urban prefect Pedanius Secundus, in Tacitus, *Ann.* 14.42–45.

Table 10.4 *Domus* and *gradus*

III	94	[10]	[9.4]	XII	363	9	40.3
II	98	4	24.5	IV	375	7	53.5
VIII	108	5	21.6	XIII	431	8	53.875
IX	116	4	29.0	VI	484	17	28.4
I	118	4	29.5	XI	503	7	71.85
XIV	167	5	33.4	X	636	12	53.0
V	184	9	20.4	VII	711	16	44.4

that of Region VI (28.4), do the ratios of the second column overlap with those in the first. As noted earlier, the number of *gradus* in Region III is doubtful; it is missing from the text of this region and is supplied from the grand total in the *Collectio Civitatis*. The number of *gradus* should probably be lower and the ratio of *gradus* to *domus* proportionately higher, but not so as to displace this region from its place as the lowest number in the first column.

The variations in the figures should not be driven too hard. Some are to be explained by inherent differences in the regions, such as their size and physical configuration; others, no doubt, by the anomalies of organization that may occur in a big city—the fourteen regions should not be seen as a perfect blueprint for city government. There is also the question of different levels of involvement in the distributions of bread; it is unlikely that the emperor himself and his noble supporters in Region I, or the occupants of other well-heeled areas like Regions II and III, were much interested in asserting their rights to the distributions, and there was less need to provide for them. Overriding all such reservations, however, is the fact that the ratio of *domus* to *gradus* rises faster than the number of *gradus* in themselves, some of which were evidently much more frequented than others by individuals qualified to receive the distributions. One can see at once that the regions in the first column generally coincide with the less densely and those in the second column with the more densely populated parts of the city. The most obvious explanation of the rapid elevation in the ratios between *domus* and *gradus* is that we are observing real differences in population density, and that the term *domus*, as used by the *Notitia*, is a variable element, encompassing different types of residence.

10.5 Living Conditions

We may use this observation as a starting point from which to address two further questions: the living conditions of the people of Constantinople and the size of the population of the city. This will introduce a feature not considered so far, the attention given to its physical security. In the first three columns of Table 10.5

Table 10.5 *Domus, Vici, Collegiati*

	domus	vici	domus:vici	collegiati	collegiati :domus	collegiati :vici
I	118 (9)	29 (4)	4.07 (12)	25 (11)	4.72 (9)	1.16 (2)
II	98 (13)	34 (3)	2.88 (13)	35 (9)	2.8 (14)	0.97 (4)
III	94 (14)	7 (13)	13.43 (6)	21 (12)	4.48 (12)	0.33 (10)
IV	375 (6)	35 (2)	10.71 (7)	40 (4)	9.375 (5)	0.875 (5)
V	184 (8)	23 (5)	8.0 (9)	40 (4)	4.6 (10)	0.575 (7)
VI	484 (4)	22 (6)	22.0 (4)	49 (3)	9.88 (4)	0.45 (8)
VII	711 (1)	85 (1)	8.36 (8)	80 (2)	8.89 (6)	1.06 (3)
VIII	108 (12)	21 (7)	5.14 (11)	17 (13)	6.35 (8)	1.24 (1)
IX	116 (11)	16 (9)	7.25 (10)	8 (6)	3.05 (13)	0.42 (9)
X	636 (2)	20 (8)	31.80 (3)	90 (1)	7.07 (7)	0.22 (12)
XI	503 (3)	8 (12)	62.88 (1)	37 (7)	13.6 (3)	0.22 (12)
XII	363 (7)	11 (10)	33.0 (2)	17 (13)	21.35 (1)	0.65 (6)
XIII	431 (5)	—	—	34 (10)	12.68 (2)	—
XIV	167 (10)	11 (10)	15.18 (5)	[37 (7)]	4.51 (11)	0.30 (11)
Total	4,388	322	13.63	560	7.84	0.575

are shown for each region the numbers of houses and streets and the ratios between them, and in the last three columns the numbers of *collegiati* and the ratio of *collegiati* to houses and streets. The rank order of the regions under each category is given in parenthesis. The regions are then discussed in four groups, following the numerical series of the *Notitia*.

10.5.1 Regions I–III

Regions I, II, and III cover the historic district at the eastern end of the peninsula and pose relatively few problems in relation to the information provided by the *Notitia*. Not surprisingly given the monumental character of this part of the city, which also contained eleven 'grand colonnades' (Table 10.1), the numbers both of streets and houses are relatively low; taken as a group they are the lowest figures among all the regions with the exception of VIII and IX, which were among the smallest. The twenty-nine streets and 118 houses of Region I yield a ratio of merely 4.1 houses to streets, no doubt reflecting the presence of the great palace and the spacious houses of the nobility mentioned by the *Notitia*. Region II, the old

acropolis, yields thirty-four streets and ninety-eight houses, a still lower ratio of
2.9, with a similar implication of a large proportion of non-residential building
(not forgetting the old temple sites, now decommissioned and confiscated by the
government), while in Region III there were a mere seven streets with ninety-four
domus with a higher ratio of 13.4 houses to streets, suggesting a denser pattern of
settlement in the parts of the region not occupied by the hippodrome with its
ancillary services, and the harbour of Julian. The numbers of *collegiati* in Regions
I–III are also at the low end of the range, falling in eighth, ninth, and tenth positions among the twelve intramural regions, with only Regions VIII and XII
below them. This no doubt corresponds to the low number of *gradus* in Regions
I and II (only four in each), catering for an evidently small number of qualifying
households. The number of ten *gradus* for the ninety-four *domus* of Region III
seems on the other hand rather high. We saw above that the figure is a restoration
in the text; if accurate it would be consistent with a denser pattern of settlement
indicated by the proportion of houses (interpreted as residential units of either
type described above) to streets.

With this possible exception relating to a part of one region, we might conclude from the lower number of *collegiati* in Regions I–III, that in this historic
part of the city, with many monuments and public institutions spanning centuries, the individual houses would be large, the side-streets few, and the risk of fire
and disorder relatively low. The similarly low proportions of *domus* to streets
would suggest that there was relatively little multi-occupation in this part of the
city, with the possible exception of the part of Region III near the harbour of
Julian, where we would expect a denser level of habitation. We can also assume
that, apart from the provision made by the city administration, the well-connected
families who lived in these areas, and of course the emperor himself, had their
own ways of guarding their material security.[24]

10.5.2 Regions IV–VII

The next group of regions takes us over to the northern side of the city. Forming
a continuous series bounded by the Mesē and the Golden Horn, these regions
include the part of old Byzantium north of the acropolis (Region IV), shading to
the west into a commercial centre with forum, warehouses, commercial harbour,
and two sets of public baths (Region V); then a dockyard with a second harbour

---

24. See for Rome the episode recorded by Amm. Marc. 27.3.5–9, with my *The Roman Empire of
Ammianus*, p. 417—the slave *familia* of an aristocratic household holding off the attack of a
disorderly crowd.

and the ferry crossing to Sycae (Region VI). Region VII contained the Thermae Carosianae, the northern sector of the forum of Theodosius, three churches, and a very large number of *domus*.

The numbers of streets and *domus* for this group of regions show fairly consistent proportions, implying a higher-range density of occupation than we found in Regions I–III. In Region IV, thirty-five streets contain 375 *domus* at a ratio of 10.7 houses to streets; in Region V, twenty-three streets contain 184 *domus* (a ratio of 8.0); in Region VI, twenty-four streets contain 484 houses (a ratio of 22.0, a higher figure than that for its neighbours but within the range for the regions as a whole), and in Region VII, eighty-five streets contain 711 *domus*, the largest number of any region, but at a ratio of a mere 8.4 houses to streets. The large numbers of *collegiati*, at forty for each of Regions IV and V, forty-nine for Region VI and as many as eighty for Region VII, confirm the impression of a dense pattern of settlement vulnerable to the risks of fire and disorder; in fact, these regions, along with their high numbers of residential units, produce four of the five largest bands of *collegiati* recorded. The numbers of *gradus* listed for the respective regions (seven, nine, seventeen, sixteen) are proportionate within rather broad limits, ranging from over fifty-three *domus* per *gradus* in Region IV to just twenty houses per *gradus* in Region V. The lower numbers of *domus* recorded for this region might reflect the presence of the commercial buildings, connected with the harbours, that are mentioned by the *Notitia*.

Speculative as they may be, there is nothing surprising in these conclusions, given the character of Regions IV–VII as it appears from the *Notitia*. We should especially note the high numbers in all categories of *domus*, streets, *collegiati*, and *gradus* for Region VII, which also contained its three churches. This is the largest number of churches in any of the regions of the city, and the presence of the foundation named after Paul, the restive bishop of Constantinople, may tell us where this popular leader found his support.[25] A likely picture is that Region VII was a lower-class residential area with many apartments, densely populated by working men who left it every day for the commercial establishments of Regions V and VI. It is also worth repeating an observation made earlier, that these four regions contain none of the great imperial palaces and 'houses of the nobility' that are listed in the *Notitia*. The contrast between this part of Constantinople and that represented by Regions I–III could not be clearer. It was not their part of town.

---

25. Again Ammianus Marcellinus, describing the popularity of Paul's contemporary, Liberius of Rome; the people 'blazed with passion' (*amore flagrabat*) for its leader (15.7.10), who had to be spirited out of the city when exiled by Constantius.

10.5.3 Regions VIII–IX

In Region VIII we come to the smallest of the regions. It presents just 108 *domus* (only Regions II and III are lower) among twenty-one streets (a low proportion of 5.1 *domus* to streets) and, at seventeen, the joint lowest number of *collegiati* of any region; the number of five *gradus* is also low. The region contained part of the forum of Constantine, the basilica of Theodosius, and the Capitolium but no very spacious monument otherwise, and the low numbers seem simply to reflect the small extent of the region. The ratio of *domus* to streets might also suggest that it was not one of the most crowded. This could however be a misleading impression given the physical configuration of the region, which sloped away quite steeply to the south of the Mesē. The region contained five colonnades (including the southern colonnade of the Mesē, which marked its border), which are more likely to have followed the level east-west contours of the land than to have plunged downhill towards the shore. If a proportion of its twenty-one streets ran across this narrow region from north to south, the low number of houses per street might just be a function of the shortness of the streets. This embarrassingly banal observation may serve as a warning against an over-schematic interpretation of the figures in other parts of the city as well.

Its southern neighbour, Region IX, was another commercial area containing two major warehouses by the harbour of Theodosius, and two churches, Caenopolis and Homonoea; the name of the first of these ('New Town') may, as we saw in Chapter 5, reflect the inclusion of a separate community of one sort of another within the city of Constantine, whether it was based on the reclamation of building land from the sea, or as suggested (p. 91), it was a main settlement of the actual builders of Constantinople. That it too was a small region is indicated by the low numbers both of streets (sixteen) and *domus* (116; a ratio of 7.25), and it has the joint lowest number of *gradus* (four) of any region; the number of *collegiati* (thirty-eight) is in the middle range overall, but quite large for the size of the region. The combination of the modest size of the region and this relatively large band of *collegiati* may express more crowded living conditions and the need to protect its important commercial installations. Like Region V, its nearest equivalent on the northern side of the peninsula, Region VIII contained warehouses and a harbour, while many of those who were employed in these facilities may have lived in adjacent parts of neighbouring regions.

10.5.4 Regions X–XII

Moving up the northern coast of the peninsula and then across it, we come to the adjacent Regions X, XI, and XII, running in an arc, veering north-easterly to

southerly, inside the wall of Constantine. Here we encounter some unusual numbers, implying a different set of issues from those we have seen so far. To begin
with their common features, all three regions show a relatively or extremely high
number of *domus* (636, 503, 363), distributed among a small number of streets
and alleys (twenty, eight, eleven). The ratio of *domus* to streets comes out at 31.8
for Region X, 62.9 for Region XI (an outlying figure, resulting from an abnor-
mally low number of streets), and 33.0 for Region XII. In fact these three regions
together provide the highest ratios of houses to streets of any of the twelve intra-
urban regions; the next highest ratio after Region X is 22.0 for Region VI, again
with a large number of *domus*.[26] Bearing in mind that Region X, on the northern
side of the peninsula, continues the sequence of largely commercial regions
(IV–VII) just surveyed and is adjacent to the most heavily populated of them,
we may suppose that it was a fully developed part of the city, with residential
properties in the area more remote from Region VII and *insulae* in the parts
nearer to it. It was a spacious region, its large area offset by three imperial residences as well as the large site of the baths of Constantine. The very large number
of *domus* given for Region X also correlates with the number of *collegiati*, which
at ninety is the highest of any region and again suggests some affinity with its
neighbour Region VII, where eighty *collegiati* are recorded.

Region X's neighbours to the south tell a rather different story. The number
of thirty-seven *collegiati* for the 503 houses of Region XI falls seventh in the order
of regions, and the little band of seventeen *collegiati* for the 363 houses of Region
XII distributed among its eleven streets occupies last position in the series, jointly
with the much smaller Region VIII. The numbers of *collegiati* for Region XII
bear a closer correlation with *domus* than with streets, which is what one might
expect since fires begin in houses, but it is not very close, and other factors may be
coming into play. The relatively small numbers of *domus* and *collegiati* might reflect the presence of monumental areas like the forum of Arcadius and of higher
land—the situation of Arcadius' forum was known as 'Xerolophos', 'Dry Ridge'—
not conducive to domestic settlement (which means in practice that it would
occur there later). The approaches to the Golden Gate via the Troadensian colonnades might also have covered a considerable portion of the available ground, and
one would expect the imperial mint (*moneta*), located between the forum of Arcadius and the golden gate, to have possessed a guarded precinct. It is true that
Region XII shared with its eastern neighbour Region IX a connection with the
harbour of Theodosius and attendant facilities, but this was a fairly recent development at the time of the *Notitia*, and it may be that the full effects of it were not

---

26. Region XIII (Sycae) has 431 houses, but the number of streets and alleys is not given.

yet felt. The explanation of the smaller number of houses in Region XII might simply be its less advanced stage of residential development, combined perhaps with the presence of some upper-class residences occupying large building lots on prime sites with a view of the Propontis, such as we know existed outside the Constantinian wall.[27]

The outstanding common feature of these three regions is nevertheless their low numbers of streets in relation to high numbers of houses, which is consistent between them and may reflect some more general aspect of the configuration of the city. Possibly they had been laid out with main avenues for a development that had not progressed very far in this newer part of the city, so that the alleyways common in its older quarters had not yet appeared. As time went on and the inhabitants of new residential developments found their way around their neighbourhoods, tracks and shortcuts would appear and, as they were established by use, form new streets and alleys that would be the focus of later development; perhaps the figures of the *Notitia* for these regions have caught such a process in its early stages. It would correspond to Themistius' description, cited earlier, of the development of Constantinople towards the west, as undeveloped parts of the city were filled in by urban settlement, a process continuing at the time of the *Notitia*.

Taking the figures in their broadest sense, the numbers of *domus*, streets, and *collegiati* reported by the *Notitia* underline the affinities between Regions I, the palace and aristocratic quarter, and its neighbours to each side, II (the acropolis) and III (containing the hippodrome). These three regions occupy low positions both as to the number of houses (ninth, thirteenth, fourteenth) and of *collegiati* (eleventh, ninth, twelfth) attributed to them. At the other extreme, three of the four intra-mural regions that possess the greatest number of *domus* (VI, VII, X) also claim the highest numbers of *collegiati* (forty-nine, ninety, eighty).[28] It was noted that these regions, which form a continuous series on the northern side of the peninsula, share the character of the commercial and harbour districts contained in Regions IV and V. This is borne out by the figures, for these predominantly commercial districts, in sixth and eighth positions in the number of houses listed, share fourth place as to the numbers of *collegiati* (forty), suggesting a high level of risk. The lower number of houses for Region V was partly explained by the suggestion that while this region was a centre of the commercial operations of

---

27. Mango, *Développement Urbain*, p. 47; see below on the possible bearing of these holdings (among other issues) on the building of the Theodosian wall.

28. The fourth of these high-scoring intramural regions is XI, which with the third highest number of 503 houses distributed among just eight streets, claims only thirty-seven *collegiati*, putting it in seventh place in this category.

the city, many those who worked there lived, not among the warehouses located in this region, but in the quarters to the west of it. The large expanse of Region X was offset by the Constantinianae baths and three imperial residences. The development of the Theodosian harbour had economic consequences for the parts of Regions IX and XII nearest to it, but it is clear that the northern shore along the Golden Horn was the most heavily populated part of the city, and likely that Regions XI and XII were the latest to be developed.[29]

10.6 The Size of the Population

This is one version of the groundwork to be done before addressing the question of the overall population of Constantinople. The general conclusions do not look as if they should be especially controversial. The housing stock was mixed as between free-standing residences and apartments, and the number of 4,388 *domus* presented by the *Notitia* covers both forms of accommodation, excluding the listed palaces and great houses of the imperial family; and there is some consistency in the proportions of the two forms of accommodation to be expected as one moves around the city and takes account of the varying character of its regions. For the reasons given earlier, it is assumed that the proportion of *domus* to *insulae* was higher at Constantinople than at Rome, and that the *domus* were more modest, reflecting the appearance of a more recent propertied class in the new city and the absence of the immense fortunes of Roman senatorial families that had accumulated over generations.[30]

Despite these encouraging observations, it remains an intractable problem with *domus* that they varied widely in size and character, from modest single-family homes (those entitled to half-inch water pipes) to opulent residences with 3-inch pipes, domestic bath-houses, and scores of servants. A possible way of approaching the problem is however suggested by Andrew Wallace-Hadrill's study of the housing stock of first-century Pompeii; for all its remoteness in place and time, and the different conditions in which these urban communities were established and evolved, the study has the advantage of being based on a concrete analysis of a physical environment of which something is known; and it may provide a model of urban development that can be modified in a controlled fashion as more is learned about Constantinople. If what follows is entirely conjectural, it is offered as a means of getting some grasp of an issue that might otherwise be inaccessible.

---

29. Comparable results are produced by Cosentino, '*Domus, vici* e demografia', p. 4, on the basis of the area of the respective regions, after the calculations of A. Berger and D. P. Drakoulis (n. 1 above and Chapter 4, n. 9).

30. See Jones, *Later Roman Empire*, p. 689, cited above, n. 14.

For the purpose of analysis, Wallace-Hadrill divides the housing stock in the excavated areas of Pompeii into four numerically equal categories of house size, of 1.4, 4.7, 8.4, and 16.4 rooms respectively, and suggests population estimates based on an assumption of one person per room. To eliminate the first and smallest category, which does not seem relevant to the level of urban planning involved at Constantinople, produces an average of ten persons per house in the remaining three categories.[31] The number of categories postulated for Constantinople will need to be extended at the higher end, for the obvious reasons that the city was an imperial capital attracting new residents to take up positions with the government, and that its upper class, without beginning to challenge the wealth of its Roman counterpart, still possessed resources of wealth far exceeding those of a modest Italian city (we should remind ourselves of those 3- and 2-inch water pipes).[32] To allow for this, I have added to Wallace-Hadrill's classification a further category of residences with an average population of twenty-five, producing an average over the four categories now in play of 13.6 persons per house.[33] I also suspect, however, that the occupancy of Pompeian houses was greater than the range of 14/20 persons envisaged for his fourth and largest category. The young Augustine's household in fourth-century Thagaste contained his parents Patricius and Monnica and their three children, together with Patricius' mother, his old nurse, and the 'ancillae' who stirred up bad blood between Monnica and her mother-in-law and with whom (or some of whom!) Patricius is claimed to have had sexual affairs. There were no doubt also male slaves, some of them attached to the *ancillae*; the total must have been of the order of fifteen persons, in a family which, of marginal curial status,[34] would not fall in the highest of Wallace-Hadrill's categories of house size. If it were to be equated with the second largest of his categories, a house of 8.4 rooms, we would need almost to double the occupancy rate of one person per room, producing an average of 27.2 (13.6 × 2) persons per house. This is assumed in what follows, reduced to twenty-five in order to use round numbers that do not convey a misleading sense of precision.

---

31. A. Wallace-Hadrill, *Houses and Society in Pompeii and Herculaneum* (1994), pp. 79–82 and 101–2 with table 4.2 at p. 81.

32. Wallace-Hadrill, pp. 88, 102 and elsewhere contrasts fourth-century BCE Olynthus as a city with a greater level of overall planning than Pompeii, the latter of which 'incorporates the expectation of inequality' (p. 102).

33. It might be thought that more than one higher category should be added to compensate for the great differences between the two cities; but I do not wish to depart too far from Wallace-Hadrill's model, and in any case take separately the great houses of the nobility, mentioned but left uncounted by the *Notitia*.

34. This is how I interpret *Conf.* 2.3.5, 'municeps admodum tenuis', meaning a modest member of the curial class; cf. 2.3.6 for an acknowledgement of Patricius' marginal financial state.

Table 10.6(a) Houses and Apartments: Hypothetical
Proportions

	houses	apartments	
at 40:60	1,755 × 25 = 43,875	2,633 × 6 = 15,798	59,673
at 50:50	2,194 × 25 = 54,850	2,194 × 6 = 13,164	68,014
at 60:40	2,633 × 25 = 65,825	1,755 × 6 = 10,530	76,355
at 75:25	3,291 × 25 = 82,275	1,097 × 6 = 6,582	88,857

The calculations will consist of a presentation of models rather than evidentially based arguments, the aim being to identify the factors that will affect the outcome and allow different assumptions to be incorporated. In what follows, the term 'residential unit' is used without further qualification to refer to the *domus* listed by the *Notitia*, on the assumption, argued above, that the housing stock at Constantinople included both free-standing houses and apartments. Relative distributions of 40:60, 50:50, 60:40, and 75:25 houses to apartments produce the results shown above for the numbers living in each type of accommodation (see above for the multipliers of 25 and 6 used for houses and apartments respectively) (Table 10.6a).

It is obvious that differing assumptions about the population levels of each type of accommodation, and the relative proportions to be assigned to each type, will affect the figures; evidently, the larger the proportion of inhabitants living in houses, the higher the overall population will be.[35] If the term *domus* were taken to include only separate houses, the total population living in them works out at 109,700 (4,388 × 25).[36]

As to which model of distribution best fits Constantinople, it is worth pausing on the figures for the five urban districts, or *grammata*, of second- or early third-century Alexandria, as they are presented in the Syriac version of a *Notitia urbis Alexandrinae* mentioned in Chapter 4 (p. 62).[37] The five *grammata* (*A–E*)

35. S. Cosentino, '*Domus, vici* e demografia', at p. 3, offers a breakdown of the two categories close to the first of those set out above, but his deduction of the 1790 *domus* given for Rome to produce a figure of 2,598 multiple occupation buildings for Constantinople and his estimate of fifty occupants of the latter seem to me equally arbitrary.

36. James Packer (above, n. 9) offers for Ostia a very different distribution from any of these, producing for the excavated part of the city a figure in excess of 3,000 residential units in *insulae* (the exact count is hard to determine) as against a mere twenty-two 'private mansions scattered throughout the site' (p. 86). However, the pattern of urban development at Ostia was very different from that at Constantinople (or Pompeii, for that matter), where we need to think of a much larger number of modest family residences.

37. P. M. Fraser, 'A Syriac *Notitia Urbis Alexandrinae*', *Journal of Egyptian Archaeology* 37 (1951), pp. 103–8—acknowledging the work of the Syriac scholar J.-B. Chabot. The five

of the city contain respectively (*A*) 1,655 'courts' and 5,058 houses, (*B*) 1,002 courts and 5,990 houses, (*Γ*) 955 courts and 2,140 houses, (*Δ*) 1,120 courts and 5,515 houses, and (*E*) 1,420 courts and 5,593 houses, to give a total of 8,102 courts and 24,296 houses. On the assumption that the word 'courts' taken over from Chabot's translation (*cours*) of the Syriac text is equivalent to the *insula* of the Roman regionaries, the overall proportions between court and house are almost precisely the 75:25 division projected in the fourth category set out in Table 10.6(a) above. The assumption is speculative, but if the housing stock of Alexandria is divided at all into two categories, it is hard to see what they can be except for free-standing houses and apartments.

There is also the question of the distribution of the two categories of domestic accommodation through the city, and of the character of its different quarters. The figures for Alexandria reflect this, in the varying proportions of 'courts' and houses in the respective *grammata*, ranging from the 1:3 and 1:2.5 courts to houses of *grammata A* and *Γ*, through 1:4, 1:5, and 1:6 for *grammata E, Δ*, and *B*. The absolute numbers listed in the Alexandrian *Notitia* are very much higher than those for Constantinople (and quite differently proportioned than those from Rome, with the latter's great preponderance of *insulae*), to which the answer might simply be that Alexandria was a bigger, older, and more crowded city. Its houses were smaller and population densities higher than those at Constantinople, in much the same way that houses in industrial Sheffield are smaller than those in leafy Tunbridge Wells.

To take up the case of Constantinople, we might begin by observing, as in Table 10.4 above, that the numbers of *domus* given by the *Notitia*, shown in two columns of equal length, display a distinct gap between the seven lowest and the seven highest numbers given for the fourteen regions; they range from 94 to 184 for the lowest and from 363 to 711 units for the seven highest regions, with totals for each group as follows (Table 10.6b).

The omission of the extra-mural Regions XIII and XIV (one in each group, with 431 and 167 units respectively) yields a proportionate result (Table 10.6c).

That the figures have a basis in the physical configuration of the city is supported by the occurrence in each group of adjacent regions possessing the same character. In fact, if Region V, which belongs with VI–VII in terms of its social configuration and offers the highest number of residential units in Group 1, were moved to Group 2, the prevalence of 'blocks' of adjacent regions would be still clearer; no region would then stand by itself. The natural assumption that the higher figures in Group 2 reflect a greater prevalence of multi-occupation in these

---

grammata are otherwise attested for the period of the *Notitia*, but exclude several quarters of the city.

Table 10.6(b) Housing Units in the *Notitia*:
Distribution by Region

Group (col.) 1:	Regions I–III, V, VIII–IX, XIV	885
Group (col.) 2:	Regions IV, VI–VII, X–XIII	3,503
		4,388

Table 10.6(c) Housing Units in the *Notitia*:
Distribution by Region

Group 1:	Regions I–III, V, VIII–IX	718
Group 2:	Regions IV, VI–VII, X–XII	3,072
		3,790

regions is supported by their socio-economic character, as described above. We must be cautious, for as we saw, the low number of residential units for Regions VIII and IX (108 and 116) is primarily a reflection of the small size of these regions, while at the other end of the scale, the high number of residential units (503) for Region XI probably exaggerates the apparent level of multi-occupation. It is not very close to the harbours and commercial facilities of the most densely inhabited regions, and one might think of it as a spacious region containing modest houses for arrivals coming to the city to work in the imperial court and administration and prepared to live a little way from their work. It is not surprising to find the busy extra-mural Region XIII (Sycae) and the more distant Region XIV, each with its own particular character, falling into different categories.

In using the figures to support population estimates, it is assumed that houses and apartments were found in varying proportions throughout the regions of the city. In the following projections the 718 residential units in Group 1 (excluding Regions XIII and XIV) are weighted 4:1 in favour of houses over apartments, and (because of the overall higher numbers in these regions) the 3,072 units of Group 2 are weighted equally as between the two categories.[38] It is a schematic distribution, and others can easily be imagined, but the differences between the two groups of regions are at once apparent (Table 10.6d).

The population levels implied by these models are more easily projected in the case of apartments because of their limited variation in size; at six occupants per

---

38. The figures from Alexandria work against a preponderance anywhere of *insulae* to free-standing residences, while those from Rome, which do show this preponderance, are atypical.

Table 10.6(d) Houses, Apartments, Population

		houses	apartments
Group 1:	Regions I–III, V, VIII–IX	574	144
Group 2:	Regions IV, VI–VII, X–XII	1,536	1,536
Totals (= 3,790)		2,110	1,680

apartment, the number of apartment dwellers is 10,080 (1,680 × 6), at 8 occupants, it is 13,440. Dividing the 2,110 houses postulated for 'intramural' Constantinople into the four economic categories described above results in a population count of 52,750 (2,110 × 25). The addition of the 10,080 (13,440) assigned to apartments yields a total of 62,830 (66,190). Adding Regions XIII and XIV on the same principles (Region XIV to Group 1 and XIII to Group 2) yields an additional count of 9,141 for Region XIII (345 houses and eighty-six apartments), or 9,313 at eight occupants per apartment, and for Region XIV (eighty-three houses and eighty-four apartments) 2,579 (2,747 at eight occupants per apartment), for a 'housed population' for the entire city of 74,550 (78,250 allowing eight occupants per apartment throughout the city). Since this is only one among many possible models and involves many assumptions, its near-equivalence to the 80,000 recipients of the bread distributions claimed by Socrates (Chapter 2 above, p. 32f.) is a mere coincidence. We might remind ourselves, however, that in the *Notitia* the numbers of *domus*, whether in the individual regions or in the city as a whole, is always followed by the number of bakeries.

Whatever value the figure may possess, and its limitations are obvious, it will refer only to that part of the population with accommodation in these particular categories. The true number of residents should certainly be higher.[39] Not included are the thousands of government officials and administrators, soldiers and guards, courtiers, servants, and maintenance staffs living in and around the imperial palaces and the mansions of the nobility, such as those lesser functionaries with their belts of office and embroidered tunics, and slaves 'in shaggy coats and hoods' mentioned in a law of 382 addressed to the urban prefect,[40] as well as the uncounted immigrants, transients, and homeless whom we saw at Rome, and building workers coming to the city for employment and living there without

39. Wallace-Hadrill, p. 102, allows that the base figures in his construction may be varied by those who would support higher or lower estimates of the population of Pompeii. Clearly, the greater effect on the overall population is achieved by varying the estimates of occupation levels in the higher categories of house size.

40. *CTh* 14.10.1 to Pancratius, a hint of the visibility of such categories of person in the life of the city; see Chapter 11 below (p. 228f.).

their families. A projected population of 120,000/140,000 would not be out of line with current estimates for the population of this new city only a century after its foundation, a figure that would equate it more, say with Ephesus, than, yet, of Antioch or Alexandria. If we further compare the number of residential units at Constantinople, at 4,388, with the combined total of *domus* and *insulae* for Rome, at 48,392, and admit a greater proportion of houses, a population of one-sixth or one-eighth of that at Rome seems to be of the right order, and is borne out by the scale of public facilities (including the number of churches) in the two cities.[41] It may be added that, whatever the reason for the building of the Theodosian wall out in the country beyond the wall of Constantine, population pressure does not seem to have been part of it.[42] Constantinople in the 420s was a busy, well-provided, and rather elegant metropolis. It had parted company from its Graeco-Roman predecessor, whose traces could still be seen, but was not yet the teeming city of Justinian or that described by Zosimus a generation earlier than Justinian's time.

It is this later city that is described, and to an extent analysed, in a little-known text from a sixth-century handbook on military strategy, summarized by Alan Cameron in his classic book on the circus factions at Rome and Constantinople.[43] The text is no doubt intended as a broader guide to statecraft in the Byzantine world, but its writer would not be a Greek if it did not evoke the ambience of a city (*polis*), in this case Constantinople. Though in certain respects anachronistic for the much earlier world of the *Notitia*, the text is worth attention as a diagnosis of the socio-political elements that would emerge from that world, and of the structure of the population. To paraphrase Cameron's summary, the elements of the state (*politeia*) are as follows:

1. the clergy (a more prominent feature of the sixth than of the fourth and early fifth centuries);
2. the administration, consisting of (i) holders of executive office, and (ii) advisers—bearing in mind that the role of adviser (*adsessor* or *symboleus*) was not a casual but a formal one, a position to which one could be appointed;

---

41. For Rome see Nordh, pp. 104–5 (figures for Constantinople in brackets); fifteen nymphaea (four), 856 balnea (153), 254 pistrinae (113/120 private and 20/21 public).

42. Mango, *Développement Urbain*, p. 49, suggesting that the construction had to do with the protection of the great cisterns outside the walls of Constantine. The cisterns in themselves document, and measure, the growth of the population (above, §6.2).

43. Alan Cameron, *Circus Factions: Blue and Greens at Rome and Byzantium* (1976), pp. 80–82. Cameron's purpose was to point out that the factions themselves (*dēmoi*) are not listed as an element in the social or political structure of the state—though they may of course have been thought of as an aspect of its theatrical activities under §8. See below, Chapter 11 for the convergence of the idea of Byzantium as a political culture with the idea of the city.

3. the judicial branch;
4. financial officials, concerned with the assessment and the collection of taxes;
5. the professional classes, including academics—men concerned with the acquisition and exercise of technical skills (see the list of occupations at p. 34 above) and the promotion of knowledge;
6. artisans and manual workers, divided into (i) traders and salesmen, (ii) craftsmen working with raw materials, and (iii) those offering services for hire, for example in transportation and delivery;
7. the unproductive or 'useless'; the elderly, children, and the infirm;
8. the theatrical profession, including charioteers, musicians, and actors—those connected with theatrical production and imperial ceremonies.

The emperor himself and his household staffs and managers are not included in the text, no doubt because they are assumed to be external to the world described rather than a part of it (or possibly to avoid placing them either above or below the clergy). Considered as participants in the life of the city, however, they were obviously an extremely significant element. Also noticeable, as a sort of pendant to the absence of the emperor, is the exclusion of the theatrical profession from the social structure of the state, which is otherwise presented in descending order; or possibly it comes last, even after those classified as 'useless', because it is still subject to the moral obloquy attaching to it in earlier periods. The profession is not as easily definable as a socio-economic class as are some of the others referred to. The text makes no mention either of a servile element, it being assumed, no doubt, that this was a juridical rather than a socio-economic category. Slaves were distributed through the social system, where they performed many different functions and were managed within it; there was no need to consider them as a separate category within the socio-economic framework of the text, as this writer understood it.

II

From the New World

THE *NOTITIA* GIVES us an image of the city of Constantinople, from its Classical Greek predecessor to the imperial capital of the author's own day—nearly a thousand years of urban history in just fifteen pages of printed Latin text. It deserves pride of place among our sources for the history of the city, but cannot be made to do more than it aspires to. It is a list, requiring, at the same time as it contains, a chronological dimension from which a story of change and development may emerge; this is what the preceding chapters of this book have attempted to do. In some ways, it resembles a stage set; not the action in itself but the physical and decorative framework within which the action is presented. It is the purpose of this final chapter to give a portrait of the city of Constantinople through some of the events that took place in the setting that has been described from the *Notitia*—not a history in the conventional sense but an attempt, somewhat in the manner of Asa Briggs' *Victorian Cities*, to present the life of the city as an expression of its physical development over the period in question.

The impact of the new city was soon apparent, and not everyone welcomed it. It grew fast, as Constantine and his successors installed their supporters there, and as people flocked in to make their fortunes 'from military service, commerce and other occupations', as the historian Zosimus put it—with a certain smirking emphasis, no doubt, on the 'other occupations' (2.35.1). Constantine was only too pleased to tax them, with the notorious *chrysargyron*, the money tax levied on professional and service providers (2.38). Their artistic counterpart, the statues imported, according to that hyper-sensitive humorist St. Jerome, at the cost of the 'nudity of other cities', were a most important part of the physical appearance of the new city, successfully claiming possession of its streets and squares and restricting their Christian successors, the saints and martyrs, to the safety of the churches. Again according to the hostile pen of Zosimus, building was hastily and often so poorly done that within a few generations some of the new structures collapsed. People fenced in parts of the sea with piles driven into the sea-bed, filled in the enclosed parts with rubble and built there; even these reclaimed areas would make a significant city (2.32.1, 35.2). By Zosimus' time of writing, the city of Constantine had been enlarged by new walls, within which the streets were still so narrow that it was impossible to move around safely for the press of people

From Byzantium to Constantinople: An Urban History. John Matthews, Oxford University Press.
© Oxford University Press 2024. DOI: 10.1093/oso/9780197585498.003.0011

and pack-animals (2.35.2). The new population described by Zosimus had been denigrated by his predecessor Eunapius as a drunken multitude, too ignorant even to pronounce Constantine's name correctly. Eunapius perhaps had in mind acclamations in the hippodrome, in which the name was chanted—as on the occasion of the grain shortage that ensued when the ships were held offshore, and the pagan protagonist Sopatros was executed for chaining the winds by magic. It was a long Latin name, which the largely Greek population perhaps found difficult![1] Others made the opposite complaint, that Constantinople attracted the best men of eastern cities, depriving the cities of the financial and other services that they provided, and enticing them to learn Latin and law rather than acquire a traditional Classical education. The issue of the grain supply was there to stay, as is shown by an event of 412, when the *praetorium* of the city prefect was burnt by the people because of a bread shortage, and his carriage forcibly dragged from the first region as far as the porticoes of Domninus. The *magistri militum* went to meet them with the consul and other high officials, and exhorted them with the words, 'Turn back and we will ordain what you wish!'[2]

In many ways, the city comes to life through the mere act of observation. It is the work of the imagination rather than historical research to picture the everyday life of the markets and harbours of Constantinople, the plying of its ferries over the Golden Horn to Sycae and Chalcedon, the commercial and business life of its forums, the noise and bustle of docks, shipyards, and baths, the endless building works that filled the city. When Themistius commented at the dedication of the forum of Theodosius, that the city was now like a woven carpet, decorated to the rim, or when Gregory Nazianzus commemorated the completion of the aqueduct of Valens, we are reading of massive and protracted building, providing work for thousands, creating an immense need for materials, filling the city with the noise of traffic and construction. The Constantinianae, the great baths in the tenth region, were begun by Constantius and not completed until the 420s. The conversion of the mausoleum of Constantine into the church of the Apostles took eleven years from 359, and the consecration of the great church of S. Sophia was thirty-four years after its initial planning. One building project (not mentioned by the *Notitia*) is illustrated by a sculptured image of how it was achieved. This was the raising of the obelisk of Theodosius on the *spina* of the hippodrome, accomplished by the urban prefect Proclus within thirty days by a complicated system of ropes and pulleys. On the base of the obelisk were other scenes, of the emperor holding court opposite the very place, the *kathisma* of the hippodrome, where he did so in real life, receiving Gothic and Persian suppliants

---

1. Eunapius, *Vitae Sophistarum* 462–63, ed. Loeb, pp. 382–85; above, p. 33.

2. *Chron. Pasch.*, s.a.; Whitby and Whitby, p. 62.

after his victories over those peoples—or at least, the treaties he had made with them (Figs 9.1–2).

It will be abundantly clear that the *Notitia* is a more like a key to the understanding of the city of Constantinople than a true representation of it. Its interpretation lies in the connection of this limited, highly structured text with the open-textured, volatile material that is otherwise available to us (compare Chapters 3 and 4 above). We are looking, and the *Notitia* provides the framework, at the emergence of an international capital city from the fabric of the Classical world. In this final chapter, the limited perspectives of the *Notitia* are enlarged by three categories of source and topic, to which more could undoubtedly be added: in first place, the information to be derived from the law code of Theodosius on the city and its senatorial order; second, descriptions of the involvements of emperors in the physical institutions of the city, particularly in relation to the obits and funerals of these emperors; and third, the picture of religious life at Constantinople that is contained in *Chronicon Paschale* and similar sources. That these selections fall short of a full description of the life of the city is self-evident, but they are not designed for that purpose; only to focus attention on certain categories of evidence that may contribute to such a description.

11.1 Constantinople in the Theodosian Code

The development of Constantinople appears in the domain of government regulation in the legislative texts collected in the Theodosian Code—itself a triumph of fifth-century Constantinopolitan legal culture, as we will see, and, as has often been said, a goldmine for the historian. The laws, assembled from various parts of the Code, provide insights on a variety of issues relating to the physical development of the city. One law, seen earlier, restricts food rations distributed to imperial officials, to those in the service who were prepared to back up their enthusiasm for living in Constantinople by building houses there (*CTh* 14.17.11). A law of Valens, which we also saw earlier, defines categories of houses in terms of the water pipes to which they were entitled, beginning with pipes 2 inches in diameter available to the finest houses possessing their own baths of the more elegant kind, or even, 'if the dignity of the owner requires it', 3 inches. Owners of less opulent houses, though still possessing baths, may use a pipe of 1.5 inches, while the most modest residences, not possessing private baths, will be content with a pipe of a half-inch diameter.[3] The implications of this for the relative size of houses were seen earlier (p. 208f.). We should think of houses built to take advantage

---

3. *CTh* 15.2.3; the law has a transmitted consular date of 382, but the urban prefect Clearchus held this office in 372–73.

of the new aqueduct and other installations allowing the comforts of residential settlement at the higher levels of the city, and, at more modest levels, of the availability of the public and private bath-houses distributed through the city.

A law of 424 attempted to regulate the proliferation of temporary shops and stalls that were springing up in the colonnades and threatening their monumental character, and one of 419 addressed the problem of pollution caused by the lime-kilns that occupied the eastern coast of the peninsula, all the way round from the old amphitheatre to the harbour of Julian.[4] Caught in the middle of the pollution was the imperial palace itself, made insalubrious by the plumes of smoke from the kilns. We may also see the kilns as an adroit response to opportunity, as they were used for the manufacture of lime cement for new building by exploiting the relics of the old city above them. This was a bountiful resource for the construction of its successor, not only in such a raw industrial activity as the making of cement, but in the re-use of architectural elements in new contexts as with columns in cisterns, or the conversion of its buildings into new uses, as with temples into prefectoral stables (pp. 182–4). The law is also important in confirming beyond reasonable doubt the location of the old amphitheatre of Byzantium implied by the *Notitia*.

At a more elevated level than amphitheatres and lime-kilns, a substantial law of 425, preserved in two excerpts in the Theodosian Code, addresses the question of higher education at Constantinople. In the first excerpt (*CTh* 14.9.3), the emperor establishes a faculty of three orators and five grammarians in Latin language and literature, five sophists and ten grammarians in Greek, one professor of philosophy and two of Roman law, with the mutually complementary restrictions that no officially recognized professor may teach in private houses, nor on the other hand may private teachers presume to give classes in the state institution at the Capitolium; the sanction is expulsion from the city.[5] The balance of Latin and Greek reflects the linguistic character of Constantinople, where Latin remained the language of administration, even as Greek gained in ascendancy as the inherited language of the streets and literary culture. The prefect of the city, who received the law, is to ensure that adequate teaching space should be assigned, 'in order that the students and teachers may not drown out each other, or the mingled confusion of tongues and words divert ears or minds from the study of letters' (a complaint still heard in ill-accommodated university departments).

---

4. Colonnades: *CTh* 15.1.52 (9 January 424), mentioning the Zeuxippon. Lime-kilns, *CTh* 14.6.5 (4 October 419); above, p. 85f. for the evidence of the law in establishing the location of the amphitheatre.

5. *CTh* 14.9.3 has no addressee, but its companion text is addressed to the urban prefect Constantius. Above, p. 93 for the location of the Capitolium.

The second excerpt (*CTh* 15.1.53), reading like the architect's report that was perhaps a source for it, describes the premises in which the new faculties were to be established. This was to be achieved by the adaptation of an existing building, judging by its description a very substantial one. The defining element is the colonnade on the northern side of the building, which opened out onto one of main avenues of the city, to be identified as the Mesē in its segment west of the forum of Theodosius (p. 115). Access from the colonnade will provide the opportunity for the suitably appointed lecture rooms referred to in the first extract of the law, while the accommodation on the eastern and western flank of the building, adjoining lesser side-streets (*vici* in the *Notitia*), was suited to the continuation of their present use as bars and restaurants. Compensation is extended to the owners of real estate displaced by the new development. Given that the location of the law school is known at some point in these years to have moved from the old basilica in the Augusteum to the Capitolium, it is natural to think of the Capitolium itself as the site of what, perhaps following the example of law schools elsewhere, can almost be described as a university.

The promotion of an advanced legal culture at Constantinople is revealed in the exercises in legal codification initiated in these same years.[6] Following an important law on judicial procedure and legal authority, addressed to the Roman senate in 426, the implementation of the major project that resulted in the Theodosian Code began in 429, with a letter of Theodosius to the senate of Constantinople, setting out the parameters of the work of collection and editorial procedure. The main phase of the work was completed by 435, when a second law reaffirmed the earlier procedures, adding some refinements for the guidance of editors. The work had been entrusted to an editorial commission of nine persons, followed in 435 by an enlarged group of sixteen. Most of the members of both commissions were administrative and political supporters of the regime, who would know the ins and outs of bureaucratic procedures, including their archival methods (and the Latin language); while the first commission included one, and the second, two persons described as legal experts. It is compelling to think of these as the two professors of Roman law established in the Capitolium by Theodosius' law of 425. The whole project was presented to the public in November 437, with copies entrusted to the eastern and western praetorian prefects for circulation in their respective jurisdictions.

The Theodosian Code, which comes to us incomplete in the first five of its sixteen books, originally contained about 3,500 constitutions, of which we

6. For what follows, see my *Laying Down the Law: A Study of the Theodosian Code* (2000), chs 1–2, esp. at pp. 26–28. On the law to the senate of Rome of 7 November 426, pp. 24–25. The circumstances are part of the re-establishment of the dynasty of Theodosius in the west after the usurpation of Iohannes in 423–25.

possess 2,700; the primary texts of imperial legislation from the time of Constantine to the present, edited to draw out the substance of the laws and arranged by date under titles relevant to subject. These were the original texts of imperial authority, the *leges*. In a planned further volume, the *leges* would be further studied, together with the writings of the jurists, for the principles of Roman law (*ius*) that they contained. No trace survives of progress on such a volume, but the Theodosian Code as it stands is, whatever its means of compilation (central archives, local sources, or combination of the two), an extraordinary accomplishment of careful scholarship. We also witness the ascendancy of the eastern court over the western, in the realization of such a monument to Roman legal culture as a project conceived and implemented at Constantinople, the editors of which probably began and surely finished their work in the Capitolium mentioned by the *Notitia*, now established as the faculty centre of the law school.

11.2 The Senate of Constantinople

It was an essential part of Constantine's intention that his city should be a new Rome, with institutions reflecting those of the old capital, including the promotion of an administration and senate to match their prototype, with the building of a new senate-house in the forum of Constantine. Historical or quasi-historical sources such as Zosimus and the *Patria* claim that Constantine invited Roman senators to follow him to Constantinople, where he built houses matching their own for them to live in and had them serve in an eastern senate housed in the city. We do not know how many Roman senators accepted this invitation, nor whether the whole idea is more than some historians' or fantasists' conception of something that must in some way have happened, if not in the simplified form of narrative claimed by these sources. The eastern Roman empire did after all acquire its senate as one of the main estates of the realm.

The senators must have come from various sources, beginning with the assignment to the new Rome of the more opulent *curiales* of Byzantium.[7] It seems unlikely that there were more than a few candidates with the resources or commit-

7. A. H. M. Jones, *The Later Roman Empire*, ch. 15, 'Senators and Honorati', surveys the origins, wealth and status of senators both in east and west, with some but not a systematic contrast between them. A critique of the primary evidence and modern literature on the senate of Constantinople (Petit, Dagron, Chastagnol) is given by Alexander Skinner, 'The Early Development of the Senate of Constantinople', in *Byzantine and Modern Greek* Studies 32.2 (2008), pp. 128–48, with André Chastagnol, 'Remarques sur les sénateurs orientaux au IVe siècle', *Acta Antiqua Hungarica* 24 (1976), pp. 341–56; Peter Heather, 'New Men for New Constantines? Creating an Imperial Elite in the Eastern Mediterranean', in P. Magdalino (ed.), *New Constantines: The Rhythm of Imperial Renewal in Byzantium, 4th–13th Centuries* (1994), pp. 11–33. For H.-G. Beck, *Senat und Volk von Konstantinopel*, see below, n. 40.

ment to play their new role, while on the other hand, it is hardly possible that the council (*boulē*) of Byzantium was continued as the local administration of the city, the old city being totally swallowed up by the new one; it is hard to imagine distinct and contemporaneous city councils of old Byzantium and new Rome. The senate of Rome in this period retained, at least notionally, the functions both of local government and imperial advisory body, and it was no doubt expected that the senate of Constantinople would become used to a similar combination of duties.

The second source was the category mentioned by Zosimus, rather differently understood; senators of Rome with origins in the east, whom it was a juridically simple matter to assign to the senate of new Rome. For some of these senators, whose distance from Rome had made them infrequent or absentee members of the *amplissimus ordo*, transference to Constantinople may have entailed an unwelcome increase in public duties, especially if financial obligations analogous to those of Roman senators were imposed upon them; they could hardly be expected to perform senatorial obligations in both cities. The emperor was well aware of this. By a law of 12 August 357 (*CTh* 6.4.11), part of a flurry of legislation concerning the senate in the form of letters addressed to that body, it was allowed that a senator who had performed the duties of magistrates at Rome should not be summoned to produce games at what can only be the new capital of Constantinople. The law then addressed the more common situation, and the real subject of the legislation; any person of senatorial status from Achaea, Macedonia, or Illyricum who had rarely or never presented himself at Rome should be sought out and assigned to Constantinople, so that the dignity of senatorial status, lacking now the inconvenience of a long journey to Rome, should be embraced by them.[8] Though somewhat assorted as to status (a proconsulship, a diocese, and a prefecture), Achaea, Macedonia, and Illyricum were the provincial entities most open to claims of absenteeism from Rome; districts further east could be assumed to fall under the senate of Constantinople. Some might protest that the journey to Constantinople was no less arduous than that to Rome, but that argument was undercut by their reluctance to go to Rome either. They might make a choice, but the reluctant senators had to choose one or the other as more convenient to them, unless they wished to be sought out by the emperor's agents.

---

8. Skinner, p. 128, like Petit and Dagron, considers that the purpose of the law was to enforce attendance of such persons at the senate of Rome, but my reading is that, having complained of the distance to Rome, they were being given the greater convenience of attending its counterpart at Constantinople. The law was 'read [in the senate]' on 12 August, but its protocol does not name the reader (unlike 6.4.8–9). It was at a time when Julian Caesar represented the imperial office in Gaul while Constantius controlled the regions of Achaea, Macedonia, and Illyricum referred to, and soon after Constantius' visit to Rome in the summer of that year.

We should add a category corresponding to that of provincial senators in the west; wealthy citizens of eastern cities willing to take up broader responsibilities in the capital, where, by ennobling their families and, in compensation for the financial obligations incurred by residence at Constantinople, they were able to exempt themselves and their families from their commitments as city councillors. It was a preoccupation of imperial legislation to prevent this outcome, but we can read the complaints of eastern cities as their most generous citizens were drawn away to become senators at Constantinople.[9]

The fourth pool of candidates was of ministers of state who had achieved a status, that of *clarissimus*, which qualified them as of senatorial rank; it remained to formally admit them to that body.[10] This also happened at Rome, though more rarely, given the distance of that city from the contemporary seats of government. At Constantinople, where the imperial court functioned in the same city as the senate, it must have been a very common situation. These active and retired imperial officials and their descendants provide some of the great names in east Roman politics and in effect transformed the senate of Constantinople into an agent of the imperial establishment, such as the senate of old Rome (distinguishing its role as a body from that of individual senators) never became.

Book 6 of the Theodosian Code has two titles containing legislation about the senates of Rome and Constantinople. The first title, 6.2 *De senatoria dignitate*, is incomplete in the manuscripts (6.1 *De dignitatibus* is missing altogether) and preserves only the last fifteen of an original twenty-six texts; the second, 6.4 *De praetoribus et quaestoribus*, has thirty-four. Of the fifteen texts extant in 6.2, only six, beginning with *CTh* 6.2.12, issued by the emperor Valens at Hierapolis in 377, apply to the senate of Constantinople, and concern the financial obligations and exemptions of senators and of ex-officials who have become senators. Of the thirty-four texts in 6.4, ten concern the western senate and twenty-two, generated by the editors from sixteen original texts, the eastern. Only two texts, parts of a single original law (6.4.22–23), are of uncertain application. The earliest text relevant to the eastern senate was issued at Antioch on 9 September 340 and is about the naming of praetorships (6.4.5–6).

The main body of regulation on this office was laid down in a law of Constantius, preserved in three extracts in the Code that clearly belong together (6.4.8–10).

9. For discussions of this aspect, incorporating examples and case-studies (and the role of Themistius in 'head-hunting' new senators), see Paul Petit, 'Les sénateurs de Constantinople dans l'oeuvre de Libanius', *L'Antiquité Classique* 26 (1957), pp. 347–82; Chastagnol, 'Remarques sur les sénateurs orientales', at pp. 351–54; Skinner, pp. 132–36.

10. Skinner, pp. 137–38; cf. at 147: '[the eastern senate] extended a new opportunity to Hellenic gentry to become part of the imperial governing order.' Imperial service at the rank of *clarissimus* (and higher) was a channel of this.

They are in the form of a letter addressed to the eastern senate from Milan on 11 April 356 and read, a month later (the time it took to get there), to the assembled body by the governor of the city, the proconsul Araxius; it is worth noting that the emperor should apply himself to legislation about Constantinople when he himself was so far away, with so many other preoccupations. He was to visit Rome in the following year, and questions of senatorial rights and procedures were perhaps on his mind. The emperor desires in his letter that no fewer than fifty men of the rank of *nobilissimus* should enter the senate, that is, be present for the conduct of business, and reviews the procedures for nominations for membership. These are to begin on the Ides (13th) of August of the current and subsequent years, and to continue for as long as necessary. There is here a nice question of protocol. That the date of the meeting is glossed as the emperor's birthday shows how far the eastern senate, created by Constantine, remains under the protection of his successor; on the other hand the misstatement of the date of Constantius' birthday, which was actually on 7 August, allows the emperor to respect the ancient convention that statutory meetings of the senate are held on the Ides of the month.[11] The law views with disfavour the acquisition of the rank of *emeritus* by bribery and endorses those who have achieved the rank of praetor, or any other, honestly and by their own merits. Finally, no man shall transfer to a son or grandson the duties that properly fall upon himself, an episode in the timeless battle between a government's best intentions to have public functions performed and the searching out of loopholes by those who wish to avoid them.

The venerable office of praetor had evolved far from its early imperial precursor, when it had been the source of public authority (*imperium*) greater than any except that of the emperor himself and the holders of consular office, for which it was itself a preparation. It was an instrument of many significant careers in the emperor's service. Commands of Roman legions, governorships of provinces, judicial office, the administration of imperial finances, public works at Rome, and the grain supply of the city—all at various times fell under the competence of men of praetorian rank. A *vir praetorius* was a senator of mature years and sufficient experience for some of the highest offices of state. In fourth-century Rome, the post had devolved into a junior position held by the scions of the great senatorial families, distinguished by the public games that it fell to the candidate, in practice his father, to provide to commemorate his election. The post was introduced into the senatorial *cursus* at Constantinople with the same purpose as the

---

11. Suetonius, *Divus Augustus* 35 refers to the establishment by Augustus of two *legitimi senatus* per month, on the Kalends and Ides, with special arrangements for September and October; Richard J. A. Talbert, *The Senate of Imperial Rome* (1984), p. 200 and in general §6.4, at pp. 200–16. The most famous example is of course the meeting on the Ides of March of 44 BCE.

quaestorship at Rome (which was not introduced at Constantinople), to provide a point of entry to the senate, and to enrol the young man's family in the work of maintaining the fabric of the city. In a very real sense, the evolution of these once important offices into expensive sinecures, after the model of provincial munificence that had underpinned the efflorescence of the Antonine age, was one of the ways devised by the emperors for the financing of their capital cities. There are moments when one can see the senatorial orders of both west and east in the role of well-heeled trustees, appointed to support the financial health of a public institution in return for a certain influence over its activities. The praetorship, defined as an entry-level qualification for membership of the senate, was usually but not necessarily a young man's position. Even quite senior candidates, entering the senate after holding high positions in the emperor's service, are encouraged not to look down on the junior rank of praetor, but to embrace it in their new identity as senators of Constantinople. Addressing the senate in a letter of 22 May 359, Constantius cites two examples of such deference to an ancient office; Facundus, who had been proconsul, and Arsenius, an ex-*vicarius* (6.4.15). By a law of a later date, even former military officers of the rank of *dux* were decreed liable for nomination for the praetorship and the provision of games—not, however, those *duces* who had served in the military for a long time or had been members of the imperial consistory (6.4.28, 23 December 396).

The procedures for the election of praetors are taken up in a further law of Constantius, again addressed as a letter to the senate (*CTh* 6.4.12–13; 3 May 361). In another nice touch of ancient procedure deferential to Rome, they are to be designated in due form by *senatus consultum*. Conditions are laid down for attendance at the nominations: there shall be present ten senators who qualify for the highest rank by virtue of having held the consulship or the office of proconsul. To them is added Themistius the philosopher, 'whose learning enhances his rank': and senators who have already held the praetorship. This singling out of Themistius is remarkable, but he was well established in the emperor's favour, having delivered an oration to him as far back as 350, when he was about 33 years of age—appropriately enough, on the subject of philanthropy. He was adlected to the eastern senate in 355, and served as its envoy to Constantius at Rome on the occasion of its granting of a gold crown to the emperor to commemorate his twenty years of rule. This was in 357, and he was proconsul of Constantinople in 358–59, his successor being the first to hold the rank of prefect, marking the elevation of Constantinople to the dignity and rank of Rome.

A further part of the regulation of 361, preserved elsewhere in the Theodosian Code,[12] established the judicial authority of the now prefect of Constantinople

---

12. *CTh* 1.6.1, under the title *De officio praefecti urbis*.

over nine neighbouring provinces, named as Bithynia, Paphlagonia, Lydia, Hellespont, the Islands and Phrygia Salutaris in Asia Minor, with Europa, Rhodope, and Haemimontus on the European side of the Hellespont. This was a replication of the situation in the west, extending the juridical responsibilities of the prefect of Rome to the hundredth milestone from the city—an antiquated definition preceding the creation of provinces in Italy, in effect giving the prefect of Rome judicial authority over central and southern Italy. The result was a judicial enclave within which appeals were deferred to the prefects of Rome and Constantinople rather than to the praetorian prefects of Italy and the east.

Constantius' regulations on the praetorship are of interest, both in their tracking of one of the earliest and most important institutions of Constantinople and in their implications for the administration of the city Where there had until now been three, there were now to be five praetors, the two new positions being honoured by the titles *Romana* and *Constantiana* (*CTh* 6.4.13).[13] Three of the five praetors had the obligation to provide games for the people. Of the other two, the first in precedence, named *Constantiniana* after the founder of the institution, was obliged to provide to the public works of the city 1,000 pounds of silver and his colleague the third, named *Flavialis* after the emperor's dynasty, 500 pounds of silver. A praetor claiming inability through youth or illness to organize his games in person was required to send a financial agent to the prefect of the city with the sum laid down in the regulation, to be spent on the completion of building works inscribed in his name. Nominations were to be made ten years in advance of the holding of the office, and a designated praetor who failed to appear to perform his obligations was penalized by the exaction of an additional one-half of the sum required of him, to be spent on public works without any recognition of the individual (there was always a need for out-of-sight infrastructural maintenance, bringing no credit to those who provided it). Provincial governors who failed to ensure that praetors living in their jurisdictions attend the city to perform their obligations are liable for monetary fines, and these sums also to go to public works; for the governor, ten pounds of gold for each delinquent praetor (how many could there be in one province at one time?), and fifteen pounds for their office staffs.

We do not know in what circumstances the five praetors of Constantius were reduced to four in the time of Valens, as appears from a law of 372 addressed to the prefect of the city, requiring 'all four praetors' to enter office together on the first day of January (6.4.20), and confirmed by a further reform of Theodosius of

13. According to the designations set out in *CTh* 6.4.5, of 340, the first praetor is Flavialis, the second Constantinian, the third Triumphalis. This law, sent from Antioch, is to be taken with 6.4.6 and is again addressed to the senate.

23 October 384 (6.4.25). In this law, Theodosius doubled the number of praetors by separating the office from its individual holders. There are still to be four praetorships (*praeturae*), each one now filled by two praetors, with a revised nomenclature in pairs corresponding to the classes: we now have Constantinian and Constantian, Theodosian and Arcadian, Triumphal and Augustal, Roman and Laureate praetors,[14] with financial contributions of 1,000 pounds of silver for the first two, and 450 and 250 pounds of silver for the third and fourth classes respectively, the expenditures to be shared between the two incumbents of each praetorship. The emperor justifies the change as offering financial relief to the individual praetors, while maintaining the total levels of contribution from the college as a whole. The reform does of course increase the number of actual candidates to be found to fill each year's *praeturae*. There is no sign that the emperor gave any thought to this, except that the very next law in the Theodosian Code, one of many extracts addressed to the then prefect of the city on 27 February 393, restores the nomination of praetorian candidates to the tax assessment office (6.4.26). It is clear that the office of praetor is becoming more and more embedded in the financial administration of the capital. Despite the new structure, a law of Arcadius can refer to the five praetors to whom had been assigned the responsibility of providing for the construction of the Theodosian aqueduct, with funds diverted from the theatrical celebrations prepared for the emperor's birthday.[15]

There is no need to follow the legislation on this subject through all its chops and changes, but one theme recurs, the emperor's concern, having defined the expenditures required of the office of praetor, that they should not be exceeded. The emperor no doubt had two motives as well as a traditionally Roman affectation of sumptuary integrity; to restrain rival expenditures in a city where he himself was the main benefactor,[16] and to ensure that the contributions, assessed in

---

14. The emperor seems to say that the titles Theodosian and Arcadian were added by the senate to the existing Constantinian and Constantian praetorships, and that he himself had added Augustal and Laureate to the historic Triumphalis and Roman. 'Flavialis' has disappeared, having lost relevance after the end of the Constantinian dynasty.

15. *CTh* 6.4.29 (29 December 396); cf. 6.4.30 (31 December ?397/9), the aqueduct being named in the second of these laws. This 'aquaeductus Theodosiacus' is not specifically identified in Crow, Bardill, and Bayliss, *The Water Supply of Byzantine Constantinople*. It could be a line extending the Valens aqueduct from the forum of Constantine to the cistern still shown as the 'cistern of Theodosius' at Crow, Bardill, and Bayliss, Map 13, F7/3, although something more elaborate (not necessarily an elevated section) seems required to justify the attentions of five praetors.

16. By a law of 372 (*CTh* 6.4.19, addressed to the senate), the emperor granted to the two praetors involved in the most important games eight horses from the emperor's Phrygian breed, to be yoked to two four-horse chariots (presumably one for each praetor, of the four mentioned above).

silver (with fines in gold), should remain fungible, able to be diverted to any area of need. The sums themselves are diminutive when compared with those spent on praetorian games at Rome—in one notorious case, 4,000, and in lesser cases, 2,000 pounds of gold respectively.[17] Both the scale of wealth and the regulatory environment were different in east and west, and were directly connected with the presence or absence of emperors.

There is also the question of the comportment of senators, how they should dress and conduct themselves—a matter of concern to emperors from the time of Augustus, who also had seen correct dress, notably the wearing of the toga, as part of the public image of the city.[18] Of the four laws that survive in title 14.10 of the Theodosian Code 'On the Correct Dress to Be Worn within the City' (*De habitu, quo uti oporteat intra urbem*), three are addressed to the people or to the prefect of Rome, but the first and most expansive was sent to the prefect of Constantinople in the early years of Theodosius, and is relevant only to that city. It begins by prohibiting the wearing of military dress by senators within the city walls, 'not excepting the early morning hours' (nor forgetting that this was the time of day for the salutation of patrons by their clients, and among members of the upper classes), and goes on to require the wearing of the white toga of their rank while attending meetings of the senate, or when they have business before a judge in a public hearing—not an uncommon situation, given the number of legal and financial issues that might arise concerning senators.[19] Lesser functionaries (*officiales*) should wear their inner garments drawn tight around them, while displaying the embroidered mantles indicating their low status, while slaves may dress in plain, that is unembroidered cloaks and hoods, as long as their masters are not holders of any public office. This regulation is best understood by the converse situation; only as long as their masters held such office were their personal servants to dress in the figured cloaks that are the mark of service. An unstated corollary would be that a senator who owed his rank to the previous tenure of a public office should not dress up his slaves to give the impression that he still held it. It is no doubt a coincidence, but the law comes just a few months after the great church council held at Constantinople in the summer of 381, at which a certain amount of modest clerical and monastic garb (not too much of it perhaps, given

---

17. Olympiodorus, fr. 44 Mueller (Blockley). The fragment has been much discussed; cf. *Western Aristocracies and Imperial Court, AD 364–425* (1975, repr. 1990), pp. 384–85 (making the contrast with Constantinople).

18. Suetonius, *Divus Augustus* 40.5.

19. Pharr's understanding of this law is misleading, in referring to senators as 'being tried' before a judge, as if for a criminal offence. This is not inherent in the Latin 'negotium eius sub publica iudicis sessione cognosci'. The travails of the early morning *salutatio* are a common feature of Roman social satire.

the taste of some highly placed prelates for conspicuous self-presentation)[20] would have been on show in the city, contrasting with the multi-coloured splendour of its secular authorities and their entourages, and no doubt to be seen in the same parts of town.

11.3 Public Events and Ceremony

A review of the occasions for public ceremony to be accommodated within the physical framework of the new city might begin at the beginning, with its dedication in November 324, and the procession led by Constantine from the Severan city to the place where he would build the walls of his new one. As we saw in Chapter 2 (p. 12f), the procession defined the configuration of the city, and was followed on the same day by the advancement of the emperor's son Constantius to the rank of Caesar, thereby asserting its dynastic character. The subsequent consecration of Constantinople was firmly tied into its physical development by races in the newly completed (or rebuilt) hippodrome, the candle-lit procession in the same place and the opening of the great baths of the Zeuxippon (p. 28), not to mention the construction of the imperial palace.

Following only a few years after this great public event, the funeral obsequies of Constantine are another showpiece of the ceremonial possibilities literally built into the new capital. Like the mausoleum of Augustus at Rome, initiated more than forty years before the first Princeps' death in 14 CE, that of Constantine was obviously begun very soon after the foundation of the city, to be ready for its founder's obsequies in 337.[21] Constantine did not actually die at Constantinople; when he fell ill there, it seemed to be no more than an indisposition which he attempted to cure by attending the baths, before leaving for the Bithynian city named Helenopolis after his mother.[22] There, according to Eusebius, he sensed that his illness was threatening and spent some time in the church of the martyrs, offering himself as a catechumen, or baptismal candidate of the church (if that is what Eusebius means). Even then, the emperor pressed on, reaching only as far as a suburb of Nicomedia before making his final dispositions—including the replacement of the purple robes of an emperor by the white garments of baptism. Constantine's death at the old Tetrarchic capital, on 22 May, was followed by the

---

20. As in Ammianus Marcellinus' memorable description of bishops of Rome at 27.3.14–15.

21. For much of the content of what follows, see Philip Grierson, 'Tombs and Obits of the Byzantine Emperors (337–1042)', *DOB* 16 (1962), pp. 1–63.

22. For these events, see Eusebius, *On the Life of Constantine* 4.60–71, with T. D. Barnes, *Constantine and Eusebius* (1981), pp. 259–63; Cyril Mango, 'Constantine's Mausoleum and the Translation of Relics', *BZ* 83 (1990), pp. 51–62 (= *Studies on Constantinople*, ch. 5). For Helenopolis, see above, p. 24.

transportation of his body to Constantinople, where it rested in a gilt coffin over-laid by a purple cover (the white robes of baptism having served their purpose) in the reception hall of the imperial palace. There it received the last respects of the military and civil authorities, senators and former office-holders, and in their turn the people of the city.

There was now a pause, since none of Constantine's three sons was in the city at the time. All were written to, together with the armies, who immediately pro-claimed all three Caesars as Augustus, and it was the second son, Constantius, who arrived to conduct the ceremonies. He led a procession of guards and sol-diers in full military array up the long, slow climb from the palace to the mauso-leum, where he installed his father's remains with all secular honours.

At this point there enters a new element in the proceedings, bringing out their double nature; someone must have planned them very carefully. Having consecrated his father with the secular honours just mentioned, Constantius and his escort withdrew from the mausoleum and made way for the clergy. Constan-tine was a baptized Christian as well as Roman emperor, and what followed was a service of blessing of Constantine and of prayers for his soul.

Eusebius' description of the mausoleum of Constantine, and of the obsequies performed within it, are distortions of the design and purpose of the building as it then stood. There is no doubt that it was built as the mausoleum of the emperor and his family; the resemblances of plan and disposition with the mausolea of Augustus and of Galerius at Thessalonica, and the very location of the monument in relation to the city, are too obvious to pass over (see Fig. 2.5). At the same time, in an indication of how the emperor wished himself to be seen, Constantine's mausoleum contained memorials of the twelve Apostles, among whom the em-peror was to be laid to rest. Eusebius, who mentions the memorials without giving a clear idea what form they took, has no difficulty in describing the building as a church. We saw in Chapter 9 (pp. 177–9), however, that it properly acquired this status only in the time of Valens, by a project initiated under Constantius. The transition from imperial mausoleum containing images of the apostles, to church of the Apostles in which the emperors were buried, is easy to understand, but it required the rebuilding of Constantius and Valens to make it liturgically coherent. Constantine was laid to rest in a mausoleum, not the church that it later became.

Eusebius says nothing about the dynastic carnage, no doubt planned at Con-stantinople whoever was responsible for it, that cleared the scene of all but the direct descendants of Constantine, his sons Constantine (II), Constantius, and Constans.[23] By the 350s only Constantius was left, and he died unexpectedly in

23. Richard Burgess, 'The Summer of Blood: The "Great Massacre" of 337 and the Promotion of the Sons of Constantine', *DOP* 62 (2008), pp. 5–51, provides a closely argued and revealing analysis of these events.

Cilicia while preparing to confront the challenge in civil war of his cousin Julian. His body was escorted to Constantinople by the future emperor Jovian to be buried beside his relatives, an event somewhat complicated, no doubt, by the current rebuilding of the mausoleum, that he himself had initiated.

Julian's stay in the city was uneventful; he was only there for six months before moving on to supervise his Persian campaign from the eastern capital of Antioch. Even the show trials of Constantius' supporters, which Ammianus singles out as one of the few unjust acts of Julian's reign, were held at Chalcedon rather than Constantinople—a measure, perhaps, of the personal popularity of some of these supporters in the city and the involvement of all too many in the activities of the previous regime: out of sight is out of mind! Julian's stay at Constantinople did leave a substantial legacy, in the important harbour of Julian on the southern side of the promontory, though as we saw, we cannot be sure whether it was a project begun earlier and dedicated by himself or initiated by Julian and completed by a successor.

It was to the senate of Constantinople, as reformed by the legislation of Constantius in the manner just described, that Cl. Mamertinus addressed his panegyric of the emperor Julian in 362 and there too, while presiding over it, that Julian committed a famous breach of etiquette. Hearing of the arrival in the city of the philosopher Maximus, whose triumphal journey through Asia Minor to join the emperor is described by Eunapius, Julian leapt up excitedly, 'forgetting who he was', went out to meet the philosopher and brought him into the senate.[24] It was a violation of the conduct expected of an emperor and of the protocols of the senate. Maximus was not a senator and should not have been introduced without a formal invitation, if only to receive its accolades.

After Julian's death in Persia, he was buried not at Constantinople but at Tarsus in Cilicia (Amm. Marc. 23.2.4–5). As things turned out, it would have been awkward in the extreme if Constantinople had been chosen. The returning Roman army would then have found itself escorting the corpses of not one but two emperors, for Jovian's reign also was a short one, before he too, returning to Constantinople with the remains of Julian's army, died in Bithynia. His body was escorted by a distant cousin of Julian, Procopius, to be buried among the remains of the Augusti, where it presumably joined the relics of Constantine and Constantius in the church of S. Acacius before their later transfer to the church of the Apostles.[25] Jovian had been seen at Constantinople before, if anyone paid attention to the tall young officer who had led the escort of the body of Constantius

---

24. Amm. Marc. 22.7.3; Eunapius, *Vitae Sophistarum*, p. 477 (ed. Loeb, pp. 442–43); *The Roman Empire of Ammianus*, p. 125.

25. Grierson, 'Tombs and Obits', pp. 40–41. Jovian was joined in his porphyry *labrum* by his wife Charito upon her death some years later.

for burial. The same service was now performed for Jovian by Procopius, whose subsequent rebellion against the unpolished Pannonian now raised to the throne is worth special attention because of the account of the uprising given by Ammianus Marcellinus, in a narrative of these events well set in the topography of Constantinople as we now know it.[26]

His duties in honour of Jovian completed, Procopius' fear of retribution as a relative of Julian led him to lie incognito at Chalcedon while the new emperors, the brothers Valentinian and Valens, established themselves and in winter 364/5, at Sirmium in Pannonia, divided army and court between them. It was the younger brother, Valens, to whom the eastern empire was committed, and to Constantinople that he returned before moving on to attempt to restore some measure of Roman authority in the east. Dismayed by the new dispensation and encouraged by the unpopularity of Valens' financial policies, Procopius was able to suborn two troop units of Valens, the Divitenses and Tungrecani (Iuniores), a product of the recent division of the army, whom Valens had sent back as reinforcements on the lower Danube and were in transit in the capital. They were billeted in the Anastasian baths, named, according to Ammianus, after a sister of Constantine; we do know of the existence of such a sister, the Anastasia who married a supporter of Licinius in the early years of the century; whether she was a full or half-sister of Constantine, and how she came to be called this (was she already a Christian?) we do not know. There is some confusion, since under the year 364, the first of Valens' reign, *Chronicon Paschale* presents the Anastasianae as one of two sets of baths built by Valens in honour of his daughters Anastasia and Carosia. It is clear from Ammianus that the Anastasianae must have existed in 366, the year of Procopius' rebellion, and they cannot have been built and inaugurated by Valens in this short period (the inauguration of the Carosianae was only in 375). Either the Anastasianae already existed in the name of the sister of Constantine, to be rededicated by Valens in honour of an identically named daughter of his own, or the *Chronicon Paschale* is simply mistaken. The baths are listed by the *Notitia* in the ninth region, on the southern flank of the city, by the new road from Regium and the military suburb of Hebdomon.

The circumstances of Procopius' proclamation are presented by Ammianus as a theatrical parody. Placed, trembling and fearful, on a tribunal by the soldiers and dressed in a gold threaded tunic (all that could be found) and purple slippers and brandishing a piece of purple cloth, Procopius was escorted through the streets by soldiers who held shields over his head for fear of stones and tiles that might be thrown at them from rooftops; the mournful clashing of

---

26. The narrative is at Amm. Marc. 26.6–9; *The Roman Empire of Ammianus*, ch. 9, at pp. 191–203.

shields was a sad travesty of the mighty noise that had attended the proclamation of Julian in Gaul (Amm. Marc. 20.5.8). The people witnessed the parade in silence, probably in ignorance of what was going on, the few hesitant acclamations that were heard being paid for by Procopius' supporters. Procopius then entered the senate (the building in the forum of Constantine) and addressed the small numbers of senators who were there, none of them of the highest rank. This was hardly surprising—the whole operation had been launched overnight by Procopius' supporters, and they could hardly have got the word out. From there, the pitiful procession went on, through the double colonnades leading to the Augusteum, to the imperial palace. Who could have believed that events so rashly and incautiously conceived, and so ridiculous in their implementation, could have produced such lamentable disasters for the republic (Amm. Marc. 26.6.19)?

The usurpation of Procopius is notable for the involvement of the physical setting of the still largely Constantinian city, and for its institutional character. Ammianus' negative portrayal shows what a real challenge to the throne would be like—the support of the army, the presentation to the public of a truly august figure in the regalia of an emperor and not the pathetic stage costume of Procopius, acclamations by a fervent populace and an enthusiastic reception by the senate, a majestic procession to the imperial palace. From the Anastasian baths to the imperial palace via the senate-house in the forum of Constantine, we can trace Procopius' movements every step of the way. There is at no point mention of a church. We would not necessarily expect this from a relative of Julian, but if the blessing of God were a regular part of an imperial inauguration, then Procopius might have deferred to it. The procession could have stopped at the recently consecrated Great Church, but there is no word of its having done so.

Valens was already on his way to the eastern frontier when the rebellion was reported to him, and he had little hope of success. His high command, and the support of great generals of the preceding generation held the day for him, however, and Procopius was surrendered and executed at Nacolia in Phrygia in June 366. Valens returned to Constantinople and by the following year was campaigning against the Goths from his field base at Marcianopolis. In 371 he returned to his interrupted campaigns on the eastern frontier, where he still was when news of the great crossing of the river by Gothic refugees drew him back to the Danube frontier, where he lost his life in the great battle at Hadrianople. The impact of his reign on the physical development of Constantinople, described in Chapter 7, was out of proportion to the amount of time he actually spent there. The needs of the city generated their own momentum, however. We should direct our attention to his supporters, notably the praetorian prefect Modestus, and the urban prefect Clearchus, whose name occurs several times in connection with the development of Constantinople (p. 131f.).

None of the emperors described so far died at the eastern capital, but elsewhere, whether on campaign or preparing for it—in the case of Constantius for a civil war. This underlines a significant aspect of the position of Constantinople and its role as an imperial capital. It was important to be accessible to the theatres of war without being at the centre of them; a successful attack on Constantinople, more so even than one on Rome, would seem to threaten the integrity of the Roman empire as such. Military operations against Persia required a presence at the eastern capital of Antioch. Julian's projected campaign against Persia limited his presence at Constantinople to just a few months, while Valens' campaigns against the Goths drew him away from the eastern frontier to Marcianopolis and Hadrianople. As long as the emperors took an active role in warfare, as was still expected of them, they would need to spend significant portions of their time in other places than Constantinople.[27] They and their armies would of course often have to travel by way of Constantinople in order to move from one theatre of war to another. It is a moment to recall the words of the deputation sent by Byzantium to the senate in the time of Claudius; theirs was a city through which all armies must march, all fleets sail and all supplies be carried (above, p. 17).

The city remained a focal point of military activity as forces moved through it to the areas of their deployment. At such times, it must have echoed with the preparations for war, like Libanius' Antioch when a Persian campaign was being prepared there—'a city noisy and bustling, crowded with men under arms and animals for war and transport', and so on.[28] In 366 and again in 376, when Valens was persuaded to defer his plans in the east in order to meet the Gothic threat in Thrace, he brought his army and administration to Constantinople and from there, via the imperial residence at Melanthias, to Hadrianople. In that city, wrote Ammianus, he installed the entire government establishment, treasuries and all, which were attacked by the Goths after their sensational victory.[29] Failing to make any impact on the fortifications of Hadrianople, the Goths turned their attention to Constantinople, with no greater success. Deterred by a feat of artillery from the city walls and a spectacular act of barbarism performed by a Saracen ally in the service of Rome (Amm. Marc. 31.16.6), the Goths withdrew; they would, much later, have better luck against Rome. If there is a temptation, in reading

---

27. See esp. the monograph and article of Sylvain Destephen, referred to at Chapter 2 above, n. 26.

28. *The Roman Empire of Ammianus*, p. 72.

29. Amm. Marc. 31.12.10: 'thesauri…et principalis fortunae insignia cetera cum praefecto et consistorianis'—all of which would normally be at Constantinople.

about this enterprise, to imagine it outside the walls of the city familiar to us, this would be a misconception. It was the earlier, now lost Constantinian walls that saved the city from the Goths.

Elevated to the throne after Valens' death at Hadrianople, Theodosius spent the first eighteen months of his reign at Thessalonica, restoring Roman authority sufficiently to prepare for a treaty with the Goths, before entering Constantinople late in 380. Theodosius' commitment to the city, together with his recent baptism in the Catholic rite, led to one of the most notable events of the history of Constantinople in these years, the council of Constantinople of 381, in which a western, 'Nicene' conception of orthodoxy was imposed on the eastern provinces. It was at the council of 381 that St. Jerome had the opportunity to view the nude statues in the streets of the city (p. 216), and, at a second church council held at Constantinople in 383, that Ulfilas, the evangelist to the Goths, passed away, delivering himself of a powerful creed of the Arian persuasion. The narrator of this event, the Arian cleric Auxentius, referred to Constantinople as better called Christianople.[30]

Exceptions to burial at the Apostles were Julian, buried at Tarsus, and Valens, whose body was lost in the chaos of the day at Hadrianople. The remains of Julian, however, were in the later years of Theodosius recovered and installed in a porphyry *labrum* (a bath-shaped sarcophagus) at the church of the Apostles and, in a sort of compensation, the body of Valens' elder brother Valentinian, who had died in the west in 375, was transported there—a powerfully symbolic act that may express the force of sentiment at Constantinople behind the regime of two brothers united in harmony.[31] In an equally striking gesture, the body of Valens' and Theodosius' adversary the Gothic king Athanaric, who had come to Constantinople to negotiate the treaty of 382 and died in the city, was also laid to rest there.

We may ignore as a curiosity an entertaining but hopelessly confused account in John Malalas and *Chronicon Paschale*, of the assassination of the emperor Gratian in 380, in an ambush set for him in the staircase at the hippodrome known as Kochlias (the Snail) by his stepmother Justina, the grounds for the murder being Justina's Arian hostility to Gratian's Catholic piety.[32] There may be some truth in the allegation of motive, but the circumstances have nothing to do with those of the death of Gratian, who was killed in Gaul three years later by the usurper Maximus. The convenience of the Kochlias for an assassination (its configuration

---

30. Translated at Heather and Matthews, *The Goths in the Fourth Century* (1991), p. 153.

31. Amm. Marc. 30.10.1: 'ut inter divorum reliquias humaretur'. The body was apparently transported in 376 but the inhumation was not until February 382. On the Philadelphion see above, Chapter 7 (pp. 134–9).

32. *Chron. Pasch.*, s.a.; Whitby and Whitby, p. 51.

preventing the effective intervention of bodyguards) recurs in a similar narrative told under the year 484.[33] Even if the body of Gratian was unavailable, its possession being disputed between the courts of Trier and Milan, that of his first wife Constantia the daughter of Constantius was laid in the Apostles on 1 December 383, having arrived in the city on 31 August.[34] Its transfer to the eastern capital was no doubt an overture of goodwill from Maximus to Theodosius, whose support the usurper hope to gain.[35]

We are on safer ground with the obsequies of Theodosius himself, who died at Milan in January 395 after the defeat of the usurpers Arbogast and Eugenius. We know of the circumstances, and of Theodosius' alleged plans for an empire united under the regency of Honorius' general Stilicho, from Ambrose's sermon *De obitu Theodosii*, delivered over Theodosius' body in his cathedral at Milan: after which, escorted by a guard of honour from the victorious western army, the remains were brought back to the east for burial in the church of the Apostles.[36] A brief notice of these events is given in *Chronicon Paschale*, which also mentions the interment of Arcadius in the church of the Apostles on 1 May 408.[37]

This is latest imperial obit to fall within the period covered by the *Notitia*, but we should add to the litany the obsequies of empresses and princesses, these too the occasions for public demonstrations of grief. The funeral of Theodosius' little daughter Pulcheria in 385 was described, with some exaggeration, no doubt, but real feeling, by Gregory of Nyssa. The description also has something to add to our understanding of the site, with its reference to the open space that stood between the church of the Apostles and its original element, the mausoleum of Constantine:

> I have seen a sea of men crammed together, the temple and vestibule of the Apostles crowded, like the open space before it; people in mourning, the nearby streets and public squares, areas, side streets and houses—wherever you look are crowds of people, as if the entire world had run together for this tragedy.[38]

---

33. *Chron. Pasch.*, s.a.; Whitby and Whitby, pp. 94–95.

34. *Chron Pasch.*, s.a.; Whitby and Whitby, p. 52.

35. J. F. Matthews, *Western Aristocracies and Imperial Court, A.D. 364–425* (1975; repr. 1990), ch. 7.

36. For subsequent events, *Western Aristocracies*, p. 249f.

37. *Chron. Pasch.*, s.a. 395, 408; Whitby and Whitby, pp. 56, 61. The translation and commentary by Michael and Mary Whitby are invaluable in the following pages.

38. Translation adapted from that cited by Croke, 'Reinventing Constantinople: Theodosius I's Imprint on the Imperial City', in McGill, Sogno, and Watts, *From the Tetrarchs to the Theodosians: Later Roman History and Culture, 284–450 CE* (2010), pp. 241–64, at 252. The topography is like that of the church complex of the Holy Sepulchre at Jerusalem; Fig. 9.5 above.

The death, within a few weeks, of Pulcheria's mother, Theodosius' first wife Flaccilla, and, in 394, the death in childbirth of his second wife Galla evoked similar scenes of lamentation. Theodosius was not present at the latter event, which occurred after he had departed on his campaign against Eugenius (he had left his wife six months pregnant). The same emergency also prevented his being present at the erection (on 1 August) of the great equestrian statue of himself on the triumphal column in the just completed forum of Theodosius. Both forum and statue are mentioned by the *Notitia*, as well as the equestrian statues of Arcadius and Honorius that flanked it. That of Arcadius, as we have seen, finished up as the statue of Justinian in the Augusteum—where Pierre Gilles saw it destined for the foundries.

Imperial tombs and obits are only one aspect of the ceremonial repertoire that was developing around the emperor and his family, which will largely define what we mean when we talk of the Byzantine monarchy. There are the celebrations of dynastic weddings, like that of Stilicho to Theodosius' niece Serena in 386, and that of Theodosius himself to his second wife in the previous year. Brian Croke, who cites these examples, adduces a law of 383 from the Theodosian Code (one of a series of five under the rubric of public *laetitia*), showing the range of occasions that could generate public rejoicing, from victory announcements or peace treaties to consulships:[39]

> We sanction that whenever any of our auspicious achievements are announced, if wars should cease, if victories should arise, if the honour of the bestowal of royal vestments should be added to the calendar [by the tenure of the consulship], if the announcement of the tranquillity of peace that has been concluded is to be spread abroad, if by chance we display the sacred imperial countenance to the eager multitudes, such occasions shall be announced and received without the payment of a fee to the bearer of the announcement.

Such announcements might be made elsewhere than at Constantinople, and the address of this law to the praetorian prefect, and the reference to the 'eager multitudes' to which the emperor displayed his countenance (that is, visited) shows that this is primarily what was in the emperor's mind. Whether at Constantinople or in the provinces, however, the law indicates the range of occasions at which such announcements might be made. They would be greeted by acclamations of the people, and by the provision of chariot races where the resources were available.

---

39. *CTh* 8.11.4, cited by Croke, p. 254, listing sixteen such occasions between 379 and 394.

It should be kept in mind, that the relationship of fourth-century Rome with the emperor was at best intermittent; only four certain and two ill-attested visits from the time of Constantine to Theodosius, none of them lasting more than a few months before the emperor left for more pressing occupations. It would be very hard to argue that Rome was the city in which they would have preferred to spend their time. The situation was different at Constantinople, where it was clear from the beginning that, even if the emperors were obliged to spend portions of their reign in cities best located for the conduct of war, this was assumed to be their preferred city of residence. Constantinople had to become familiar, as Rome did not, with the idea of an emperor-in-residence, whose influence in political and cultural (including religious) matters was more consistently expressed than it ever could be at Rome, and whose power base in the city—emperor, court and administration, senate and people—became ever more closely integrated, as the city itself developed to accommodate them.[40]

11.4 Secular and Sacred in Chronicon Paschale

We have already had occasion to acknowledge *Chronicon Paschale* for its account of the consecration of the city (pp. 27–30) and its predecessor, the *Chronicle* of John Malalas, for the fate of its pagan temples (pp. 182–4). These examples are part of an extensive selection offered by these sources, of political events and natural disasters affecting the city, recorded not as continuous history (any more than the chronicles themselves are historical texts as we understand the term), but as an assortment of episodes and anecdotes from diverse sources and of varying significance, that seemed one time or another to be worth recording. We may think of them as history in the style of a popular newspaper, combining headlines and text in a more or less informative fashion, but with transparent bias and little in the way of critical analysis.

There is an obvious danger in using such texts by rearranging their material to suit the diverse topics that they cover, in that one may finish up with something very like what one started with, isolated episodes organized in different ways from the original but offering little sense of organic development. On the other hand, the episodes provide moments of common experience through which the life of the city can be understood. What we may call the natural or divine element

---

40. The political and other consequences of the emperors' sustained residence in the city are a point of emphasis of H.-G. Beck, *Senat und Volk von Konstantinopel: Probleme der byzantinischen Verfassungsgeschichte* (1966), as of Paul Magdalino, *Studies on the History and Topography of Byzantine Constantinople* (2007), p. 151. Both studies look to a later period than that covered by this book, but the phenomena that they observe can already be seen in it. See too the publications of Sylvain Destephen mentioned above (n. 27).

is in some cases the counterpart of the registers of portents and unnatural occurrences recorded in Roman republican sources, now recorded not as portents but as acts of the 'mercy of God'—either because the mercy of God has been allowed to moderate the justice of his punishments, or because through the mercy of God the afflictions were less serious than they might have been. They include preternatural outbreaks of severe weather, such as the storms of 367 and 404, when God scattered hailstones 'the size of nuts' upon the city, or the fearful cold of 401, when the sea was frozen for twenty days. In a storm of April 407 mentioned earlier, hurricane-force winds blew bronze tiles from the basilica of Theodosius as far as Caenopolis and tore off the emblem of Christ on the Capitolium, while ships foundered at sea; victims' corpses came to shore as far away as Hebdomon.[41] Earthquakes are recorded in 408, 417, and 422, with many tremors in the following year.[42] According to the *Chronicle* of Marcellinus, the earthquake of 417, on 20 April, was felt as far away as Cibyra in south-western Asia Minor, which speaks to a great deal of intermediate destruction. In 416 a large stone fell from the lower part of the porphyry column of Constantine, which was then bound together with metal hoops, as it can be seen today.[43] Not mentioned by the *Chronicon* or any related source is the sad story of the church of S. Mocius falling into disrepair no great interval of time after its building, and then collapsing on the Arian heretics who had restored it (above, pp. 173–5). This is to set aside earthquakes affecting other places, like the earthquake that devastated Nicomedia in 359, or one that affected Nicaea in 368 and completed the destruction of Nicomedia. It was suggested in Chapter 7, that the statue group known as the Venice Tetrarchs had formed part of a larger monument that was transported from Nicomedia to Constantinople after this date and incorporated into the architectural feature known as the Philadelphion, commemorating the harmonious reign of the brothers Valentinian and Valens.

Divine intervention aside, a constant threat on the human level, reflected in the appointment of *collegiati* for the regions as described in the previous chapter, was fire, whether purely accidental or whether, as sometimes happened, connected with public or ecclesiastical disorder. The most notorious case, entered in *Chronicon Paschale* under the year 404, was the burning of the great church of S. Sophia and the senate-house in the Augusteum by those in possession of the church at the time. These were the dissidents known as Xylocircites, supporters of the recently exiled bishop John Chrysostom, so called because they had met in

41. *Chron. Pasch.*, s.a.; Whitby and Whitby, pp. 46, 58, 59, 60–61. On the location of the Capitolium see above, pp. 90, 93.

42. Whitby and Whitby, pp. 61, 65, 69 (in the last case coinciding with a comet).

43. Whitby and Whitby, p. 65 (28 March).

some sort of wooden enclosure resembling a circus outside the (Constantinian) walls. The burning of the senate-house was at the cost of the destruction of statues that stood there, though the pagan historian Zosimus could celebrate the preservation, as if by an alternative form of miracle, of statues of Zeus and Athena; it is however worth more than a passing note that the senate still contained them.[44] The inauguration of a new great church, as rebuilt by Theodosius after the fire, was celebrated on 10 October 415.[45] In 406 a fire damaged the entry gates of the hippodrome and in 433 there was a serious conflagration beginning at the Neorion, the old shipyard and harbour on the northern side of the promontory, which went on to consume the adjacent granaries and the baths of Achilles.[46] The baths, in a part of the old Graeco-Roman city, may be those that appear, rebuilt and renamed after the empress Eudocia, in Region VI of the *Notitia*, where the granaries too are mentioned.

The progression of Christianity at Constantinople is a cumulative story, and advances on many fronts and in many places. No one would imagine that the pursuit of the religion, with its disputes and controversies, dissenting groups and conventicles, private chapels and sympathetic great houses, aristocratic patronage of holy men and all the other public and private activities described in the richly documented article by Brian Croke, was entirely contained within the twelve or fourteen churches listed by the *Notitia* for the early fifth century.[47] It was not the purpose of the *Notitia* to characterize the living history of the church of Constantinople, though as we saw in Chapter 9, it is sometimes possible to relate individual churches to the socio-economic character of the regions in which they stood. The presence of five of the twelve listed churches in regions most closely connected with harbours, warehouses, and the more crowded living conditions associated with these should say something about the penetration of Christianity into the working population of the city. If this process, as was suggested, ran on a separate track from the Christianization of the imperial house and ruling classes, these tracks do seem to have converged in the later decades of the fourth century, and especially during the reign of Theodosius.

---

44. Zosimus 5.24.6–8; *Chron. Pasch.*, s.a. 404; Whitby and Whitby, p. 59 with n. 196.

45. Whitby and Whitby, p. 59. John's successor, Arsacius, was consecrated on 26 June in the church of the Apostles.

46. Whitby and Whitby, pp. 60, 71.

47. 'Reinventing Constantinople' (above, n. 38), esp. pp. 247–57. Private acts of piety of influential laymen such as Fl. Rufinus, or the generals Saturninus and Victor (see below), do not fall within the purview of the *Notitia*, while expressing the Christian evolution of the city; Croke, pp. 260–62.

We saw in Chapter 9 the beginnings of the process of the collection of holy relics at Constantinople, in the installation in the Holy Apostles (before its consecration as a church) of the remains of Timothy the follower of St. Paul and legendary first bishop of Ephesus, and in the following year of the apostles Luke and Andrew 'through the zeal of Constantius Augustus', amid the singing of psalms and hymns in their honour (p. 177f.). Later and increasingly imaginative importations, like the remains of the prophet Samuel in 411 and of Joseph the son of Jacob and Zacharias the father of John the Baptist in 415,[48] were received in the great church, pending permanent installation elsewhere. The arrival of such relics at Constantinople offered yet another occasion for public ceremony. Those of the prophet Samuel, again according to *Chronicon Paschale*:

> …were conveyed to Constantinople by way of the Chalcedonian jetty, in the month Artemisios, on the 14th day before the Kalends of June [19th May], with Arcadius Augustus leading the way, and Anthemius, praetorian prefect and former consul, Aemilianus, city prefect, and all the senate; these remains were laid to rest for a certain time in the most holy Great Church.

They were later transferred to a new sanctuary at Hebdomon. Similar protocols attended the arrival of the relics of Joseph and Zacharias, which were conveyed in two caskets by Atticus, patriarch of Constantinople, and Moses, bishop of Antaradus in Phoenicia (presumably where they had been found), and deposited in the Great Church with the city prefect and the whole senate in attendance. The date, as given by *Chronicon Paschale*, preceded by just a few weeks the formal re-inauguration of the rebuilt church after its destruction by the fire of 404.[49]

Conspicuous in these episodes is the panoply of celebration that accompanied them, with city prefect and senate attending the ecclesiastical dignitaries in the processions, the latter riding in carriages, just like their urban counterparts. If it had earlier been lacking, Constantinople is making up for its deficiencies in respect for the holy dead, not limited to saints, martyrs, and Old and New Testament heroes from the remoter past. Already in 383, Theodosius had ordered the body of Isaac, the deceased first monk of Constantinople, to be laid in state in S. Irene before being conveyed for burial, presumably in his monastery, by the bishop Nectarius and his clergy. The monastery was just outside the city wall, on property donated by the emeritus general Saturninus after a pious competition with his former colleague Victor, won, needless to say, by the less ostentatious

48. *Chron. Pasch.*, s.a. 411, 415; Whitby and Whitby, pp. 62, 64.

49. Whitby and Whitby, pp. 60, 64 (s.a. 406, 415).

benefactor—two prominent lay Christians from the ranks of the military.⁵⁰ Built in a semi-rural area of private estates, the monastery would become part of the urban landscape of Constantinople after the construction of the city wall of Theodosius, a significant moment in the emergence of a truly Byzantine city.

The prize item does not directly involve Constantinople. In 391 someone acting for Theodosius (who was in the west at the time) recovered from the possession of a 'Macedonian' woman—a follower of the bishop deposed in 360—living at Cyzicus, no less a relic than the head of John the Baptist. The original 'discovery' had apparently been made by Macedonian monks back in the days of Valens, who had wished to install it at Constantinople but were frustrated, after which the head reverted to the possession of the lady of Cyzicus. Having laid the precious item to rest for a time at Chalcedon, the emperor installed the relic, on 18 February of an unknown year, in a new church of the Baptist he had built at Hebdomon; installation at Constantinople would obviously have upset the established rank order of the Holy Apostles.⁵¹ The story is enriched by an alternative version, in which the relic was discovered in the Syrian city of Emesa in 453.⁵² How it got there we do not seem to know. We are in the reconstructed fantasy world of Umberto Eco's enchanting (and enchanted) novel *Baudolino*, in which the hero, a man of proud and confessed mendacity, goes east to find the kingdom of Prester John, carrying for diplomatic purposes seven identical heads of John the Baptist, only one of them genuine. The image of the emperor Theodosius processing on foot from Constantinople to Hebdomon with the head of John the Baptist enfolded in the imperial purple, would strike as bizarre parody any person, if there were such, who could recall the image of Augustus as *pontifex maximus*, leading the priests and the imperial family to sacrifice on the Altar of Peace at Rome. Such a person might also recall the statue images of Roman heroes in the republic arrayed in galleries on each flank of Augustus' temple of Mars Ultor. The New Rome too is collecting its heroes, appropriately disposed among the monuments of its new religion.

Tempted by multiple heads of John the Baptist, we have come a long way from a late Roman inventory to the kingdom of Prester John; but there is reason for it.

---

50. Croke, 'Reinventing Constantinople', p. 256; *Western Aristocracies and Imperial Court*, pp. 120–21, with the full story at 130.

51. *Chron. Pasch.*, s.a. 391; Whitby and Whitby, p. 54. Other sources say that the lady was from a village in the territory of Chalcedon. On the day that I draft these paragraphs (29 November 2019), I read that the Pope has returned to the Holy Land a wooden fragment of the crib of baby Jesus, in the possession of the Vatican since 640 CE. It is reported to be in fragile condition.

52. *Chron. Pasch.*, s.a. 453 (to be corrected to 452), with a longer account in the *Chronicle* of Marcellinus; Whitby and Whitby, p. 82.

The *Notitia* of Constantinople reveals the development of a Greek and Graeco-Roman city, enjoying the benefits of imperial munificence in the days of Septimius Severus and Caracalla, as later of Constantine. Throughout this period, and even after the religious policies of Constantine and his successors began to have an impact, the city, with its forums and triumphal columns, statues of gods, heroes and dignitaries, colonnaded streets and public buildings, presented to the world an essentially Classical identity; one could find one's way around it with the usual directions for such a place. At the same time, behind this image of a still Classical city, can be seen a new world awaiting the light of day. This final chapter is not an attempt to write the history of fourth- and early fifth-century Constantinople, but to indicate the trajectory of change between the *Notitia*, with its view of a Classical city enhanced by its emperors, between Roman administrative law as we see it in the Theodosian Code, the continuing role of public education in the city and its literature, owing so much to Classical and Hellenistic precedent—between all these things and the world of *Chronicon Paschale*, and to remind ourselves of the continuing presence of a more ancient tradition, as Roman Constantinople is transformed into the Byzantine city.

Bibliography

1. ABBREVIATIONS AND FREQUENT TITLES

Standard abbreviations are used. The following are the more frequent or cumbersome titles; those that occur on only one or two occasions are given in full in the footnotes to the book and in §2 below.

Bruns, *FIRA*⁷	K. G. Bruns, *Fontes Iuris Romani Antiqui*, 7th edn by O. Gradenwitz, 1909
Barnes, *New Empire*	T. D. Barnes, *The New Empire of Diocletian and Constantine* (Cambridge, MA, and London, 1982)
Berger	See *Patria*
CCL	*Corpus Christianorum, series Latina* (Turnhout)
Chron. Pasch.	M. and M. Whitby, *Chronicon Paschale, 284–628 AD* (TTH 7, Liverpool, 1989)
CIL	*Corpus Inscriptionum Latinarum*
CJust	*Codex Justinianus*, ed. P. Krüger, *Corpus Iuris Civilis*, vol. 2 (Berlin 1877; repr. Aalen, 1969); B. Frier (ed.), *The Codex of Justinian: A New Annotated Translation with Parallel Latin and Greek Text, Based on a Translation by Justice Fred H. Blume* (Cambridge, 2016)
CTh	*Theodosiani libri XVI, cum Constitutionibus Sirmondianis*, ed. Th. Mommsen, with P. Meyer and P. Krüger (Berlin, 1905; repr. 1962); trans. Clyde Pharr, *The Theodosian Code and Novels, and the Sirmondian Constitutions: A Translation, with Commentary, Glossary, and Bibliography* (Princeton, 1952; repr. Westport, CT, 1969)
DOP	*Dumbarton Oaks Papers*
GCS	*Die Griechischen Christlichen Schrifsteller der ersten drei Jahrhunderte*
IGR	*Inscriptiones Graecae ad Res Romanas Pertinentes*
ILS	H. Dessau, *Inscriptiones Latinae Selectae* (Berlin, 1892–1916)

Janin, *Constantinople Byzantine*	R. Janin, *Constantinople Byzantine: Développement urbain et repertoire topographique* (2nd edn, Paris, 1964)
JRS	*Journal of Roman Studies*
Malalas	E. Jeffreys, M. Jeffreys, R. Scott, et al., *The Chronicle of John Malalas: A Translation* (Byzantina Australiensia 4; Australian Association for Byzantine Studies, Melbourne, 1986)
Müller-Wiener, *Bildlexikon*	W. Müller-Wiener, *Bildlexikon zur Topographie Istanbuls* (Tübingen, 1977)
Parastaseis	A. Cameron and J. Herrin, *Constantinople in the Early Eighth Century: The 'Parastaseis Syntomoi Chronikai'* (Leiden, 1984)
Patria	Th. Preger, *Scriptores Originum Constantinopolitanarum* (ed. Teubner 1901 and 1907; repr. in one volume, 1989); trans. A. Berger, *Accounts of Medieval Constantinople: The Patria* (*DOP* 24; Cambridge, MA and London, 2013)
PIR/PIR²	*Prosopographia Imperii Romani*; 1st edn, ed. E. Klebs et al. (Berlin, 1897–98); 2nd edn, ed. E. Groag et al. (Berlin, 1933–)
Platner-Ashby, *Topographical Dictionary*	S. B. Platner and T. Ashby, *A Topographical Dictionary of Ancient Rome* (Oxford, 1929, repr.)
PLRE	*The Prosopography of the Later Roman Empire*, Vol. I: *A.D. 260–395*, ed. A. H. M. Jones., J. R. Martindale, and J. Morris (Cambridge, 1971); Vol. II: *A.D. 395–527*, ed. J. R. Martindale (Cambridge, 1980); Vol. III A & B: *A.D. 527–641*, ed. J. R. Martindale (Cambridge, 1992)
Preger	See *Patria*
RE	Pauly-Wissowa, *Real-Encyclopädie für Altertumswissenshaft*
RIC	*The Roman Imperial Coinage*
TTH	Translated Texts for Historians (Liverpool)
ZPE	*Zeitschrift für Papyrologie und Epigraphik*

2. BOOKS AND ARTICLES

Alföldi, A., *The Conversion of Constantine and Pagan Rome* (Oxford, 1948)

Aydingün, Ş., *see under* Rose, Mark

Atasoy, Nurhan, *see* Stanley, Tim

Bardill, J., 'The Palace of Lausus and Nearby Monuments in Constantinople: A Topographical Study', *American Journal of Archaeology* 101 (1997), pp. 67–95

Bardill, J., *Divine Emperor of the Christian Golden Age* (Cambridge, 2012). *See also* Crow, James

Barnes, T. D., *Tertullian: A Historical and Literary Study* (Oxford, 1971)

Barnes, T. D., *The Sources of the* Historia Augusta (Collection Latomus 155; Brussels, 1978)

Barnes, T. D., *Constantine and Eusebius* (Cambridge, MA, and London, 1981)

Barnes, T. D., *The New Empire of Diocletian and Constantine* (Cambridge, MA, and London, 1982)

Barnes, T. D., 'Publilius Optatianus Porfyrius', *AJP* 96 (1975), pp. 173–86

Barnes, T. D., and Bevan, G., *The Funerary Speech for John Chrysostom: Translated with an Introduction and Commentary* (TTH 60; Liverpool, 2013)

Bassett, S., *The Urban Image of Late Antique Constantinople* (Cambridge, 2004)

Bauer, F. A., *Stadt, Platz und Denkmal in der Spätantike* (Mainz, 1996)

Bayliss, R., *see* Crow, J.

Baynes, N. H., 'Constantine the Great and the Christian Church', *Proceedings of the British Academy* 15 (1929), pp. 341–42; reissued with a preface by H. Chadwick, (Oxford, 1972)

Beck, H.-G., *Senat und Volk von Konstantinopel: Probleme der byzantinischen Verfassungsgeschichte* (Bayerische Akademie der Wissenschaften, Philosophisch-Historische Klasse, Sitzungsberichte 5; Munich, 1966)

Beck, H.-G. (ed.), *Studien zur Frühgeschichte Konstantinopels* (Munich, 1973)

Behrwald, R., *Die Stadt als Museum? Die Wahrnehmung der Monumente Roms in der Spätantike* (Berlin, 2009)

Benelli, L., 'Osservazioni sul P.Ct.YBR Inv. 4000', *ZPE* 193 (2015), pp. 53–63

Benelli, L., 'The Age of Palladas', *Mnemosyne* 69 (2016), pp. 978–1007

Berger, A., 'Regionen und Straßen im frühen Konstantinopel', *Istanbuler Mitteilungen* 47 (1997), pp. 349–414

Berger, A., 'Streets and Public Squares in Constantinople', *DOP* 54 (2000), pp. 161–72. *See also* §1 above, s. *Patria*

Browning, R., *The Emperor Julian* (London, 1975)

Bruun, P., *The Roman Imperial Coinage*, Vol. VII: *Constantine and Licinius, A.D. 313–337* (London, 1966)

Burgess, R., 'The Summer of Blood: The "Great Massacre" of 337 and the Promotion of the Sons of Constantine', *DOP* 62 (2008), pp. 5–51

Cakmak, A. S, *see* Freely, J.

Cameron, Alan, *Circus Factions: Blues and Greens at Rome and Byzantium* (Oxford, 1976)

Cameron, Alan, 'Palladas and Christian Polemic', *JRS* 55 (1965), pp. 17–26

Cameron, Alan, 'Palladas and the Nikai', *JHS* 84 (1964), pp. 54–82

Cameron, Alan, 'The Date of Palladas', *ZPE* 198 (2016), pp. 49–52

Cameron, Alan, and Long, J., *Barbarians and Politics at the Court of Arcadius* (Berkeley, Los Angeles, and Oxford, 1993)

Cameron, Averil, and Herrin, J., *see* §1 above (*Parastaseis*)

Çelik, Z., *The Remaking of Istanbul: Portrait of an Ottoman City in the Nineteenth Century* (Los Angeles, 1986)

Chastagnol, A., *La Préfecture urbaine à Rome sous le Bas-Empire* (Paris, 1960)

Chastagnol, A., *Les Fastes de la Préfecture de Rome au Bas-Empire* (Paris, 1962)

Chastagnol, A., *Le Sénat sous le règne d'Odoacre: recherches sur l'épigraphie du Colisée au Vᵉ siècle* (*Antiquitas*, Reihe 3, Band 3; Bonn, 1966)

Chastagnol, A., 'Remarques sur les sénateurs orientaux au IVe siècle', *Acta Antiqua Hungaricae* 24 (1976), pp. 341–56

Corcoran, S., *The Empire of the Tetrarchs: Imperial Pronouncements and Government, AD 284–324* (Oxford, 1996)

Cosentino, S., '*Domus, vici* e demografia nella *Notitia Urbis Constantinopolitanae*: alcune osservazioni', in I. Baldini and C. Sfameni (eds), *Atti del Covegno Internazionale del Centro Interuniversitario di Studi Abitative Tardoantica nel Mediterraneo* (Bari, 2018), pp. 1–6

Croke, B., *Count Marcellinus and His Chronicle* (Oxford, 2001)

Croke, B., 'Reinventing Constantinople: Theodosius I's Imprint on the Imperial City', in S. McGill, C. Sogno, and E. Watts (eds), *From the Tetrarchs to the Theodosians: Later Roman History and Culture, 284–450 CE* (Yale Classical Studies 34; Cambridge, 2010), pp. 241–64

Crow, J., J. Bardill, and R. Bayliss, *The Water Supply of Byzantine Constantinople* (*JRS* Monograph 11; London, 2008)

Crow, J., J. Bardill, and R. Bayliss, 'Water and Late Antique Constantinople', in L. Grig and G. Kelly, (eds), *Two Romes: Rome and Constantinople in Late Antiquity* (Oxford, 2012), pp. 116–35

Dagron, G., *Naissance d'une Capital: Constantinople et ses Institutions de 330 à 451* (Paris, 1974)

Dagron, G., 'Aux origins de la civilisation byzantine: langue de culture et langue d'état', *Revue Historique* ccxli (1969), pp. 23–56. *See also* Mango, C.

Daim, F. (ed.), *Die byzantinischen Häfen Konstantinopels: Byzanz zwischen Orient und Okzident* 4 (Mainz, 2016)

Dark, K. R., 'Houses, Streets and Shops in Byzantine Constantinople from the Fifth to the Twelfth Centuries', *Journal of Medieval History* 30 (2004), pp. 83–107

Dark, K. R., and Özgümüş, F., *Constantinople: Archaeology of a Byzantine Megapolis* (final report on the Istanbul Rescue Archaeology Project; English language report by Ken Dark (Oxford and Oakville, CT, 2013))

Davis, R., *The Book of Pontiffs (Liber Pontificalis)* (2nd edn, TTH 6, Liverpool, 2000)

Destephen, S., *Le Voyage Impérial dans l'Antiquité Tardive: des Balkans au Proche-Orient* (De l'Archéologie à l'Histoire 67; Paris, 2016)

Destephen, S., 'From Mobile Center to Constantinople: The Birth of Byzantine Imperial Government', *DOP* 73 (2019), pp. 9–23

di Vita-Evrard, G., 'Les dédicaces de l'amphithéatre et du cirque de Lepcis', *Libya Antiqua* 2 (1965), pp. 29–37

Downey, G., 'Constantine the Rhodian: His Life and Writings', in K. Weitzmann (ed.), *Late Classical and Mediaeval Studies in Honor of Albert Mathias Friend, Jr.* (Princeton, 1955), pp. 212–21

Drakoulis, D. P., 'The Functional Organization of Early Byzantine Constantinople according to the *Notitia Urbis Constantinopolitanae*' (English version), in P. Doukellis et al., *Openness: Historical and Philosophical Studies in Honour of Prof. Emeritus Vasiliki Papoulia* (Thessaloniki, 2012), pp. 153–82

Effenberger, A., 'Konstantinopel/Istanbul—die frühen bildlichen Zeugnisse', in F. Daim (ed.), *Die byzantinischen Hafen Konstantinopels: Byzanz zwischen Orient und Okzident* 4 (Mainz, 2016), pp. 19–31

Elsner, J., 'The Itinerarium Burdigalense: Politics and Salvation in the Geography of Constantine's Empire', *JRS* 90 (2000), pp. 181–95

Feissel, D., 'Tribune et colonnes impériales à l'Augusteion de Constantinople', in *Constantinople réelle et imaginaire: Autour de l'oeuvre de Gilbert Dagron* (Travaux et Mémoires 22/1; Paris, 2018), pp. 121–55

Fraser, P. M., 'A Syriac *Notitia Urbis Alexandrinae*', *Journal of Egyptian Archaeology* 37 (1951), pp. 103–8

Freely, J., *Istanbul: The Imperial City* (Viking, Harmondsworth, 1996; repr. Penguin Books, 1998)

Freely, J. and A. S. Cakmak, *Byzantine Monuments of Istanbul* (Cambridge, 2004)

Freshfield, E. H., 'Notes on a Vellum Album Containing Some Original Sketches of Public Buildings and Monuments, Drawn by a German Artist Who Visited Constantinople in 1574', *Archaeologia* 22 (1922), pp. 87–104 with plates XV–XXIII

Frier, B., *see* §1 above (*Codex Justinianus*)

Gilles, P. (Petrus Gyllius), *De Topographia Constantinopoleos* (*The Antiquities of Constantinople, based on the translation by John Ball*) (2nd edn with new introduction and bibliography by R. Musto; New York, 1988)

Grierson, P., 'Tombs and Obits of the Byzantine Emperors (337–1042)', *DOP* 16 (1962), pp. 1–63

Grig, L. and G. Kelly, *Two Romes: Rome and Constantinople in Late Antiquity* (Oxford and New York, 2012)

Haldon, J. F., *Constantine Porphyrogenitus: Three Treatises on Imperial Military Expeditions* (Vienna, 1990)

Haselberger, L. et al., *Mapping Augustan Rome* (*Journal of Roman Archaeology*, Supplementary Series 50; Portsmouth, Rhode Island, 2002)

Haynes, D. E. L., *An Archaeological and Historical Guide to the Antiquities of Tripolitania* (Antiquities Department of Tripolitania, Libya; Tripoli, 1956; 2nd edn, 1959)

Heather, P. and J. Matthews, *The Goths in the Fourth Century* (TTH 11; Liverpool, 1991)

Heather, P., 'New Men for New Constantines? Creating an Imperial Elite in the Eastern Mediterranean', in P. Magdalino (ed.), *New Constantines: The Rhythm of Imperial*

Renewal in Byzantium, 4th–13th Centuries (Aldershot and Brookfield, VT, 1994), pp. 11–33

Henck, N., 'Constantius ὁ Φιλοκτίστης', *DOP* 55 (2001), pp. 279–304, esp. 284–93

Hermansen, G., 'The Population of Ancient Rome: The Regionaries', *Historia* 27 (1978), pp. 129–68

Herrin, J., *see* Cameron, Averil

Holloway, R. R., *Constantine and Rome* (New Haven and London, 2004)

Holum, K. G., *Theodosian Empresses: Women and Imperial Dominion in Late Antiquity* (Berkeley, Los Angeles, and London, 1982)

Hunt, E. D., *Holy Land Pilgrimage in the Later Roman Empire, AD 312–460* (Oxford, 1982)

Hurbanič, M., 'The Topography of the 14th Region of Constantinople: A Critical Reexamination', in S. Turlej et al. (eds), *Byzantina et Slavica: Studies in Honour of Maciej Salamon* (Krakow, 2019), pp. 129–37

Janin, R., *Constantinople Byzantine: développement urbain et repertoire topographique* (2nd edn; Paris, 1964)

Jeffreys, E., B. Croke, and R. Scott (eds), *Studies in John Malalas* (Byzantina Australiensia 6, Australian Association for Byzantine Studies; Sydney, 1990). *See also* §1 above

Johnson, M., *The Roman Imperial Mausoleum in Late Antiquity* (Cambridge, 2009)

Jones, A. H. M., 'Notes on the Genuineness of the Constantinian Documents in Eusebius' *Life of Constantine*', *JEH* 5 (1954), pp. 196–200 [= *The Roman Economy*, ed. P. A. Brunt (Oxford, 1974), pp. 257–62]

Kaldellis, A., 'The Works and Days of Hesychios the Illoustrious of Miletos', *Greek, Roman, and Byzantine Studies* 45 (2005), pp. 381–403

Kaldellis, A., 'The Forum of Constantine at Constantinople: What Do We Know about Its Original Architecture and Adornment?', *Greek, Roman, and Byzantine Studies* 56 (2016), pp. 714–39

Kelly, G., *see* Grig, L.

Krautheimer, R., *Three Christian Capitals: Topography and Politics* (Berkeley, Los Angeles, and London, 1983)

Külzer, A., 'Der Theodosioshafen in Yenikapı, Istanbul: ein Hafengelände im Wandel der Zeit', in F. Daim (ed.), *Die byzantinischen Hafen Konstantinopels: Byzanz zwischen Orient und Okzident* 4 (Mainz, 2016), pp. 35–50

Kulikovsky, M., 'Constantine and the Northern Barbarians', in N. Lenski (ed.), *The Age of Constantine* (Cambridge, 2006), pp. 347–76

Lenski, N. (ed.), *The Age of Constantine* (Cambridge, 2006)

Lenski, N., *see also* Ramskold, L.

Liebeschuetz, J. H. W. G., *Antioch: City and Imperial Administration in the Later Roman Empire* (Oxford, 1972)

Liebeschuetz, J. H. W. G., *Barbarians and Bishops: Army, Church and State in the Age of Arcadius and Chrysostom* (Oxford, 1990)

Long, J., *see* Cameron, Alan

Magdalino, P. (ed.), *New Constantines: The Rhythm of Imperial Renewal in Byzantium, 4th–13th Centuries* (Aldershot and Brookfield, VT, 1994)

Magdalino, P., *Studies on the History and Topography of Byzantine Constantinople* (Aldershot and Burlington, VT, 2007)

Mamboury, E., *Constantinople: Tourist's Guide* (Constantinople, 1925)

Mango, C., *The Brazen House: A Study of the Vestibule of the Imperial Palace at Constantinople* (Copenhagen, 1959)

Mango, C., *Le développement urbain de Constantinople (IVe–VIIe siècles)* (Travaux et Mémoires du Centre de Recherche d'Histoire et de Civilization de Byzance, Monographies 2; Paris, 1985; 3rd edn, 2004)

Mango, C., *Byzantium: The Empire of the New Rome* (New York, 1980)

Mango, C., *Studies on Constantinople* (Aldershot and Brookfield, VT, 1993)

Mango, C., and G. Dagron, with G. Greatrex (eds), *Constantinople and Its Hinterland: Papers from the Twenty-Seventh Symposium of Byzantine Studies, Oxford, April 1993* (Aldershot, 1995)

Mango, C., 'Justinian's Equestrian Statue', *Art Bulletin* 41 (1959), pp. 351–56 [= *Studies on Constantinople* (Aldershot and Brookfield, VT, 1993), ch. 11].

Mango, C., 'Antique Statuary and the Byzantine Beholder', *DOP* 17 (1963), pp. 53–75

Mango, C., 'Constantinopolitana', *Jahrbuch des Deutschen Archäogischen Instituts* 80 (1965) [*Studies on Constantinople* (Aldershot and Brookfield, VT, 1993), ch. 2]

Mango, C., 'Constantine's Mausoleum and the Translation of Relics', *BZ* 83 (1990), pp. 51–62 [= *Studies on Constantinople* (Aldershot and Brookfield, VT, 1993), ch. 5]

Mango, C., 'The Fourteenth Region of Constantinople', in *Studies on Constantinople*, (Aldershot and Brookfield, VT, 1993), ch. 7

Mango, C., 'The Water Supply of Constantinople', in *Constantinople and Its Hinterland* (Aldershot and Brookfield, 1995), pp. 9–18

Mango, C., 'The Triumphal Way of Constantinople and the Golden Gate', *DOP* 54 (2000), pp. 173–88

Mango, C., 'Le Mystère de la XIVᵉ Région de Constantinople', *Mélanges Gilbert Dagron* (Travaux et Mémoires 14; Paris, 2002), pp. 449–55

Mango, C., 'Septime Sévère et Byzance', *Comptes Rendus de l'Académie des Inscriptions et Belles-Lettres* (2003), pp. 593–608

Mango, M. M., 'The Commercial Map of Constantinople', *DOP* 54 (2000), pp. 189–207

Mango, M. M., 'The Porticoed Street at Constantinople', in N. Necipoğlu (ed.), *Byzantine Constantinople: Monuments, Topography and Everyday Life* (Leiden, Boston, and Cologne, 2001), pp. 29–51

Manners, I. R., 'Constructing the Image of a City: The Representation of Constantinople in Christopher Buondelmonti's *Liber Insularum Archipelagi*', *Annals of the Association of American Geographers* 87 (1997), pp. 72–102

Manners, I. R., *European Cartographers and the Ottoman World 1500–1750: Maps from the Collection of O. J. Sopranos* (Chicago, 2007)

Martiny, G., 'The Great Theatre, Byzantium', *Antiquity* 12 (1938), pp. 89–93

Matthews, J. F., *Western Aristocracies and Imperial Court, A.D. 364–425* (Oxford, 1975; repr. with postscript, 1990)

Matthews, J. F., *The Roman Empire of Ammianus* (London and Baltimore, 1989; repr. Ann Arbor, MI, 2007)

Matthews, J. F., *Laying Down the Law: A Study of the Theodosian Code* (New Haven and London, 2000)

Matthews, J. F., *The Journey of Theophanes: Travel, Business and Daily Life in the Roman East* (New Haven and London, 2006)

Matthews, J. F., *Roman Perspectives: Studies in the Social, Political and Cultural History of the First to Fifth Centuries* (Swansea, 2010)

Matthews, J. F., 'A Last Will and Testament', in *Roman Perspectives* (Swansea, 2010), pp. 111–56

Matthews, J. F., 'The Cultural Landscape of the Bordeaux Itinerary', in *Roman Perspectives* (Swansea, 2010), pp. 181–200

Matthews, J. F., 'The Notitia Urbis Constantinopolitanae', in L. Grig and G. Kelly (eds), *Two Romes*: *Rome and Constantinople in Late Antiquity* (Oxford, 2012), pp. 81–115

Matthews, J. F., *see also* Heather, P.

Mattingly, D., *Tripolitania* (Ann Arbor, MI, 1994)

Mayer, E., *'Rom ist dort, wo der Kaiser ist': Untersuchungen zu den Staatsdenkmälern des Dezentralisierten Reiches, von Diocletian biz zu Theodosius II* (Römisch-Germanisches Zentralmuseum, Monographien 53; Mainz, 2002)

McCormick, M., *Eternal Victory: Triumphal Rulership in Late Antiquity, Byzantium and the early Medieval West* (Cambridge and Paris, 1986)

McGill, S., C. Sogno, and E. Watts, *From the Tetrarchs to the Theodosians: Later Roman History and Culture, 284–450 CE* (Yale Classical Studies 34; Cambridge, 2010)

McKay, A. G., *Houses, Villas and Palaces in the Roman World* (London, 1975)

Meiggs, R., *The Athenian Empire* (Oxford, 1972)

Müller-Wiener, W., *Bildlexikon zur Topographie Istanbuls* (Tübingen, 1977)

Musto, R., *see* Gilles, P.

Naumann, R., 'Vorbericht über die Ausgrabungen zwischen Mese und Antiochus-Palast 1964 in Istanbul', *Istanbuler Mitteilungen* 15 (1965), pp. 135–48

Nicolet, C., *Space, Geography and Politics in the Early Roman Empire* (English trans.; Ann Arbor, 1991)

Nixon, C. E. V. and B. Saylor Rodgers, *In Praise of Later Roman Emperors: The Panegyrici Latini* (Los Angeles, 1994), p. 252

Nordh, A., *Libellus de Regionibus Urbis Romae* (Lund, 1949)

Özgümüş, F., *see* Dark, K. R.

Packer, J. E., 'Housing and Population in Imperial Ostia and Rome', *JRS* 57 (1967), pp. 80–95 with plates

Paschoud, F., *Zosime: Histoire Nouvelle*, ed. Budé, vol. 1 (Paris, 1971)

Petit, P., 'Les sénateurs de Constantinople dans l'oeuvre de Libanius', *L'Antiquité Classique* 26 (1957), pp. 347–82

Platner, S. B. and T. Ashby, *A Topographical Dictionary of Ancient Rome* (Oxford, 1926, repr.)

Ramskold, L., 'Coins and Medallions Struck for the Inauguration of Constantinople, 11 May, 330', *Niš and Byzantium* 9 (2011), pp. 125–58

Ramskold, L., and N. Lenski, 'Constantine's Dedication Medallions and the Maintenance of Civic Tradition', *Numismatische Zeitschrift* 10 (2012), pp. 31–58

Rebenich, S., 'Zum Theodosius obelisken in Konstantinopel', *Istanbuler Mitteilungen* 41 (1991), pp. 447–76

Reynolds, L. D. (ed.), *Texts and Transmission: A Survey of the Latin Classics* (Oxford, 1983)

Robinson, O. F., *Ancient Rome: City Planning and Administration* (London and New York, 1992)

Rose, M. and Ş. Aydingün, 'Under Istanbul', *Archaeology* (July/August 2007), pp. 34–40

Russell, T., *Byzantium and the Bosporus: A Historical Study, from the Seventh Century BC until the Foundation of Constantinople* (Oxford, 2017)

Saylor Rodgers, B., *see under* Nixon, C. E. V.

Sherwin-White, A. N., *The Letters of Pliny: A Historical and Social Commentary* (Oxford, 1966)

Skinner, A., 'The Early Development of the Senate of Constantinople', *Byzantine and Modern Greek Studies* 32.2 (2008), pp. 128–48

Sogno, C., *see under* McGill, S.

Stanley, Tim, 'Painting the map green', *Cornucopia* 55 (2017), pp. 35–43

Steinby, E. M. (ed.), *Lexikon Topographicum Urbis Romae* IV (Rome, 1999)

Syme, R., *Ammianus and the Historia Augusta* (Oxford, 1968)

Taddei, A., 'La Colonna di Arcadio a Constantinopoli. Profilo Storico di un monumento attraverso le fonti documentali dale origine all età moderna', pdf text available on Academia.edu.

Thompson, E. A., *A Roman Reformer and Inventor: Being a New Text of the Treatise De Rebus Bellicis with a Translation and Introduction* (Oxford, 1952)

van Millingen, A., *Byzantine Constantinople: the Walls of the City and Adjoining Historical Sites* (London, 1899)

Wallace-Hadrill, A., *Houses and Society in Pompeii and Herculaneum* (Princeton, 1994)

Ward-Perkins, J. B., 'Severan Art and Architecture at Leptis Magna', *JRS* 38 (1948), pp. 59–80

Watts, E. J., *Hypatia: The Life and Legend of an Ancient Philosopher* (Oxford, 2017); *see also* McGill, Scott

Weiss, P., 'Die Vision Constantins', in *Colloquium aus Anlass des 80. Geburtstages von Alfred Heuss* (Frankfurter Althistorische Studien 13; Kalmünz, 1993), pp. 143–69

Weiss, P., 'The Vision of Constantine', *Journal of Roman Archaeology* 16 (2003), pp. 237–59

Whitby, M. and M. Whitby, see §1 above (*Chron. Pasch.*)

Wilkinson, K. W. (ed.), *New Epigrams of Palladas: A Fragmentary Papyrus Codex (P.Ct.YBR inv. 4000)* (*American Studies in Papyrology* 52; 2012); reviewed Rodney Ast, *Bryn Mawr Classical Review* 2014.02.03

Wilkinson, K. W., 'Palladas and the Age of Constantine', *JRS* 99 (2009), pp. 36–60

Wilkinson, K. W., 'Palladas and the Foundation of Constantinople', *JRS* 100 (2010), pp. 179–94

Wilkinson, K. W., 'More Evidence for the Date of Palladas', *ZPE* 196 (2015), pp. 67–71

Wilkinson, K. W., 'Πρύτανις and Cognates in Documentary Papyri and Greek Literature', *ZPE* 196 (2015), pp. 88–93

Wilton-Ely, J. and V. (translators; many authors) *The Horses of San Marco, Venice* (The Royal Academy, London and Procuratoria di Sa Marco, Venice, 1977 and 1979)

Woods, D., 'Palladas, Constantinople, and the Power of Money (AP 16.262)', *Mnemosyne* 68 (2015), pp. 836–42

Yoncaci-Arslan, P., 'Towards a New Honorific Column: The Column of Constantine in Early Byzantine Urban Landscape (1)', *METU* (Middle East Technical University) *Journal of the Faculty of Architecture* 33.1 (Middle East Technical University, Ankara, 2016), pp. 121–45

Yoncaci-Arslan, P., 'Registrars of Urban Movement in Constantinople; Monumental Columns of the Mese', *Annual of Istanbul Studies* 7 (2018), pp. 7–29

General Index